Mittani Palaeography

Cuneiform Monographs

Editors

VOLUME 48

The titles published in this series are listed at *brill.com/cumo*

Mittani Palaeography

By

Zenobia S. Homan

BRILL

LEIDEN | BOSTON

Library of Congress Cataloging-in-Publication Data

Names: Homan, Zenobia, author.
Title: Mittani palaeography / Zenobia Sabrina Homan.
Description: Leiden ; Boston : Brill, 2020. | Series: Cuneiform monographs, 0929-0052 ; vol. 48 | Includes bibliographical references. | Summary: "In Mittani Palaeography, Zenobia Homan analyses cuneiform writing from the Late Bronze Age Mittani state, which was situated in the region between modern Aleppo, Erbil and Diyarbakır. The ancient communication network reveals a story of local scribal tradition blended with regional adaptation and international political change, reflecting the ways in which written knowledge travelled within the cuneiform culture of the Middle East. Mittani signs, their forms, and variants, are described and defined in detail utilising a large digital database and discussed in relation to other regional corpora (Assyro-Mittanian, Middle Assyrian, Nuzi and Tigunanum among others). The collected data indicate that Mittanian was comparatively standardised - an innovation for the period - signifying the existence of a centralised system of scribal training"—Provided by publisher.
Identifiers: LCCN 2019037966 (print) | LCCN 2019037967 (ebook) | ISBN 9789004417236 (hardback) | ISBN 9789004417243 (ebook)
Subjects: LCSH: Mitanni (Ancient kingdom)—History—Sources. | Cuneiform writing. | Cuneiform inscriptions.
Classification: LCC DS66.4 .H66 2020 (print) | LCC DS66.4 (ebook) | DDC 935/.4—dc23
LC record available at https://lccn.loc.gov/2019037966
LC ebook record available at https://lccn.loc.gov/2019037967

Typeface for the Latin, Greek, and Cyrillic scripts: "Brill". See and download: brill.com/brill-typeface.

ISSN 0929-0052
ISBN 978-90-04-41723-6 (hardback)
ISBN 978-90-04-41724-3 (e-book)

This book is printed on acid-free paper and produced in a sustainable manner.

Printed by Printforce, the Netherlands

Contents

Acknowledgements IX
Abbreviations X
List of Figures XI
List of Tables XII
List of Maps XVII

1 **Introduction** 1
1.1 Cuneiform Palaeography 2
1.2 Mittani Palaeography 3
1.3 Middle Assyrian Palaeography 5
1.4 Nuzi Palaeography 6
1.5 Palaeography of Northern Mesopotamia 7

2 **Writing and Identity** 10
2.1 Tablets as Artefacts 10
2.2 The Archaeology of Knowledge 13
2.3 Social Networks 14
2.4 Social Identity 16
2.5 Semiotics 18
2.6 Categorisation 20
2.7 Digital Humanities 25
2.8 Sign-composition 29
2.9 Sign-organisation 31
2.10 Methodology 32
2.11 Summary and Conclusions 33

3 **Mittani and Assyro-Mittanian** 35
3.1 Introduction 35
3.2 The Corpus 38
3.2.1 *The Tušratta Letters* 40
3.2.2 *The Other Mittani Tablets* 47
3.2.3 *The Assyro-Mittani Tablets* 56
3.3 Comparative Palaeography of Mittani 59
3.3.1 *Divergent and Diagonal Wedges* 60
3.3.2 *Cross-corpus Sign-form Diversity* 70
3.3.3 *Inter-corpus Sign-form Diversity* 78
3.3.4 *Variants* 85

3.4 Comments 106
3.4.1 *Summary* 106
3.4.2 *Tablet Format* 109
3.4.3 *Relevance of Hurrian* 112
3.5 Final Remarks 114

4 **Middle Assyrian** 116
4.1 Introduction 116
4.2 The Selected Middle Assyrian Corpus 116
4.2.1 *Aššur 14446* 118
4.2.2 *Aššur 14410* 121
4.3 Middle Assyrian Tablet Format 123
4.4 Comparative Palaeography of Middle Assyrian 125
4.5 Comparison of Key Signs between Scribes 143
4.6 Comments 144
4.6.1 *Summary* 144
4.6.2 *Assyrian Amarna Correspondence* 146
4.7 Final Remarks 148

5 **Nuzi and Tigunanum** 149
5.1 Introduction to Nuzi 149
5.1.1 *Archaeological Context* 151
5.1.2 *Social Context* 151
5.2 The Selected Nuzi Corpus 154
5.3 Comparative Palaeography of Nuzi 155
5.3.1 *Note on the Old Copies* 155
5.3.2 *Differences between the Corpora* 162
5.3.3 *Differences between Scribes* 170
5.4 Comments 178
5.4.1 *Summary* 178
5.4.2 *Individual Scribal Hands* 179
5.4.3 *Historical Background* 181
5.5 Introduction to Tigunanum 182
5.6 The Tigunanum Corpus 183
5.7 Comparative Palaeography of Tigunanum 186
5.8 Comments 210
5.8.1 *Summary* 210
5.8.2 *Comparing Tigunanum to Other Script-groups* 212
5.9 Final Remarks 217

6 **Comparative Palaeography** 219
6.1 Introduction 219
6.2 Complete Comparison 220
6.2.1 *Analysis* 250
6.2.2 *Are They Mittanian?* 254
6.3 Other Writing from Northern Mesopotamia 261
6.4 Final Remarks 264

7 **Conclusions** 265
7.1 Introduction 265
7.2 Writing as a Marker of Identity 266
7.3 Defining Mittani Script 270
7.4 The Organisation of Society 278

Appendices 285
A Complete Mittani Corpus 285
B Selected Assyro-Mittanian Corpus 287
C Selected Early Middle Assyrian Corpus 288
D Selected Later Middle Assyrian Corpus 291
E Selected Nuzi Corpus 292
F Published Tigunanum Corpus 296
G Mittani Sign-list 297
H Middle Assyrian Sign-list 312
I Nuzi Sign-list 322
J Tigunanum Sign-list 333
K Comparative Sign-list 343
Bibliography 367
Index of Places 393
Index of Names 394
Index of Subjects 395

Acknowledgements

As I am writing this, my research has shifted from archaeology to international security. It is one of the many unexpected consequences of the ongoing war in Syria. The versatility of an archaeologist's skillset means we often end up elsewhere than the field – bartenders, publishers or diplomats, to name just a few possibilities. Whatever happens, we all share a passion for the past; we try to disentangle how humankind got to the present and wonder where it will go next; and history remains the foundation of any line of enquiry.

To me, the big question of life, the universe and everything has invariably been about communication. In particular: why and how do people write? Assisting me on my mission to find answers, my PhD thesis, on which this book is based, was supervised by Mark Weeden. I think the essence of a successful PhD project is connecting with a good supervisor, and I am so happy we found each other. I am also grateful to my second supervisor, Andrew George, MPhil supervisor Nicholas Postgate and BA supervisors Tony Wilkinson and Graham Philip. In addition, I want to thank those who, over the years, taught me my first Syriac, let me sit in on Akkadian, and hosted evening Hieroglyphics. Even before this, I owe so much to Yvonne Geiss for supporting me through secondary school Latin and Greek. Although unfamiliar grammar may never come to me naturally, I am glad that all these individuals dared to help me pave the way to studying ancient writing systems.

To realise this project, I hugely benefited from digital databases, including CDLI, HethPort and InscriptiFact. The specific database for this project was written by Dr Leszek Świrski at a kitchen table in Cambridge. I was also allowed access to some of the most exciting collections of cuneiform tablets in the world. For this, I am especially indebted to Joachim Marzahn at the Vorderasiatisches Museum Berlin and Jon Taylor at the British Museum London.

Financially, this project was supported by a generous grant from Alida Beekhuis through the Prins Bernhard Cultuur Fonds, the Fund for International Information and Communication (Stichting I.I.C.) and the fund KETEL 1 from Leiden. While the School of Oriental and African Studies (SOAS) has been my home for this work, an environment I can recommend to anyone, I am also grateful to have been made welcome at Fitzwilliam College, Cambridge, and its Middle Combination Room, as well as the Department of Altorientalistik of the University of Würzburg where I had the opportunity to learn from Daniel Schwemer and Gerfrid Müller.

Finally, I want to thank my friends and family; for sofas, floors, cups of tea, copying, editing, advice and even technical support. It has meant a great deal to me that so many people believed this research was worth pursuing.

Abbreviations

AASOR	Annual of the American Schools of Oriental Research
AfO	Altorientalische Forschungen
AlT	Alalaḫ; *The Alalakh Tablets* (Wiseman 1953)
Am-Mit	Amarna Mittanian
As-Mit	Assyro-Mittanian
BM	British Museum, London, UK
Bz	Tall Bazi; *Die zwei Urkunden aus Tall Bazi am Mittleren Euphrat* (Sallaberger et al. 2006)
CDLI	Cuneiform Digital Library Initiative
CMAWR	Corpus of Mesopotamian Anti-Witchcraft Rituals
CTH	Catalogue of Hittite Texts
CUSAS	Cornell University Studies in Assyriology and Sumerology
EA	El-Amarna; *Die Tontafeln von El-Amarna* (Schröder 1915)
EMA	Early Middle Assyrian
HMM	Tell Hammam et-Turkman; *Three Tablets from Tell Hammam et-Turkman* (Van Soldt 1995)
HPM	Hethitologie Portal Mainz
HSS	Harvard Semitic Series
KAJ	Keilschrifttexte aus Assur juristischen Inhalts
KAV	Keilschrifttexte aus Assur verschiedenen Inhalts
KBo	Keilschrifttexte aus Boğazköy
KUB	Keilschrift Urkunden aus Boghazköi
LMA	Later Middle Assyrian
MAH	Musée d'Art et d'Histoire, Geneva, Switzerland
MARV	Mittelassyrische Rechtsurkunden und Verwaltungstexte
MRAH	Musées royaux d'Art et d'Histoire, Brussels, Belgium
MS	Schøyen Collection
MZ	*Mesopotamisches Zeichenlexikon* (Borger 2004)
O-Mit	Other Mittanian
RIAA	*Recueil des inscriptions de l'Asie Antérieure* (Speleers 1925)
SCCNH	Studies on the Civilization and Culture of Nuzi and the Hurrians
SMN	Harvard University Semitic Museum, Cambridge, USA
TB	Tell Brak; *Excavations at Tell Brak* (Oates *et al.* 1997)
UEM	Tell Umm el-Marra; *A Mittani-Era Tablet from Umm el-Marra* (Cooper *et al.* 2005)
VAT	Vorderasiatisches Museum, Berlin, Germany

Figures

2.1 Categorisation of cuneiform signs 24
3.1 Proportional comparison of the number of instances and signs in each corpus 61
3.2 Comparison of Mittani KA 65
3.3 Comparison of Mittani TI 66
3.4 Comparison of Mittani LÚ, ŠAR and IN 75
3.5 Comparison of Mittani UM, DUB and MES 77
3.6 Comparison of Mittani QA and NA4 89
3.7 Placement of the horizontal in NA 91
3.8 Comparison of placement of horizontals in NA between tablets 91
3.9 Comparison of placement of horizontals in RU 92
3.10 Combined comparison of placement of horizontals in NA and RU 93
3.11 Comparison of co-occurrence of Mittani TA and RU 99
3.12 Stacked comparison of key Mittani signs 107
3.13 Size-comparison of all other Mittani documents 110
3.14 Size-comparison of all Mittani Amarna tablets 111
4.1 Comparison of Early Middle Assyrian UM, DUB and KIŠIB 135
4.2 Comparison of key Middle Assyrian sign-forms 145
5.1 Comparison of Nuzi UM, DUB and KIŠIB 161
5.2 Comparison of Old Assyrian and Tigunanum sign-forms with Mittanian 215
6.1 Comparison of BA, ZU and SU 223
6.2 Comparison of KA 225
6.3 Comparison of LI 226
6.4 Comparison of RU 230
6.5 Comparison of TI 234
6.6 Comparison of UM, DUB and MES 239
6.7 Comparison of DA and ŠA 242
6.8 Comparison of IL 245
6.9 Abridged comparison of Mittani and Middle Assyrian sign-forms 251
6.10 Abridged comparison of Mittani, Middle Assyrian and Nuzi sign-forms 253

Tables

2.1 Comparison of Middle Assyrian UM, DUB and KIŠIB 20
2.2 Comparison of fundamental and dispensable wedges 21
3.1 Overview of Mittani rulers 38
3.2 The divergent wedge 61
3.3 The divergent wedge in BAL 62
3.4 The divergent wedge in BA, ZU and SU 63
3.5 The divergent wedge in KA 65
3.6 The divergent wedge in TI 66
3.7 The diagonal wedge 66
3.8 The divergent wedge in SAG 67
3.9 The diagonal wedge in RI 68
3.10 The diagonal wedge in TA and ŠA 69
3.11 The diagonal in AḪ 70
3.12 The diagonal in AR 71
3.13 Mittani GAB 72
3.14 Mittani IL 72
3.15 Mittani MU 73
3.16 Mittani LÚ, ŠAR and IN 74
3.17 Mittani UM, DUB and MES 76
3.18 Instances of TI on KBo 1.2 80
3.19 Mittani ID 82
3.20 Mittani UGU 82
3.21 Mittani NA 82
3.22 Mittani RU 83
3.23 Mittani TI 83
3.24 3D comparison of number of wedges in TI 84
3.25 Mittani TIM 84
3.26 Mittani MEŠ 85
3.27 Mittani TAR 86
3.28 Mittani NU 86
3.29 Mittani LI 88
3.30 Mittani QA and NA4 88
3.31 Mittani AK 94
3.32 Mittani SA 95
3.33 Mittani Ú 95
3.34 3D scans of Mittani Ú 96
3.35 Mittani TA 98

3.36 3D-scans of Mittani TA and RU 98
3.37 Mittani É, DAN and UN 100
3.38 Mittani RA 101
3.39 Mittani MA 102
3.40 Mittani DA 102
3.41 Mittani ŠA 103
3.42 Mittani ŠU 103
3.43 Mittani ŠE and TE 104
3.44 Mittani ḪI, 'A, IM and AM 105
3.45 Mittani EŠ 106
4.1 Directory of Middle Assyrian Kings 117
4.2 Middle Assyrian BAL 126
4.3 Middle Assyrian BA and ZU 127
4.4 Middle Assyrian ARAD 127
4.5 Middle Assyrian ITI 128
4.6 Middle Assyrian KA 129
4.7 Middle Assyrian LI 129
4.8 Comparison of RU from EA 15 131
4.9 Middle Assyrian QA and NA4 132
4.10 Middle Assyrian RU 132
4.11 Middle Assyrian TI 132
4.12 Middle Assyrian SA 134
4.13 Middle Assyrian SAG 134
4.14 Middle Assyrian UM, DUB and KIŠIB 135
4.15 Middle Assyrian TA, DA and ŠA 138
4.16 Middle Assyrian DUMU 138
4.17 Middle Assyrian IN, LUGAL and ŠAR 139
4.18 Middle Assyrian IL 139
4.19 Middle Assyrian RA 141
4.20 Middle Assyrian ḪI, AM, AḪ and IM 141
4.21 Middle Assyrian UGU 142
4.22 Middle Assyrian EŠ 142
4.23 Middle Assyrian MEŠ 142
4.24 Comparison of sign-forms between different scribes from Ass. 14410 143
4.25 Comparison of sign-forms between possible 15th century tablets from Ass. 14446 144
4.26 Key sign-forms from EA 15 147
5.1 Nuzi signs photographed from different angles 156
5.2 Nuzi BAL: comparison between generations 157
5.3 Nuzi LI: comparison between generations 157

5.4 Nuzi LI: comparison between scribes 157
5.5 Nuzi RU: comparison between generations 158
5.6 Nuzi RU: comparison between scribes 159
5.7 Nuzi AK: comparison between generations 159
5.8 Nuzi AK: comparison between scribes 159
5.9 Nuzi UM and DUB: comparison between generations 160
5.10 Nuzi UM, DUB and KIŠIB: comparison between scribes 161
5.11 Nuzi BA and ZU: comparison between generations 162
5.12 Nuzi BA and ZU: comparison between scribes 163
5.13 Nuzi KA: comparison between generations 163
5.14 Nuzi DUMU: comparison between generations 164
5.15 Nuzi DUMU: comparison between scribes 164
5.16 Nuzi IN, ŠAR and SUM: comparison between generations 165
5.17 Nuzi IN, ŠAR and SUM: comparison between scribes 166
5.18 Nuzi LUGAL and LÚ: comparison between generations 166
5.19 Nuzi IL: comparison between generations 167
5.20 Nuzi IL: comparison between scribes 167
5.21 Nuzi ḪI: comparison between generations 168
5.22 Nuzi ḪI: comparison between scribes 169
5.23 Nuzi QA: co.mparison between scribes 170
5.24 Nuzi comparison between scribes 170
5.25 Nuzi MEŠ: comparison between generations 171
5.26 Nuzi MEŠ: comparison between scribes 171
5.27 Nuzi NA: comparison between generations 172
5.28 Nuzi NA: comparison between scribes 172
5.29 Nuzi NU: comparison between generations 173
5.30 Nuzi NU: comparison between scribes 173
5.31 Nuzi TI: comparison between generations 174
5.32 Nuzi TI: comparison between scribes 174
5.33 Nuzi RI: comparison between scribes 175
5.34 Nuzi TA and ŠA: comparison between generations 175
5.35 Nuzi TA and ŠA: comparison between scribes 176
5.36 Nuzi NA4: comparison between generations 177
5.37 Nuzi NA4: comparison between scribes 177
5.38 Nuzi MUNUS: comparison between generations 177
5.39 Nuzi MUNUS: comparison between scribes 178
5.40 Comparison between Nuzi scribal hands 180
5.41 Tigunanum BAL 187
5.42 Tigunanum BA, ZU and SU 187
5.43 Tigunanum ITI 189

5.44 Tigunanum KA 189
5.45 Tigunanum LI 189
5.46 Tigunanum TU and MU 191
5.47 Tigunanum LA 191
5.48 Tigunanum QA 192
5.49 Tigunanum NA 192
5.50 Tigunanum RU 192
5.51 Tigunanum NU 194
5.52 Tigunanum TI 194
5.53 Tigunanum AK 194
5.54 Tigunanum IG 195
5.55 Tigunanum GI 196
5.56 Tigunanum EN 196
5.57 Tigunanum TIM 196
5.58 Tigunanum SA 198
5.59 Tigunanum ŠUM 199
5.60 Tigunanum UM 199
5.61 Tigunanum TA 199
5.62 Tigunanum ḪÉ 201
5.63 Tigunanum LUGAL 201
5.64 Tigunanum IL 201
5.65 Tigunanum DU and IŠ 202
5.66 Tigunanum AL 202
5.67 Tigunanum UN 203
5.68 Tigunanum RA 204
5.69 Tigunanum MA 205
5.70 Tigunanum ID and DA 205
5.71 Tigunanum ŠÀ 206
5.72 Tigunanum ḪI and IM 206
5.73 Tigunanum AR 207
5.74 Tigunanum DI and KI 208
5.75 Tigunanum MEŠ 208
5.76 Tigunanum KU and LU 209
5.77 Tigunanum ḪA 209
5.78 Tigunanum numerals 210
5.79 Sign-forms which differ between Mittani and Tigunanum 213
5.80 Sign-forms which are comparable between Mittani and Tigunanum 213–214
5.81 Sign-forms which match between Mittani and Tigunanum 216

6.1 Comparison of BAL 221
6.2 Comparison of ARAD 221
6.3 Comparison of ITI 222
6.4 Comparison of BA, ZU and SU 222
6.5 Comparison of KA 225
6.6 Comparison of LI 226
6.7 Comparison of NA 227
6.8 Comparison of NA_4 228
6.9 Comparison of RU 229
6.10 Comparison of NU 231
6.11 Comparison of AK 231
6.12 Comparison of SA 232
6.13 Comparison of TI 233
6.14 Comparison of SAG 236
6.15 UM, DUB and KIŠIB as recorded by Labat 237
6.16 Comparison of values and forms of UM and similar signs in the database 238
6.17 Comparison of UM 238
6.18 Comparison of UGU 239
6.19 Comparison of TA, DA and ŠA 240–241
6.20 Comparison of DUMU 243
6.21 Comparison of IL 244
6.22 Comparison of LÚ, ŠAR and IN 246–247
6.23 Comparison of ḪI 248
6.24 Comparison MEŠ 249
6.25 Comparison of MUNUS 250
6.26 Significant signs from KUB 4.53 255
6.27 Comparison of key signs from KUB 4.53 and KUB 3.80 255
6.28 Comparison of key signs from KUB 37.55 and KUB 37.43 256
6.29 Comparison of KUB 47.41 to Mittani, Assyro-Mittanian and Middle Assyrian 258–259
6.30 Comparison of signs between the Amarna Mittani Letters and HMM 86-014 261
6.31 Comparison between Mittani, Ugarit, Qaṭna and Emar 263
7.1 Recognising Mittani 271
7.2 Recognising Assyro-Mittanian 272
7.3 Recognising Early Middle Assyrian 272
7.4 Recognising Later Middle Assyrian 273
7.5 Recognising Nuzi 274
7.6 Recognising Tigunanum 274
7.7 Mittanian, Assyro-Mittanian or Middle Assyrian? 276

Maps

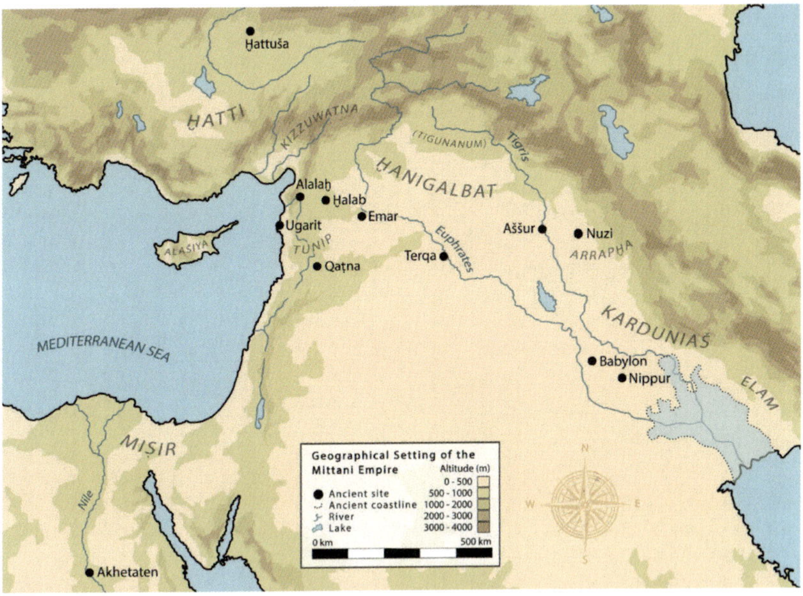

MAP 1 Geographical setting of the Mittani Empire
DRAWN BY AUTHOR

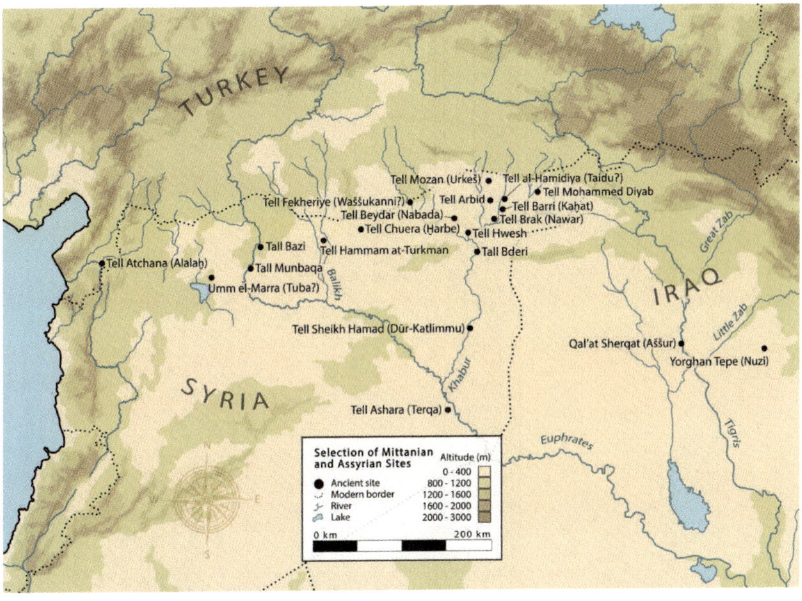

MAP 2 Mittanian and Assyrian archaeological sites
DRAWN BY AUTHOR

CHAPTER 1

Introduction

Who would not want to unravel the secrets of the Phaistos Disc, decipher the messages on the Rosetta stone, or read letters exchanged between royals over three millennia ago? These are the documents that bring history to live. Palaeography is the study of ancient handwriting (παλαιός, old; γράφειν, to write), and will take centre stage in the chapters to come.

In the broadest sense, this work aims to explain some of the ways in which writing relates to human identity. Understanding the forms and processes of ancient and historical handwriting is intertwined with different systems of administration and cultural relationships. It can be used to investigate links between power and identity, and how far this is reflected in writing. Similar questions have been posed in the past, which is what this project can build on. For example, the reasons for using Ogham script in ancient Ireland, the relationship between Roman writing and Norse Runes, the use of *kanji* in Japanese, and the invention of modern Korean. Each script has a developmental story with centuries of history surrounding it. More narrowly, this work will explain how palaeography can be used to identify the ways in which written knowledge travelled within the cuneiform culture of the Middle East and beyond (Wilhelm 1984). The use of the different sign-forms can be a reflection of local scribal tradition blended with regional adaptation and international political change (Gordin 2014).[1]

Sometimes, palaeography is in fact one of the only ways by which we can learn more about an ancient society. The following chapters will look at cuneiform writing used in the Late Bronze Age Mittani state, located roughly in what is now eastern Turkey, northern Syria, and northern Iraq – or Kurdistan. It makes a challenging case-study, because so little is known about it and so little besides cuneiform has survived.[2] Subsequently, this work presents a new methodology, taking an archaeological (object-based), digital humanities approach to find a different way of producing profiles of scribal hands.

1 Gordin has also investigated what changes in inscriptions say about Hittite institutions of literacy and transmission of knowledge (Gordin 2014: 57).

2 Subject to future excavations.

 | DOI:10.1163/9789004417243_002

1.1 Cuneiform Palaeography

Unlike scripts such as Latin and Greek, knowledge of cuneiform was lost for a long time. The writing was observed by Medieval travellers, and some tablets were kept in private collections. Only in the middle of the 19th century were the secrets of cuneiform writing unlocked, through studies of the Bisitun inscription in western Iran and the Assyrian records of King Tiglath-pileser I. For this reason, the study of cuneiform palaeography lingers far behind its Classical and Medieval counterparts. The genesis of Greek and Latin palaeography took place as early as the 17th century, when monks began to organise handwriting found in manuscripts into type and date (*Palaeographia Graeca; Nouveau Traité de Diplomatique*).[3]

Because of the head-start given to Classical palaeography, the discipline has been equated with epigraphy (the study of inscriptions incised on hard surfaces), and the primary purpose of palaeography is usually considered to be the dating of documents (Delorez 2003: 1). However, in reality, dates can often only be established when writing is related to particular persons or places – especially in the case of cuneiform, where in some corpora, such as those under discussion here, very few tablets are securely dated. It then matters who wrote the tablet; why; where; how; and so forth. In other words, palaeography becomes a study of the context of handwriting. Certainly, this raises multiple theoretical and methodological questions which will be addressed briefly over the course of this introduction. This includes an overview of existing research in cuneiform palaeography, followed by some notes on archaeological theory and philosophy, and finally a description of the used methodology.

To delve right into it: when it comes to cuneiform palaeography, it is essential to consider the composition of the signs. There are three primary works on cuneiform which may be consulted for sign evolution and development: Fossey's *Manuel d'assyriologie* (1926), Labat's *Manuel d'épigraphie akkadienne* (1948), and Borger's *Mesopotamisches Zeichenlexikon* (2004).[4] While these works are in some places based off other publications and copies, as well as copies of copies, together they form a basis for finding and understanding sign-forms.[5] However, it is particularly relevant to Mittani palaeography to be

3 See Bischoff 's *Latin Palaeography* (1990) for a relatively recent overview.

4 Other early ventures into cuneiform palaeography, often focussing on specific text-groups, include Strassmayer (1886), Clay (1906), Messerschmidt (1906), Barton (1913), Mercer (1918), Bayer (1927), and Ungnad (1927). More general works include Amiaud & Méchinau (1887) and Thureau-Dangin (1898).

5 Early lists include Westergaard (1845), Botta (1847), Hincks (1848), Norris (1868), Smith (1871), and Brünnow (1889; concordance in Borger).

able to distinguish between individual manuscripts. At present, few publications of specific sub-corpora of cuneiform undertake such analyses.[6] In-depth studies and detailed projects on cuneiform palaeography did not appear until the 1990s, and even then they are often limited to articles or single chapters.[7,8,9] Many excellent sign-lists are added onto the end of text-corpus publications which focus on transcription and translation.[10]

In more recent years, books such as *Palaeography and scribal practices in Syro-Palestine and Anatolia in the Late Bronze Age* (2012) and *Current Research in Cuneiform Palaeography* (2015) have joined the list of available literature on cuneiform palaeography. Here authors comment on very specific subsets of cuneiform corpora, analysing details not normally considered in broader publications – for example, writing at Alalaḫ level VII (Van den Hout 2012) or the Amurru scribes in Amarna (Vita 2012). This is particularly significant from a methodological perspective. Papers show photographs rather than copies and refer to particular tablets and lines (Ernst-Pradal 2015: 108; Jursa 2015: 192). In addition, it has become more common to take an abstract approach and consider writing space (Bramanti 2015: 31), wedge order (Taylor 2015: 1) and wedge angle (Cammarosano 2015: 166). While such articles are not accompanied by full sign-lists, they question and analyse scribal choices and thus contribute to understanding the development of cuneiform signs overall. Rapid progress has been made over the last decade, and workshops continue to be organised, so presumably this list will only grow further the coming years.

1.2 Mittani Palaeography

Paving the way for Mittani palaeography, Jensen (1890: 166) once commented that "*das Wort Entzifferung seinen magischen Schimmer* [*hat*] *verloren*" and expresses his "*allergrößte Freude*" upon the discovery of the Hurrian Mittani letter in Amarna. He attempts a first transcription of Hurrian (then still called Mittanian) based on ideograms loaned from Assyrian ('city', 'land', 'gold') and simply ascribes the writing system to Assyria as well (1890: 169). In the same volume of *Zeitschrift für Assyriologie*, Brünnow provides his own transcription and an overview of word-endings (1890: 209), while Sayce (1890: 260) instantly

6 For example, Clay (1893) and Hinke (1911).
7 See Steve (1992), Sommerfeld (1999), a brief note by Jursa (1999).
8 This is a common complaint in many palaeographic studies, see e.g. Jursa (2015: 187).
9 An outstanding exception to this is Mittermayer's *Altbabylonische Zeichenliste* (2006).
10 Such as the sign-lists for Middle Assyrian from Šeḫ Ḥamad and Tell Chuera discussed in **Chapter 4**.

relates the new language to Urartian (which he calls Vannic), and also makes out "a wee bit" (1890: 275) of the Hurrian letter. Since these three authors did not yet have the luxury of exchanging e-mails, much of their work overlaps (also see Jensen 1891: 56; and Messerschmidt 1899: 175). However, they have in common that they only attempted decipherment of Mittanian language and paid little or no attention to Mittani script.

One of the first studies of Mittani script can be found in the *Tontafeln von el-Amarna* published by Schröder in 1915. It has a detailed sign-list comparing between most but not all Amarna letters – but his list does not consider more subtle differences, particularly between different scribes.[11] In the case of Mittani at Amarna this means the tablets in the Vorderasiatisches Museum Berlin – which Schröder labelled tablets 8–12 and 199–201, now better known as EA 18, EA 20, EA 21, EA 22, EA 24, EA 25, EA 27, EA 29. He did not consider the remaining six tablets in the British Museum London – EA 17, EA 19, EA 23, EA 26, EA 28 and EA 30. Schröder did confidently add that, despite this, the list 'should be nearly complete' and that if a sign-form does not occur in the Berlin-texts it would probably be 'coincidence' (1915: 73). He also wrote that he did not consider any 'certainly erroneous' or broken forms. On the same page, Schröder included one side-comment on Mittanian: because he follows the organisation of Delitzsch' sign-list, who lists Assyrian first (1900), Schröder put 'Assyria's neighbour' first. Notably, Schröder did not study the two currently known Assyrian Amarna tablets, which is why an Assyrian column is missing – but he seemed to think that Mittanian is most closely related.

Most of the groundwork for palaeography of Mittani was established by Wilhelm, as part of his study of the tablets of Boğazköy (1991b, 1992, 1994, 2010) and a Hurrian tablet from Tell Brak (1991a). Then, in 1998, Schwemer published an invaluable sign-list as part of his work on Akkadian rituals from Boğazköy. It compares so-called Assyro-Mittanian, Mittanian and Middle Assyrian – but with the footnote that the latter two do not represent a sign inventory of the respective text-groups. Weeden (2012) built on these previous projects and created a new sign-list of diagnostic forms by personally reviewing a large number of Mittani and Middle Assyrian tablets – drawing into question whether Assyro-Mittannian should be considered a separate script-group at all. Further remarks appear in Klinger (2003), Cooper *et al.* (2005), as well as a small sign-list in Sallaberger *et al.* (2006).

In summary: while certain aspects of cuneiform palaeography and Mittani have been studied before, the script has not previously been rigorously

11 Exactly 100 years later Marzahn still summarises the palaeography of the Amarna archives as "all of these documents are written in Babylonian cuneiform" (2015: 149).

described or defined in comparison to different script-groups. Although limited sign-lists exist, there has been no complete commentary on the corpus of available signs; there has been no categorical overview or definitions of all its features, nor a comparison of these features between tablets within the same corpus or compared statistically to other corpora.[12] Thus, there are many mysteries left to unravel in this particular area of research. To make a start on working toward a complete palaeography of Mittani, this book includes a review of *all* currently known tablets, including those which have been tentatively or erroneously labelled Mittanian.

1.3 Middle Assyrian Palaeography

In addition to the Mittani documents, a chapter dedicated to Middle Assyrian will follow as well. This should distentangle some of Mittani's connections to other script-groups and it will be used for statistical comparison. The Middle Assyrian texts are roughly contemporary and geographically similar to the Mittani texts under discussion; by pointing out what they have in common, and how they differ, particularly regarding palaeography, it has been possible to gain a better understanding of the choices made by the scribes in each society. It has already been noted that there are many similarities between 14th century Middle Assyrian and Mittani cuneiform (Wilhelm 1992); in fact, they might be one and the same. In their work on Assyro-Mittanian signforms, Schwemer (1998) and Weeden (2012) each included circa 15 tablets from the 15th–14th century Middle Assyrian archives of Aššur.[13] However, thus far no sign-lists for early Middle Assyrian as a whole have been available. Published sign-lists of later Middle Assyrian, besides Cancik-Kirschbaum (1996) and Jakob (2009), are a small list of key signs in Weidner (1952: 201), Maul's work on Tall Bderi (1992) and Ṭaban (2005) and Radner's work on Giricano (2004). These have also been used in the more recent *Cuneiform spotlight of the Neo- and Middle-Assyrian signs* by Gottstein and Panayotov (2014). Bderi's tablets are 12th century, and Giricano's tablets 11th century. Gottstein and Panayotov do not mention leaving out the 15th and 14th centuries and as a result their work often does not include what could be developmentally older forms (such as the 'small' or 'short' version of TI). All of this critically

12 A full description of the Mittani state and history of its research will be given in **Chapter 3**.

13 Schwemer also studied MARv 1.19, MARv 1.37, MARv 1.38, MARv 1.41, MARv 1.60 which are not included in the database used here.

complicates the use of terms such as 'older' and 'younger' and the category 'Middle Assyrian' as a whole. To indicate changes between earlier and later development in the script-group, the comparison made in this book includes 13th century Middle Assyrian too. While the chapter on Middle Assyrian was not intended to result in a full and accurate database or sign-list of the script-group, it will hopefully form a significant up to date contribution to the existing literature.

1.4 Nuzi Palaeography

Besides Aššur, it is also of interest to discuss Nuzi. The small Kingdom of Arrapḫa was a vassal of the Mittani state yet used a notably different script, more comparable to Middle Babylonian than Middle Assyrian. This means Nuzi was Mittanian in a geo-political but not in a palaeographical sense. Nuzi tablets can be used to reflect on wider social influences contemporary to Mittani. In addition, in an attempt to illuminate boundaries between features within different script-groups, Nuzi can be used to compare how much variation occurs in the signs.[14] Only when it is clear how much script-groups can differ, can it be said whether Mittanian and Middle Assyrian belong to the same group or not. Since many scribes at Nuzi were named, it is also possible to comment specifically on variation between scribal hands, in order to find boundaries between small individual differences and larger socio-cultural differences.

What is more, the Nuzi texts have received considerable attention in scholarship. This makes Nuzi palaeography a much more accessible field of study, compared to the current literature available on its suzerain Mittani. Lacheman, for one, devoted his entire career to the study and publication of the cuneiform tablets from Nuzi (see the HSS and SCCNH series). However, it is challenging to unravel fifty years of continuous study. Lacheman never published an overarching volume of transliterations matching the tablets or, more importantly, a sign-list. Contenau (1926) has thus far published the only Nuzi sign-list. It consists of exactly 150 signs, with a broad comparison to other cuneiform scripts (Assyrian, Neo-Babylonian, Amarna and Boğazköy).[15] This list has not been edited in almost a century and no detailed follow-up commentary on it exists.

14 Script-group: a collection of sign-forms which shares distinct features, ranged or considered together as being related in some way, and can be distinguished as a unit diverging from other collections of sign-forms.

15 This round number could be unintentional coincidence but taking into account the overall work it may be suspected that the number can be attributed to the author intentionally selecting signs to be included and excluded.

The publication as a whole focussed on the 'origins of the Assyrian civilisation', which lead to a comparison of 2nd millennium cuneiform. Contenau wrote that the tablets from Kerkuk form an 'interesting' stage in the evolution of cuneiform (1926: 11) and that the writing of Boğazköy, Amarna and Kerkuk are comparable (1926: 88). He then briefly made mention of Babylonian and Assyrian influence on the signs and dated the tablets to the 14th century (1926: 89). Contenau did not number his work and he did not justify any of his Nuzi sources: there is no explanation which specific tablets he used for his analysis and he did not discuss why he selected the examples that he did. Although Contenau did not explicitly state how he studied the tablets he apparently based himself primarily on copies, giving a brief bibliography of published tablets earlier in the book (1926: 13). For his comparison he consulted the works of Forrer (1922) and the previously described list by Schröder (1915).

This is where the chapter on Nuzi will try to make a small contribution to scholarship. While it is not Mittani script, so to speak, it is part of the Mittani identity and it is certainly worth reviewing some of the sign-forms. When comparing Lacheman's line-drawings (1989; 1993) to Contenau, it is already possible to adjust a third of the signs. Another third appears accurate, while the final third is too difficult to trace back. In the present stage of Nuzi research, it is barely possible to palaeographically distinguish between different scribes, let alone their different positions in society.[16] Since Nuzi is often included among Middle Babylonian rather than categories such as Middle Assyrian or 'Other' (see, for instance, Koschaker (1928), Pedersén (1998), or also the 'Bibliography' of the Cuneiform Digital Palaeography Project 2004) it does not fall into the same category or group of writing as Mittanian. It is a tantalising prospect to work out *why* this is the case.

1.5 Palaeography of Northern Mesopotamia

Considering the bigger picture, the idea of an Upper Mesopotamian or Syrian scribal tradition has surfaced, with Schwemer comparing Mittanian, Assyro-Mittanian and Assyrian to Ugarit and Emar as well (1998: 16). On the similarity between Mittanian and Assyro-Mittanian Weeden, too, suggested they "belong to a much broader script that flourished in northern (peripheral)

16 However, some attempts are being made, such as the *Nuzi_e-DUB.SAR* project by Negri Scafa (2015). This project is concerned with analysing a specific family corpus, by integrating text mining technologies and network analysis and visualisation, finding similarities and differences between the three scribes making up the archive.

Mesopotamia during the 14th century" (2011: 21, 51, 69, 372). Rutz in turn proposes that writing at both Ugarit and Emar may have been inspired by the cuneiform scribal culture of a number of sources, including Babylonia and Mittani (2006: 610), and speaks of "a certain uniformity" of the scribal curriculum throughout the western periphery (Cohen 2009: 241), abbreviated by Huehnergard as Late Bronze texts in West Peripheral Akkadian: WPA (1983: 11).

Among these Upper Mesopotamian sites is Ugarit (Ras Shamra, see **Maps**), a close neighbour of Mittani. Ugarit was controlled first by the Egyptians and then by the Hittites and thus, seemingly, never strictly Mittanian. Nevertheless, script at Ugarit shows strong Hurrian influence in writing and personal names among other things. Fragmentary Hurrian musical tablets in syllabic script were found in the palace libraries, which have morphology and some orthography in common with the Hurrian Mittani Amarna letter EA 24 (Dietrich & Mayer 1999: 63). It would be interesting if the Hurrian tablets from Ugarit could be dated to the 15th century and tied in with script development during this period. However, currently available dated documents at Ugarit (any language) all originate from the 14th century or later (Van Soldt 1999: 29), including three letters from Ugarit in the Amarna correspondence. It has been suggested that work by students would have probably (but not certainly) been composed close to the collapse of Ugarit in the 12th century, as these tablets were not usually saved – but whether the Hurrian musical tablets should be attributed a similar date, or were composed earlier, or elsewhere, remains to be answered.

Another contemporary site within the Mittani sphere of influence is Qaṭna (Tell el-Mishrife) (Pfälzner & Maqdisī 2015). The first excavations took place in the 1920s, but only during the 2002 field season a collection of tablets dating to King Idadda (or Idanda) was discovered. This ruler lost his throne during the campaign of Šuppiluliuma in the mid-14th century BCE (Richter & Lange 2012: xxv). The documents are primarily administrative, but also include five letters. The letters show a high degree of Hurrian influence, with linguistic forms comparable to contemporary EA 24 (Richter 2005: 114; Richter & Lange 2012: xxvi).[17] Due to its location between Egypt and Anatolia, Qaṭna grew into an important commercial centre during the Middle Bronze Age. This is evidenced by the construction of a massive palace, where finds have included the so-called Nuzi ware (Novák 2004). Qaṭna became a vassal of Mittani but maintained the ability to create its own policies to some degree (Klengel 2000).

A final member of this Upper Mesopotamian group which is of interest here is Emar (Tell Meskene), which "probably fell under Mittannian dominion" or

17 A publication on the *ductus* is in progress (August 2016).

"felt its political influence" (Cohen 2009: 15; d'Alfonso & Cohen 2008: 21). The script found at Emar has been divided into two groups, usually described as older 'Syrian', with traces of Old Babylonian, and younger 'Syro-Hittite', more comparable to contemporary Middle Babylonian (Cohen 2009: 29).[18] The first has been dated to the 14th–13th centuries while the second has been placed in the 13th–12th centuries BCE (d'Alfonso & Cohen 2008). The latter, dating after the collapse of Mittani power, has been said to be "similar, although not identical to the Karkamiš and the Mittani scripts" (Cohen 2012: 34). The documents primarily record every-day activities such as debt settlements, but also include tablets attributed to a family of diviners (Zu-Ba'la) (Cohen 2009: 36). Some of these tablets are clearly concerned with Anatolian deities and ritual procedures known from Ḫatti, thus reflecting the political situation of Emar at the time: the end of local Emar dynasties and the installation of Hittite control (Cohen 2012: 37; Van Exel 2010: 66).

Lastly, to compose a more cohesive narrative of the considered corpora in their regional and chronological context the role of scripts such as Old Assyrian and Old Babylonian should be considered as well. However, it is of course impossible to produce a palaeography of all cuneiform within this volume. Therefore, the small corpus of Tigunanum has been incorporated instead. Tigunanum will be joining the chapter on Nuzi, as both are distinctly not Mittanian or Middle Assyrian, the corpora have only been studied to a limited extent for the purpose of this project, and it is possible to compare to existing sign-lists to some degree. Tigunanum was a c. 17th–16th century BCE (city-)state located somewhere east of the Euphrates – corresponding to the western territory of the later Mittani Empire. It may have been a neighbour of a very early Mittani state, or even a predecessor of some sort. Tigunanum's currently only known King was a Hurrian-named Tunip-Teššup, a contemporary of Ḫattušili I of the Hittites. Since it remains unclear how much the different powers emerging in the 15th century based themselves on old Babylonian methods or their own, comparing to Tigunanum makes it possible to augment understanding of the development of sign-forms during this time and the unique features of each script. For example, Babylonian influence – rather than Old Assyrian – on the script-groups under discussion highlights the disparity between broader southern and northern writing traditions. This provides a basis for making statements both about the internal aspects of Mittani script (how it was learned and used) but also about its geographical and historical aspects (the lines of transmission resulting in its presence and development in Northern Mesopotamia).

18 See Kämmerer (1998) for 'Middle Babylonian from Emar'.

CHAPTER 2

Writing and Identity

2.1 Tablets as Artefacts

Whereas palaeography can quickly turn technical, the reason for studying this aspect of cuneiform tablets is much more philosophical. There are certainly many perspectives from which to investigate these fascinating ancient documents; some factors can be analysed, and some cannot. This chapter will give a general outline of different streams of archaeological thought, followed by more specific approaches to material and social analysis.

The traditional approach to cuneiform tablets is first and foremost to undertake textual analysis (see Albright 1934; Glock 1971). However, to understand cuneiform documents and the culture in which they came to be we must consider object as well as the content; we have to figure out how and why the object was made. While this is a generally accepted course of action today, it was not always so. During the 'Deep Theoretical Sleep' many archaeologists thought artefacts could only be catalogued, described, and used to create timelines (Childe 1925). In the 20th century this method began to receive critique, and the New Archaeologists, or later processualists, posed that it was possible to go beyond the limits of the archaeological record and learn something about how the people who used the artefacts lived (the processes involved) (Clarke 1973; Watson 1972). Their method was more explicit, more systematic, more analytical and more varied; it established archaeology as a science. However, the scientific framework of this school was questioned almost immediately. Since archaeologists are not perfectly objective, the conclusions they reach will always be influenced by personal biases (Trigger 1989: 379). This post-modern or post-processual archaeology argues that personal biases inevitably affect the very questions archaeologists ask and direct them to the conclusions they are predisposed to believe (Hodder 1985). While this could be considered overly critical, it is not dismissible. Significantly, the post-processualists placed great emphasis on the study of human agency; they rejected the opposition between material and ideal and the idea that people are passive (Giddens 1984). With palaeography, there is a certain tension between processualism and post-processualism: between wanting to find secure boundaries and knowing it is impossible to grasp all factors on which they depend.

 | DOI:10.1163/9789004417243_003

As a result of the evolution of archaeological thought, emphasis on tablets as artefacts has increased in recent years and it has become clear that there is more than text which conveys meaning. Significant features of tablets include medium (colour, matrix, inclusions, vegetal material and firing temperature, as well as scribal skill), layout (palaeography, orthography, shape, size), language (period and political context, as well as formulae and abbreviations) and sealing practices (also see Cancik-Kirschbaum 2012: 27). It is uncommon to find detailed, unambiguous information regarding all of these characteristics for a single artefact. While present-day field epigraphers do consider artefactual features of tablets, the data is usually not systematically recorded or published. Where clay provenance is studied, palaeography may be lacking – and although context may be known, colour cannot be derived from a hand-drawn copy. To use a modern example: while computers have become a common medium, rarely do authors record the make of their laptop, from whom they purchased it, which company created it and where the materials were sourced; let alone who developed the writing software, the font used and the reasons for choosing particular paragraph spacing.[1] There are dozens if not hundreds of people involved just in providing the means. Artefacts have (had) a life: it is worth considering the ways in which known characteristics intersect with other studies and contemplating phenomena beyond the artefact itself (also see Ashby 2010). In doing this, a dialogue must exist between archaeology and history: material analysis and social significance.[2]

The study of artefacts was revolutionised by the concept of operational chains of artefact production, allowing for reconstruction of technology and use (Kopytoff 1986; Leroi-Gourhan 1964). With the advent of processualism and then post-processualism, analysis has been extended further, beyond the purely functional, to consider social aspects of artefact production and consumption (Gosden & Marshall 1999: 169). Even so, a distinction has to be made between artefact biography and background: the first traces the transformation of objects over time (Schiffer 1972), while the research described here is concerned with the social transformation of the world around them. Instead of studying only the 'life' of the artefact, emphasis should also be placed on the world it 'lived' in. For example, consider the clay the tablets were made of. Clay was not an expensive or exotic material that required import or

1 In a commentary on the description of aesthetic profiles of script Cancik-Kirschbaum and Mahr (2005) discuss issues such as the configuration of orthographic elements, as well as the configuration of demarcated spaces on writing surfaces.

2 Artefacts in this case defined as objects altered or made by humans.

export across Empires or Kingdoms, which often gives clay artefacts a unique local character. In highly specialised pottery it is more likely to find a selective choice of raw materials, while non-specialised ceramics are usually made from opportunistic, rougher, materials. The ideal clay for tablets is bright (highlighting the script), has a low shrinkage rate and should include fine temper (enabling drying without cracking), but should also be smooth (no large grits or fibres) (Goren *et al.* 2004: 6); although, of course, not every situation was ideal. Furthermore, clay and temper were not usually taken from a distance of more than 10 km around a site (*ibid*) – unless there was access to easy transportation (by water), or constraint (due to political territory).[3]

Thus, a more comprehensive recording of cuneiform tablets as artefacts is necessary. Eidem suggests the creation of an inventory of tablet 'styles': he groups the Old Babylonian Tell Hariri (Mari) tablets into Type A (thick tablet, greyish/light-brown clay, fine writing) and B (smaller, darker grey/brown/reddish, less consistent writing) (Eidem 2002: 80). Waal (2012) similarly distinguishes between Old to Late Hittite tablets Type A (I through VII, permanent records) and B (often discarded, poor clay quality). Whether in Babylonian Mari or Hittite Ḫattuša, there is a general relationship for cuneiform tablets between importance of content and clay quality, as well as development of scribal skill and standardisation. It is currently not possible to make these classifications for Early Middle Assyrian or Mittani tablet shapes, as there is not enough evidence – but it was nevertheless kept in mind whilst analysing the tablets selected for this project.[4]

Moreover, it is essential to consider not only the surface receiving the writing and the person doing the writing, but also the person who composed the original text – because they may not be one and the same.[5] Similar complications apply to audience. There are fully literate readers, but also those who only read a little, and those who cannot read a particular text at all. The past and present have (had) different audiences. Some people experience texts

3 The way the clay was treated may also imply significant administrative practices. The ancient Minoans and Mycenaeans (circa 2100–1450 BCE) adopted the logical practice of cutting clay tablets. On some tablets it is apparent that clay was cut where the first letter began and where the last letter ended (Tomas 2013: 178). On other tablets, it seems that large sets of information were impressed on a single piece of clay, which was then cut into smaller documents.

4 Also see Paoletti (2015: 52) and Maiocchi (2015: 79) for comments on tablet shape.

5 It has rightfully been pointed out (see e.g. Quirke 2010: 288) that it is rarely possible to definitively establish the identity of a scribe, because this depends on the assumption that the handwriting of no two persons is the same (and that one person would only employ one style of handwriting). That does not however mean that it is not relevant to question, depending on a variety of parameters, whether several texts were written by the same person; what they have in common; and how they differ.

through oral performances, yet other people have no way of understanding a text except knowing it is important in some way (Piquette & Whitehouse 2013: 6). This could be dependent on physical abilities or disabilities, but also on language and education, position and purpose, time and place.

2.2 The Archaeology of Knowledge

Up to this point, these are all factors which can be traced back through archaeological detective-work to some degree – and they will receive further attention in the following paragraphs and chapters. However, the final document and its contents are only a few of many aspects worth considering, and, even then, understanding the document is not as straightforward as it may seem. This leads to the question: to what extent is it possible to understand a tablet? Which aspects can be studied and which cannot?[6,7] A manifestation of this thought-process is seen in the principles of New Materialism, according to which there are various non-human actors (such as neurological structures dedicated to reading, ergonomics of clay) which interact with and constrain scribal agency (Olsen 2003: 95; and more critical Johnson & Johnson 2012: 67). While the writing of a tablet undoubtedly involves unconscious decisions and non-human actors, these aspects are impossible to detect and define and not attainable in the framework of palaeographic research. It is simply not possible to analyse the brain function of a scribe who lived three millennia ago, or to smell wet clay on a spring morning in ancient Waššukanni.

This project takes a pragmatic approach. While Descartes questioned how it is that we can be certain about what we perceive at all (*Discours de la Méthode*), Pierce, a fierce opponent of Descartes, found it pointless to doubt all knowledge (*Collected Papers* 5.265). What we feel confident about today may well be proved false tomorrow – but if that were the premise of all inquiries, particularly in archaeology with excavations unearthing new finds every day, no research would matter. Foucault therefore promoted the study of shifts, changes and readjustments (*L'archéologie du Savoir*). These aspects are valuable in their own respect, as opposed to straightforward narratives and loose notions of continuity. Foucault uses the term 'archaeology' to describe the

6 According to the principles of phenomenology, interpretation requires consideration of sensory experiences (Tilley 1994); yet there is generally no scientifically accurate way to establish these experiences.

7 James Gibson proposed that visual perception is often unconscious; the mind perceives environmental stimuli without additional cognitive construction or processing (Gibson 1979).

examination of discursive traces of the past as a way of understanding the processes that have led to where we are today. He further argues that the meaning of these expressions depends on the conditions in which they emerge. He values this over the 'truth' of history as a whole. Bourdieu in turn takes a closer look at social context and individual agency. Social agents develop strategies in response to their entire social environment, which includes interaction, negotiation, conflict, interest, motivation, competition and symbolic power. Central to his philosophy is practical sense, or *habitus* (*Esquisse d'une Théorie de la Pratique*). *Habitus* is structured by the experiences in the social life of the person it belongs to and it structures the field in which the person moves. These are aspects in Near Eastern Archaeology which are accessible: there are volumes of books on hegemony, spatial organisation, technological innovation, and cultural appropriation.[8] Although cuneiform is first and foremost a means to write, this is not restricted to the expression of language alone. The relationship between social structure and human agency is both possible to analyse and central to this project.

2.3 Social Networks

Palaeographic research has long been trapped "into the bondage of subjectivity" (Cammarosano 2015: 147): the problem is not *what* to look for, but *how*. Determining the date, origin or significance of a tablet simply by one individual's visual judgement sidesteps all scientific analysis. It is thus important to consider using methods like quantitative and statistical analysis. This can be used to answer questions such as 'Do more signs / sign-forms occur on larger / longer tablets?' and 'Are these sign-forms more common in diplomatic or in economic correspondence?' This often means building large digital databases, as has been done for the project presented here. However, describing and defining phenomena found through data and databases in culturally meaningful terms remains complicated.

According to Social Network Analysis (SNA), ideas and technology are transmitted through social interconnections: changes in, for example, culture can be understood as emergent phenomena through analysis of the variability and dynamics of these interconnections (Collar 2007). SNA is supposed to describe basic structures of social life in precise terms and measure them. In ideal situations, this means SNA can aid in pointing out which actor functioned as a bridge, who was influenced by that, and who was not (Waerzeggers 2014: 116).

8 For an overview of related works on Mittani, see Cancik-Kirschbaum *et al.* (2014).

Common network properties are density and centralisation as well as reachability and balance (e.g. how cohesive the society is); tie properties within this include strength, multiplexity, direction and symmetry (e.g. how often one person meets another person, how many different relationships they have and whether these are one-sided).

Social networks are nowadays quickly associated with the internet, rather than cuneiform tablets buried in the deserts of the Middle East. An example is the social media network *Twitter*. *Twitter* limits users to a specific number of characters when they compose messages. In research on online linguistics these users are often reduced to communities: speech communities, discourse communities, communities of practice (Herring 2004: 338). Thus, while it is possible to show that Spanish is the most tweeted language amongst world leaders (Lüfkens 2015), individual actors are drowned out in these data. However, it has also been possible to analyse virtual diplomatic networks. The UK Foreign Office has a large network and maintains a public *Twitter* list with a record of hunderds of ambassadors, embassies and missions (*ibid.*). These all connect (or, consciously do not connect!) to other ambassadors, embassies, and so forth, and in turn reflect on the global diplomatic *status quo*. A more specific example of SNA from archaeology is the quantification of pottery (Kotsonas 2011). It is often possible to analyse quantitative distribution of single types over time (a normal distribution) and to investigate mutual behaviour of two related types against each other (Schoop 2006: 218). Following on from this, SNA can be applied to certain cuneiform archives by studying personal names, relationships between persons, the places they visited, how frequently they visited, and so forth. There are also some examples of attempts at statistical analysis in cuneiform palaeography, such as the search for the origin of Hittite cuneiform (e.g. Van den Hout 2012: 163) or characterisation of scribal hands (e.g. Cammarisano 2015: 166).

Of course, the applicability of different theories and methods depends on the available data. Therefore, a major problem in the context of social analysis is the availability of (surviving) material. Whereas a digital database could remain complete and up to date, cuneiform will never be. A much-quoted paragraph by Westenholz summarises the situation: "I reckon that of all the texts that were produced, 99 per cent were destroyed, most of it quite soon – the clay of the tablets was recycled. Of the 1 per cent that survived and is still buried in the ground, about 1 per cent has been recovered in excavations; and of that, about one-half has been made available to scholarship in often less-than-adequate publications. A sample of one in 20,000, quite unevenly distributed by random chance!" (2002: 23). While this makes any research appear quite hopeless, the reality is less bleak. Any surviving tablet contains a wealth of information and its lack of statistically satisfying companions does not obliterate its value. It simply means that large-scale generalisations can only be theorised through arguments based on the available evidence, which is something that must be understood for all generalisations.

2.4 Social Identity

As touched upon briefly with regard to post-processualism, some aspects of history remain unknown, simply because they no longer exist. Although Magritte once said that a picture of a pipe will never be a pipe, or in the words of Korzybski, a map will never be the territory (1933: 58), representation can be valuable in and of itself. The past has left traces, which can help answer even the more conceptual questions such as 'What is writing?' and 'Who was writing?', as well as 'What is a sign?', 'What is a script-group?' and 'What are the boundaries?' There can be no categories such as Mittanian and Middle Assyrian, or form and variant, without examining these questions.

One of the broadest queries in the context of this project is what motivates people to adapt to or deviate from a common style of writing. It is not peculiar for the Mittani Empire to have produced documents primarily in Akkadian rather than Hurrian: the Italian term *lingua franca* dates to the 17th century Mediterranean, where a common language was needed for commercial exchanges. Long before this, and long afterwards, various languages have fulfilled this role.[9] Linguistic divisions are commonly based upon significant political events and clearly perceptible cultural shifts, instead of perhaps more subtle long-term social developments (Woodard 2008: xv). In addition, a language might flourish when it is spoken by more high-status people, or simply the surrounding communities (Baker 2011: 77). Considering social phenomena, rather than answering the philosophical question 'Who am I?', we should ask 'Who are you?' (Vignoles *et al.* 2011: 2): identity comprises not only who we think we are (whether individually or collectively), but also who we act as being in interpersonal and intergroup interactions.

Social psychologists have been working on the concept of a social identity as a way to explain intergroup behaviour and boundaries between groups (Tajfel and Turner 1986). It has been proposed that people have an inbuilt tendency to categorise themselves into one or more groups, building a part of their identity

9 Notably, Von Dassow (2004: 641) has suggested the *lingua franca* of the Amarna letters was Canaanite and not Akkadian. Regardless, the common language does not seem to ever have been Hurrian.

on the basis of membership of that group and enforcing boundaries with other groups. In this theory a person does not have one 'self' but rather several 'selves' which correspond to widening circles of group membership (e.g. family, city, region, country) (Turner *et al.* 1987). In other words, social identity is what links people to society. This has resulted in three generally applicable variables which contribute to the emergence of intergroup favouritism and group boundaries: 1) identification with a group 2) comparison between groups and 3) the perceived relevance of the comparison group. These variables can be used to investigate when and how social (political, religious, etc.) structures have an impact on the behaviour of people, bridging social identification and collective action (Reicher *et al.* 2010). A group may be the producer of a social representation, such as overall script or subsidiary script. Equally, a social representation can be produced outside of the group. Most often, a social representation will be co-produced by different groups of people, changing over time as the social representation develops. This process can likewise be divided into three steps: 1) exposure, 2) acceptance and 3) use (Breakwell 1993: 3) – which is why a script-group can be considered a collection of sign-forms which shares distinct features, aranged or considered together as being related in some way. Equally, a script-group should also be distinguished as a unit diverging from other collections of sign-forms; none of which is static and may change depending on factors such as influence, area and time.

Studies of social identity in turn relate closely to postcolonial theory. When Classical historians explored this topic (for example, Webster & Cooper 1996) it sparked the 'Romanisation' debate (Mattingly 2002; Woolf 1997). The Roman Empire, like most Empires, was not a union, but an assemblage of different peoples. 'Romanisation' and 'Roman' are not synonymous, because being Roman was far more socially complex. The same applies to any '-isation'. Even acculturation and adaptation are big words to apply to entire societies, and power-relations involved in group-identification are not necessarily a one-way flow (Stein 2002: 903). Thus, is it even possible to try and connect nation, writing and identity?

Post-collonial examples of writing as a form of behaviour, in which script serves as an index for a particular social or political context, include the debate over using the Cyrillic or the Latin alphabet in Turkic Central Asia, and Arabic or Latin alphabet in Persian Tajikistan, as well as the use of Kurdish language by ethnic Kurds (Abazov 2005: 159; Kassymova *et al.* 2012: 173; Babak *et al.* 2004: 315; Bennett 2011: 100; Smagulova 2008: 178; Roshani 2010). Notably, finding such patterns for Central Asia and Kurdistan does not mean they are generally applicable. However, adapting to or deviating from a particular style of writing can at least in these cases be connected to identity construction. It has been found that when a script is allocated the role of an identity marker for a speech community, it strengthens the language, and even helps to preserve minority languages (Brandt 2014; Brenzinger 2007). The local cultural sphere (whether imaginary, symbolic or real), which is accessible by a given individual, will usually dictate which identities can be formed or adopted (see Stavrakakis 2004). Each individual subject takes on a number of signs and re-fashions the relationships between those signs to create a unique identity. Above anything else, this leads question 'What is a sign?'

2.5 Semiotics

The two scholars most famous for contemplating 'What is a sign?' are Ferdinand de Saussure and Charles Sanders Peirce. When they discuss signs, this means any kind (see *Collected Papers* 1.339) – from mathematical signs to hailing a bus and presenting an Oyster card. According to de Saussure a sign is composed of a signifier (the form it takes) and the signified (the concept it represents): the dyadic model (*Cours de Linguistique Générale* 1.1). Peirce went further in explaining his thought-process and theorised that the way we interpret a sign is what allows it to be signified: the triadic model. Although we are surrounded by an infinite number of signs, they may be classified according to qualities ('icon'), conventions ('symbol') and facts ('index') (*Collected Papers* 2.254).[10] The iconic sign possesses some of the qualities of the object it resembles or imitates, so its relationship with the object and the way in which it is interpreted do not necessarily have to be learned; e.g. a portrait or a statue. The symbolic sign is accepted as social convention or assigned arbitrarily, therefore it is important to understand its object or what it refers to; e.g. mathematical signs and letters of the alphabet. An indexical sign is directly connected to the object but does not consequently resemble it, so what it refers to, as well as the way in which it is interpreted, may have to be learned (correlation in space and time); e.g. footsteps or flavours. It is also essential to note that these three modes are not mutually exclusive; cuneiform is covered by all of them (although, it developed from more iconic to more symbolic over time).

10 Peirce divides these three categories in three again: qualities into the qualisign, the icon, and the rheme; facts into the sinsign, the index, and the dicent; and conventions into the legisign, the symbol, and the delome. Combinations of these categories result in e.g. rheme-icon-sinsign: 'an individual diagram'; or rheme-index-sinsign: 'a spontaneous cry'. N.b Peirce published three accounts on sign structure (Early, 1867–68; Intermediate, 1903; and Final, 1906–10), in each experimenting with new terminology, usually describing the same phenomena from different angles.

This in turn leads to the question of differentiating between signs in general and their particular impressions. Peirce addressed this problem in his 1906 type-token distinction. This is a distinction between universals and particulars; or, abstract types, and concrete tokens. He comments that the word 'the' can occur on a page dozens of times (tokens) but the single word 'the' itself is otherwise invisible (type) (*Collected Papers* 8.334). The way a 'type' is shown in Borger's cuneiform sign-list, in an abstract computer-generated font, is based on, but never identical to, the many 'tokens' found across different periods and in various places. Because of this invisible overarching 'type', nominalists such as Goodman renounce the idea of universals and abstract objects. Instead, Goodman argues, we should speak of collections of individuals (1956; 1940). There are no general things, there are only general *words*, and such words simply apply to more than one thing: a word type is just the class, or set, of its tokens (Barber & Stainton 2010: 370). In cuneiform, problems between type and token, the universal and particular, are exemplified by signs such as UM, DUB and KIŠIB.[11] They each receive their own value and number in e.g. Borger (three types?), yet the values are often all impressed with the same number and composition of wedges (one type?), which simultaneously looks different depending on the scribe impressing them (token?) (**Table 2.1**). It can be difficult for the modern reader to comfortably identify what the ancient scribe had in mind.

A further problem with the type-token distinction is the addition of new tokens. It should not be assumed that collected data pre-suppose that any future discoveries will occur identically. The described properties of, for example, Mittanian are based only on the 'tokens' which are available at the moment. Of particular interest to comparative palaeography are Goodman's 'grue' and 'bleen' – where two different inductions can be true and false under the same conditions (as in Middle Assyrian and Mittanian). Something is 'grue' if and only if it has been (or will be) observed to be green before a certain time and blue after that time (1954: 73). Where one token is considered to belong to the type Middle Assyrian now ('green'), the discovery of a new archive could show it was Mittanian all along ('blue') (or, as has already been suggested 'Assyro-Mittanian'; 'grue').

11 Although other signs can occur in the same form (e.g. KU and TÚG) the described situation is relatively rare.

TABLE 2.1 Comparison of Middle Assyrian UM, DUB and KIŠIB

UM	DUB	KIŠIB
238	242	486

These signs will be discussed more in-depth in the following chapters.

2.6 Categorisation

De Saussure and Peirce were not the first, nor the last, philosophers to debate how something is or is not a part of a category (consider also Aristotle *Περὶ Ψυχῆς*, III.IV; Locke *An Essay Concerning Human Understanding*, II.V; Kant *Kritik der reinen Vernunft*, Bxvi). However, by the 20th century propositions that objects do not *have* to be classified as members of a particular set arose (such as Wittgenstein *Philosophische Untersuchungen*, 66; Heidegger *Sein und Zeit*, 32; Whitehead *Process and Reality*, 15). Whitehead aptly stated, "If we desire a record of un-interpreted experience, we must ask a stone to record its autobiography". It is true that there is a certain "fuzziness" which is encountered whenever we try to apply categorisational ideas in a social context (Miller 1985: 8). Although this may be perceived as scientifically disorganisational, similarities and overlap are socially valuable. Unsurprisingly, it has been difficult to establish objective boundaries to differentiate between different script-groups, major sub-groups, or minor sub-groups in cuneiform palaeography (i.e. 'it has to look *this* different to belong in *that* category').[12] It is even more complicated to distinguish between categories and to define each.

In sociology, dividing lines lie at the difference between the effort of an individual and a collective (Marwell & Oliver 1993: 2). In script-identification, the border stands between the two major sub-categories 'scribal tradition' and 'scribal hand' (Cammarosano *et al.* 2014: 4). Yet, when exactly is this border

12 There are however some specific case-studies. For instance, Maiocchi divides sign variants of the 3rd millennium into three levels: a) variation in the total number of wedges, b) variation in the direction of certain wedges composing the sign and c) variation in wedge alignment (2015: 83).

TABLE 2.2 Comparison of fundamental and dispensable wedges

ZU	SU	ŠU	Still ŠU
15	16	567	

crossed? Moreover, signs do not stand separately from the overall appearance of the script.[13] Appearance encompasses the way in which signs are impressed in the clay, whether these impressions are deep or shallow, how sharp the stylus was, what size the signs are, how far signs are spaced apart, their relation to rulings, and how closely the wedges are crowded together (Cammarosano 2015: 155; Weeden 2012: 229).

As Taylor already wrote, the general shape of a cuneiform sign is, perhaps, the key to its identity, rather than the exact number and placement of its component wedges (2011: 13). It is true that some wedges are essential to the shape of the sign (e.g. one vertical for ZU and two verticals for SU) while others would not change its meaning (e.g. number of horizontals used in ŠU) (**Table 2.2**). At the same time, the number and placement of wedges can be the distinguishing factor between different sign-forms (e.g. placement of the *Winkelhaken* inbetween or in front of the verticals in DA). Similarly, wedges can be impressed at a variety of angles without changing the meaning of the sign – but the preferred angle could be specific to an individual scribe (see Cammarosano 2015).

Taking into account the philosophical and practical discussion in combination with the specific corpora under consideration, the following categories will be used in this book:

1) Sign: a general abstract entity, used to refer to the value of a written mark regardless of period, place, tradition, school or individual. A sign refers to a representation or understanding rather than a real wedge-shaped

13 Known variously as *ductus, Schriftductus, Schriftbild, Struktur*, aspect, tracing, style or even *equilibrium* (see Cammarosano 2015: 149, 155–156; as well as Van den Hout 2012: 152, n. 125): broadly, the characteristic or distuinguishing features of the written work. Medievalists assign a drastically different meaning to *ductus*, using it to refer to letter formation – the order of strokes used to construct a letter (John 1992: 8).

stroke impressed in clay – although that will be the context in which signs will be discussed in this study. The signs in this project are ordered by number according to Borger 2004 (for example, '118 TI').

2) Sign-form (sub-categories primary and secondary): frequently occurring form, or forms, of a sign; often, but not always, indicative of overarching school or tradition.[14] The form must either differ in composition entirely (e.g. additional or missing wedges in the fundamental components (those without which it would be a different sign) of the sign-form), or wedges must be *consistently* placed at a specific angle (e.g. always, in all cases, diagonal wedges instead of horizontals), in a particular shape (e.g. always *Winkelhaken* instead of horizontals), or a unique number (e.g. always four horizontals instead of three horizontals). The term sign-form indicates that a sign can have one or several appearances, and in the project presented here forms will be marked with numbers, e.g. (1) (for example, 'TI_1 and TI_2'). The primary form (1) constitutes the statistically most commonly occuring form in the main corpus under comparison, and any secondary form, or forms (2, 3, and so forth), are those which occur statistically less often than the primary form.[15] Not all signs have more than one form.

3) Variant (sub-categories frequent and infrequent): these are occurrences which are notably different, but not different enough to constitute their own form-category. Variants can be, but are not always, indicative of individual scribal hands. While variation can be specific to a school or tradition as well, this category is used when differences are *inconsistent* (not in all cases the same) on or between tablets.[16] Variation includes manner of impression (spaced or crowded, e.g. whether the broken

14 Schools should be understood in relation to wider circles of group membership, intergroup behaviour and boundaries. A school in this case refers to a cluster of more than one person having learnt the same material (whether through an institution, family or separate teacher) (on scribal education in ancient Mesopotamia see for instance George 2005; Negri Scafa 1999; Robson 2001; and Veldhuis 1999). However, an individual can be taught by different teachers and of course express the knowledge in his or her own way. The overarching term 'school' is thus used here in cases where a source of shared knowledge is indicated by multiple scribes expressing themselves in notably similar ways.

15 The tables in the following chapters are cumulative, from top-left to bottom-right. This means that the primary form from another corpus may sometimes have the number 2 or 3 (see for example LÚ or UM) so that the inter-corpus frequency of these forms may be analysed more clearly.

16 There is of course a danger of miss-labelling an infrequently occurring form as a variant, or an odd variant as an erroneous instance. In this project judgements were made based on the available statistics following the criteria described above (frequency of occurrence, similarities on or between tablets, and so forth). The label could change if more data were added into the database to alter these statistics.

horizontal in AK is clearly visible or not), angle of the impression (but in this case per tablet / scribe rather than overall script-group, e.g. whether NU is impressed more vertically or diagonally) or potentially the order of impression (although this is difficult to detect). Here, variants will be marked with letters, e.g. (a). The variants show that each sign-form itself can also occur in different ways. Some of these variants occur frequently – more than twice – (for example 'TI$_{1a}$ appears 43 times out of 312') and others infrequently – twice or less – (for example, 'TI$_{1b}$ appears 2 times out of 312').

4) Instance: this is a case or occurrence of any of the thousands of signs in the database (for example, 'TI, EA 19, obverse, line 14'). This term will also be used to describe any occurance that does not meet the described criteria of 'form' or 'variant' (avoiding the creation of endless sub-categories for anything that is not). This includes uncommon or rare instances which are not likely to be indicative of a script-group *or* scribal hand, but more likely the consequence of a mistake, an awkward edge impression, or damage to the tablet.

As illustrated in **Figure 2.1**, the overall appearance of a document can be the defining factor, determining when a sign-form becomes a variant and vice versa. At first sight TI$_3$ and TI$_4$ are variants of TI$_1$ and TI$_2$. However, the definitions used here are corpus-based. Looking at the three Mittani corpora under discussion, TI$_3$ and TI$_4$ occur *only* and *consistently* in just one of them, while being used by (what looks like) separate scribes on different occassions. In this case, these are differences which can be attributed to a systematic trend or tradition and they can be considered sign-forms. Another example is ḪI, which in these corpora can occur with anything between four and eight wedges. Although one corpus shows a specific preference for the use of a large number of wedges, these vary on and between tablets within the corpus (e.g. six, seven, or eight). While this fits in with the broader characteristics of the corpus, the number of impressions is not identical throughout the corpus, not isolated, and *not consistent* on or between individual tablets; therefore, this has been classified as variation.

While this kind of system can be applied to a single corpus, it is difficult to use the same numbers and letters when comparing across corpora.[17]

17 In her 2008 doctoral thesis, Ernst-Pradal presents a similar system, using photographs, abstracted copies, and numbered forms and variants. She assigns numbers and letters to forms based on their frequency (rare, common) as well as length of the impressions (short, long), and the depth and angle of the wedges – depending whether these factors are present or relevant per sign (Ernst-Pradal 2015: 113).

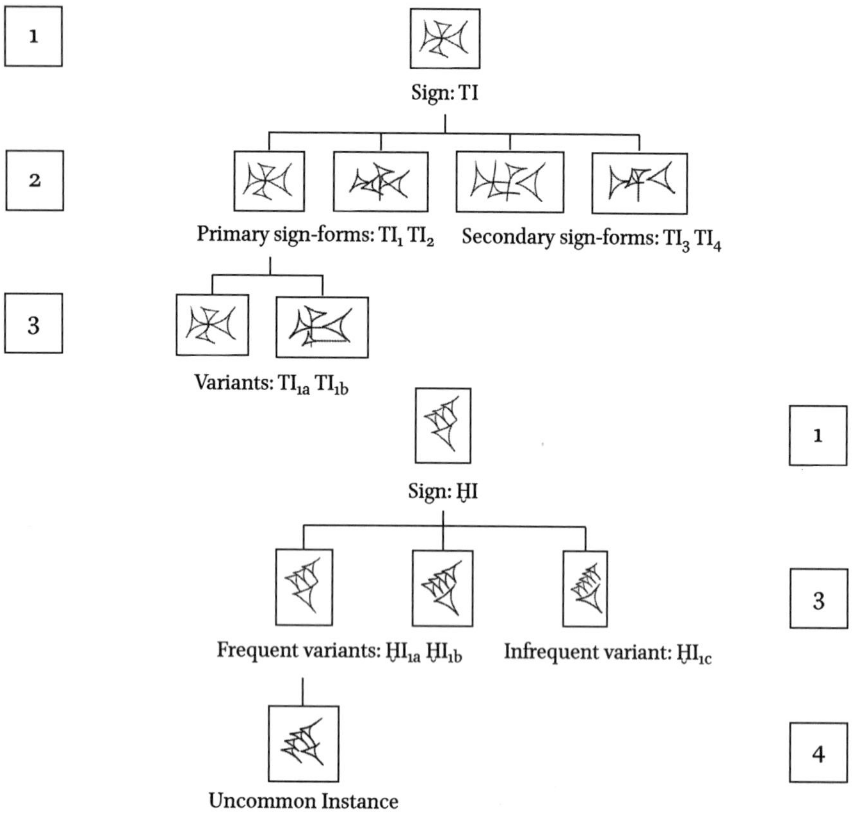

FIGURE 2.1 Categorisation of cuneiform signs
The form is described by a number (e.g. 1), the variant is described by a letter (e.g. a). See **Chapter 3** for a full explanation of each form and variant shown here.

For example, the primary form of TI for Mittani differs from 13th century Middle Assyrian. So, labelling each primary form as (1) causes confusion in a broader comparison. Yet, if the Mittani form were labelled (1) and the Middle Assyrian form (2) it becomes unclear which is more common for which corpus, therefore complicating cross-corpus frequency comparison. Forms occuring equally often is rare, but for clarity the number of times any sign was included in the database has been added to table descriptions, and, where significant, graphs show the number of times different forms occur; this will help with distinguishing whether a second or third (and so forth) form is similarly or particularly less common than the primary form. In addition, if forms were labelled sequentially (Mittani (1), Middle Assyrian (2), etc.), signs with different forms in each corpus, such as KA and LI, would end up being numbered up to (8) or more, with (8) possibly only occurring once on a single Nuzi tablet. While large numbers of forms are not necessarily a problem, it would cause the analysis to become increasingly more abstract and difficult to follow for the reader, which does not fit the descriptive socio-historical nature of this project. As a result, for the analysis presented in this book, numbers and letter have been adapted per corpus for statistical inter-corpus comparison. Therefore, Mittani TI_1 can differ from Middle Assyrian TI_1 and from Nuzi TI_1. In the comparison in **Chapter 6**, descriptions are used rather than numbers, to avoid confusion and to place emphasis on the character of the discussed sign-forms, documents, scribes and systems rather than numbers.

2.7 Digital Humanities

Taking the discussed archaeological and philosophical theory into account, it is possible to consider the practicalities of cuneiform palaeography. This includes the physical composition and organisation of signs, but also the modern methods available to analyse them.

To accurately determine and analyse variation in signs, a palaeographer will always want to physically examine the tablets in question. Shining light from different angles, distinguishing scratches from wedges, and becoming familiar with the perceived depth of impressions are all essential to getting to know and understand the material at hand. During this project it was possible to study several tablets from Amarna and Nuzi in the British Museum, London, and the Vorderasiatisches Museum, Berlin, contributing to the accuracy of the analysis. However, as mentioned previously, the corpora under discussion are currently spread over four continents (Europe, Asia, Africa and North America), some of which inaccessible; and basing a study on one person's set of eyes may reduce its objectivity.

While intellectual aspects of palaeography will likely never (need to) be automated or eliminated, this does not detract from the fact that using computer programmes can facilitate accessibility and increase precision, not to mention speed up the process. One of the forerunners of digital palaeography is the Epigraphic Survey of the Chicago Oriental Institute (see Vertés 2014). Their first step is photography (and, where necessary, rubbings), followed by pencilling on an enlargement, inking, blueprinting, scanning, and digitally inking. In the Survey, 'digital epigraphy' does not include further digital processing or analysis. It cannot be denied, however, that during the last two decades the computer has played an increasingly important role in the field of epigraphy (and indeed palaeography). In the nineties, there was already talk of digital epigraphy in "portable form" and the use of "future generations of laptop computers" (Der Manuelian 1998: 113). It is essential to continuously report on innovations, because "the rise of the internet" (Strudwick 2014: 500) is old news by now.

Of great significance to the creation of cuneiform databases is the Cuneiform Digital Library Initiative (CDLI, 2000). This project has established an online catalogue of more than 300,000 cuneiform tablets (and counting), including collections from dozens of museums. Another such catalogue is InscriptiFact (2003). Its data goes beyond cuneiform and includes papyri, and its focus is specifically on high resolution imaging: it has no entries without images. Finally, dedicated specifically to Hittite texts, there is the Hethitologie Portal Mainz (HPM, 2001), which includes, in particular, images of so-called 'Assyro-Mittanian' fragments and the Mittani texts from Boğazköy. All of these databases were of great value to the present research.[18,19]

Challenges in scanning and photographing cuneiform tablets include the density of inscriptions and text running over rounded edges.[20] This makes a complete 2D capture problematic, even with many exposures from different angles. Several new methods to completely capture the detail on cuneiform tablets have been developed or are under development. These include the Reflectance Transformation Imaging for the Study of Ancient Documentary Artefacts – RTISAD or RTI, by universities of Oxford and Southampton, as well

18 A small number of photographs and scans was obtained via other routes as well. Many museums, such as in this case the British Museum, London, the Vorderasiatisches Museum, Berlin, and the Metropolitan Museum, New York, all have excellent online collections and may be contacted for further images.

19 The British Museum has allowed the publication of the specific extracts of photographs taken there; extracts from photographs taken by the British Museum itself are licensed and have been purchased for this publication (March 2019). The Vorderasiatisches Museum has kindly given permission to publish details of their clay tablets (March 2019). The Metropolitan Museum image falls under 'Public Domain': it can be copied, modified and distributed, even for commercial purposes.

20 It is possible to photograph cuneiform tablets more clearly by coating them with a fine white layer of ammonium chloride (see Hameeuw & Willems 2011). This gives the surface of the tablet a stark white appearance which highlights the wedges. Ammonium chloride is toxic and may only be used by trained personnel; it can be removed by gently brushing it away or simply allowing it to evaporate. Examples of this can be seen from the photos published in *A Late Old Babylonian Temple Archive from Dūr-Abiešuḫ* (Van Lerberghe & Voet 2009).

as the Portable Light Dome (PLD) of the University of Leuven.[21,22] However, these relatively large and unique systems cannot easily be adopted by any researcher for their own projects (e.g. to capture tablets for the project presented here); and despite different exposures they do not solve problems such as detailing signs running over tablet edges. When considering the curvature of tablets and the depth of impressions in digital format, 3D poses an effective solution (Woolley *et al.* 2001: 107). Yet, equipment costs can be astounding, and many methods are still slow and time-consuming. Moreover, the file-sizes of such models are not suitable for uploading onto the internet (to easily search and access for research) and the developed software is rarely made available to the public for downloading.

Nevertheless, several methods have been developed and refined over the past decade. The Stanford Cuneiform Tablet Visualisation Project (2002) opted for laser range data to obtain a high-resolution 3D computer model (Duncan *et al.* 2007: 2839).[23] Johns Hopkins' Digital Hammurabi Project (1999) choose to develop a prototype scanner making use of photometric stereo to calculate the surface normal map of a tablet, incorporating structured light data (Hahn *et al.* 2006).[24] Separate projects have been looking at the piecing together of broken tablets and the matching of fragments (Kampel & Sablatnig 2004; Papaioannou *et al.* 2002; Zhu *et al.* 2008), the recognition of degraded signs (Diem & Sablatnig 2009; Lettner *et al.* 2008), as well as automating collation and sign-extraction (Kleber *et al.* 2008; Lettner *et al.* 2007) and attempting 3D cuneiform character extraction (GigaMesh 2010).[25] Significant accomplishments in this field have also been made by the University of Würzburg, with their CuneiformAnalyser (Fisseler *et al.* 2014: 165) and the Virtual Cuneiform Tablet Reconstruction (VCTR) Project. This last project aims to solve many of

---

21 The system's hardware consists of a segmented black dome, measuring one metre in diameter. Photography involves a sequence of 76 shots for a single object (or side of an object), each taken with a different LED turned on while the rest are turned off – lasting for about 2.5 minutes (Piquette *et al.* 2011).

22 Available at http://www.kmkg-mrah.be/nl/digitalisatie-van-spijkerschrifttabletten (August 2019), 'Digitalisatie van Spijkerschrifttabletten / Digitization of Cuneiform Tablets'.

23 This was then unwrapped and flattened on a plane model, to represent scalar displacement, and rendered non-photorealistically using accessibility and curvature colouring (Anderson & Levoy 2002: 82).

24 Tablet scans are typically acquired at 60° view increments by manually repositioning the tablet – and it takes a total of ten scans to image the entire artefact (Hahn *et al.* 2006).

25 This can be achieved using integral invariant filtering, a robust technique known from signal processing and shape matching in 2D-space. In 3D-space the state-of-the-art systems roughly estimate integral invariants for determining small numbers of highly distinctive features to solve puzzles of fractured objects (Mara 2012).

the common complaints made above, developing a low-cost, lightweight, 3D photogrammetry acquisition system that does not require user expertise or calibration – capturing tablets in under 5 minutes using a camera or smartphone. Be that as it may, the VCTR project was launched after data collection and analysis for the study presented here were completed and it was not realistic to include anymore.[26] However, one of the most interesting tablets studied (EA 24) has already been scanned by the Würzburg team, as well as three tablets for comparison (KBo 28.66, KBo 28.65 and KUB 37.50). Because the Department of Altorientalistik generously provided access to the software at the University, it has been possible to carry out a small case-study on the potential of applying this kind of technology to the studied materials.

Another issue to address in the context of digital humanities is the acquisition of copies of tablets. They have traditionally been drawn by hand (and nowadays scanned and/or traced using illustration software), by scholars bending over tablets in museum archives; but more recently scientists have also been exploring the automation of this process.[27] For example, an added benefit of the PLD developed by the University of Leuven is that researchers were able to generate digital line-drawings of the tablets. This allows for a comparison between scans, computer-generated line drawings, and hand-illustrated copies (Van Lerberghe & Voet 2009). It is clear that the 'digital drawings' show much more (accurate) detail than the hand-drawn copies. However, the inclusion of every scratch makes the drawings difficult to read. Particularly when it is not possible to view the original artefact or the scans, it is not necessarily easy to distinguish wedges from damage or mistakes. The opposite can occur too: the naked eye might distinguish only one impression where there are really two.

For an experienced reader of cuneiform it is tempting to copy signs the way in which they are already known, rather than noting exceptions.[28] This is human: almost nothing looks the same when viewed more than once. Precisely *because* of this, hand-drawn copies are a tremendously useful guide to reading cuneiform tablets. However, a note of caution must be made for the use of copies in palaeographical analysis. While drawings may be used as the basis

26 The first tablet acquisitions took place in the British Museum during 2015–2016 and the project website was launched late in the summer of 2016 (personal communication with Dr Sandra Woolley, July 2017).

27 The same has been done in the project presented here.

28 Most present-day students in fact learn to read cuneiform from copies rather than photographs or scans and memorise standardised forms such as those published by Borger. Small differences, such as shorter versus longer verticals or horizontals, which are especially important in, for instance, Old Babylonian, may not be observed and forgotten.

for research questions, or for comparison when the original tablet is no longer accessible, they must never be assumed to be totally accurate representations.

In most cases (also in the research presented here) there is not the luxury to compare between photographs or scans, digital drawings and hand-copies. Furthermore, original artefacts may have gone missing over the years, high-quality, clear, images were never obtained and many copies date back to the early 20th century – when neither illustration nor publishing techniques were as fully developed as they are now. This is an important problem to consider in light of this project, as the location of Mittani tablet HSS 9, 1 or SMN 1000, from Nuzi, is currently unknown and only a copy and low-quality, unclear, photograph of the final few lines of the reverse exist – and several other Mittani tablets were not photographed or scanned in high resolution, or are so damaged, that they can only be read together with their copies. This does not deduct from the value of these copies *per se* but at the same time, they do not necessarily serve the purposes of palaeography. As an example: if we were to follow the copies of Middle Assyrian tablets made by Ebeling in 1927, there would be many different forms of the sign RU (111), with most of them occurring mixed across the 15th–13th centuries. However, up-to-date photographs suggest that the copies are sometimes incorrect (e.g. fewer forms than suggested) and other times too damaged to draw any conclusions at all.

2.8 Sign-composition

There are several issues to consider when it comes to studying sign-composition. As briefly mentioned, it remains difficult to establish sequences of impression and thus far the topic has received little attention. One of the earliest commentaries comes from Messerschmidt (1906), who was interested in the stylus and how impressions were made. In 1973, Biggs conducted a detailed case-study, and a paragraph is also included in the *Reallexikon der Assyriologie* (1980: 557). A comment from Edzard turns up at the end of a 1993 book review and Daniels (1995: 84) dedicated a sub-chapter to Neo-Assyrian wedge-order. Finally, Sallaberger devoted a (sub-)chapter to the topic of wedge-sequence, in his analysis of the Tell Beydar tablets. He points out that by drawing a wedge, the stylus does not cut out the clay of the tablet, but instead drives it away.[29] He proposes that the sequence of wedges can most

29 In Sallaberger's example of MAR, the clay surrounding the upper wedge of two horizontals narrows the head of the lower horizontal, which means that the latter has been impressed first. The upper left corner of the right vertical wedge was covered by a very

easily be observed at the crossing of two wedges. However, he demonstrates that the stronger, deeper wedge is always going through without interruption, be it written before or after the more shallow one (1997: 61). Through experimental archaeology, the Cuneiform Digital Palaeography Project (CDP) (Woolley *et al.* 2001: 103; Woolley *et al.* 2002: 310; Arvanitis *et al.* 2002) has established that the wedge which is impressed deepest always *appears* to have been impressed last – also if it was actually impressed first. Clearly this greatly complicates analysis from photographs or scans and even observations made in person.

The investigation of impression sequence and position has seen a revival in the last decade (see e.g. Bramanti 2015; Taylor 2015). Taylor has studied wedge order in Neo-Assyrian, contextualising this within the broader 'rules' for writing cuneiform generally, as well as looking at scribal practices across time based on the Archaic to late Babylonian tablets from Ur. He discovered a lack of variation according to scribe, place or date: not only was the order of impression consistent for an individual scribe, it was also consistent between scribes active throughout Assyria and the Neo-Assyrian period (Taylor 2015: 1). In fact, there was probably already a standard Mesopotamian wedge order in the second millennium (and, crucially, not before the Ur III period). The order of the stroke system according to Taylor is as follows: wedges flow from left to right, stacks of any type other than verticals flow from bottom to top (verticals top to bottom), when diagonals cross the ascending strokes are made before descending strokes, parallel equal strokes are impressed together before returning to the next wedge, basal character-spanning strokes are impressed last (when the wedge is at the base, not in the centre), containers are completed before their contents, major structural wedges are impressed before minor decorative wedges, and, finally, in approximately square signs verticals are impressed before horizontals (in elongated or rectangular signs horizontals come before verticals) (Taylor 2015: 19). Critically, Taylor has proposed that there is no set sequence for *crossing* wedges, meaning that the order in which these are impressed may reveal scribal choice. He has tested this on Middle Assyrian (13th–11th century BCE), Middle Babylonian (14th–13th century BCE) and also Mittanian (EA 30).

Hence, while it seems easy to see how wedges cross when using photographs or scans, it has been proven that this is not the case. At the moment, it requires

---

thin layer of clay displaced by the left wedge, which means that the right was impressed before left. He also shows that the ends of the two parallel horizontals lead into the left vertical showing a slight impression – which means the horizontals were impressed later, because the vertical would have otherwise crushed them.

studying the original artefacts, and it remains to be seen whether 3D-scanning will be able to make any progress in this area. Consequently, it may be useful to compare wedge *emphasis* instead, as it has been established that deep wedges often obscure the sequence of impression.

2.9 Sign-organisation

Besides wedge impression it is also of interest to briefly linger on sign organisation, which is needed to find signs according to their graphic parameters and to group them for analysis. For example, in the context of palaeography, signs beginning with a 'ḪI' element (e.g. AḪ, IM) will often be impressed similarly depending on certain factors (such as scribal school). Traditionally, the organisation of cuneiform depends on the 'five elements of cuneiform script'. For instance, Borger organised his sign-list according to the horizontal wedge (), the top to bottom diagonal wedge (), the bottom to top diagonal wedge (), the *Winkelhaken* (), and the vertical wedge ().[30] He admits that this organisation is based on Neo-Assyrian, and while it should not be very different from, for example, Middle Assyrian, it is 'practically impossible' to arrange other script-types this way (2004: 1). However, since sign-lists such as Borger's by no means reveal all possible graphic variation in a sign, there are a few more options to consider. For example, the Gottstein system organises by specific sign-forms rather than abstract signs.[31] It is more representative of the reality of signs as they appear in the clay. In this case, the 'elements of cuneiform script' are the vertical wedge (a), the horizontal wedge (b), to the left falling wedge (or *Winkelhaken*) (c), and the to the right falling wedge (d). Whereas Borger will always call the sign LI '118', in the Gottstein system Middle Assyrian LI could equally be 'a2b4c2', 'a2c6', 'a2b7c2' or 'a2b4c6', among others. This organisational principle should theorethically be more applicable in digital palaeography and the creation of sign-lists, because it allows the user to include or exclude sign-forms without affecting the coherence of the list, and it should bring similar sign-forms together automatically. However, due to ambiguity in wedge identification (e.g. left-diagonal, slanted horizontal or *Winkelhaken*?), forms and variants of the same sign could end up with significantly different 'parameters'. In other words, the 'elements of cuneiform' are

30 Also see Cammarosano (2015: 151) on the naming of primary wedge components.

31 For those who are interested, Panayotov has applied the Gottstein System to a bilingual literary text from Karkamiš (2014: 337).

most useful for studying broad dating, rather than subtle variation between contemporary texts.

In the database used for this project, files were given the more abstract numbers according to Borger (2004), awaiting classification of sign-form, variant, or otherwise. When instances are discussed, they are ordered by file-name: Sign Number (MZ), Sign Value (Tablet Abbreviation + Number, Tablet Side, (Tablet Column), Tablet Line, (Instance Number); for example, '10 AN (KAJ20 o l7)' or '552 MA (EA24 o c1 l70 i2)'.[32] Using a bulk renaming utility, these file-names are easily adaptable, despite their large number. In future, the general signs named '110 NA' could easily be changed to, for instance, form 'a1b1c2 NA' if this were desired.

2.10 Methodology

Considering innovations in database-design, availability of high-resolution images and recent discussions on sign-categorisation and composition, the following interactive database concept was created for the project presented here.[33]

The database script makes it possible to show signs in a sign-list and allows the user to select a sign (the primary sign-form from the particular corpus). A page then shows all instances of the selected sign. It allows for the user to drag and drop sign instances into different categories, in order to visually distinguish between sign-forms, variants, and instances of minor variations or exceptions. Taking into account human error, the script was expanded with a 'counting' option, listing the number of times a sign occurs on a tablet and the number of times a sign occurs in general. It also automatically lists files which have been misnamed (e.g. typing mistakes), allowing for correction. In this project, the database *only* contained extracts from good quality, clear, images, and in a few exceptions (the Mittani tablets mentioned earlier) copies. The final database includes over 50,000 unique entries. Further written analysis also considers original artefacts, 3D scans and 2D copies.

To extract instances from the tablets, graphic editing software was used. The files include oddly shaped or especially elongated wedges, even if they cross over into the next sign. While this may make it difficult to apply 3D character

32 Ernst-Pradal uses a similar filing system in her analysis of the Ugarit tablets: "*Le numéro de la tablette d'où il était issu, le numéro de la ligne, le genre du texte et le nom du scribe quand il figurait sur la tablette*" (2008: 50).

33 The database used for this project was written using Python by Dr Leszek Świrski (University of Cambridge, UK). If you would like access to the database for research purposes, please contact the author.

recognition to the files – if it is ever developed well enough – it ensures that no features can escape from palaeographic analysis. To keep track of the instances included in (and excluded from) the database, separate text documents were created for each tablet. This also made it possible to count how many instances per tablet were excluded, and to easily compare images to copies, line by line. Instances were only ever excluded when completely illegible due to damage to the tablet. Finally, using copies and transliterations, it was possible to compare the number of instances per line visible on the tablet and estimate instances per line when restored (in case of damage). Counting all (expected) instances per line allows for a full understanding of the composition of the tablet as the scribe intended it, rather than the often damaged or broken version we have today. The text documents also included meta-data such as the publication and collection numbers of each individual tablet, measurements (where possible), subject or genre, and translations.

The data has been used to compare the number of instances on a tablet to the number of instances per line, and to compare the number of instances on a tablet to the total number of lines – as well as to compare both of these to tablet format. This has allowed for reflection on factors such as tablet composition, sign density and sign usage. More specifically, it was possible to compare the number of times certain sign-forms occur and whether they co-occur with other sign-forms – and then to compare this between tablets. Thanks to the counting function of the database, it was possible to quickly show results combined from thousands of instances. No special programming language is needed, and it is possible to create graphs using easily accessible software. Perhaps in the future, graphs could be integrated into the database design too.

2.11 Summary and Conclusions

In this chapter approaches to archaeological thought, material analysis, and the confines of what is and is not possible to study received some consideration. Digging deeper into the theoretical framework, problems of categorisation were explored – for writing as a whole and signs on their own. On a micro level this involves the composition of signs themselves and on a macro level how they are organised. For the practical framework it was investigated how palaeography fits into digital humanities and the various methods and techniques available, as well as their accompanying shortcomings and issues. Finally, theory and practice were joined by reflections on social networks and the possibilities of quantifying them. As a result, this project has based itself around the following research narrative:

The subsequent chapters will explore in what ways writing can be considered a marker of identity and how is it possible to tell the difference between scribal hands. They will discuss how a distinct Mittani script may be described, what defines it, what it relates to, and whether there are sub-groups, as well as the influences that can be detected in these groups. They will question whether Mittani and Middle Assyrian could have been the same script, and what could possibly explain similarities to or differences from other scripts. They will examine the motivations for use of certain types of script, and finally they will illuminate, in some way, how script reflects on the organisation of society and cultural identity during the Late Bronze Age in Northern Mesopotamia.

Of course, the discussed theory raises its own set of discussion points. For example, about the relationship between institutions (e.g. imperial (palace) structures) and script-type. Or, in what ways script-choice could have been a conscious decision. More specifically, this brings into question whether people could have used a certain script-type because they grew up with it (education), because it was promoted in a certain area (geography), or because it was used by the government (politics). It is also fascinating to consider that writing at contemporary Nuzi differs so much from Mittanian. Plus, there is this so-called 'Assyro-Mittanian' writing with its various similarities and differences to Mittanian. This calls into question whether we are using the right labels, what we should distinguish as separate script-groups and sub-groups, and what the boundaries between them are.

All in all, this is a substantial set of objectives to start out with. While you will find some explanations in the conclusions at the end of this book, undoubtedly you will also encounter new questions as well as suggestions on where to go with those next.

CHAPTER 3

Mittani and Assyro-Mittanian

3.1 Introduction

The emergence of Mittani is unclear, but hints can be drawn from various documents and known historical events. Van Koppen (2004: 21) points out the occurrence of the name Ḫanigalbat in Late Old Babylonian, indicating that there was a Hurrian presence during this time. There are also general mentions of continuous strong resistance by the Hurrians against the Hittites (De Martino 2014: 63). It has even been suggested that the Mittani Kingdom was already powerful in the 16th century. Old Kingdom documents such as KBo 3.46 and KBo 3.60 mention a 'King of the Hurrian troops.' Furthermore, a treaty between Ḫatti and Ḫalab (Aleppo) (CTH 75) has a historical introduction which describes manoeuvring the polities of Aštata and Nuḫašši between Ḫatti and Ḫanigalbat (obverse, line 15–20) (Beckman 1999: 93).[1]

Ḫalab had been part of the powerful Middle Bronze Age Kingdom Yamḫad, with vassals such as Alalaḫ, Ebla and Ugarit. The Hittite King Ḫattušili led several campaigns against Yamḫad, significantly weakening it. Ḫattušili died soon after the last campaign, but his grandson Muršili came back to destroy Ḫalab, and continued to even sack Babylon. However, upon his return to Ḫatti he was assassinated by his brother-in-law, inaugurating a period of social unrest amongst the Hittites. With Ḫalab, Ḫatti and Babylon now all struggling, the rising Hurrian power found opportunity to expand.

The name Mittani itself (*Mtn*) only occurs for the first time in an Egyptian source dated to the 15th century BCE (Tuthmosis I) (De Martino 2004: 35). Late Bronze Age archaeological records of the region show that Late Old Babylonian materials were gradually replaced by Mittani pottery (Reiche 2014; Soldi 2008). Although the precise geographical reach of the Mittani territory is not known, it eventually stretched up to Lake Van in eastern Turkey, followed the Upper Khabur in northern Syria, and spread down to modern Kerkuk and the middle Euphrates in Iraq (see **Maps**).[2]

1 However, while the events of CTH 75 are meant to have taken place around the 16th century, this tablet is a 13th century replacement and it is not unthinkable that the contents of the old and the new treaty are not identical.

2 Texts which describe Mittani domination over various areas, and treaties with neighbouring regions, include the Amarna letters (**Paragraph 3.2.1**) and KBo 1.2 (**Paragraph 3.2.2**). While Mittani and Middle Assyrian pottery are not always separated, it is now acknowledged that

 | DOI:10.1163/9789004417243_004

Naming and describing the Mittani socio-political structure has been subject to debate: it has been called 'Empire', 'polity', 'Kingdom' and 'state' (Cancik-Kirschbaum *et al.* 2014: 2). In studying the Middle East, we typically see overarching political structures as imperial formations, which is why we most commonly refer to this structure as the Mittani Empire.[3] At its greatest extent, the Mittani Empire encompassed various urban centres, including but not limited to Başiru (Tall Bazi), Taidu (Tell Hamadiya), Nawar (Tell Brak), Kaḫat (Tell Barri), Urkeš (Tell Mozan), Tell Bderi, Tell Chuera, Tall Munbaqa, and Tell Fekheriye, as well as the smaller Tell Arbid, Tell Beydar, Tell Hwesh and Tell Mohammed Diyab (Pfälzner 2007; Reiche 2014) (see **Maps**). Mittani also included at least the realms of Aššur, Alalaḫ, Arrapḫa, Kizzuwatna, Tunip, and probably Yamḫad (Ḫalab) and Ḫana (Terqa) (Von Dassow 2014). These were semi-independent, and sometimes ruled by their own Kings under the overlordship of Mittani. Models of governance seem to have been adapted on a case-by-case basis. For example, the King of the land of Ḫana is mentioned alongside the Mittanian King (see Charpin 2002), while Ḫalab was assigned a governor (Von Dassow 2014: 20) and at Başiru documents address the (council of) people. Many of the mentioned Kingdoms were incorporated during the reign of King Šauštatar (**Table 3.1**),[4] who features in tablets from Alalaḫ, Bazi, Nuzi and Umm el-Marra and which are currently some of the earliest Mittani tablets available for study.

While Akkadian was the primary language used in official correspondence, it looks like the first language of major parts of the Mittani population was Hurrian.[5] Hurrian is the earliest indigenous language attested in ancient Anatolia (Woodard 2008: 3) and Hurrian texts found at Tell Mozan (ancient Urkeš) date to circa 2100–2000 BCE.[6] Although there is no firmly established palaeography for Old Akkadian, Maiocchi reasons the script used to write Hurrian

---

Nuzi ware, stump bases, fine painted goblets, red band plates, piecrust pot-stands, red-edged bowls, large shallow bowls and some distinctive painting styles may be associated with Mittani layers, and surveys identifying Mittani sites have been conducted throughout northern Syria and northern Iraq (see Koliński (2014: 180) for an overview).

3 According to the original Roman understanding of the word, an *imperium* referred to the geographical expansion and temporal extension of power.

4 Also described in CTH 51 (KBo 1.2).

5 Wilhelm (1989) provides a valuable 35-page history of the Hurrian people. In particular, a lot of research bases itself on tracing Hurrian personal names throughout history – with the footnote that linguistic derivation of a name does not lead to certainty about the nationality of its owner (Wilhelm 1989: 13). In addition, it is possible to detect Hurrian lexicon, grammar, and personal names even in Akkadian documents (Wilhelm 2008: 83).

6 Most famous of which is the Tišatal inscription, on display at the Louvre (August 2016).

at Urkeš belongs to this group, albeit in a different hand from Akkadian tablets (2011: 193). Notably, Urkeš yielded both monumental and administrative documents; and the Hurrian language was adapted to the existing cuneiform used at the time.

Thus far, most Hurrian texts have been found at Ḫattuša (see HPM). These are primarily myths, prayers, omens and Hittite rituals with Hurrian incantations, which were written in the script common for Ḫattuša.[7] Wilhelm notes that Hurrian magical documents "enjoyed high cultural prestige" (1989: 52, 70). Late Hurrian texts have been found at Ugarit. These are also all religious texts (incantations, hymns, offerings) (Vita 2009: 220), some composed using syllabic cuneiform[8] and some using the Ugaritic alphabetic cuneiform (Vita 2013: 208). It is likely that Hurrian was more frequently written than spoken in the end; which is comparable to the demise of, for instance, Latin. Hurrian is an "isolated language without a genetic relation to any other known ancient Near Eastern language" (Wilhelm 2008: 81). A cognate language of Hurrian is Urartian, which likewise died out over two millennia ago (around the 6th century BCE).

Speaking and 'being' Hurrian formed an important part of the ethnic, cultural and social identity of the people that together made up the Mittani Empire. This is reflected by the use of Hurrian personal names, but also in international politics. As mentioned in relation to the emergence of the Empire, early sources refer to the King of Mittani as 'King of Hurri(-land)' or 'King of the Hurrian troops'. The 43.5 × 25 × 1.8 cm Amarna letter EA 24, from the Mittani King to the Egyptian Pharaoh, deviates from the diplomatic standard Akkadian, and is instead written entirely in Hurrian. The Mittani Empire is the only known power to have communicated in Hurrian at this scale. When the Empire succumbed to Assyrian and Hittite attacks circa 1350 BCE, Hurrian language faced a downward spiral too and slowly disappeared from history.[9]

Besides language, much about Mittani identity remains a mystery. The area has been difficult to access in recent times[10] and emerging states are often less visible in the archaeological record to begin with (Schwartz 2014: 265). Even in recent surveys, archaeologists still combine Mittani and Assyrian data rather than separating between them (e.g. Kolińksi's Upper Greater Zab Archaeological Reconnaissance Project 2012–2015 and Pfälzner's Eastern Habur

7 With the exception of KUB 47.41 (see **Paragraph 6.2.2**).

8 Ernst-Pradal has been studying the palaeography of the syllabic cuneiform (2015). She uses a similar method to the one in this chapter, comparing wherever possible instances taken from high-quality images.

9 Also see Wilhelm (2015) on the decline of Mittani.

10 Due to, amongst others, the 2003–2011 Iraq War and the 2011-present Syrian Civil war.

TABLE 3.1 Overview of Mittani rulers

Ruler	Reign
Parattarna	1500–1480 BCE
	1470 BCE
Paršatatar	1460–1440 BCE
	1440 BCE
Šaustatar	1480–1460 BCE
	1420 BCE
Artatama I	1400 BCE
	1400–1375 BCE
Šuttarna II	1380 BCE
	1375–1355 BCE
Artašumara	1380 BCE
	1355–1350 BCE
Tušratta	1365–1335 BCE
	1350–1335 BCE

Dates as suggested by Maidman (2010) and Wilhelm (1982). Parattarna was potentially preceded by Šuttarna I circa 1500 BCE (Novák 2007) and Tušratta succeeded by Artatama II, Šuttarna III and Šattiwaza circa 1335 BCE (Wilhelm 1982). For further discussions on the reigns of the Mittani Kings see Kühne (1999), Von Dassow (2005: 19–64) and De Martino (2015).

Survey in Iraqi-Kurdistan 2013–2015). To date, neither a royal archive, such as that of Aššur, nor the capital Waššukanni has been found (with certainty).[11] However, this does not mean that the available evidence can be overlooked. The handful of Mittani tablets are a small but valuable source of information, but, while transcribed and translated, their material composition and the writing of the signs themselves has received very little attention.

3.2 The Corpus

Terminology of the initial analysis will be based on existing judgements, where scholars have distinguished between 'Mittani', 'Assyro-Mittani' and 'Middle Assyrian'. However, as will be illustrated over the following chapters, when

11 A serious contender is Tell Fekheriye in northern Syria (Opitz 1927: 300).

compared, these labels are sometimes arguably inaccurate or in need of re-interpretation. The tablets considered in this chapter have been divided into three corpora: 1) the Mittani Amarna letters (diplomatic correspondence), 2) other tablets classified as Mittani (shorter correspondence from different sites) and 3) a selection of Assyro-Mittani tablets (witchcraft and rituals found at Boğazköy).

The label Assyro-Mittanian was introduced by Wilhelm (1991b), in his notes on four Boğazköy tablets (KBo 36.11, KBo 36.28, KBo 36.29, and KBo 36.34).[12] He explains that the script was inspired by Mesopotamian traditions, "presumably by a north Babylonian variant of writing that spread north to Arrapḫa and Assyria" (Wilhelm 2010: 257). Wilhelm himself refers to Schwemer (1998) for a palaeographic comparison between Middle Assyrian, Assyro-Mittanian and Mittanian. The compound implies that the script should have features of Mittani and Assyrian yet stand out from both. Since Mittani and Early Middle Assyrian share many features to begin with, this calls into question when something is a separate script-type, how it becomes another script-type, and when it is a sub-type. Weeden (2012) has suggested a terminological re-calibration, using Assyro-Mittanian as the over-arching category which includes Early Middle Assyrian and Mittanian (i.e. not as a category on its own). Anything that is neither Early Middle Assyrian nor Mittanian, but shares features with both, can be defined as belonging to the larger script group (primarily because there is not enough information to define it any more closely). For this reason, the following chapters on Middle Assyrian (Early and Later) and Nuzi will be used for thorough comparison, with the following questions taking centre stage:

How many different sign-forms were there in other contemporary scripts; how do they differ; and how did they evolve? When does an old script-group end and a new script-group begin? What are the factors that determine variation; can variation be attributed to scribal school; can variation be attributed to scribe; and when is it possible to tell the difference between school and scribe?

To begin with, this chapter will carefully outline and describe the features of (what we think is) Mittani script. At the time of writing (2018), the total number of tablets labelled Mittani is fewer than 40. They include 14 tablets from el-Amarna, 4 tablets from Boğazköy (and 2 other possible tablets from Boğazköy), 6 tablets from Alalaḫ (IV), 1 tablet from Umm el-Marra, 2 tablets from Tall Bazi, 6 tablets from Tell Brak, 1 tablet from Nuzi, and 2 tablets from the Schøyen Collection (as well as 1 possible tablet from Tell Hammam at-Turkman).

12 KBo 36.11, KBo 36.29 and KBo 36.34 are also included in the database; KBo 36.28 is both fragmentary and damaged and only referred to in the written analysis.

3.2.1 *The Tušratta Letters*

The Mittani el-Amarna tablets, also known as the Tušratta letters, are 14 tablets from the famous Amarna correspondence, which consists of 382 documents in total. Nearly all Amarna documents are epistolary in nature, with a few classed as poetry. The site was a New Kingdom capital city, both constructed and abandoned in a period of 15–30 years (Stevens 2015). The archives provide a record of the interaction between the Egyptian Empire and other great powers (Babylonia, Mittani, Ḫatti, Arzawa, Alašiya) as well as smaller Kingdoms (Amurru, Ugarit) and Canaanite 'city-states' (Adams 2008: 88). The Mittani documents record correspondence between King Tušratta and Amenhotep III (circa 1391–1353 BCE) and Amenhotep IV (Akhenaten) (circa 1353–1335 BCE).[13]

Named after their find-place, the clay tablets were discovered in 1887 by the local inhabitants of el-Amarna (Egypt). Some were then purchased by museums, and some by private collectors. Today, the Mittani documents are all located in the British Museum (London) and Vorderasiatisches Museum (Berlin). Due to the initial accidental discovery of the tablets, the archaeological context of most Amarna tablets has not been documented. However, the site also has a long history of legal excavations: Petrie in 1891–92, the Deutsche Orient-Gesellschaft in 1913, as well as the Egypt Exploration Society from 1920–36 and again from 1977 onwards. A handful of Amarna tablets was found in or near 'block of chambers #19', also tentatively named 'Foreign Office' (Sayce 1894: 34), 'Records Office' (Pendlebury 1951: 130), or 'Royal Bureau' (Mynářová 2007: 37), and some in residential buildings further away (Izre'el 1997: 3). None of the tablets were Mittani however, so whether these documents were also originally located in the 'Records Office' remains speculative. Furthermore, many of the Amarna letters pre-date the foundation of Akhenaten's city, which means they could have originally been stored in the palace of Amenhotep III, in Malqata in western Thebes. Due to the abandonment of Amarna after Akhenaten's death, part of the royal archive may have then been moved back to Thebes or Memphis again (Bard 2015: 421).

It has been possible to do a provenance study on the Mittani documents, which places them in the Khabur basin. Petrographically, the materials of the tablets supply little information about the precise location where they were originally created (Goren *et al.* 2004: 40). However, the material and suggested geology of all Mittani tablets are almost identical and their composition does not match Egyptian or Babylonian tablets. Furthermore, chemical analysis also indicates strong similarities between all Mittani tablets. Researchers have

13 With the exception of EA 26 (written to the widow Tiye) and EA 30 (where the Mittani King is not identified).

sampled both the Hurrian letter (EA 24) and an Akkadian document (EA 18): although EA 24 and EA 18 differ somewhat, they are made of two related clay types that are markedly different from those of the Babylonian and Egyptian letters. In other words, while these two tablets are both from the same area, it is possible that they were made in different locations within the Khabur region (Goren *et al.* 2004: 43). Although the provenance study focuses on speculation about the location of the Mittanian capital Waššukanni, it is impossible to determine the exact place in which any of the tablets were created.[14] In summary, it is not known precisely where the Mittani Amarna tablets were found, or where they were written. However, their corresponding purpose and material ensure that it is possible to view the 14 documents as belonging to a cohesive collection.

As mentioned in the introduction to this book, the only sign-list based on the Tušratta letters which has been published so far was created by Otto Schröder in 1915.[15] The author does not comment on the signs and the work includes no descriptions or discussion. In addition, Schröder only looked at the tablets in the Vorderasiatisches Museum Berlin – by him labelled tablets 8–12 and 199–201, now better known as EA 18, EA 20, EA 21, EA 22, EA 24, EA 25, EA 27, EA 29. He did not consider the remaining six tablets in the British Museum London – EA 17, EA 19, EA 23, EA 26, EA 28 and EA 30. While, for instance, EA 29 (Berlin) is a very long text and EA 30 (London) very short, the number of available signs should not be thought to equal the usefulness of the tablet; likewise, a sign appearing on the side of a tablet should not be discounted because it may be more difficult to read.[16] For this reason it is of great significance to include the British Museum tablets in any further discussion of the palaeography of the Tušratta correspondence.

EA 17 (BM 029792, 12.3 × 7.7 × 1 cm) is a relatively short letter from Tušratta to Amenhotep III, rekindling their diplomatic alliance. The message recounts Tušratta's family history and places emphasis on their friendship. It mentions enemies, gifts, and messengers. Tušratta refers to the Pharaoh as 'my brother'. This family metaphor is used throughout the entire Amarna correspondence,

---

14 Although it has been suggested that Waššukanni can be identified with Tell el-Fekheriye on the Turkish border in Syria, sufficient evidence is still lacking (see for example Bonatz & Bartl 2013: 266).

15 Dietrich & Mayer (2010) have also published a sign-list exclusively for EA 24, and as mentioned Schwemer (1998) has used the Amarna tablets in his study of Assyro-Mittanian palaeography.

16 However, methodologically it is of little use to include damaged instances (from any location on a tablet), unless the characterising part of the sign-form survives (e.g. it is clearly 118 TI_1 and not TI_2, despite damage).

modelling international relations on a 'family-village-neighbourhood' structure (Liverani 2000: 18). Addressing someone as 'brother' indicates that they have the same level of power – or otherwise at least a desire to be just as powerful. Protection from Egypt against the Hittite power was essential to the Mittani state, which made every effort to be on good terms. The quality of the tablet is excellent: only the upper right corner on the obverse has suffered damage. It has 54 lines, with an average of 10 signs per line. For the database it was possible to collect 536 instances, comprising 98 signs. The images used in this database came from the British Museum online collection (nr. E29789),[17] and the transcription (Izre'el) and copy (Knudtzon 1915) from CDLI (nr. P270895).[18]

EA 18 (VAT 01880 + VAT 01879, 8.3 × 7.6 cm)[19] is a short message from the Mittani King Tušratta to Amenhotep III about a gift. This tablet is the most damaged in the whole collection, and it was not possible to extract more than 16 instances (12 signs) in total. The tablet has 16 lines with an average of 7 signs per line. Although the key sign-forms will be considered, this makes it difficult to include EA 18 in any type of comparative analysis. Low-quality, fuzzy, photographs were available via the Vorderasiatisches Museum, Berlin; but CDLI has recently also published a high-resolution image (nr. P271171). A transcription (Izre'el) and copy (Knudtzon 1915) have likewise been available through CDLI.

EA 19 (BM 029791, 22.2 × 12.7 cm) is a letter from Tušratta to Amenhotep III, acknowledging friendly letters and announcing despatch of gifts. It has been nicknamed 'love and gold', as its contents describe the relationships between various family members and requests for gold (referring to the rich Nubian gold-mines) (Edzard 1960: 43). Tušratta claims a large quantity of gold should be sent as payment for expenses of his grandfather in sending gifts to the King, and he asks for a gift in return for his daughter, whom Amenhotep marries. The combination KÙ.SIG$_{17}$ (*ḫurāṣu* = gold) appears on the tablet frequently. The writing on the tablet is clear and distinct, and one of the best-preserved in the entire Tušratta correspondence. The tablet has 85 lines, with an average of 13 instances per line. It was possible to record 1,463 instances (128 signs), with an average of less than 1 instance per line missing (mostly

17 The collection can be accessed through http://www.britishmuseum.org/research/collection_online/search.aspx (August 2019). When entering a number, replace the '0' with an 'E': e.g. not '029792' but 'E29792'. Images not available on the website may be requested via e-mail.

18 The CDLI database can be searched online at http://cdli.ucla.edu/ (August 2019).

19 Tablets were measured in person by the author where possible. EA 18 is too damaged to make an accurate estimation of its thickness.

damage on the edges). The image used in the database came from the British Museum online collection, and another high-resolution image has been available on InscriptiFact (nr. 01762).[20] A transcription (Izre'el) and copy (Knudtzon 1915) were accessed via CDLI (nr. P270894).

EA 20 (VAT 00191, 17.8 × 11.5 cm) is a letter from Tušratta to Amenhotep III, about the marriage of his daughter Taduḫepa to the Pharaoh. It appears that Amenhotep III had sent an official named Mane to escort the King's daughter to Egypt. However, there was a delay before the princess could be sent and Tušratta dispatched Haramašši, a man known to the Pharaoh, with a message explaining the situation. 'Diplomatic delays' are a common occurrence in the Amarna correspondence, indicating an unwillingness to communicate (Jönsson 2000: 202). Tušratta writes that he had gathered all the significant people in his court for the unveiling of the Egyptian gifts, only to realise the statues were not in fact made of solid gold. However, he writes, the Egyptian delegation was as distraught as he was and defended the good intentions of their master. Of course, this may be a tactical way for Tušratta to suggest to Amenhotep to send the appropriate statues after all. The tablet is crumbling, but the sign instances that survive are of good quality. The tablet has 84 lines, with an average of 18 instances per line. In total 333 instances were recorded (82 signs). The images used in the database are from InscriptiFact (nr. 01571), but images can also be found through the Vorderasiatisches Museum,[21] and CDLI (nr. P271179). The transcription (Izre'el) and copy (Knudtzon 1915) were accessed through CDLI.

EA 21 (VAT 00190, 9.2 × 7.6 × 1.1 cm) is another letter from Tušratta to Amenhotep III about a gold statue. They seem to have resolved the marriage and gift situation, and Tušratta says he is sending gifts to Amenhotep now. He praises the Egyptian messengers saying, 'I have never seen men with such an appearance' (line 24–32). These messengers, or court officials, can also be recognised as diplomats. The way in which they are treated reflects state relations (Jönsson 2000: 202). The care and maintenance of messengers was an integral part of Amarna-period diplomacy. To strengthen the position of the host – both locally and on an international level – foreign messengers were fed and cared for in an elaborate public display; their arrival was an excuse to throw a grand party in support of the King's prestige (Head 2011: 84). This tablet is very

20 The InscriptiFact viewer can be downloaded from http://www.inscriptifact.com/ (August 2019). Using the database requires registration and entering a username and password. It may not be compatible with all operating systems.

21 Previously available at http://web.archive.org/web/*/http://amarna.filol.csic.es 'Las tablillas de El Amarna en el Vorderasiatisches Museum de Berlín' (website offline).

worn, but it has 41 lines with an average of 10 instances per line. The total number of instances collected was 242 (74 signs). Initially images from InscriptiFact (nr. 01572) and the Vorderasiatisches Museum were used in the database, but CDLI has recently published higher resolution images (nr. P271178). The transcription (Izre'el) and copy (Knudtzon 1915) can be found on CDLI as well.

EA 22 (VAT 00395, 50.5 × 17.5 × 1.8 cm) is a long gift-list from Tušratta to Amenhotep III, primarily concerned with presenting the dowry and personal gifts. The tablet includes many logograms such as ANŠE.KUR.RA.MEŠ (*sīsî*, horses) and determinatives like KUŠ (*mašku*, leather). Tušratta now refers to Amenhotep III as 'brother-in-law' as well. The tablet is large and reasonably well-preserved; it has 246 lines spread over 4 columns, with an average of 11 instances per line. In total 1,853 instances were gathered (175 signs). The photographs used were taken by the author in the Vorderasiatisches Museum, Berlin (March 2014). A transcription (Izre'el), copy (Knudtzon 1915), and a low-quality, grainy, image have been available through CDLI (nr. P271213).

EA 23 (BM 029793, 8.9 × 6.7 × 0.9 cm) is a letter from Tušratta to Amenhotep III, with regard to the royal marriage. The Hurrian goddess Šauska (written using ^{d}INANNA) is called upon to bless the marriage. The tablet is very well-preserved and has sustained no damage. On the reverse there are 3 lines of Hieratic writing which have nearly worn away. The Hieratic was probably added once the letter was stored in the Egyptian archive (Hagen 2011). The tablet has 32 lines with an average of 11 instances per line. The total number of instances collected was 295 (81 signs). The images used for the database came from the British Museum online collection (nr. E29793), the transcription (Izre'el) and copy (Knudtzon 1915) from CDLI (nr. P270896).

EA 24 (VAT 00422, 43.5 × 25 × 1.8 cm) is a letter from Tušratta to Amenhotep III about accompanying Taduḫepa to Egypt. This is the only letter in the Amarna correspondence which was written in Hurrian and the only Hurrian document found to date of such significant size and length. Tušratta spends much of the letter complaining that he has not received enough, or expensive enough, gifts from Amenhotep III. The letter discusses the historical background of the marriage, with the aim to emphasise political integration. Tušratta mentions the 'Hittite enemy' (column 1, line 15) and talks about a mutual defence treaty (while the defence can be assumed to be intended against the Hittites, they are not named in this context). Tušratta writes 'If on the other hand my archenemy should present himself – behold, he should definitely not present himself! – and I report it to my brother, (then) my brother will send (help), (by) sending (all forces) of Egypt, the armoured ones and all the irregulars against my enemy' (column 3, line 114–117). Tušratta also stresses unity, with statements such as 'Just as we (now) (are) united in our mutuality, (so will) we be united in the future, and the Ḫurri country (and) the country of Egypt will, through all this in their unity, be content with each other in the future, as if I were the lord of Egypt (and) my brother lord of the Ḫurri country' (column 1, line 67–71). Tušratta is strategic in his political approach: he says he will only trust Mane (establishing a secure line of communication) and asks for the movement of envoys to be unhindered and fast (see EA 30). EA 24 by far yielded the most sign instances of any of the tablets (5,086 instances) but does not have the largest repertoire of signs (only 106). It has 495 lines spread over 4 columns, with an average of 16 instances per line. The tablet is also so large and heavy[22] that it may not have been carried by one person alone. Considering its size and context (royal wedding) the tablet was likely intended to impress. Photographs of the tablet were taken by the author at the Vorderasiatisches Museum, Berlin (March 2014). A copy (Knudtzon 1915) has been available on CDLI (nr. P271214) and a transcription in Dietrich and Mayer (2010).

EA 25 (VAT 00340 (+) VAT 02191 + fragments, 37 × 21.5 × 2.3 cm) is another gift-list from Tušratta to Amenhotep III. The document is similar to EA 22, and it is especially noteworthy that these two gift-lists are some of the biggest tablets in the Tušratta collection. Although large portions of EA 25 are damaged, the surviving signs are all of very good quality. It was possible to collect 2,056 instances (146 signs), from 289 lines, with an average of 16 instances per line. Photographs of the tablet were taken by the author at the Vorderasiatisches Museum, Berlin (March 2014). A transcription (Izre'el) and copy (Knudtzon 1915) have been available on CDLI (nr. P271202).

EA 26 (BM 029794 + A 09356, 14.7 × 9.5 × 2.4 cm) is a letter from Tušratta to Queen Tiye of Egypt. The majority of the letter consists of formulaic well-wishing, re-iterating friendship between Mittani and Egypt, and it ends by asking for a gift of gold. Tiye was wife to Amenhotep III, who had died at the time this letter was written. She was a powerful figure in the Egyptian court and Tušratta probably expected her to assert some influence with regard to their good diplomatic relations, and particularly the gold gift as well. Although the tablet has survived relatively well, the left bottom corner is broken. The tablet has 2–3 lines of Hieratic, which read 'Lady of the Two Lands (Wife of the King)' (translated in Rainey 2015: 281). The total number of instances was 453 (83 signs), from 59 lines, with an average of 13 instances per line. High resolution images have been available through the British Museum

22 Precise weight currently not known. However, other examples of very large cuneiform tablets include the Ur III tablets, which can measure 30 cm square and weigh up to 7 kg (e.g. BM 110116, dating to Ibbi-Sin, about the management of land). Walker comments "how they handled them is itself a mystery" (1987: 22).

online collection (nr. E29794) and a transcription (Izre'el) and copy (Knudtzon 1915) through CDLI (nr. P270897).

EA 27 (VAT 00233 + VAT 02197 + VAT 02193, 24.8 × 13.6 cm) is a letter from Tušratta to Amenhotep IV (Akhenaten), complaining about gold statues. As has become clear from the previous letter, Tušratta and Amenhotep IV did not get off on the right foot. Akhenaten had sent him gold plated statues rather than statues made of solid gold. These statues formed part of the bride price which Tušratta received for the marriage of his daughter Taduḫepa. This letter stands out in particular for Tušratta's exclamation that in Egypt 'gold is as plentiful as dirt / dust' (reverse, line 46). Despite large parts of the tablets having broken, the surviving signs are very clear. The tablet has 114 lines, with an average of 20 instances per line. It was possible to collect 1,259 instances (118 signs). The images used came from InscriptiFact (nr. 01573), and the transcription (Izre'el) and copy (Knudtzon 1915) from CDLI (nr. P271181).

EA 28 (BM 037645, 14.6 × 10.2 × 2.4 cm) is a letter from Tušratta to Amenhotep IV, about a dispute regarding their messengers. Since Tušratta's messengers Pirissi and Tulubri were detained in Egypt, he decided to hold back the Egyptian official, Mane. Tušratta clearly seems more comfortable with his old ally, Queen Tiye, and the final part of the letter is addressed to her. He explains to the Pharaoh that 'she can tell you' to trust the messengers. The tablet has survived well, with minor damage on the right edge and a small section of the bottom broken off. It has 49 lines with an average of 11 instances per line. The total number of instances gathered was 527 (97 signs). Images have been available through the British Museum online collection (nr. E37645) and InscriptiFact (nr. 01231), the transcription (Izre'el) and copy (Knudtzon 1915) through CDLI (nr. P270967).

EA 29 (VAT 00271 + VAT 01600 + VAT 01618 + VAT 01619 + VAT 01620 + VAT 02192 + VAT 02194 + VAT 02195 + VAT 02196 + VAT 02197, 43.2 × 24.9 cm) is the last (known) letter sent from Tušratta to Amenhotep IV. Tušratta begins by declaring a long list of gifts he has sent to Akhenaten and expresses his sadness over the death of Amenhotep III. Note that this is another very large document. He then brings up the golden statues once more. In the letter Tušratta also expresses his astonishment that Ḫaramašši has managed to make a round-trip between the Mittani capital and Egypt in 3 months – an important side-note on the frequency at which the correspondence was possible to take place. It was possible to collect 2,500 instances (137 signs) from 188 lines (no columns) with 25 instances per line. Images have been available through the Vorderasiatisches Museum, Berlin, and Inscriptifact (nr. 01574). The transcription (Izre'el) and copy (Knudtzon 1915) were taken from CDLI (nr. P271184).

Finally, EA 30 (BM 029841, 4.8 × 6 cm) is the only letter not addressed to the Egyptian Pharaoh or his wife; instead it is from Tušratta to 'the Kings of Canaan'. It is a short letter of credentials of a Mittanian envoy and the smallest tablet in the Mittani Amarna correspondence. Despite the tablet's size its 13 lines (8 instances per line) have survived very well and it was possible to record nearly all sign instances appearing on the tablet (105 instances, 52 signs). In addition, its size allowed for a very high-quality image to be created (available through InscriptiFact, nr. 01732) making it possible to study the impression of wedges at almost four times the size of the other tablets. A less large image has also been available through the British Museum online collection (nr. E29841) and a transcription (Izre'el) and copy (Knudtzon 1915) on CDLI (nr. P270943).

So, while this is a coherent collection of Mittani documents, most tablets differ from one another in content, shape, size and writing-style. As a result, there are a few questions which are particularly important with regard to this corpus. For example, this chapter considers in which ways the writing styles of each tablet differ; and whether differences can be related to the shape, size or content of the tablet. It will discuss how sign-forms could be connected to tablet-genre; and whether there is a significant difference between letters and gift-lists. Furthermore, it may be of interest to work toward a tablet-shape-genre typology; for instance, considering the tablet as a prestige object may have impacted writing style. Finally, some time will be spent discussing how the Hurrian letter (EA 24) differs from the Akkadian documents.

3.2.2 *The Other Mittani Tablets*

KBo 1.2 (manuscript B of CTH 51, 14.4 × 17.1 cm) is one of three (known) copies of a treaty between Šuppiluliuma I of Ḫatti and Šattiwazza of Mittani. This treaty was created shortly after the events described in the Tušratta letters and it is an important source on the expansion of Ḫatti into northern Syria in the middle of the 14th century BCE (Beckman 1999: 37). When Tušratta was murdered during the coup, his son Šattiwazza fled to Ḫatti – where Šuppiluliuma jumped at the chance to incorporate him into his own Empire. The other two copies of the treaty[23] were written with more (but not exclusively) typical Hittite sign-forms (Weeden 2012: 233). Besides CTH 51, there is another version of the treaty, CTH 52.[24] The first includes numerous of provisions (succession, fugitives, and frontiers), while the second focusses on history, curses and blessings,

23 Manuscript A: KBo 1.1. Manuscript C: KUB 3.1a, KBo 28.114, KUB 3.1b, KBo 28.111, KBo 28.112, KUB 3.1c, KUB 3.1d, KBo 50.27.

24 Manuscript A: KBo 1.3 and KUB 3.17.

and emphasises there should be no co-operation with Assyria while justifying the conduct of Šattiwazza with Ḫatti. Its purpose may have been to preserve some pretence of Mittani independence and therefore increased co-operation (Beckman 1999: 38). KBo 1.2 is written completely in Akkadian and like most Mittani Amarna letters it is not separated into columns. While it was found in Boğazköy its exact find-spot is unknown. Transcription (after Weidner 1923) and images were taken from the HPM (VAT 13024), via the Vorderasiatisches Museum Berlin where the tablet is currently also located.

KBo 28.66 (10.6 × 4.7 cm) is a fragmentary Akkadian letter from the Mittanian King to the Hittite King or a dignitary. The addressee is referred to as his 'brother', indicating equal relations between Ḫanigalbat and Ḫatti and thus places the tablet prior to the subjugation of Ḫanigalbat by Assyria. However, the letter also features Narigalli (or Nerikkaili), whom Hagenbuchner suggests was the son of Ḫattušili III and brother of Tudḫaliya IV (1989: 311), which indicates the period during which Assyria conquered Ḫanigalbat. Either the identity of Narigalli has to be reconsidered, or this tablet was written during the very final years of Mittani power.[25] The contents of the letter are otherwise very unclear and involve not returning and not reaching something. It includes the reference 'oath tablet' (ša ma-mi-ti, obverse lines 4 and 15), suggesting perhaps the subject is diplomatic in nature. It also includes the phrases 'he said words which were not good' (a-ma-te.MEŠ la-a DU_{10}.GA.MEŠ, line 18) and 'you will not revenge him' (la-a tù-ta-ar-šu, line 13) which may be indicative of tension amongst the various powers. Alexandrov (2014: 53) comments that the order in which the addressee and the sender are mentioned (*ana* A *qibīma umma* S-*ma*) is typical for Mittanian (rather than the Syro-Anatolian tradition). However, the line is broken (only [... bi]-ma survives) so both the addressee and the formula are uncertain. Alexandrov also suggests that the Akkadian has 'Assyrianisms' such as vowel harmony (la-a tàš-pá-ra, obverse line 7), forms of enclitic accusative pronouns (la-a tu-tá-ar-ra-šu-nu, also line 7) and possibly also Hurrian influence (agreeing feminine and masculine forms, such as KUR-ti and ša-ni-i in line 6) (*ibid*). At the moment the tablet is located in Ankara. A transcription can be found in Hagenbuchner (1989: #211) and photographs as well as a 3D-scan have been made available through the HPM (nr. 1603/c), via the Vorderasiatisches Museum Berlin.

KBo 28.65 (5.9 × 4.8 cm) is likewise fragmentary and difficult to decipher. However, it is possible to read the signs LUGAL-ti ḫa-ni-[gal ...] (line 3), and also to see a seal of the King of Ḫanigalbat (Güterbock 1942: 37). It further mentions the city Taide (URU ta-i-te, reverse, line 5). The addressee is now 'my

25 At the end of the reign of Šattuara I, who became a vassal of the Assyrian King Adad-nirari.

father', indicating that, if understood diplomatically, Ḫanigalbat had become dependent on Ḫatti.[26] Photographs and a 3D scan have been made available through the HPM (n. 2539/c) via the Akademie der Wissenschaften und der Literatur Mainz and the Vorderasiatisches Museum Berlin, and the tablet itself is currently in Ankara. Own transcription was used.

IBoT 1.34 (12.8 × 9.7 cm) is a letter from a King of Ḫanigalbat to a King of Ḫatti. They are only referred to by their titles, not their personal names.[27] An Eḫli-šarrumma and Ḫalpa-ziti are mentioned however. The first is probably the Eḫli-šarrumma who became King of Isuwa during the reign of Tudḫaliya IV and was contemporary with Šalmaneser I and Tukulti-ninurta I (Beckman 1999: 142; Glocker 2011: 255).[28] The second was a likely a priestly King in Aleppo during the reign of Tudḫaliya IV (Alexandrov 2014: 67). The addressee is again 'my father', implying that Ḫanigalbat is a vassal of Ḫatti here and that this is a very late Mittani document. The Mittanian King is having diplomatic difficulties and he is being accused of disloyal behaviour by Eḫli-šarrumma and Ḫalpa-ziti. In line 13, the King compares the Assyrian ruler to the Hurrian god and patron Teššub (ki-i-me-e ^{d}IŠKUR EN-ia), as a reference to his power over Mittani (Alexandrov 2014: 62). However, in addition to damage to the obverse, the entire reverse of the letter is broken and it is difficult to use in palaeographic analysis. The tablet is currently in Istanbul and images can be obtained through the HPM (Bo 10401). A transcription can be found in Hagenbuchner (1989: #213).

KUB 3.80 (5.5 × 4.2 cm) is another broken fragment, where only the middle of the text has been preserved. Although almost nothing of the first line survives, it is probably from the King of Ḫanigalbat to a Hittite King (Weeden 2012: 232) or alternatively from a King to a vassal (Weeden 2014: 60). The tablet is currently in Istanbul and images are available through the HPM (Bo 1271), via the Akademie der Wissenschaften und der Literatur Mainz and the Vorderasiatisches Museum Berlin. A transcription can be found in Hagenbuchner (1989: #212), who thinks the letter was sent by (a) King Šattuara. However Mora and Giorgieri (2004: 149) argue that rather than

26 Güterbock (1942: 38) also suggests the phrase could be interpreted literally, in which case it would be a letter from Šattiwaza to his father-in-law Šuppiluliuma I.

27 Possibly Šattuara II and Tudḫaliya IV, since Ḫanigalbat was a vassal of Ḫatti during that time (Klengel 1963), with further notes in Van den Hout (1995: 125) and Cancik-Kirschbaum (2008: 210).

28 It is possible that a different, otherwise unknown, Eḫli-šarrumma is meant here (Alexandrov 2014: 65) and that Ḫalpi-ziti became King straight after the battle of Qadeš (Singer 2011: 165) – in which case the document may be dated slightly earlier.

^{DIŠ}Ša-at-[du]-a-[ra] the name should be read ^{DIŠ}Za-[ad-du-a], making the sender Zadduwa, and not the King of Ḫanigalbat.

KUB 4.53 (8.7 × 6.1 cm) was identified as a Mittanian school-tablet by Wilhelm (1994: 6) – which would make it the only known Mittanian school-tablet. The scribe has the Hurrian name Aki-teššup. However, Rutz later suggested it could be a collection of texts, with an incantation prayer on the obverse and terrestrial omens on the reverse (2012: 171). The tablet is currently in Istanbul and images were taken from the HPM (Bo 1384), via the Akademie der Wissenschaften und der Literatur Mainz and the Vorderasiatisches Museum Berlin. Transcriptions are available in both Wilhelm (1994) and Rutz (2012).[29]

Ancient Alalaḫ (Tell Atchana) is located in the Hatay province of modern Turkey, which borders Syria (see **Maps**). It was first surveyed in the 1930s and excavated by Sir Leonard Woolley from 1936–1939 and 1946–1949, followed by the Oriental Institute from 2003–2004 and since 2006 the Mustafa Kemal University in Antakya (Fink 2010: 14). Alalaḫ was an important urban centre and a vassal of Mittani during the 15th–14th centuries BCE. 15th century 'Alalaḫ IV' was also one of the two strata of the site yielding most textual finds (Von Dassow 2005: 1). A dynasty had been established by Idrimi (according to his statue inscription) (see Dietrich & Loretz 1981: 204).[30] This is a mythical rather than a strictly historical account and several events do not match up; for instance, the inscription announces that Idrimi's son and designated successor was one Addu-nirari, but Addu-nirari does not re-appear in any other records.[31] Besides the statue, a handful of tablets makes mention of Idrimi (AlT 3, AlT 99, AlT 71), one of which indicates Parattarna as Idrimi's overlord. This would date his accession to circa 1475 BCE (Von Dassow 2008: 42). The story of Idrimi's son Niqmepa (AlT 15) is less shrouded in mystery. More than half of the documents found at Alalaḫ level IV were drawn up in his presence. They attest to a treaty with Tunip (AlT 2) and legal cases involving Šauštatar of Mittani (see below). These tablets are composed in a Middle Babylonian form of cuneiform.[32] Postgate has suggested that similarities between Mittani and

---

29 KUB 3.80 and KUB 4.53 were included here due to their original classification as Mittanian by other scholars; however, upon refection, their labels will be discussed further in **Paragraph 6.2.2.**

30 Note: it is unclear when the statue was made and inscribed, who authored the inscription and who authorised it (Von Dassow 2008: 31).

31 Wiseman suggests this is because he either ruled for a very short period of time, or took on different responsibilities such as religious service (1953: 5).

32 Niedorf (2008) has published all 606 tablets from this period. On CDLI images are available of AlT 17, 46, 48, 50, 70, 73, 81, 87, 89, 108, 110, 114, 128, 133, 136, 142, 147, 148, 149, 160, 172,

other documents could only be attributed to shared heritage under Mittani domination rather than cross-border influence (2013: 382) and also that the Mittani documents were 'probably not written at Alalaḫ' (2013: 387).

AlT 13 (ATmB 31.1, BM 131452, 5.1 × 5.3 cm) is a letter with a judgement from King Sauštatar. A man called Irip-ḫazi had claimed 'Ḫanigalbatean' status. Citizenship of Ḫanigalbat was apparently more desirable than citizenship in one of the subject Kingdoms (Von Dassow 2014: 26). The tablets do not reflect legal or semantic opposition between 'slavery' (*ardūtu*) and 'status of Ḫanigalbatean' (*ḫanigalbatūtu*) (Von Dassow 2008: 51): it was possible to be a subject to the King of Alalaḫ without being a slave or a Ḫanigalbatean. In this document allegiance and subordination to the King of Alalaḫ is contrasted with allegiance and subordination to the King of Mittani. With the status of a citizen of Ḫanigalbat, Irip-ḫazi would owe no service to the King of Alalaḫ. However, the King judges him a subject of Alalaḫ and returns him to the service of Niqmepa (Von Dassow 2014: 22). The tablet also bears the seal of Šuttarna I – who may altogether have been one of the earliest known Mittanian rulers (De Martino 2014: 69). While little is known about Šuttarna, it has been suggested that it was common practice to use the seal of an earlier ruler (Postgate 2013: 386). It is unclear why the King would seal the tablet – but possibly as authentication (*ibid*). The tablet was found in palace room 7, below the pavement level (Von Dassow 2005: 14). A high-resolution image was requested via the British Museum (nr. 131452), where the tablet is currently located. A transcription has been published by Niedorf (2008: 239).

AlT 14 (ATmB 31.2, ca. 4.2 × 4.4 cm) is another judgement of Sauštatar, with the seal of Šuttarna. Here, the Mittanian King tries to settle a dispute between Niqmepa and Sunassura of Kizzuwatna in relation to a place called Alawari. The tablet was found in palace room 21, above floor level (Von Dassow 2005: 15). Half of the obverse of the tablet is broken. An image was downloaded via the HPM (Alalach-Archiv, 31.2, AlTqi70), and the tablet itself currently resides in the Archaeological Museum of Antakya, Hatay, Turkey. A transcription can be found in Niedorf (2008: 245).

AlT 108 (ATmB 2.5, BM 131497, 4.5 × 5.4 cm) has less clear protagonists. It is a letter from the King to someone called Utti, asking for exemption from transit tax for asses belonging to Niqmepa. The seal is not obviously one of a Mittanian King, but it was likely that people meant him when referring to 'the King', and no other King at the time was in a position to give orders to Niqmepa (Von Dassow 2014: 16). The tablet was found in palace room 33,

179, 183, 185, 190, 191, 192, 199, 207, 218, 220, 222, 226, 228, 230, 232, 284, 290, 296, 298, 300, 302, 309, 312, 313, 315, 323, and 446 (August 2016).

on the floor (Von Dassow 2005: 17). A high resolution photo provided by the British Museum, where the tablet is currently located, was obtained via CDLI (nr. P348075). Own transcription was used.

AlT 110 (5.2 × 4.9 cm), AlT 111 (ATT/8/9, 4.5 × 4 cm) and AlT 112 (4.8 × 3.8 cm) are letters to Niqmepa from Tiriṣ-ra (or Tirisrama), a Mittanian official (Von Dassow 2014: 16). In AlT 110 Tiriṣ-ra instructs Niqmepa to seize some (unknown) people and then send them to him. The tablet, which is both damaged and broken, is currently in the British Museum, London. An image can be downloaded from CDLI (nr. P348077) and a copy and transcription can be found in Wiseman (1953: 59). AlT 111 asks for various provisions (asses, an ox, cloth, a hammer) to be deposited in a village by the name of Takuia (Ta-ku-ia, line 7). An image has not been published, but a copy and transcription are available in Wiseman (1953: 59). The tablet is currently in the Archaeological Museum of Antakya, Hatay, Turkey. AlT 112 informs Niqmepa of the outcome of a lawsuit. The right and lower edges are broken. A low resolution black and white image was obtained via the HPM (Alalach-Archiv, 2.9, AlTqviii17) and a copy and transcription likewise appear in Wiseman (1953: 59).

Umm el-Marra[33] is located in the Jabbul plain of western Syria, east of Aleppo (see **Maps**). It was first excavated by a Belgian team in the 1970s–1980s and since 1994 by the Johns Hopkins University and the University of Amsterdam (Ascalone & D'Andrea 2013: 221). Umm el-Marra was a regional administrative centre, dating back to the Early Bronze Age (contemporary with Ebla and Alalaḫ VII texts) (Curvers & Schwartz 1997: 204). Compared to other Bronze Age urban centres it was relatively small, indicating that it was a 'second-tier' centre, dominated politically by more powerful cities (Maskevich 2014: 2). Little is known about the social and political circumstances of Umm el-Marra at this time but, partially thanks to the single tablet, it looks like the dominant Late Bronze Age power was Mittani.

UEM T1 (4.3 × 5.2 cm) has much in common with the Alalaḫ (and Tell Brak) tablets. It is a contract by a man called Kubi, who released someone called Azzu, as well as her children. They were granted the coveted 'Ḫanigalbatean' status (see Alalaḫ) and given an estate. It was written in the presence of Šuttarna II and bears the seal of Šauštatar. While Cooper *et al.* argue they were freed from slavery (2005: 48), von Dassow counters that it would have been unusual to see the King about this (2008: 49). It was necessary to execute an act like this in the presence of the King because whoever it was – freed slave, adoptee, concubine, family, or other subordinate – needed the King's authorisation to receive the Ḫanigalbatean status. The tablet was found not far from the city

33 Possibly ancient Tuba/Dub (see Schwartz 2010: 376).

wall on the edge of the site (but in a wheelbarrow, not *in situ*) (Cooper *et al.* 2005: 41). Cooper *et al.* cautiously suggest the tablet may have been composed in the Mittani capital however (2005: 52). Low-quality, fuzzy, black and white images, a copy and a transcription are all published in Cooper *et al.* (2005) – contact with the authors confirmed there are no other photographs or scans (July 2014). The last known whereabouts of the tablet is the National Museum of Aleppo, Syria, which is inaccessible at the time of writing.

Tall Bazi is located in the ar-Raqqa governate of northern Syria, very close to the Tišrin dam (see **Maps**). Rescue excavations were conducted from 1993 to 1998 on behalf of the Damascus Branch of the Deutsches Archäologisches Institut. The Tišrin dam was closed in 1999 and the western part of the site was flooded. The citadel is still accessible and further excavations were conducted by the Ludwig-Maximilians-University Munich from 1999 to 2010 (Otto 2014: 85). As with Umm el-Marra, the tablets of Tall Bazi are one of the primary pieces of evidence of Mittani domination over the region. It looks like it was not a Kingdom and the Mittani King does not deal with a local King but the collective people of the town (Von Dassow 2014: 19). The tablets were both found in the 'central building' of the acropolis. Whereas there is some debate as to the function of the building, it was large, it had thick walls and it contained expensive finds (Sallaberger *et al.* 2006: 74). The tablets were found on the floor inbetween debris of ceramics and traces of fire. It appears they fell down when the buildings collapsed; one of the two tablets was broken (Sallaberger *et al.* 2006: 77). Again, the excavators assume the tablets were not written at Tall Bazi itself but rather composed in the Mittani capital (Sallaberger *et al.* 2006: 78).

Bz 50 (4.3 × 5.0 × 2.0 cm) only has four lines, which say that Šauštatar granted the town Baidali to the people of Baṣiru. Šauštatar here is spelled the same as on AlT 14 (sa-uš-sa-ta-at-tar). The seal on the tablet also belongs to Šauštatar. Bz 51 (3.2 × 4.1 × 1.7 cm) is slightly longer, but its upper right corner is missing. It is another grant of a town to the people of Baṣiru, but this time by Artatama I, although the seal still belongs to Šauštatar. While Sallaberger *et al.* (2006: 98) argue this 'town' was a fortress, Von Dassow proposes it refers simply to a place in the district of Ḫalab (2014: 19). The central building in which the tablets were found was destroyed nearly two centuries after Šauštatar's rule, when the site was already under Hittite domination. The importance of the building, combined with the absence of other tablets, indicates these were significant documents to the townspeople: they took great care to securely store and preserve them. Black and white photographs, copies and transcriptions are published in Sallaberger *et al.* (2006). The last known location of both tablets is the National Museum of Aleppo, Syria.

Tell Brak (ancient Nagar/Nawar) lays in the upper Khabur region of Syria, north of al-Hasaka (see **Maps**). It has a long history going back to the 5th millennium BCE and up to the Early Abbassid period (Ur *et al.* 2011: 1). The site was first excavated by Max Mallowan from 1937–38 and features in Agatha Christie's *Come, Tell Me How You Live*. The modern project was established in 1976 and from 1984 a large Mittani 'palace and temple' complex was uncovered (Oates *et al.* 1997: XV). Excavations continued until 2011, when it became impossible to return due to the Syrian Civil War. While Tell Brak was a smaller site in the 2nd millennium than it had once been, it was still a substantial urban centre covering at least 40 ha (Oates *et al.* 1997: 141). Archaeologists have found no evidence for a King of Nawar during the Mittani period and it seems to have been under direct Mittani domination. Traces of its Hurrian past date back to Ur III, 1970 BCE (Oates *et al.* 1997: 144) and it is one of very few sites which has revealed a fragment of a Hurrian tablet.

TB 11021 (ca. 6.5 × 9.5 × 3.5 cm) is this rare Hurrian fragment. It was found during the 1990 excavation season in the 'Mittani palace', in corridor 6 amongst Adad-nirari I destruction debris (Eidem 1997: 40). Only about 16 lines survive, obverse and reverse combined, but it looks like it was a larger document which in some ways resembles EA 24 (e.g. paragraph division by double lines) (Wilhelm 1991a). It is almost impossible to translate or make any sense of the remaining text, but it includes the unknown places Kusam and Satayam, as well as a person named Šenuni, and the verbs 'hearing', 'dispatching' and 'coming'. A black and white image and transcription are published in Wilhelm (1991a).

TB 6001 (12.0 × 7.2 × 3.2 cm) is an administrative document divided into two columns. It was found in 14 fragments under a pot-stand on the floor of corridor 3 of the 'palace' (Finkel 1985: 194). It originally listed roughly 100 names of workmen grouped into six sections under the supervision of foremen. The 24 names which survive are all Hurrian. Finkel (*ibid*) described the script as a 'cursive Middle Babylonian'. A black and white image and transcription are published in Finkel (1985).

TB 6002 (4.2 × 5.2 × 1.8 cm) is a real-estate transaction. It was found on the floor of room 3 in the 'palace' and survived completely intact. It describes an agreement between Intarutti, and a woman called Zunzilla and her sons. The document names several key royal figures: it was written in the presence of Artašumara, son of Šuttarna II, and it has the seal of Šaustatar, son of Paršatatar. Artašumara was the older brother of Tušratta, also mentioned in EA 17 and possibly AlT 108 (obverse, line 9). Very little is known about him; he was murdered, and it is unclear whether he ever ruled (Kitchen 1998: 257). A black and white image and transcription are published in Finkel (1985).

TB 7035 (3.3 × 4.5 × 1.8 cm) is a short private letter. It was found in a loose ashy fill at floor level in room 5 (Finkel 1988: 84). The document reads 'Tie him up! Nobody may release his handcuffs!' with regard to a certain Uaššu of Mittani (mi-ta-ni). Finkel cautions the names of persons involved are all provisional, due to damage to the tablet, but they include a Pattip-šarri, Nadna, and Kilip-papni. A black and white image and transcription are published in Finkel (1988).

TB 8001 (7.2 × 5.8 × 2.5 cm) is another document addressing 'Ḫanigalbatean' status. It was found in room 11 of the 'palace' at the bottom of charred debris in the floor. Purame, the son of Yabbi's concubine, has been freed and become heir to the estate. The tablet specifically names the town Nawar and the special Mittani *mariannu*-warrior. The letter states it was written in the presence of Tušratta, the King, and it is sealed with the seal of Šaustatar, son of Paršatatar. Illingworth (1988: 100) comments that the layout and structure compare to other contemporary documents in northern Syria, including TB 6002 and tablets from Alalaḫ and Nuzi. A black and white image and transcription are published in Illingworth (1988).

TB 8002 (2.4 × 3.6 × 2.1 cm) finally, is a very small document about the issue of reeds or arrows – either in exchange for services or as a substitute for payment (Illingworth 1988: 105). It was likewise found on the floor of room 11 of the 'palace'. Significantly, it mentions Ta'ide (Taidu) – with which Tell Brak has previously been identified – and Nawar. A black and white image and transcription are published in Illingworth 1988. In addition, black and white images, copies and transcriptions of all Mittani Tell Brak tablets are also available in Eidem (1997). These images were all difficult to work with and, surely, retrieving the tablets and obtaining new photographs or scans would greatly improve analysis, particularly with regard to comparison between the texts. However, the tablets were last known to be in either the National Museum of Aleppo, or Deir ez-Zor, Syria, and are not accessible at the time of writing.

Nuzi, southwest of modern Kirkuk in northern Iraq, will be discussed further in **Chapter 5**. This chapter will focus only on HSS 09, 001 (SMN 1000, 5.7 × 7.0 × 2.2 cm). The tablet was found in 1927, in room A26, an archival room in the house of prince Šilwa-teššup (Stein 1989: 36). It is a letter addressed to Itḫia, about the boundary adjustment of property belonging to Amminaya. Significantly, it is sealed with the seal of Šaustatar, son of Paršatatar, King of Mittani.[34] The tablet was studied at the Semitic Museum, Harvard University,

34 Stein has explained this does not necessarily date the letter directly to Šauštatar; she argues it could have been sent by any one of four Mittanian Kings who ruled during the 15th–14th centuries BCE (1989: 45).

but then returned to Baghdad. Due to political unrest the collection has become disorganised and it is currently not possible to locate the tablet. The only known photo is of the 5 lines of the reverse, published in Starr (1937) (who was interested in the seal). A transcription is available in Speiser (1929: 270) and a copy in Pfeiffer (1932: 2).

Finally, Lambert identified two potential Mittani tablets in the Schøyen Collection (published in the CUSAS series). They both come from private and anonymous owners and nothing is known about their provenance. However, the script, names and language are all consistent with circa 1400 BCE Northern Mesopotamia. MS 1848/1 (4.2 × 4.7 × 1.2 cm) is a letter from Uaššu to Ekakke, about the people of Ašlakka – a known town in the Ḫabur triangle. The name Uaššu also featured in TB 7035, and a variant of Ekakke, Ekeke, is common at Nuzi. MS 1848/2 (2.3 × 4.2 × 1.1 cm) is a private letter about a debt. It was sent by someone called Parašše to Zupite. It also mentions an Arippa and Arip-araššiḫ, both names known at Nuzi, and a fourth person called Yammar. Images of both tablets were taken from CDLI (nrs. P250522 and P250523) and copies and transcriptions were kindly provided by A.R. George (May 2015).

A last tablet tentatively labelled Mittani is HMM 86-014 from Tell Hammam at-Turkman. This severely damaged document measures only 4.2 × 3.4 × 1.8 cm and was published by Van Soldt in 1995 (transcription, translation and copy). A scan of a transparent slide of the obverse was generously provided by Prof. D. Meijer (May 2016). The tablet only has four lines, which read 'Speak to Šatuwatri, thus says the King. Let Karukka(ma) come quickly.' It was found in square M 23, area 45, level 22, incorporated in the mudbricks of a wall which belonged to the second sub-phase of the first phase of the Late Bronze Age palace; and, therefore, has to have been written prior to this period. Van Soldt comments that the names Šatuwatri and Karukka have not otherwise been attested but relates them to Hurrian and names used at Nuzi (1995: 278). He also poses that, because the ruler writes to a subject of the city, the letter probably came from elsewhere; in which case, if the tablet was written during the very early Mittani period, it could have been sent by a Mittani King. The seal is discussed by Van Loon & Meijer in *Akkadica* 52, who identify a long-robed deity wearing a tall hat, a three-leaved plant, a kilted god above a humped bull with a large sphere and, finally, a long-robed worshipper wearing a triple-crested helmet and holding an indistinct object (1987: 9).

3.2.3 *The Assyro-Mittani Tablets*

To address the issue of Mittanian versus Assyro-Mittanian, as many Assyro-Mittanian tablets as possible have been added into the database as well. They present a few unique issues: they were all found in Boğazköy; their original place of writing, and who wrote them, may differ; they are difficult to date and could be decades apart; and they are concerned with witchcraft rituals rather than economy or diplomacy. In addition, they are all divided by columns (whereas few of the Mittani tablets are) and at the same time virtually all of them are fragmentary. For this reason, it is generally difficult to reconstruct their contents and size and to compare their format to the other corpora in the database.

These Assyro-Mittanian documents are CTH 803 (KUB 37.55+KBo 36.32), CTH 804 (KUB 37.43, KUB 37.52 and KBo 9.47), CTH 805 (KUB 37.100a + 100b + 103 + 106), and CTH 812–813 (KBo 36.29 (Ms. A) + KBo 36.34 (Ms. B) + KUB 37.57 (Ms. X1) + KUB 37.62 (Ms. X2) + KUB 37.65 (Ms. X3) + KUB 37.72 (Ms. X6) + KUB 37.74 (Ms. X4) + KUB 37.66 (Ms. X5) + KUB 37.86 (Ms. X7) + KUB 37.97 (Ms. X8) as well as KUB 37.9 and KUB 4.16).

KUB 37.55 (fragments 323c, 373b, 423c, 450c, 472c and 468c) and KBo 36.32 (fragment 2693c) form 'Manuscript A' of a collection of anti-witchcraft therapies, described as 'Assyro-Mittanian of the 14th–13th century' in the printed version of the CMAWR (Schwemer & Abusch 2011: 67). However, the CMaWRo marked it as 'Middle Assyrian', and both Wilhelm (1992: 88) and Weeden (2012: 231, 244) make arguments in favour of this classification. The tablet looks to have had 6 columns, but the entire 3rd/4th column is missing. The fragments were found separately: five in room 5 of the 'large building' along the southern half of the eastern wall, amongst tablet debris; one fragment in the northern section of room 4, also amongst tablet debris; and one in the Phrygian layer, north of room 2–3 (HPM 2016). KUB 37.9 (fragment 166/d) forms 'Manuscript B' of KUB 37.55 + KBo 36.32. This tablet was originally 2–4 columns rather than 3–6, found in the western section of room 5 r/14. The images were accessed via HPM and the Vorderasiatisches Museum, the transcriptions can be found in CMAWR, Volume 1 (Schwemer and Abusch 2011).

KUB 37.43 (fragment 231/g) is an incantation ritual, describing the undoing of witchcraft. In the CMAWR (printed and online) it is labelled 'Middle Babylonian' but the HPM has called the script 'Assyro-Mittanian'. The tablet had two columns, and was found in room 11 of building M, in a brick rubble layer. KUB 37.52 (fragment 337/e) is a small section of a tablet with ritual instructions. It was 'bought by the commissioner' (HPM 2016) so the tablet's find-spot is unknown. Only 13 broken lines survive, but it was identified as 'Assyro-Mittanian of the 14th–13th century' based on its similarity to KUB 37.43 (Schwemer & Abusch 2011: 43). KBo 9.47 (fragment 212/n) is a therapeutic ritual, followed by a description of undoing witchcraft via figurines. It was found in a Phrygian layer. The CMAwRo describes it as Middle Assyrian, but the printed CMAWR calls it 'Assyro-Mittanian'

(Schwemer & Abusch 2011: 46). Images are available from HPM, via HPM and the Vorderasiatisches Museum, with transcriptions in CMAWR, Volume 1 (Schwemer and Abusch 2011).

KUB 37.100a (fragments 1016/c, 656/c) + 100b (fragment 241/c) + 103 (fragment 523/b) + 106 (fragments 536/b, 640/b) (also published as KBo 36.11) is a Sumerian incantation about a 'bad man'. The fragments were found amongst tablet debris scattered through rooms 4–6 of the 'big building'. Cooper classified it as a Middle Babylonian *ductus* (1971: 11), but this is rejected by Weeden (2012: 231) who compares the sign-forms to Middle Assyrian. In addition, because there are some irregularities in translation, sign-values and sign-forms, Cooper suggested that the tablet was written in Boğazköy (1971: 20) – but Weeden comments irregularities may be better explained as Mittanian manuscript transmission (2012: 245). The images were obtained from the HPM, via the Akademie der Wissenschaften und der Literatur, Mainz, and the Vorderasiatisches Museum; most of the transcription has been published by Cooper (1971).

KBo 36.29 (fragments 166/e, 73/b, 285/a, 2533/c, 34/k, 1017/c, 399/d, 2555/c, 97/q, 510/d, 743/c, and 1039/c), or 'Manuscript 'A', is the largest 'Assyro-Mittanian' text. All fragments were found in or near building A, primarily in rooms 3, 5 and 6, and used to make up a tablet with four columns. The text includes recipes against stomach aches and rituals to expel the demons causing suffering. This requires creating a figure from reeds, to banish the spirit which possesses the patient. There is a magical marriage between a patient and a reed figure, which eventually causes the spirit to depart. KBo 36.34 (fragments 829/c, 842/c, 254/e), or 'Manuscript B' was likewise found in or near building A, rooms 4–6, as were KUB 37.57 (Ms. X1, fragment 359/c), KUB 37.62 (Ms. X2, fragment 626/b), KUB 37.65 (Ms. X3, fragment 1428/c), KUB 37.72 (Ms. X6, fragment 38/a), and KUB 37.74 (Ms. X4, fragment 2622/c), KUB 37.66 (Ms. X5, fragment 1402/c), KUB 37.86 (Ms. X7, fragment 1792/c), and KUB 37.97 (Ms. X8, fragment 400/b). Images were sourced from the HPM, via the Akademie der Wissenschaften und der Literatur, Mainz, and the Vorderasiatisches Museum. The transcriptions are published in Schwemer (1998).

Finally, KUB 4.16 (fragment Bo 6345) is an '*utukku lemnutu*' incantation, a form of demon exorcism. It is the Akkadian fragment of a probably bilingual two-column tablet, with Sumerian on the left and its Akkadian translation on the right. Each line is divided by a horizontal line across the width of the tablet, as was the custom for line-by-line translations in Ḫattuša (Fincke 2009: 53). The HPM and Weeden (2012: 230) classified it as 'Assyro-Mittanian', but Fincke (2009: 53) says it is written "*in mittanischem Duktus*". Images were downloaded from the HPM, via the Akademie der Wissenschaften und der Literatur, Mainz, and the Vorderasiatisches Museum, and the transcription is published in Fincke (2009).

Known Assyro-Mittanian tablets (as of 2014) which were not included in the database, because they were severly damaged, did not include sign-forms interesting to add to the comparison, or did not otherwise include significant new information for the analysis are KUB 37.54: 420/c (frg. X12), Kbo 36.63: 829/f (frg. X14), KUB 37.93: 374/b, KUB 37.96: 424/c (frg. X9), CTH 809 (KUB 37.7 + 3 + 2 + 9 + 4 + 5 + 6 + 8), and CTH 801 (KBo 36.28: B1325/d). According to the HPM, other possible – but not certain – Assyro-Mittanian fragments are CTH 794 (KUB 37.115: 481/e, KBo 7.1: 70/k, Kbo 7.2: 71/k), CTH 802.2 (KUB 37.81: Bo 5885), CTH 804 (KUB 37.50: 167/b), CTH 805 (KUB 37.107: 683/c), CTH 806 (KUB 37.95: 194/c), CTH 809 (KUB 37.12: 188/a, KUB 37.14: 566/b, KUB 37.15: 659/f, Kbo 8.1: 199/m, Kbo 8.2: 8/1), CTH 812 (Kbo 36.37: 59/r), CTH 813 (KUB 37.10: 26/c, KUB 37.11: 117/d, KUB 37.21: 1315/c, KUB 37.22: Bo 7407, KUB 37.23: 336/d, KUB 37.24: 194/a, KUB 37.25: 2461/c, KUB 37.27: 2530/c, KUB 37.29: 735/c, KUB 37.33: Bo 8675, KUB 37.58: 415/b, KUB 37.91: 189/c, KUB 37.94: 258/c, KUB 4.52: Bo 4833, Kbo 8.4: 233/m), and CTH 819 (KUB 37.137: Bo 1524, KUB 4.27: Bo 5013, KUB 4.54: Bo 6037, KUB 4.98: Bo 5189, Kbo 47.41: 1291/v). A few of these have been included in the analysis in this chapter, as well the final chapter, where key sign-forms (not broken or damaged) have been compared.

3.3 Comparative Palaeography of Mittani

The discussion of signs in this chapter has been divided from broad to narrow, into sign-forms and variants whose shape is dependent on single wedges, sign-forms whose shape is determined by other factors, and, least common, sign-forms which differ within the same corpus, followed by a description of smaller variants.

The total number of extracted Amarna instances adds up to 17,380, with 215 different signs. Of these 215 signs, 22 were recorded only once and another 20 less than 5 times, bringing the more balanced total of the corpus to the frequent use of circa 180–200 signs. This fits in well with other contemporary corpora, which generally make use of a similar or slightly smaller number of signs.[35] None of the tablets display all 215 signs; the maximum is 175 on

35 Based on considering existing sign-lists. Although these do not usually show how often a form was attested or what may have been excluded, the lists indicate smaller collections of 15–30 tablets generally yield between 110–140 signs used, with 15–20 different

EA 22.[36] On average most tablets have 100 signs, with fewer than 80 on the smaller tablets and over 120 for the bigger tablets. There are important exceptions to this: the limited number of signs on EA 24, and also a limited number of signs from those tablets which are very damaged (particularly EA 18) as well as more signs on especially well-preserved tablets (such as EA 19). Of these 215 primary signs, few also have different sign-forms, and perhaps 20 show variation. This is unusual, as will be discussed throughout the following chapters.

The remaining Mittani tablets resulted in 2,811 instances (and 413 copies of instances where photographs or scans were not available), with 156 different signs. 28 were recorded only once and another 27 less than 5 times, making a balanced total of circa 130–140 frequently used signs. The tablet with the greatest number of signs is KBo 1.2 with 130 signs (1,272 instances), but on average most tablets have only 30–40 signs due to their small size. It is difficult to determine whether the number of signs on TB 11021 is limited, as on EA 24, since only such a small fragment survives.

The total number of Assyro-Mittani instances, from the tablets selected, is 3,487, with 210 signs. 39 were recorded only once and 57 less than 5 times, making a balanced total of 170–190 frequently used signs.[37] Most signs were recorded from KBo 36.29 and its fragments – circa 170 signs (1,701 instances). Since all tablets are fragmentary, and it is unclear what size they would have been, it is not possible to provide information on the average number of instances or signs per tablet. Although the number of instances extracted from each corpus – including those presented in the following chapters – varies greatly, the number of signs is fairly balanced (**Figure 3.1**).

3.3.1 *Divergent and Diagonal Wedges*

Assyro-Mittanian

A typical feature of Assyro-Mittanian is the development of a wedge which appears heavily emphasised or angled differently; this can apply both to initial horizontal wedges (which therefore look more like a vertical) and mid-composition horizontal wedges (which therefore look more like a *Winkelhaken*

forms (Tell Bderi, Giricano) (Maul 1992; Radner 2004). Larger archives of 100 tablets and over show 160–180 signs and 30–40 different forms (Tell Šeḫ Ḥamad, Tell Chuera) (Cancik-Kirschbaum 1996; Jakob 2009).

36 Quite likely due to the nature of the contents (gift-list): the letter includes more logograms than the other tablets.

37 These are likewise less common logograms, which can be attributed to the subject matter of the corpus (rituals). For example, from KUB 37.100a ASAL was recorded only once (obverse, column 1, line 32) – as part of the name Asalluḫi, a god of incantations and magic.

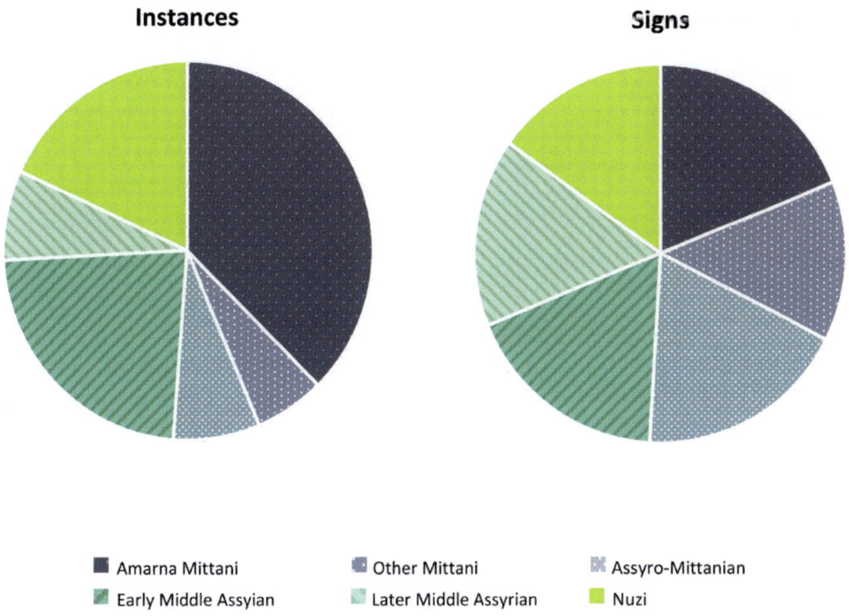

FIGURE 3.1 Proportional comparison of the number of instances and signs in each corpus

TABLE 3.2 The divergent wedge

BAL	TI	SU	KA	SAG

Mittani (left) versus Assyro-Mittani (right). BAL and TI with a horizontal divergent wedge, SU, KA and SAG with a vertical divergent wedge.

which extends through the horizontal above) (**Table 3.2**). This wedge may be formed by switching the corner of the stylus (Weeden 2012: 238), which is not necessarily reflected accurately by the components of cuneiform. Cuneiform signs in the context of this chapter thus consist of the horizontal wedge (), the top to bottom diagonal wedge (), the bottom to top diagonal wedge (), the *Winkelhaken* (), and the vertical wedge () as well as a horizontal divergent wedge () and vertical divergent wedge (). Because this changes the appearance of some signs drastically, the switch in stylus angle is the cause of several different forms in Assyro-Mittanian script; particularly BAL (5), BA (14), ZU (15), SU (16), KA (24), TI (118), SAG (184) and UGU (663).

The Divergent Wedge in BAL (5)

From the Mittani Amarna (Am-Mit) tablets, instances of BAL were recorded only from EA 22, 24, 25 and 29. The instances always begin with a broken horizontal and end with two *Winkelhaken*. The only variation is in the lower part of the sign: all instances either have a bottom *Winkelhaken* (BAL_{1a}) or a horizontal wedge (BAL_{1b}) (**Table 3.3**). It appears as if the variants differ per tablet (BAL_{1a} on EA 24 and 29, BAL_{2b} on EA 22 and 25), but it is difficult to tell as more than half of the recorded instances are damaged. Only one instance of BAL was recorded from the Other Mittani (O-Mit) tablets (KBo 1.2, reverse, line 5) and it has a bottom *Winkelhaken* (BAL_{1a}). The sign also occurs only six times in the Assyro-Mittani (As-Mit) collection considered here. In all cases, the bottom wedge was turned so that it extends through the horizontal above it (BAL_2).[38]

The Divergent Wedge in BA (14), ZU (15) and SU (16)

Plenty of instances of BA, ZU and SU were recorded from the Am-Mit tablets. However, SU was only recorded from the larger tablets (EA 22, 24, 25, 29), and BA was not recorded from EA 24 at all. The upper horizontal wedge of these signs is often emphasised (1a), sometimes extremely so (2a), but it is difficult to tell whether the entire wedge has been impressed at a different angle, as in the

TABLE 3.3 The divergent wedge in BAL

Am-Mit		O-Mit	As-Mit
BAL_{1a}	**BAL_{1b}**	**BAL_{1a}**	**BAL_2**

Am-Mit (recorded 10 times): EA 24, reverse, column 2, line 23; EA 25, reverse, column 3, line 72. **O-Mit** (recorded 1 time): KBo 1.2, reverse, line 5. **As-Mit** (recorded 6 times): KBo 36.34, fragment 829c, obverse, column 2, line 16.

38 BAL_{1a} and BAL_{1b} appear variously throughout the Amarna and Mittani corpora and are probably – but not certainly due, to the limited number of instances collected – particular to certain scribes (see **Paragraph** 2.6: "inconsistent ... between tablets" and "can be ... indicative of individual scribal hands"); while BAL_2 is consistently isolated to the Assyro-Mittanian corpus under consideration. Hence the distinguishment between variant and form in this particular case.

TABLE 3.4 The divergent wedge in BA, ZU and SU

Amarna Mittani Letters					
BA_{1a}	**ZU_{1a}**	**BA_{2a}**	**ZU_{2a}**	**BA_{1b}**	**ZU_{1b}**

Other Mittani Documents					
ZU_{1a}	**SU_{1a}**	**BA_{3a}**	**ZU_{3a}**	**BA_{1b}**	

Assyro-Mittanian					
BA_{2a}	**ZU_{2a}**	**BA_{3b}**	**ZU_{3b}**	**BA_{2b}**	**ZU_{2b}**

Am-Mit (recorded 25, 81 and 110 times), **1a**: EA 19, obverse, line 9 (second instance); EA 26, obverse, line 27. **2a**: EA 28, reverse, line 12; EA 27, reverse, line 44. **1b**: EA 20, reverse, line 16; EA 19, reverse, line 28 (second instance). **O-Mit** (recorded 10, 20 and 9 times), **1a**: KBo 1.2, obverse, line 14; KBo 1.2, obverse, line 21. **3a**: KBo 1.2, obverse, line 8; AlT 14, obverse, line 3. **1b**: KBo 28.66, obverse, line 7. **As-Mit** (recorded 29, 29 and 4 times), **2a**: KBo 36.29, fragment 285a, obverse, column 2, line 10; KUB 37.55, fragment 373b, reverse, column 6, line 5. **3b**: KUB 37.55, fragment 373b, reverse, column 6, line 6; KBo 36.29, fragment 1017c, obverse, column 1, line 17. **2b**: KUB 37.43, reverse, column 4, line 10; KUB 37.43, reverse, column 4, line 11.

As-Mit tablets (**Table 3.4**). Although the horizontal wedges are usually straight, they do also occur at a slight angle (1b), which is typical for Babylonian forms of the signs (see Labat 1988: 42–44). EA 22 is the only tablet on which it is clear a mixture of the sign-forms and variants was used. In Schröder's Mittani sign-list (1915: 75) the signs are all drawn without emphasised horizontal or divergent wedges and with relatively straight lines. Similarly, Dietrich and Mayer (2010:

282) record these signs from EA 24 with straight wedges. O-Mit BA, ZU and SU follow the same pattern of variation as the Amarna documents. A new form also appears: the middle impression occurs so high up that the top wedge looks like a broken horizontal instead (3a). In the Amarna tablets, only EA 22 hints at this sign-form. On the As-Mit tablets there is a clear and important difference, which is that the most common sign-forms are those with the divergent wedge (2a), which vary by occasionally occurring at an angle too (2b). It is sometimes difficult to tell whether the signs were composed with the divergent wedge, or simply heavy emphasis. Occassionally the third form can also be found, but likewise with emphasised initial impression (3b).

The Divergent Wedge in KA (24)
KA only has one sign-form across all Am-Mit tablets. A common variation is for the *Winkelhaken* not to be attached to the top horizontal (KA_{1a}) but moved further down to a more central position (KA_{1b}) (**Table 3.5**). Every instance has two parallel horizontals followed by a *Winkelhaken* however. On the O-Mit tablets KA primarily occurs as in the Amarna correspondence, but also with a broken horizontal on KBo 28.66 (KA_2) and possibly TB 6001 (the single instance collected is damaged and the image was not taken in high resolution). On the As-Mit tablets KA again emerges with a divergent wedge – and in the primary form of the sign the *Winkelhaken* has vanished (KA_3) – although KUB 37.43 does have KA_1 (also see **Figure 3.2**). A secondary form of the sign does have *Winkelhaken*, but differs from KA_1, since the initial horizontal is centred (KA_4). The second form occurs on its own on KUB 37.55 and together with KA_3 on KBo 36.29.

The Divergent Wedge in TI (118)
TI is the sign which most clearly has different sign-forms in the Am-Mit corpus. These will be discussed further in **Paragraph 3.3.3**, because here the key issue is the divergent As-Mit wedge (**Table 3.6**). The Am-Mit tablets have a form with a bottom *Winkelhaken* (TI_1), which is the most common form in the corpus; but also a more elongated form, starting with a horizontal wedge attached to a *Winkelhaken*, then a vertical, and finally another horizontal wedge followed by a *Winkelhaken* (sometimes crossing through the vertical) (TI_2). From the O-Mit tablets TI most commonly occurs as TI_1 but in a few cases also TI_2. As-Mit TI however, occurs with a bottom *Winkelhaken* or horizontal which is turned or impressed at a different angle and extends through the wedge above it, like in BAL (TI_3). Sometimes the lower impression is placed so high up along the vertical that it almost takes the form of a broken horizontal. In addition, the elongated form of TI in this corpus misses (or completely obscures)

TABLE 3.5 The divergent wedge in KA

Am-Mit		O-Mit		As-Mit	
KA_{1a}	KA_{1b}	KA_{1a}	KA_2	KA_3	KA_4

Am-Mit (recorded 173 times): EA 19, obverse, line 18; EA 24, reverse, column 2, line 12. **O-Mit** (recorded 16 times): KBo 1.2, obverse, line 2; KBo 28.66, obverse, line 9. **As-Mit** (recorded 52 times): KBo 36.34, fragment 254e, obverse, column 2, line 5; KUB 37.55, fragment 373b, reverse, column 6, line 4.

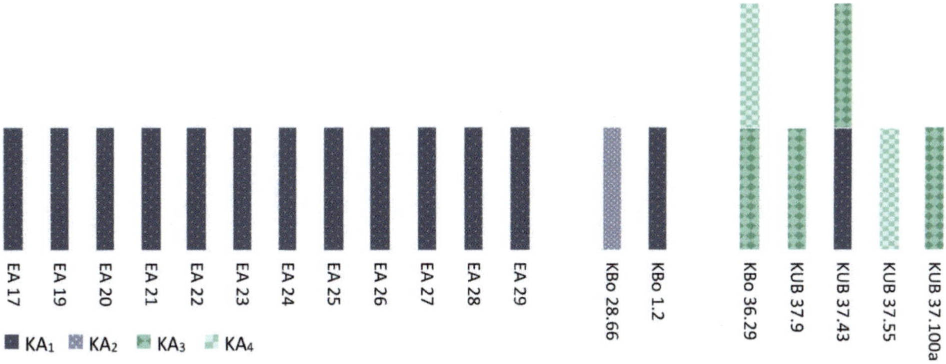

FIGURE 3.2 Comparison of Mittani KA
Note the similarity between Am-Mit tablets, and the variation on KBo 36.29 and KUB 37.43.

its final horizontal wedge (TI_4) (also see **Figure 3.3**). The only exception is KUB 37.43, which has TI_1.

The Vertical Divergent Wedge in SAG (184)

Am-Mit SAG was recorded only from the large tablets EA 22, EA 25 and EA 29. The initial horizontal is emphasised, but not divergent as in the As-Mit documents (SAG_{1a}) (**Table 3.7**). There SAG was consistently recorded with a divergent wedge (KBo 36.29, KBo 36.34, KUB 37.9, KUB 37.100a, KUB 37.55 – the instances from KBo 36.29 and KUB 37.43 are unclear) (SAG_2). From the O-Mit documents SAG was only recorded 3 times, all from KBo 1.2 with a lower or more central horizontal without emphasis (SAG_{1b}).

TABLE 3.6 The divergent wedge in TI

Am-Mit		O-Mit		As-Mit		
TI_1	TI_2	TI_1	TI_2	TI_1	TI_3	TI_4

Am-Mit (recorded 333 times): EA 19, reverse, line 34, second instance; EA 24, reverse, line 3, second instance. **O-Mit** (recorded 94 times): KBo 1.2, obverse, line 40; KBo 1.2, obverse, line 15. **As-Mit** (recorded 81 times): KUB 37.43, reverse, column 4, line 10; KUB 37.106, fragment 536b, obverse, column 2, line 27; KUB 37.43, obverse, column 1, line 14.

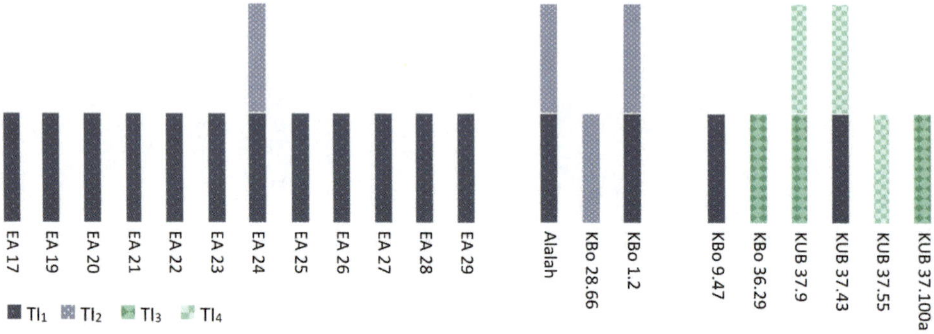

FIGURE 3.3 Comparison of Mittani TI
Note the similarity between Am-Mit tablets with the exception of EA 24, and the variation on KUB 37.9 and KUB 37.43.

TABLE 3.7 The diagonal wedge

RI	TA	AḪ	AR

Mittani/Assyro-Mittani (left) versus KBo 1.2 (right).

KBo 1.2

On Mittanian KBo 1.2 the scribe often places a diagonal wedge quite early into the composition of the signs (**Table 3.8**), which would be an obvious *Winkelhaken* in all other Assyro-Mittanian and Mittanian signs, particularly in RI, TA, ŠA, AḪ, and AR. This calls into question the line between sign-form and variant. If there was only one Assyro-Mittanian tablet, would the signs with divergent wedges still be different sign-forms? Why not signs with diagonal wedges in that case? The answer is, because this is only one tablet; none of the other As-Mit or O-Mit tablets share the same use of diagonal wedges, therefore making it more likely that this is a tablet-consistent variation, attributed to scribal hand, rather than the mark of a scribal school.

The Diagonal in RI (142)

RI does not occur in different forms on the Am-Mit tablets. The *Winkelhaken* is always placed inbetween the final two verticals (RI$_{1a}$) and there is only occasional accidental variation (one instance of a *Winkelhaken* placed a little further to the left, one instance of a *Winkelhaken* with a particular flourish through the final vertical). From the O-Mit documents many instances of RI are damaged, but the clear instances match the Am-Mit tablets. However, on KBo 1.2 the *Winkelhaken* is extended into a diagonal and placed after the first vertical (RI$_{1c}$) (**Table 3.9**). On the As-Mit tablets again only RI$_{1a}$ occurs. There is a minute, detectable variation between scribal hands: on KUB 37.106 and KBo 36.29 the *Winkelhaken* is consistently impressed low down in the composition while on KUB 37.43 the *Winkelhaken* is always impressed higher up in the composition.

TABLE 3.8 The divergent wedge in SAG

Am-Mit	**O-Mit**	**As-Mit**
SAG$_{1a}$	**SAG$_{1b}$**	**SAG$_{2}$**

Am-Mit (recorded 21 times): EA 25, obverse, column 1, line 29. **O-Mit** (recorded 3 times): KBo 1.2, obverse, line 35. **As-Mit** (recorded 11 times): KUB 37.100a, fragment 656c, column 1, line 29.

TABLE 3.9 The diagonal wedge in RI

Am-Mit		O-Mit		As-Mit
RI_{1a}	**RI_{1b}**	**RI_{1a}**	**RI_{1c}**	**RI_{1a}**

Am-Mit (recorded 149 times): EA 28, obverse, line 12; EA 30, obverse, line 9. **O-Mit** (recorded 56 times): AlT 13, obverse, line 8; KBo 1.2, obverse, line 34, second instance. **As-Mit** (recorded 41 times): KBo 36.29, fragment 510d, obverse, column 2, line 36.

On a separate note: on some tablets the final vertical of RI occurs taller or deeper than the first two (RI_{1b}). This is the case on EA 19, 25, 26 and 30, but not on EA 22, 23, 27, 28, or AlT 13, TB 11021, KBo 1.2, KBo 36.39 and KUB 37.106; on most other tablets it is unclear (not enough instances, damage, crowdedness of script, or possibly accidental differences). Taylor (2015: 15) determined that typically a final vertical which is taller or deeper was impressed last, which was common from the Early Dynastic to Old Babylonian and Old Assyrian period. Taylor also shows that the variations he studied for the Middle Babylonian and Middle Assyrian periods occur with the *Winkelhaken* or horizontal impressed last, rather than the vertical (2015: 7). The taller final vertical can be considered more common in Older Babylonian than Later Assyrian. That said, because of the inconsistencies, the RI with a taller final vertical should here be considered a possible variation in scribal hand, rather than a chronologically different sign-form.

The Diagonals in TA (248) and ŠA (566)

Once one deviating wedge is identified, it becomes easier to see it in other signs. Variants of TA and ŠA will be discussed further in **Paragraph 3.3.4.** Am-Mit TA and ŠA occur in only two variants (more / less space between the verticals) (TA_{1a}, $ŠA_{1a}$). From the O-Mit tablets TA was recorded 78 times and ŠA 56 times, with the same variants as the Am-Mit documents – apart from KBo 1.2 (**Table 3.10**). Here the bottom *Winkelhaken* in TA has extended into a diagonal and moved in front of the initial vertical (TA_{1b}, $ŠA_{1b}$). Additionally, the composition of ŠA is slightly more crowded and the centre two horizontals are smaller or less emphasised than the top and bottom impressions, matching the way the scribe impressed, for instance, MA. As-Mit TA and ŠA were

TABLE 3.10 The diagonal wedge in TA and ŠA

Amarna Mittani Letters		**Other Mittani Documents**	
TA$_{1a}$	**ŠA$_{1a}$**	**TA$_{1a}$**	**ŠA$_{1a}$**

KBo 1.2		**Assyro-Mittanian**	
TA$_{1b}$	**ŠA$_{2}$**	**TA$_{1c}$**	**ŠA$_{1c}$**

Am-Mit (recorded 383 and 489 times): EA 19, obverse, line 34; EA 19, obverse, line 14. **O-Mit** (recorded 78 and 56 times): KBo 28.66, obverse, line 21; AlT 13, reverse, line 1; KBo 1.2, reverse, line 26. KBo 1.2, obverse, line 31. **As-Mit** (recorded 85 and 82 times): KBo 36.29, fragment 2533c, reverse, column 3, line 26; KUB 37.55, fragment 423c, column 5, line 25.

recorded in the same variants as the Am-Mit letters. The bottom *Winkelhaken* on KUB 37.43 are possibly also impressed as diagonals but less obviously. As with other signs in this corpus the initial horizontal wedge is generally heavily emphasised (although not clearly divergent) (TA$_{1c}$, ŠA$_{1c}$).

The Diagonal in AḪ (636)

The only variation in AḪ from the Am-Mit tablets is that the scribes of EA 22 and 29 consistently impress the ḪI element with five (AḪ$_{1b}$) rather than four (AḪ$_{1a}$) *Winkelhaken*; this is also the case for a few (but not most) instances from EA 24. AḪ was recorded with the same limited variation from the O-Mit tablets (not comparable between tablets due to the limited number of instances collected). However, on KBo 1.2 AḪ is a different sign-form altogether: it has a diagonal crossing through the verticals and four verticals (as opposed to three) (AḪ$_{2}$) (**Table 3.11**). On the As-Mit tablets AḪ often occurs with more than four *Winkelhaken* (see ḪI, **Paragraph 3.3.4**) – on KBo 36.29 and KBo 36.34 consistently with six or more *Winkelhaken* (AḪ$_{1b}$).

TABLE 3.11 The diagonal in AḪ

Am-Mit		O-Mit		As-Mit
AḪ$_{1a}$	AḪ$_{1b}$	AḪ$_{1b}$	AḪ$_{2}$	AḪ$_{1b}$

Am-Mit (recorded 52 times): EA 30, obverse, line 7; EA 29, obverse, line 32. **O-Mit** (recorded 15 times): KBo 28.66, obverse, line 12; KBo 1.2, obverse, line 8. **As-Mit** (recorded 22 times): KBo 36.34, fragment 254e, obverse, column 2, line 4.

The Diagonal in AR (726)

Cuneiform AR can be found written with an IGI + RI combination, resulting in a broken horizontal; but also unified, with a single horizontal wedge. All instances recorded from the Mittani corpus as a whole occurred with two horizontal impressions. It is possible for the second of the two to occur larger (AR$_{1b}$), probably because this was the first wedge impressed when writing RI (Taylor 2015: 8).

AR hardly varies on the Am-Mit tablets and has the same form throughout the O-Mit documents (AR$_{1a}$). However, as with RI and AḪ, the form on KBo 1.2 has a more extended diagonal beginning after the first vertical (AR$_{1c}$) (**Table 3.12**). From the As-Mit tablets AR was likewise recorded with little variation – except that the scribe of KUB 37.43 preferred to impress the final *Winkelhaken* high up and the scribe of KBo 36.29 preferred to impress it low down through the second to last vertical.

3.3.2 *Cross-corpus Sign-form Diversity*

Formation of MU (98)

From the Am-Mit tablets MU was recorded completely without variation (MU$_1$) (**Table 3.15**). However, in the O-Mit documents, MU occurs with four *Winkelhaken* in a 'square' composition around the horizontal, much closer to the way it usually appears in older script-groups such as Babylonian or Tigunanum and therefore potentially a different sign-form (MU$_2$). It was only recorded from KBo 1.2, KBo 28.65, KBo 28.66, MS 1848 2 and TB 6001 respectively. Although the latter two are unclear, it looks like all tablets display MU$_1$ apart from KBo 1.2 which has MU$_2$. From the As-Mit documents the sign

TABLE 3.12 The diagonal in AR

Am-Mit	O-Mit		As-Mit
AR_{1a}	AR_{1b}	AR_{1c}	AR_{1b}

Am-Mit (recorded 31 times): EA 27, obverse, line 12. **O-Mit** (recorded 18 times): KBo 28.66, obverse, line 7; KBo 1.2, reverse, line 28. **As-Mit** (recorded 26 times): KUB 37.55, fragment 373b, reverse, column 6, line 3.

seemingly only looks like MU_1. It appears that MU_2 may occur on KUB 37.43. However, the placement of wedges in this case could be attributed to crowdedness of the script on the tablet, as on EA 24.

Forms of GAB (148)

GAB (148) was recorded from the Am-Mit letters without variation (GAB_1) (**Table 3.13**). From the O-Mit documents the sign was only recorded a few times, with two instances from KBo 1.2 in a completely different sign-form, matching a Babylonian version (GAB_2) (Labat 1988: 78). From the As-Mit tablets all instances of GAB follow the first form with an initial *Winkelhaken* between the verticals, albeit with more variation between the two tablets it was recorded from.

Winkelhaken *and Diagonals in IL (348)*

On the Am-Mit tablets the broken diagonal in IL is not always obvious (especially on EA 19) – but there are no clearly different sign-forms and very little variation (IL_1) (**Table 3.14**). From the O-Mit tablets instances were recorded from ALT 13, IBoT 1.34, TB 11021 and TB 8002 – but they are all damaged and unclear. However, on KBo 1.2 the sign has a broken diagonal followed by a *Winkelhaken* or diagonal rather than vice versa (IL_2). In the As-Mit documents there is a form which seems common across the three tablets from which the sign was recorded, where the broken diagonal has become horizontal and the *Winkelhaken* is placed directly above the initial horizontal (IL_3). However, one instance on KBo 36.29 also exists with a small cluster of *Winkelhaken* instead (IL_4).

TABLE 3.13 Mittani GAB

Am-Mit	O-Mit	As-Mit	
GAB$_{1a}$	GAB$_{2}$	GAB$_{1a}$	GAB$_{1b}$

Am-Mit (recorded 33 times): EA 19, reverse, line 40. **O-Mit** (recorded 3 times): KBo 1.2, obverse, line 20. **As-Mit** (recorded 5 times): KBo 36.29, fragment 97q, obverse, column 2, line 44; KUB 37.43, reverse, column 4, line 13.

TABLE 3.14 Mittani IL

Am-Mit	O-Mit	As-Mit	
IL$_{1}$	IL$_{2}$	IL$_{3}$	IL$_{4}$

Am-Mit (recorded 32 times): EA 28, obverse, line 18. **O-Mit** (recorded 8 times): KBo 1.2, obverse, line 18. **As-Mit** (recorded 6 times): KUB 37.43, reverse, column 4, line 6; KBo 36.29, fragment 510d, obverse, column 2, line 20.

Winkelhaken *in LÚ (514) and Similar Signs*

On the Am-Mit tablets these signs occur with upper *Winkelhaken* or possibly diagonals, not horizontals (1a, 1b) (**Table 3.16**). Occasionally the cluster of *Winkelhaken* is angled so that it resembles a 'ŠE' shape (no consistent differences between tablets however) (1a, 1b). Many of the O-Mit instances collected were damaged, but they look like they follow the same pattern of variation as in the Amarna letters. The scribe of KBo 1.2 had a preference for diagonal impressions, as seen in other signs on the tablet. The As-Mit scribes on the other hand had a preference for straight horizontals rather than more diagonal wedges (2). The second form of LÚ occurs on all tablets the sign was recorded from: KUB 37.55, KUB 37.43, KUB 37.9, KUB 37.100a + 106, KBo 9.47, and KBo

TABLE 3.15 Mittani MU

Am-Mit	O-Mit		As-Mit	Tigunanum
MU_1	MU_1	MU_2	MU_1	MU_2

Am-Mit (recorded 153 times): EA 19, obverse, line 14; EA 24, obverse, column 1, line 92. **O-Mit** (recorded 9 times): KBo 28.66, obverse, line 3; KBo 1.2, obverse, line 33. **As-Mit** (recorded 24 times): KUB 37.65, obverse, line 3; KUB 37.43, obverse, column 1, line 14. **Tigunanum:** MS 2799, obverse, line 2.

36.34 + KUB 37.73 + KUB 37.66. The second form of IN occurs on KBo 36.29 and KUB 37.103, but it looks like KUB 37.43 has a form more like the first. ŠAR (541) was recorded from KBo 36.29 and 36.34 (2), and KUB 37.9 and 37.43 (1) (also see **Figure 3.4**). The less frequent occurrence of the first form is significant, because it leaves room for the possibility that Assyro-Mittanian scribes could also have impressed LÚ in this way, despite the instances not occuring in the database.

Verticals and Horizontals in UM (238), DUB (242) and KIŠIB (486)
It is not always possible to distinguish the signs UM, DUB and KIŠIB (or MES) from one another (further see **Paragraph 6.2**), so in the initial analysis here they will be referred to and divided by their value and form according to the corpus under consideration. This means **Table 3.17** essentially shows the same sign and its sign-forms twice in the case of UM and DUB, and **Figure 3.4** artificially assumes three forms of MES in order to indicate co-occurrence.

On EA 19, EA 21, EA 24, EA 26, EA 29 and EA 30 the small verticals of UM (238) are boxed in by the horizontals (UM_1), on EA 17, EA 22, EA 23, EA 27 and EA 28 the verticals are extended above or over the upper horizontal (UM_{2a}) (**Table 3.17**). However, from EA 22 and EA 27 only one instance was recorded and on EA 28 one out of two instances is completely damaged. From the O-Mit documents many of the instances of UM are damaged and it is unclear

TABLE 3.16 Mittani LÚ, ŠAR and IN

Amarna Mittani Letters

LÚ$_{1a}$	LÚ$_{1b}$	ŠAR$_{1a}$	ŠAR$_{1b}$	IN$_{1a}$	IN$_{1b}$

Other Mittani Documents

LÚ$_{1b}$	ŠAR$_{1a}$	IN$_{1a}$
		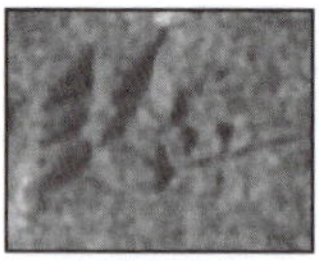

Assyro-Mittanian

LÚ$_{2}$	ŠAR$_{1b}$	ŠAR$_{2}$	IN$_{1b}$	IN$_{2}$

Am-Mit LÚ (recorded 40 times): EA 26, reverse, line 19, second instance; EA 28, obverse, line 12. **O-Mit LÚ** (recorded 7 times): KBo 1.2, obverse, line 34. **As-Mit LÚ** (recorded 21 times): KUB 37.9, obverse, column 2, line 4. **Am-Mit ŠAR** (recorded 24 times): EA 25, obverse, column 2, line 7; EA 22, obverse, column 1, line 31. **O-Mit ŠAR** (recorded 5 times): KBo 1.2, obverse, line 21, second instance. **As-Mit ŠAR** (recorded 5 times): KBo 36.29, fragment 166e, reverse, column 4, line 12. **Am-Mit IN** (recorded 119 times): EA 24, obverse, column 1, line 74; EA 19, reverse, line 39. **O-Mit IN** (recorded 4 times): TB 6002, obverse, line 3. **As-Mit IN** (recorded 13 times): KUB 37.43, obverse, column 1, line 10; KBo 36.29, fragment 1017c, obverse, column 1, line 28.

whether verticals are shorter or longer on purpose or by accident. IBoT 1.34, TB 6002 and UEM T1 could be UM$_1$ while AlT 108, MS 1848 1, TB 8001 and SMN 1000 could be UM$_{2a}$. On KBo 1.2 and KBo 28.65 the form occurs with the horizontals extended before (rather than along) the verticals (UM$_{2b}$). From the As-Mit documents UM was recorded only a few times: on KUB 37.55 the verticals are

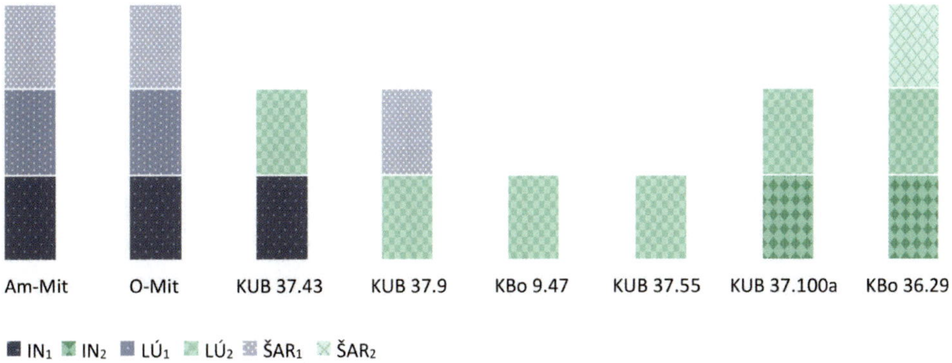

FIGURE 3.4 Comparison of Mittani LÚ, ŠAR and IN
Note the difference between the Amarna Mittani and Other Mittani tablets, and Assyro-Mittanian.

boxed in (UM_{1a}), on KUB 37.62 the verticals are extended (UM_{2b}), and on KUB 37.43 the middle verticals are obscured or absent ($UM_{3?}$).

On EA 24 and EA 25 the sign DUB (242) can be found with boxed verticals (DUB_1) and EA 27 (one instance) with extended verticals (DUB_2) (**Table 3.17**). This means that on EA 24 and EA 27 UM and DUB are essentially the same sign-form (the first with boxed verticals, the latter with extended verticals). Instances from the other corpora are few and far between. From EA 25 no instances of UM were recorded to compare. DUB was recorded only once from the O-Mit tablets, with extended verticals (DUB_2) on KBo 28.66. No instances of UM were recorded from this tablet to compare either. Likewise, DUB was recorded only once from the As-Mit tablets, from KUB 37.103. Although it has extended verticals ($DUB_{2?}$), only three horizontal wedges are clearly visible (with the middle wedge centred) and no instances of UM were recorded to compare.

Finally, belonging to the same group is KIŠIB or MES (486). The value KIŠIB refers to seals, which are absent from the Mittani Amarna letters, thus MES has been used in **Table 3.17**. On EA 22 and EA 25 the recorded instances had the value $KIŠIB_3$, while the instances from EA 19 had the value MIŠ or $MEŠ_3$. On EA 23 there was another $MEŠ_3$ and on EA 27 a MIŠ. MES is (meant to be) distinguished from UM and DUB by lacking an upper horizontal and it is never impressed with small, enclosed verticals. Thus, on EA 19, the scribe clearly distinguishes between MIŠ and UM, using the form without an upper horizontal for the first and the form with small, 'boxed' verticals for the second. However, the scribe of EA 25 does not differentiate his respective $KIŠIB_3$ and DUP, and uses a form with short, enclosed verticals for both; he does not utilise the form

TABLE 3.17 Mittani UM, DUB and MES

Amarna Mittani Letters				
UM$_1$	UM$_{2a}$	DUB$_1$	DUB$_2$	MES

Other Mittani Documents				
UM$_1$	UM$_{2a}$	UM$_{2b}$	DUB$_2$	MES

Assyro-Mittanian				
UM$_1$	UM$_{2b}$	UM$_{3?}$	DUB$_{2?}$	MES

Am-Mit UM: EA 19, obverse, line 32; EA 23, obverse, line 13. **O-Mit UM:** TB 6002, obverse, line 4; TB 8001, obverse, line 14; KBo 1.2, obverse, line 4. **As-Mit UM:** KUB 37.55, fragment 423c, column 2, line 7; KUB 37.62, obverse, line 3; KUB 37.43, reverse, column 4, line 13. **Am-Mit DUB:** EA 24, reverse, column 1, line 38. EA 27, obverse, line 13. **O-Mit DUB:** KBo 28.66, obverse, line 15. **As-Mit DUB:** KUB 37.103, fragment 523b, obverse, column 1, line 28. **Am-Mit MES:** EA 19, obverse, line 28. **O-Mit MES:** KBo 1.2, reverse, line 6. **As-Mit MES:** KBo 36.29, fragment 285a, obverse, column 2, line 14.

without an upper horizontal at all. Since the scribes of EA 22, EA 23 and EA 27 use extended verticals in all cases (which could obscure an upper horizontal), the difference there is less clear; but it looks likely the upper horizontal is absent in the case of MIŠ or MEŠ$_3$ and present in the case of KIŠIB$_3$ (EA 22), ṬUP (EA 27) and UM (EA 22, 23 and 27). From the O-Mit tablets two instances of MIŠ, without an upper horizontal, were collected from KBo 1.2. This scribe

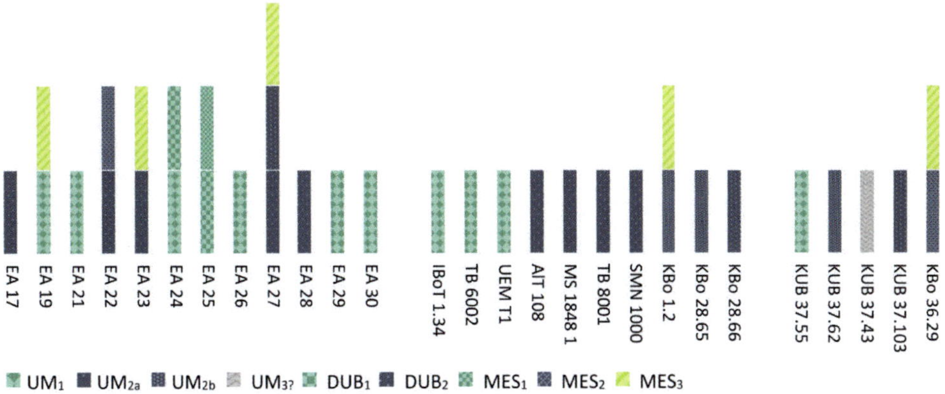

FIGURE 3.5 Comparison of Mittani UM, DUB and MES
Note: Most O-Mit instances are uncertain. The scribes of EA 19, EA 23, EA 27, KBo 1.2 and KBo 36.29 use different sign-forms, while the scribes of EA 24 and EA 25 do not differentiate. Overall, 'form 1' is most common in Mittanian, whereas 'form 2' is more common in Assyro-Mittanian.

used extended verticals, but four horizontals, for UM, therefore distinguishing between MIŠ and UM. From the As-Mit tablets only KBo 36.29 yielded any instances for comparison. MIŠ was recorded once, without an upper horizontal, but it can be distinguished from KIŠIB, which was recorded twice, with upper horizontal.

In summary, across the discussed corpora, the values KIŠIB$_3$ and KIŠIB match the forms of UM (238) and DUB (242), with are impressed variously with small, 'boxed' verticals (form 1) or extended verticals (form 2). Individual scribes sometimes differentiate between UM and DUB by using form 1 for one and form 2 for the other, but not always (**Figure 3.5**). Both are differentiated from MES (486), which is impressed with extended verticals and lacks an upper horizontal wedge.

ID (560)

The only variation in Am-Mit ID (ID$_1$) is that sometimes five rather than four *Winkelhaken* are impressed, but this is not consistent. Due to the way the wedges are impressed, the broken horizontal is often obscured and appears like a regular horizontal wedge. O-Mit ID matches the form from the Amarna documents. However, KBo 1.2 has a different form, with an additional small and central vertical wedge (ID$_2$). Schröder's Amarna sign-list (XII, p. 86, nr. 133) shows that this form also occurred at Byblos, a vassal of Egypt, from where letters were sent by Rib-addi to the Pharaoh (EA 68–140). Fossey further illustrates that the second vertical in ID has been attested for several 13th century Kassite Kings (1926: 658–659) and traces it back to as early as 18th century Babylon (1926: 653–654). In the As-Mit corpus there is a dominant variant where the broken horizontal is placed more clearly central-right in the composition and the initial horizontal is once again emphasised (ID_{1b}).

UGU (663)

UGU (663) was recorded from four Am-Mit letters without variation (UGU_1) (**Table 3.20**). While the instances collected from O-Mit MS 1848 2 and KBo 1.2 match the form from the Amarna letters, on KUB 3.80 the initial horizontals are organised differently (UGU_2). Where Babylonian forms often have a *Winkelhaken* (Labat 1988: 190), Middle Assyrian forms of the sign likewise leave out the *Winkelhaken* and replace it with a horizontal or broken horizontal. On As-Mit KUB 37.43 UGU occurs as in the Amarna letters, but on KBo 36.29 and KBo 36.34 also with a different combination of horizontals – particularly, with an emphasised initial horizontal wedge like in other signs in this corpus (UGU_3).

3.3.3 *Inter-corpus Sign-form Diversity*

Winkelhaken *of NA (110)*

There are over five hundred instances of NA (110) in the Am-Mit database, but, despite that, variation is minimal (as will be discussed further in **Paragraph 3.3.4**). Two new forms of NA occur on the O-Mit tablets. The first divides the *Winkelhaken* much more clearly and centrally between the horizontal wedge (NA_2) and the second replaces the bottom *Winkelhaken* with a horizontal (NA_3) (**Table 3.21**). All forms occur mixed throughout the corpus: AlT 13 has NA_1, AlT 14 has NA_3, IBoT 1.34 has NA_2, KBo 1.2 has thirty-nine instances of NA_2 and four instances of NA_3, KBo 28.65 has NA_1, KBo 28.66 has NA_1, KUB 3.80 is unclear but seems to have NA_1 as well, MS 1848 1 has NA_3, MS 1848 2 has one instance of NA_1 and one instance of NA_2, SMN 1000 according to Lacheman has NA_2, and all Tell Brak tablets have only instances of NA_1 (with the exception of TB 8001 which looks like it could have a variation of NA_2). As-Mit NA, like the Amarna documents, was collected only in the form NA_1 – with the exception of KUB 37.43 which has NA_2.

Since the instances occur mixed, which is uncommon for signs in all three corpora, particularly in 'Mittani' documents, the different forms of NA may be classified as variants instead. The reason they are currently in this category is due to Nuzi NA (see **Chapter 5**), where the form is clearly different – illustrating that the placement and shape of wedges in the case of contemporary cuneiform NA was at the very least not completely accidental.

Winkelhaken *and Verticals of RU (111)*

Am-Mit RU occurs in two different forms. On most tablets composition is dominated by the verticals (two, impressed over or more strongly than the *Winkelhaken*) (RU_{1a}), whereas on EA 24, EA 25 and EA 29 the overall composition is determined by the *Winkelhaken* (three, impressed over or deeper than the verticals) (RU_2) (**Table 3.22**). From the O-Mit documents the only tablet yielding clear and undamaged instances was KBo 1.2, which uses a form with two *Winkelhaken* impressed before the verticals (RU_3). Copies by others suggest that this may not be the case for other tablets. According to the copies MS 1848 2 and Bz 50 have RU_3, but SMN 1000 and TB 6001 have either RU_1 or RU_2. TB 11021 also has RU_2. The As-Mit tablets introduce an entirely new form with two smaller verticals (RU_4) and a different variation of the primary form with *Winkelhaken* so obscured that only a single one is observable on the surface (RU_{1b}). RU_4 occurs on KUB 37.43 and KUB 37.55 while RU_{1b} occurs on KBo 36.29, KBo 36.34, KUB 37.106, KUB 37.65, and KUB 37.72. The single instance recorded from KUB 4.16 is the only occurrence of RU_2 in this corpus.

A similar observation was made by Schwemer (1998: 11, 20) who saw RU as a distinguishing feature between 'Mittanian' and 'Assyro-Mittanian'. The first is meant to have clearer *Winkelhaken* while in the second they are barely visible. It is true that in the database used here, all Am-Mit forms of RU have obviously distinguishable *Winkelhaken*, while on some As-Mit tablets the *Winkelhaken* are hardly visible. Although the sign does not occur on any of the relevant tablets that have been 3D scanned, an example from EA 24 shows how the *Winkelhaken* might be hard to see at first, but present nonetheless (**Table 3.36** in the following paragraph). Schwemer did not include a copy of RU_4 as it is found here (1998: 20), and Weeden (2012: 241) observes that the variation of RU he has recorded from the Assyro-Mittanian Boğazköy tablets is also one with *Winkelhaken* rather than without.

Composition of TI (118) (again)

In the Am-Mit letters each individual document consistently uses only one form, with two similar variants, of 118 (TI) and does not mix them – apart from EA 24. EA 19 has a TI with a bottom *Winkelhaken* (TI_{1a}), which is the most common form in the corpus. EA 26 stands out for using a TI with a bottom horizontal wedge in every single case of its collected instances (TI_{1b}). EA 17 has a TI where the bottom wedge is impressed so shallowly it is almost non-apparent (TI_{1c}); traces are visible in a quarter of the collected instances, which indicate the intention to make a horizontal impression rather than a *Winkelhaken*. In EA 22 and EA 29 the bottom wedge is either a *Winkelhaken* or diagonal (TI_{1d}). The same applies to EA 20 and 21, but the recorded instances of TI are all damaged. On EA 24, TI appears both with a bottom horizontal / vertical wedge and with a bottom *Winkelhaken* (more common) – as well as the previously mentioned elongated form (TI_2) (see **Table 3.23**). This is also the most frequently used form of TI on EA 24.

From the O-Mit tablets, TI_{1a} occurs on KBo 1.2, KBo 28.66, SMN 1000, TB 6002, TB 8001 and maybe TB 8002; TI_{1b} occurs on AlT 108, AlT 14, KBo 28.65, KBo 28.66, possibly TB 8001 and TB 8001, and probably UEM T1 (damaged); and TI_2 occurs only on KBo 1.2, KBo 28.66, and AlT 13. In summary: TI_2 rarely occurs in isolation in any available 'Mittani' documents. KBo 28.66 has TI_{1a}, (one third of instances) TI_{1b} (one sixth one instances) and TI_2 (one half of instances). KBo 1.2 has both TI_{1a} (almost three quarters of instances) and TI_2 (around one quarter of instances) (**Table 3.18**). There is some consistency in spelling: 'A-ra-ḫa-ti' occurs three times and is written with TI_2 in all cases. 'Šat-ti-ú-az-za' occurs six times and is written with TI_1 in all cases. 'Ḫat-ti' occurs six times as well and is written with TI_1 in all cases. 'Ḫa-at-ti' occurs seven times and is written once with TI_2 and the remainder with TI_1. There are inconsistencies in word-endings however; the two forms occur within the same line in the same setting several times (**Table 3.18**). For EA 24 there are no distinguishable patterns for the use of different forms of TI. AlT 13 is the only tablet on which TI_2 occurs in isolation, but it is a short text and not many instances were recorded.

TABLE 3.18 Instances of TI on KBo 1.2

Line	Form	Word
Obverse line 4	TI_1	ending 'šu-nu-ti' (x2)
	TI_2	ending 'šu-nu-ti'
Obverse line 16	TI_1	'Ḫat-ti'
	TI_2	'it-ti' and 'Ḫa-at-ti'
Obverse line 25	TI_1	'šu-nu-ti', 'Ḫat-ti'
	TI_2	'šu-nu-ti'
Obverse line 26	TI_1	'Ḫat-ti', the ending 'ḫu-ut-ti''
	TI_2	'šu-nu-ti', '[ša-a]t-ti'

From the As-Mit tablets TI was again recorded in a variety of forms. As discussed, a new form of TI appears, with the bottom impression extending through the horizontal (TI_3), much like in As-Mit KA (24). This form occurs on KBo 36.29, KUB 37.66, KUB 37.72, KUB 37.86, KUB 37.97, KUB 37.106 and KUB 36.34. At first sight KUB 37.55 and KBo 9.47 seem to have TI_{1c}, but in some cases it is clear that the vertical obscures the *Winkelhaken* of TI_4 instead. The only tablet on which it is obvious that multiple forms occur is KUB 37.43 which uses TI_{1a} (less than half of the collected instances) and TI_4 (slightly more than half of the instances).

Since the Mittanian TI with five wedges is rare, it was worth checking whether the additional wedge was really impressed, or only tricking the eye. Using 3D scans (**Table 3.24**), it was possible to both distinguish this wedge and measure that it was impressed at a different depth from the other wedges. Whereas it is not obvious in the original image, the vertex image clearly shows the additional wedge. Thus, this impression is not simply an extension of the initial horizontal, or the *Winkelhaken*. The same was done for an apparent TI with four wedges, to see if a fifth impression was not obscured by a different wedge such as the vertical. The depth of the initial horizontal, the vertical, and the final *Winkelhaken* are otherwise comparable between the two sign-forms.

Additional Winkelhaken *of TIM (167)*

TIM (167) was recorded only a few times from the Am-Mit letters, and occurs most clearly on EA 19, where it has a broken vertical, followed by straight horizontals which are crossed by two verticals (TIM_1) (**Table 3.25**). On EA 17 however, these key components of the sign are all less obvious: it is unclear whether the vertical is broken, if there is a vertical impression at all; the horizontal wedges are either slanted or diagonal; and it is not possible to detect whether the two verticals are absent or obscured due to clay displacement (TIM_2). Very few other instances were recorded: the instances on EA 20 are all damaged and the single occurrence on EA 21 has not been photographed or scanned well enough to study. No instances were recorded from the O-Mit tablets or the As-Mit documents either. Significantly, the clear version from EA 19 is not recorded in Labat (1988) or Borger (2004) at all.

'Attached' and 'Detached' Forms of MEŠ (754)

Most Am-Mit tablets have a form of MEŠ with an initial horizontal wedge, detached from the vertical, followed by a more closely impressed cluster of horizontals ($MEŠ_1$) (**Table 3.26**). EA 24 and 25 both have a form where the

TABLE 3.19 Mittani ID

Am-Mit	O-Mit		As-Mit
ID_{1a}	ID_{1a}	ID_2	ID_{1b}

Am-Mit (recorded 21 times): EA 19, reverse, line 9. **O-Mit** (recorded 32 times): AlT 13, reverse, line 2; KBo 1.2, obverse, line 35. **As-Mit** (recorded 22 times): KBo 9.47, obverse, line 17.

TABLE 3.20 Mittani UGU

Am-Mit	O-Mit		As-Mit	
UGU_1	UGU_1	UGU_2	UGU_1	UGU_3

Am-Mit (recorded 7 times): EA 27, obverse, line 12. **O-Mit** (recorded 8 times): KBo 1.2, obverse, line 35; KUB 3.80, obverse, line 10. **As-Mit** (recorded 3 times): KUB 37.43, reverse, column 4, line 19; KBo 36.29, fragment 2533c, reverse, column 3, line 21.

TABLE 3.21 Mittani NA

Am-Mit	O-Mit			As-Mit	
NA_1	NA_1	NA_2	NA_3	NA_1	NA_2
	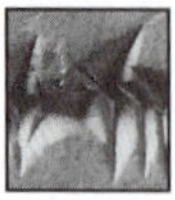				

Am-Mit (recorded 539 times): EA 29, obverse line 15. **O-Mit** (recorded 113 times): KBo 28.66, obverse, line 15; KBo 1.2, obverse, line 34; MS 1848 1, obverse, line 3, edge. **As-Mit** (recorded 95 times): KBo 36.29, fragment 1017c, obverse, column 1, line 24; KUB 37.42, reverse, column 4, line 19.

TABLE 3.22 Mittani RU

Am-Mit		**O-Mit**		**As-Mit**		
RU_{1a}	**RU_2**	**RU_3**	**RU_2**	**RU_{1b}**	**RU_3**	**RU_4**

Am-Mit (recorded 95 times): EA 26, obverse, line 24; EA 25, obverse, column 1, line 61. **O-Mit** (recorded 15 times): KBo 1.2, obverse, line 5; TB 11021, obverse, line 5. **As-Mit** (recorded 23 times): KUB 37.65, obverse, line 6; KUB 4.16, obverse, line 6; KUB 37.43, reverse, column 4, line 9.

TABLE 3.23 Mittani TI

Amarna Mittani Letters				
TI_{1a}	**TI_{1b}**	**TI_{2a}**	**TI_{2b}**	**TI_3**

Other Mittani Documents			**Assyro-Mittanian**		
TI_{1a}	**TI_{1b}**	**TI_3**	**TI_{1a}**	**TI_3**	**TI_4**

Am-Mit – TI_{1a} and TI_{1b}: EA 19, reverse, line 34, second instance; EA 28, reverse, line 18. **TI_{2a} and TI_{2b}**: EA 26, obverse, line 7, second instance; EA 17, reverse, line 7, second instance. **TI_3**: EA 24, reverse, line 3, second instance. **O-Mit – TI_1**: KBo 1.2, obverse, line 40. **TI_2**: KBo 28.66, obverse, line 20. **TI_3**: KBo 1.2, obverse, line 15. **As-Mit – TI_1**: KUB 37.43, reverse, column 4, line 10. **TI_3**: KUB 37.43, obverse, column 1, line 14. **TI_4**: KUB 37.106, fragment 536b, obverse, column 2, line 27.

TABLE 3.24 3D comparison of number of wedges in TI

		TI (118)		
Tablet	Photograph	3D-scan face colours	3D-scan vertex	3D-scan measurements
EA 24			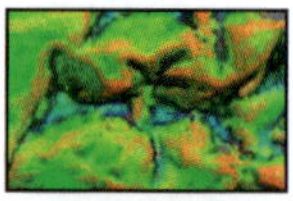	
KBo 28.66				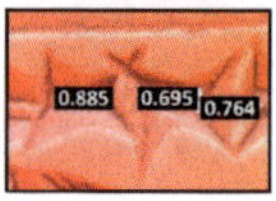

Four versus five in 'long' form: EA 24, reverse, column 4, line 34. KBo 28.66, obverse, line 4. With thanks to the Department of Altorientalistik, Universität Würzburg.

TABLE 3.25 Mittani TIM

Amarna Mittani Letters	
TIM$_1$	TIM$_2$

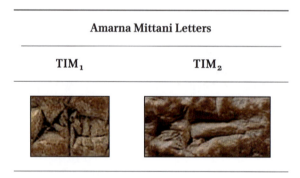

Am-Mit only (recorded 9 times): EA 19, obverse, line 29; EA 17, obverse, line 22.

initial horizontal is impressed into the vertical and followed by a sequence of *Winkelhaken* (MEŠ$_2$). In O-Mit MEŠ the horizontal wedges are generally all impressed evenly and within equal distance to one another, but sometimes there is a slight difference between the initial impression and the following sequence, betraying the form MEŠ$_1$. The As-Mit tablets also always have MEŠ$_1$. These forms are not completely exclusive to specific tablets – for example, at least 2 instances (out of 26) of MEŠ$_2$ also occur on EA 22, and 1 instance (out of 4) on KBo 28.66; however, this seems incidental.

TABLE 3.26 Mittani MEŠ

Am-Mit		O-Mit	As-Mit
MEŠ$_1$	MEŠ$_2$	MEŠ$_1$	MEŠ$_1$

Am-Mit (recorded 221 times): EA 19, obverse, line 6; EA 25, reverse, column 4, line 57. **O-Mit** (recorded 50 times): KBo 1.2, reverse, line 29. **As-Mit** (recorded 26 times): KUB 37.55, fragment 423c, reverse, column 5, line 17.

3.3.4 *Variants*

Angle and Placement of Wedges in TAR (9)

In Am-Mit TAR the placement of wedges is fairly consistent without noticeable variants between tablets. The broken horizontal is nearly always straight, with a straight or angled bottom horizontal which is usually attached to it but sometimes detached (TAR$_{1a}$) (**Table 3.27**). O-Mit TAR likewise occurs with little variation. On AlT 14 and on Bz 51 the wedges are shorter and resemble *Winkelhaken* more than horizontals, and the composition looks more like an initial impression followed by a top and a bottom impression (TAR$_{1b}$). At least four instances of As-Mit TAR are TAR$_{1a}$ and at least two are TAR$_{1b}$, but the differences could possibly be attributed to coincidence. Both variants appear on KBo 36.29 and there is no clear distinction between tablets. However, variants with a less clear broken *Winkelhaken* and more obvious higher placed second wedge are also more common in Early Middle Assyrian (**Chapter 4**).

Winkelhaken *of LI (85)*

LI is a remarkably stable sign for the quantity in which it was recorded and the number and shape of its component wedges. In Middle Assyrian and Amarna Babylonian a form with horizontal wedges (ŠE+ŠA) and one without are used alternately. From the Am-Mit documents LI was recorded from all tablets apart from EA 18. None of these instances have horizontal wedges. The only variation is in the impression and spacing of the centre *Winkelhaken*, which is in line with scribal hand – for example, on EA 19 and EA 27 the top *Winkelhaken* is usually obscured by the vertical or possibly missing (LI$_{1a}$), whereas on EA 24

TABLE 3.27 Mittani TAR

Am-Mit	O-Mit		As-Mit	
TAR_{1a}	TAR_{1a}	TAR_{1b}	TAR_{1a}	TAR_{1b}
	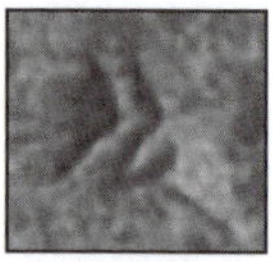	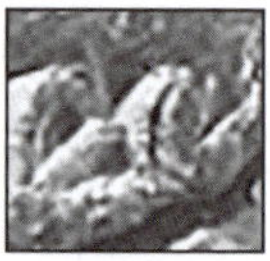		

Am-Mit (recorded 13 times): EA 22, obverse, column 2, line 23. **O-Mit** (recorded 10 times): TB 6002, obverse, line 3; Bz51, obverse, line 2. **As-Mit** (recorded 10 times): KBo 36.29, fragment 2533c, reverse, column 3, line 9; KBo 36.29, fragment 399d, reverse, column 4, line 3.

TABLE 3.28 Mittani NU

Am-Mit			As-Mit		
NU_{1a}	NU_{1b}	NU_{1c}	NU_{1a}	NU_{1b}	NU_{2}

Other Mittani Documents					
NU_{1a}	NU_{1b}	NU_{1c}	NU_{2}		

Am-Mit (recorded 267 times): EA 19, obverse, line 32; EA 25, obverse, column 1, line 36; EA 29, obverse, line 64. **As-Mit** (recorded 60 times): KUB 37.9, reverse, column 3, line 1; KUB 37.43, obverse, column 2, line 5; KUB 4.16, reverse, line 8. **O-Mit** (recorded 63 times): AlT 108, obverse, line 5; MS 1848 1, obverse, line 3; TB 11021, reverse, line 5; KBo 28.66, obverse, line 11.

and EA 25 it is easier to distinguish (LI_{1b}). In O-Mit LI the only difference is that it is often the top *Winkelhaken* that is clearer than the bottom one (LI_{1c}). In As-Mit LI the bottom *Winkelhaken* is frequently extended into a vertical impression (LI_{1d}).

On the reverse of KUB 37.5 (not included in the database) an instance of LI occurs with horizontal wedges (**Table 3.29**). Weeden (2012: 240) has commented that this could be evidence of the rare occurrence of this form in Assyro-Mittanian, and possibly even be proof that it is simply coincidence that it has not yet been found for Mittanian. However, Köcher (1953) originally identified the script as Middle Babylonian, where this form of LI is much more common. This is repeated by Schwemer (1998: 9), Haas (2003: 117) and Sassmannshausen (2008: 265), although Schwemer later calls it 'Syrian *ductus*' … 'not written by a Hittite scribe' (2005: 224). Schwemer (1998: 9) also says he found a RU with three *Winkelhaken* (e.g. reverse, line 3), but, upon inspection of the project database, this is not the same as the form found in the large Mittanian Amarna letters. On KUB 37.5 it is further possible to find an AK with a divergent initial wedge typical for Assyro-Mittanian or Middle Assyrian (e.g. obverse, line 2), and a 'long' TI with four wedges (e.g. obverse, line 4). On the reverse (line 6) MEŠ occurs with a horizontal impression, pause, *Winkelhaken*, but on the obverse (e.g. line 7) this is much less clear. Also see **Paragraph 6.2.2** for the occurrence of this form on KUB 47.41.

Height of Wedge-placement in NA (110) and RU (111) (again)

Due to the very large number of instances of NA in the Am-Mit database it was possible to conduct a detailed analysis of variation. The initial horizontal wedge of NA can occur low (NA_{1c}), in the middle (NA_{1b}) and high (NA_{1a}) in the composition (**Figure 3.7**, **Figure 3.8**). The height of the horizontal (or length of vertical) differs between tablets. It is also notable that in all compositions the upper *Winkelhaken* is nearly always written with a flourish, and crossing through paragraph dividing lines (when present), which is also a feature of Middle Assyrian. The vertical never extends into the line below, making it clear that the appearance of higher horizontals is not (necessarily) accidental. The same observation can be made about the O-Mit tablets – that the horizontal impressions are impressed consistently at the same height along the vertical wedge per tablet. Most variants of As-Mit NA_1 are either NA_{1a} or NA_{1b}, but, while primarily consistent, the impression along the verticals is less obvious than in the Amarna letters.

Like NA, the lower horizontal of RU occurs both at the bottom, in the middle and at the top of the composition (**Figure 3.9**). On EA 25 the bottom

TABLE 3.29 Mittani LI

Am-Mit		O-Mit		As-Mit	
LI$_{1a}$	**LI$_{1b}$**	**LI$_{1c}$**	**LI$_{1b}$**	**LI$_{1d}$**	**LI$_{2?}$**

Am-Mit (recorded 175 times): EA 19, obverse, line 15; EA 25, obverse, column 1, line 26. **O-Mit** (recorded 26 times): KBo 1.2, reverse, line 17; AlT 108, obverse, line 7. **As-Mit** (recorded 37 times): KUB 37.106, fragment 640b, obverse, column 2, line 13; KUB 37.5, fragment 601d, reverse, line 2.

TABLE 3.30 Mittani QA and NA4

Am-Mit		O-Mit		As-Mit	
QA$_{1a}$	**QA$_{1b}$**	**QA$_{1a}$**	**QA$_{1b}$**	**QA$_{1c}$**	**QA$_{1d}$**

Am-Mit		As-Mit	
NA$_{4\text{-}1a}$	**NA$_{4\text{-}1b}$**	**NA$_{4\text{-}1c}$**	**NA$_{4\text{-}1d}$**

Am-Mit QA (recorded 13 times): EA 22, reverse, column 2, line 28; EA 22, reverse, column 2, line 17. **O-Mit QA** (recorded 13 times): KBo 1.2, obverse, line 23; TB 6001, obverse, line 17. **As-Mit QA** (recorded 6 times): KUB 37.55, fragment 423c, reverse, column 6, line 24; KUB 37.106, fragment 640b, obverse, column 2, line 13. **Am-Mit NA$_4$** (recorded 163 times): EA 25, obverse, column 1, line 62; EA 22, obverse, column 1, line 50; EA 22, reverse, column 2, line 17. **As-Mit NA$_4$** (recorded 9 times): KUB 37.52, obverse, line 8. KBo 36.29, fragment 1017c, obverse, column 1, line 14, second instance; KBo 36.29, fragment 166e, reverse, column 4, line 17.

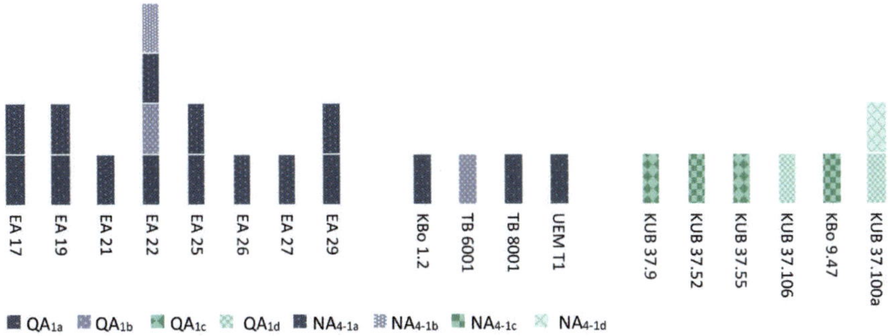

FIGURE 3.6 Comparison of Mittani QA and NA4
Note the correlation between variants in each corpus.

horizontal wedge is almost always crossed by the final vertical (impressed after or deeper than the horizontal). The differences in height of the horizontal can also be compared per tablet. There is no clear pattern which emerges when comparing NA to RU, but some observations can be made: EA 17, EA 24 and EA 27 form a middle-low category, EA 22 and EA 29 middle, EA 20, EA 26 and EA 28 middle-high. EA 29, EA 21 and EA 25 all have a NA with a high horizontal wedge and RU with a low horizontal wedge (**Figure 3.10**). While the illustrated differences are all minute, the placement of wedges has an impact on the overall appearance of each tablet; particularly the group with horizontals which were placed consistently higher up along the vertical stands out.

Angle of QA (99) and NA4 (385)

QA is an interesting sign with regard to the angle of impressions. Cammarosano (2015: 166) found that differences in the angle of NA were indicative of scribal hand, separating tablets written by the Hittite scribes Tarḫunmiya and Šuriḫili. Most collected Am-Mit instances of QA have a strong angle (QA_{1a}), with the exception of two examples from EA 22 (QA_{1b}) which seem to be co-incidental (**Table 3.30**). The difference between scribal hands is very clear in the O-Mit documents. QA was recorded only from KBo 1.2, TB 6001, TB 8001 and UEM T1. However, on KBo 1.2 the scribe used a straight lower horizontal but angled upper wedge (QA_{1a}) and on TB 6001 the scribe preferred only straight (horizontal) impressions (QA_{1b}). Of the As-Mit documents QA was recorded from KUB 37.9 and KUB 37.55, which show a preference for a short upper impression (QA_{1c}) – while KBo 36.29 and KUB 37.106 have a more elongated upper wedge (QA_{1d}).[39]

39 The sign occurs on none of the relevant tablets of which 3D scans have been made so it is not possible to measure this more technically.

NA_4 was also recorded with very little variation from the Am-Mit tablets. Sometimes it has a short diagonal impression ($NA_{4\text{-}1a}$) and occasionally a slightly longer and more horizontal impression ($NA_{4\text{-}1b}$) – again particularly on EA 22. From the O-Mit tablets no instances of NA_4 were recorded. As-Mit NA_4 was recorded from KBo 9.47 and KUB 37.57 with the short *Winkelhaken* impression as in QA (99) ($NA_{4\text{-}1c}$), but from KBo 36.29 with a more extended and protruding diagonal wedge ($NA_{4\text{-}1d}$) (although the single instance from KUB 37.52 is less clear). Recorded instances of NA_4 and QA only co-occur on KBo 36.29, where the wedges are both extended and match (**Figure 3.6**).

Angle of NU (112)

Am-Mit NU occurs in three clear variations. On EA 17, EA 19 and EA 30 the middle wedge is impressed straight rather than slanted or diagonal (NU_{1a}) (**Table 3.28**). On EA 20, EA 21, EA 23, EA 25, EA 26, EA 27 and EA 28 the middle wedge is slanted slightly (NU_{1b}), and on EA 22, EA 24 and EA 29 the slant is more noticeable (almost diagonal) (NU_{1c}). This is a consistent variation per tablet and thus possibly representative of scribal hand. That said, this does not automatically identify each group of tablets as having been written by the same scribe; as discussed throughout this chapter, other forms and variants may differ between these tablets. From the O-Mit documents NU was likewise recorded straight on some tablets and slanted on others. NU_{1a} appears on AlT 108 and primarily KBo 1.2, NU_{1b} on MS 1848 1, MS 1848 2, TB 6001, and TB 8001, and NU_{1c} on SMN 1000 (according to the copy), KBo 28.66 and TB 11021. However, the instances on KBo 28.66 could also be seen as a different form of NU altogether, since the diagonal wedge is consistently impressed through or almost above the horizontal (NU_2). From the Assyro-Mittani tablets NU_{1a} occurs on KBo 9.47, KUB 37.9, KUB 37.106, KUB 37.57, KUB 37.65 (only one instance each) and KUB 37.55, NU_{1b} on KUB 37.72, KUB 37.86, KUB 4.16 and primarily on KBo 36.29 and KUB 37.43. There are no clear examples of a completely diagonal NU_{1c} in this corpus, but KUB 4.16 is another contender for NU_2.

Spacing in AK (127)

While the sign-forms of Am-Mit AK do not differ, a very subtle shift in the broken horizontal creates two distinct variants. The horizontal in AK_{1a} begins crossed through or obscured by the initial vertical, while the horizontal in AK_{1b} is clearly detached from it or impressed with more emphasis and takes a central position in the composition (**Table 3.31**). AK_{1b} only occurs on EA 24 and EA 25 (the instances from EA 22 and EA 29 are unclear). From the O-Mit documents most instances are damaged, but it looks like AK_{1a} was used. Copies by others suggest a much larger variety in variation or even sign-form but this

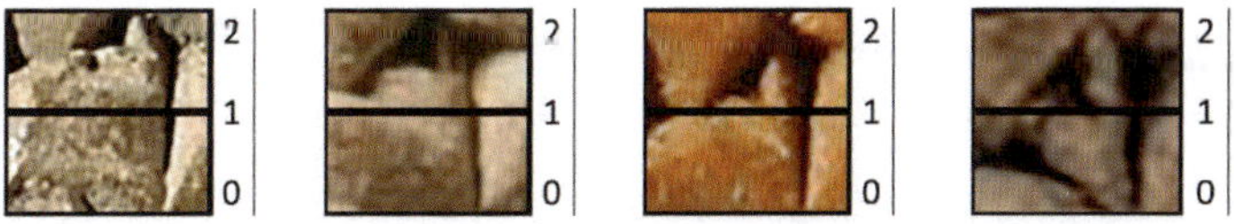

FIGURE 3.7 Placement of the horizontal in NA (four variants). The vertical has been re-sized to 1.33 cm in each image (EA 26, obverse, line 4; EA 26 reverse, line 18; EA 29 obverse, line 15; EA 19, obverse, line 30). The final variant occurs infrequently however. Image scale 2:3.

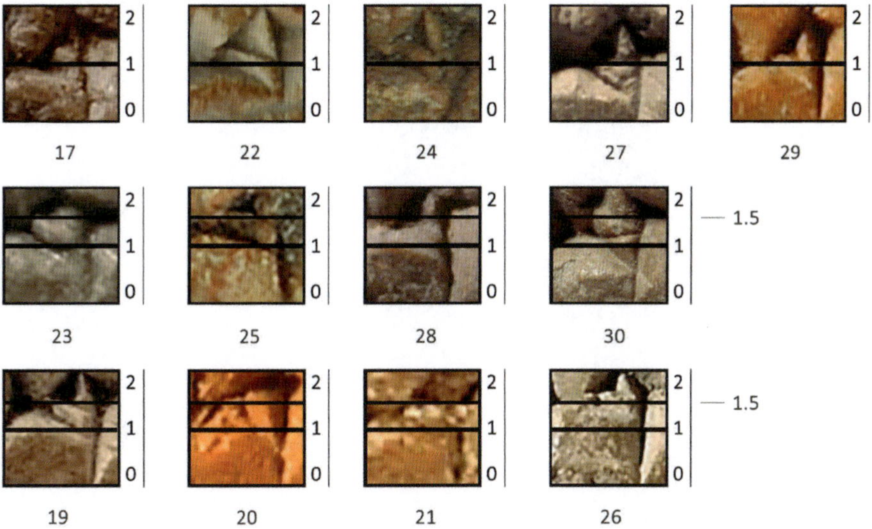

FIGURE 3.8 Comparison of placement of horizontals in NA between tablets. Verticals re-sized to 1.33 cm. The placement of the horizontal can be given a standard deviation of 1.5 mm, but overall group 1 is decidedly lower and group 3 decidedly higher. Image scale 2:3.

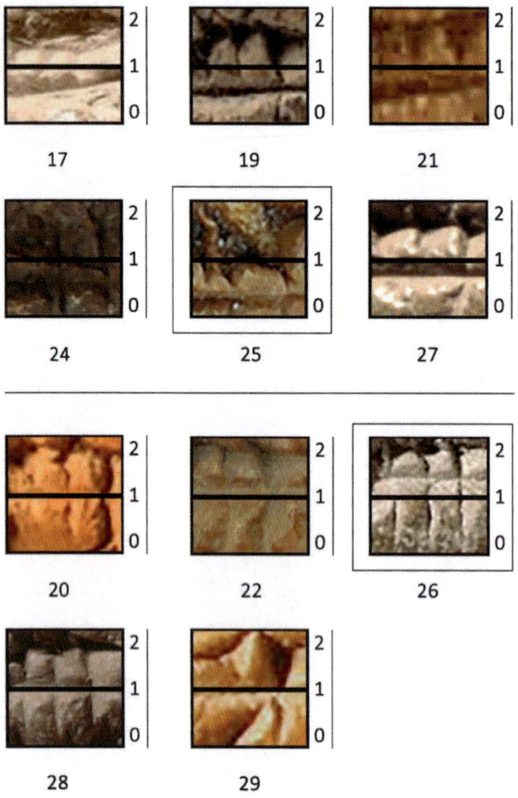

FIGURE 3.9 Comparison of placement of horizontals in RU. All verticals re-sized to 2 cm. The placement of the horizontal can be given a standard deviation of 1.5 mm, but overall group 1 is decidedly lower and group 2 decidedly higher. Image scale 2:3.

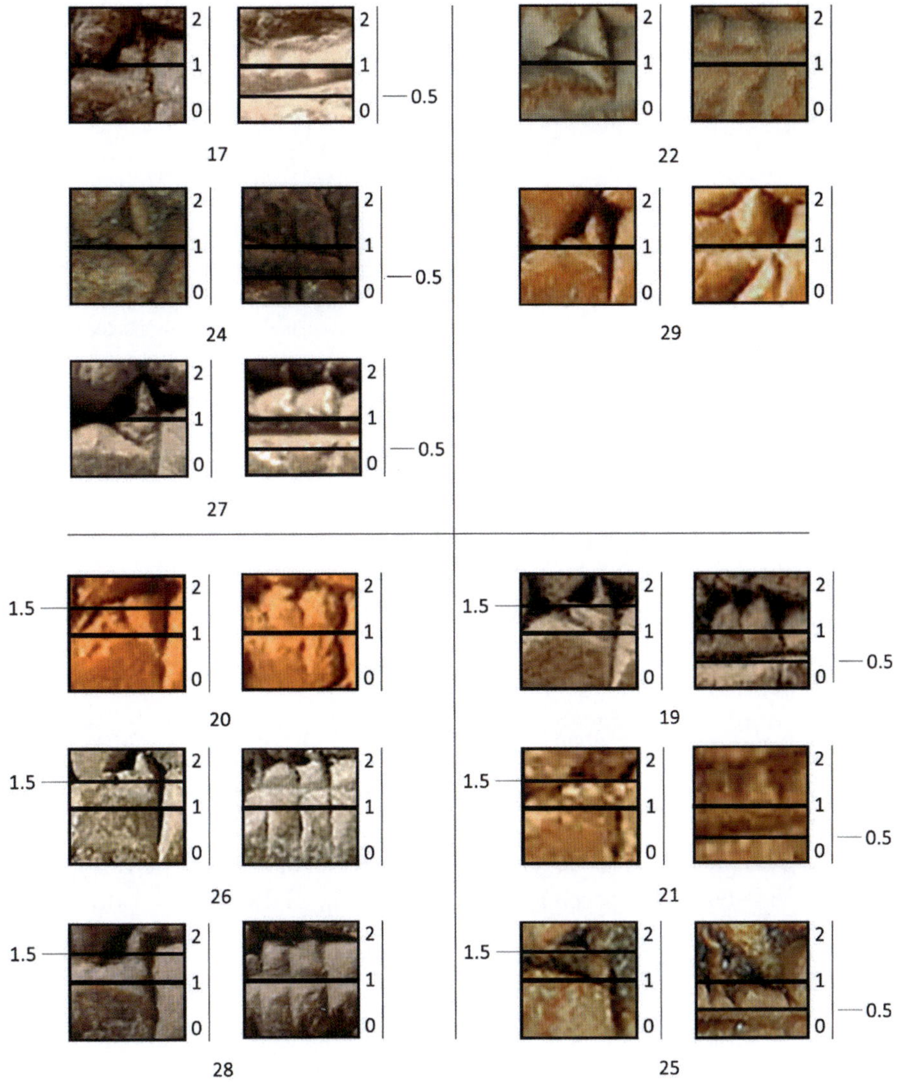

FIGURE 3.10 Combined comparison of placement of horizontals in NA and RU
All verticals re-sized to 1.33 cm. Image scale 2:3.

TABLE 3.31 Mittani AK

Am-Mit		O-Mit	As-Mit
AK_{1a}	AK_{1b}	AK_{1a}	AK_{1a}
		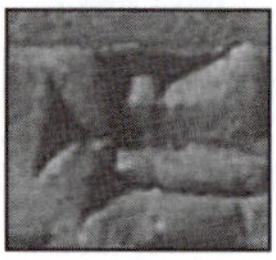	

Am-Mit (recorded 40 times): EA 19, obverse, line 30; EA 25, obverse, column 2, line 26. **O-Mit** (recorded 10 times): KBo 1.2, obverse, line 6. **As-Mit** (recorded 20 times): KBo 36.29, fragment 2533c, reverse, column 3, line 26.

cannot be confirmed from the available photos. While on the As-Mit tablets the position of the broken horizontal is that of AK_{1a}, it is often impressed more strongly than the variant in the Amarna letters.

Verticals of SA (*172*)

SA was not recorded many times from any of the corpora under consideration, but nonetheless the form is interesting. From the Am-Mit tablets SA was recorded only from EA 22, 24 and 29; and from more O-Mit tablets, but always the same as in the Amarna letters. On As-Mit KUB 37.55 it occurs the same (SA_{1a}), but on KUB 37.100a and KBo 36.29 with four consecutive verticals (without a larger or more spaced initial vertical) (SA_{1b}) (**Table 3.32**).

Spacing in TA (*248*) (*again*)

In **Paragraph 3.3.1** TA was only mentioned in relation to KBo 1.2. There are smaller variations between all tablets and all corpora to reflect on as well. Amarna TA has a variant where the verticals are impressed closely together, obscuring the *Winkelhaken*, which occurs on most tablets (TA_{1a}) (see **Table 3.35**). It also has a variant where the final two verticals are spaced further apart, clearly revealing the two *Winkelhaken*, only on EA 24, EA 25, EA 26 and EA 29 (TA_{1b}). On the O-Mit tablets TA_{1a} occurs on KBo 28.65, KBo 28.66, TB 11021, and probably the other Tell Brak tablets too (instances very damaged). TA_{1b} occurs on AlT 108, probably the other Alalaḫ tablets (instances damaged), MS 1848 1, SMN 1000 according to the copy but not the image, and possibly Bz 51 (instances damaged). The instances from IBoT 1.34 and UEM T1 are too damaged to judge altogether. As mentioned, TA for KBo 1.2 was already

TABLE 3.32 Mittani SA

Am-Mit	O-Mit	As-Mit	
SA_{1a}	SA_{1a}	SA_{1a}	SA_{1b}
			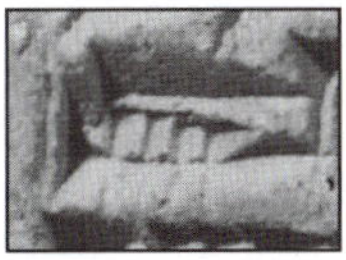

Am-Mit (recorded 6 times): EA 22, reverse, column 1, line 38. **O-Mit** (recorded 10 times): AlT 14, obverse, line 1, second instance. **As-Mit** (recorded 7 times): KUB 37.55, fragment 423c, reverse, column 5, line 19; KUB 37.100a, fragment 656c, obverse, column 1, line 28.

TABLE 3.33 Mittani Ú

Am-Mit			O-Mit		As-Mit
$Ú_{1a}$	$Ú_{1b}$	$Ú_{1c}$	$Ú_{1b}$	$Ú_{1a}$	$Ú_{1b}$
				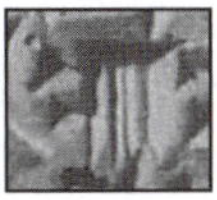	

Am-Mit (recorded 442 times): EA 30, obverse, line 7; EA 29, obverse, line 35; EA 19, obverse, line 16. **O-Mit** (recorded 66 times): KBo 1.2, obverse, line 36; TB 11021, obverse, line 5. **As-Mit** (recorded 75 times): KUB 37.43, obverse, column 1, line 11.

discussed in **Paragraph 3.3.1** ($TA_{2?}$). On the As-Mit tablets TA_{1a} occurs on KBo 36.29, KUB 37.9, KBo 36.34, KUB 37.43, and KUB 37.72. TA_{1b} only occurs very clearly on KUB 4.16. On KUB 37.106 the two variants are mixed. Finally, on KUB 37.55 a variant appears with smaller verticals (TA_{1c}).

The 'slipping' of the verticals in TA (whether they are placed below, level with, or above the horizontal) has been used as a diagnostic element in dating Hittite script (Starke 1985: 24).[40] An example of the level placement of these impressions can be seen on AlT 108 (**Table 3.35**, O-Mit, TA_{1b}). This (almost)

40 Forrer (1922: 34) documents two forms for Hittite TA: one with verticals even with the upper horizontal, and one with verticals below the upper horizontal.

TABLE 3.34 3D scans of Mittani Ú

Ú (490)				
Tablet	**Photograph**	**3D-scan face colours**	**3D-scan vertex**	**3D-scan measurements**
EA 24			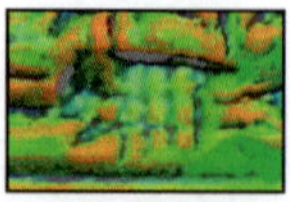	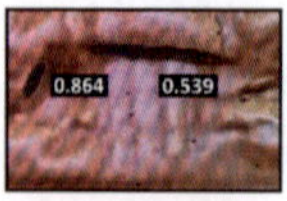
KBo 28.66				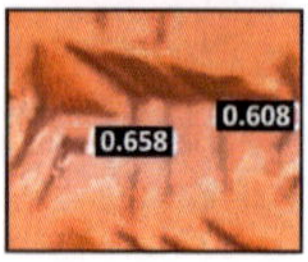

Depth of impression can affect whether verticals of horizontals are dominant in a sign. EA 24, reverse, column 4, line 39, second instance. KBo 28.66, obverse, line 5.

never occurs in the Amarna documents. On the other Mittanian tablets it is difficult to distinguish, due to the low number of instances collected (i.e. impressed as such on purpose, or by coincidence). One instance each was collected from the other Alalaḫ tablets, both of which are contenders, but not as obvious as AlT 108. The same can be said for the Mittani tablets from the Schøyen collection and Tall Bazi. The vertical of ŠA (566) equally seems to have been impressed level on these tablets, as well as the one instance recorded of GA (491). In the Amarna documents, all of these signs are generally impressed with the verticals well above the horizontals (especially GA). Since most of the other tablets mentioned can potentially be dated earlier than Tušratta, it might be tempting to connect dating to the level of the verticals, as for Hittite. However, the one instance of TA collected from Nuzi (a tablet with a seal of Šaustatar) clearly has verticals above the horizontal (**Table 3.35**, O-Mit, TA_{1a}). Weeden (2011: 46) suggests the use of a sliding scale in dating tablets: the fewer old features a tablet possesses, the later it was written, thereby eliminating the rule that a tablet *must* possess certain features. Perhaps the same is true here, where tablets with higher verticals are likely to be more recent, but not exclusively so.

Tablets on which RU and TA co-occur generally follow the same form (primary versus secondary; obscured *Winkelhaken* versus visible *Winkelhaken*) (**Figure 3.11**). Because it is often difficult to find the *Winkelhaken* and to count their number, 3D-scans were used to check some of the impressions –

particularly with regard to the depth of impression of the *Winkelhaken* (**Table 3.36**). Normally the *Winkelhaken* are visible on EA 24 but in the example selected here they are barely distinguishable in the photograph. In the vertex image, however, they are very clear. The depth of impression of both the initial horizontals and the *Winkelhaken* here is 0.8 mm, whereas the depth of all three verticals is 0.4 mm. In the instance selected for RU from the same tablet, likewise difficult to read from the photograph, the *Winkelhaken* also become visible in the vertex image and impressed deeper than the other wedges (**Table 3.36**). On KBo 28.66 the *Winkelhaken* are usually less clear, but they are distinguishable on the instance selected here. The horizontal wedges are impressed with a depth of circa 0.7 mm, while the verticals and *Winkelhaken* are impressed with a depth of circa 0.9 mm, contributing to the dominance of the verticals in this form. It is interesting that the large Amarna tablets (apart from EA 22) all share a preference for forms which place emphasis on spaced and deep *Winklehaken*, and also that they form a minority. KUB 4.16 however follows the same pattern, but otherwise generally has more typical Middle Assyrian sign-forms; therefore, this cannot be used to distinguish between more and less 'Assyrian' scribes.

Order or Depth of Impression of Ú (490), É (495) and Similar Signs

As discussed in **Paragraph 2.6**, it is complicated to comment on order of wedge impression. However, Ú is a clear indication that scribes had preferences for wedge-placement – be it order of impression, depth of impression, or otherwise (**Table 3.35**). To begin with the Am-Mit tablets: the horizontals in Ú often completely obscure the verticals, but on some tablets the verticals appear to have been impressed either last or with more pressure. For example, on EA 30 the horizontal wedges stand out so much that the middle of the verticals has vanished. On EA 29 on the other hand, it is the horizontal wedges that have disappeared. On EA 19 the bottom horizontal is consistently more visible than the top horizontal. Not all tablets are as consistent, but each reveals hints of a primary preference of impression. While this is a general observation rather than a Mittani-centred one, it helps in distinguishing between individual scribes and the same can be said about the other two corpora under discussion. From the O-Mit tablets Ú was recorded with, for example, a consistently vertical-focussed variant on KBo 1.2 and an evenly crossed variant on TB 11021. On the As-Mit tablets, the verticals are dominant in nearly all cases, but particularly on, for example, KUB 37.43.

Since depth of impression is difficult to observe accurately from regular images, a selection of instances was also measured from the 3D-scans (**Table 3.36**). On the instance from EA 24 the verticals are impressed at circa

TABLE 3.35 Mittani TA

Am-Mit		O-Mit		As-Mit		
TA_{1a}	TA_{1b}	TA_{1a}	TA_{1b}	TA_{1a}	TA_{1b}	TA_{1c}

Am-Mit (recorded 383 times): EA 19, obverse, line 34; EA 24, reverse, column 1, line 107, second instance. **O-Mit** (recorded 75 times): KBo 28.66, obverse, line 21; AlT 108, obverse, line 9. **As-Mit** (recorded 85 times): KBo 36.29, fragment 2533c, reverse, column 3, line 26; KUB 4.16, reverse, line 5; KUB 37.55, fragment 423c, reverse, column 5, line 8, second instance.

TABLE 3.36 3D scans of Mittani TA and RU

TA (248)				
Tablet	Photograph	3D-scan face colours	3D-scan vertex	3D-scan measurements
EA 24			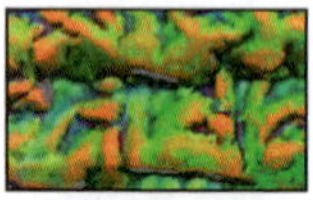	
KBo 28.66				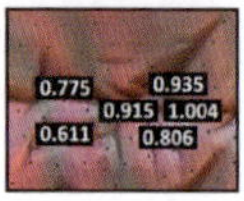
RU (111)				
EA 24			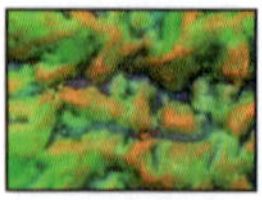	

Revealing obscured *Winkelhaken*. **TA:** EA 24, reverse, column 4, line 38, KBo 28.66, obverse, line 4. **RU:** EA 24, reverse, column 4, line 38.

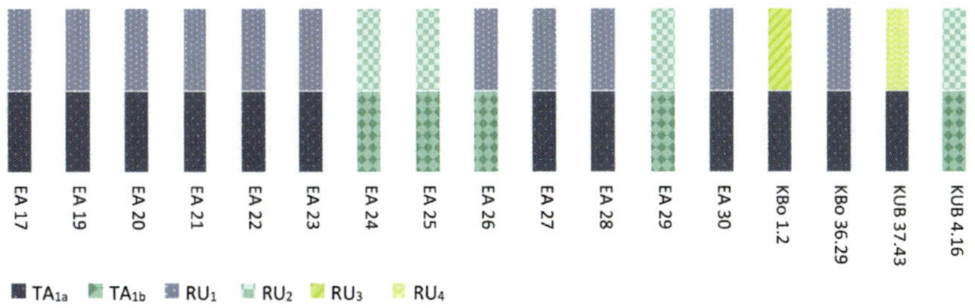

FIGURE 3.11 Comparison of co-occurrence of Mittani TA and RU

0.5 mm deep and the horizontals at circa 0.9 mm deep; thus, the verticals do not obscure the horizontals entirely. On the example from KBo 28.66 the verticals and horizontals are both impressed at circa 0.6 mm deep, and the verticals almost completely obscure the horizontals. The same applies to similar signs such as É (495), DAN (496) and UN (501) (**Table 3.37**). For example, on the Am-Mit tablets É often has strong horizontal impressions. However, on EA 28 the lines cross a little more clearly – as do the lines in all similar signs on the tablet. From the O-Mit tablets not many instances co-occur, but where they do, as on KBo 1.2, they match. Equally, on the As-Mit tablets, co-occurring instances match.

The Horizontals of RA (511)

There is some variation between tablets for Am-Mit RA. For example, the scribe of EA 27 consistently used four instead of three initial horizontal wedges. At other times, the initial broken horizontal extends out in front of the composition (RA$_{1b}$) (**Table 3.38**). This is particularly clear on EA 26. The variant may also occur on EA 24 and EA 29 but due to the crowded nature of the script on these tablets it is more difficult to establish. On the O-Mit tablets RA occurs with very little variation, except that the scribe of KBo 1.2 seems to have had a preference for using four horizontals, and a bottom wedge with a more diagonal angle (consistent with the manner in which the other signs are impressed) (RA$_{1c?}$). The scribe of KBo 28.66 preferred a variant with a small initial vertical (RA$_{1d?}$). From the As-Mit tablets the primary variant is RA$_{1b}$: it consistently occurs on KUB 37.72, KUB 37.74, KUB 37.100a, KUB 37.106, and KBo 36.34. RA$_{1a}$ occurs on KUB 37.43, KUB 37.55, KBo 36.32, KUB 37.9.

Emphasis in MA (552)

Despite a very large number of instances recorded (nearly 600), there is very little variation in Am-Mit MA, apart from slight differences in wedge emphasis between tablets. On EA 26 and EA 27 the top horizontal is impressed with

TABLE 3.37 Mittani É, DAN and UN

EA 28		
É (495)	DAN (496)	UN (501)

KBo 1.2		
É (495)	DAN (496)	UN (501)
		–
KUB 37.106		
É (495)	DAN (496)	UN (501)

Am-Mit: EA 28, reverse, line 14, second instance; EA 28, obverse, line 14; EA 28, obverse, line 7. **O-Mit:** KBo 1.2, obverse, line 37; KBo 1.2, obverse, line 27. **As-Mit:** KUB 37.106, fragment 640b, obverse, column 2, line 6; KUB 37.106, fragment 640b, obverse, column 2, line 14; KUB 37.106, fragment 640b, obverse, column 2, line 13.

more emphasis than the lower two wedges (MA_{1c}), while on EA 19 the top and bottom horizontal are both impressed with more emphasis (MA_{1b}), and on EA 28 all wedges are impressed with equal emphasis (MA_{1a}) (**Table 3.39**). From the O-Mit tablets the MA on KBo 1.2 and KBo 28.66 has a middle horizontal which is also clearly less emphasised or shorter (MA_{1b}), while on other tablets, such as those from Tell Brak, the emphasis is even (MA_{1a}). From the

TABLE 3.38 Mittani RA

Am-Mit		O-Mit		As-Mit	
RA_{1a}	**RA_{1b}**	**RA_{1d}**	**RA_{1c}**	**RA_{1a}**	**RA_{1b}**

Am-Mit (recorded 123 times): EA 19, obverse, line 7; EA 26, obverse, line 29. **O-Mit** (recorded 28 times): KBo 28.66, obverse, line 10; KBo 1.2, obverse, line 15. **As-Mit** (recorded 45 times): KUB 37.55, fragment 423c, reverse, column 6, line 21; KUB 37.74, obverse, line 3.

As-Mit tablets nearly all cases are completely even (MA_{1a}), apart from KUB 37.43 where the top horizontal has more emphasis (MA_{1c}).

Winkelhaken *of DA (561)*

In all instances of DA on Am-Mit EA 19 and EA 27 the *Winkelhaken* is placed before the verticals (DA_{1a}) while in the instances of EA 17 and 25 the *Winkelhaken* is placed decidedly inbetween the two verticals (DA_{1b}) (**Table 3.40**). While inconsistencies do occur, each tablet displays a primary preference for the placement of the *Winkelhaken*. From the O-Mit tablets DA was recorded only once, from KBo 28.66 (DA_{1b}). However, in As-Mit DA, like ID, the broken horizontal is more pronounced. The *Winkelhaken* is nearly always placed in front of the verticals with two exceptions (out of twelve instances) on KBo 36.29.

Winkelhaken *of ŠA (566) (again)*

As mentioned, Am-Mit ŠA varies very little. Generally, the top horizontal is more emphasised than the other horizontal impressions. The two *Winkelhaken* are always placed carefully and visibly between the two verticals ($ŠA_{1a}$) (**Table 3.41**). However, on EA 27 almost half the instances have a bottom *Winkelhaken* impressed more to the left ($ŠA_{1b}$). In O-Mit ŠA the *Winkelhaken* also receive space between the verticals, apart from the different form from KBo 1.2 discussed already (**Paragraph 3.3.1**). In As-Mit ŠA, as with most signs from this corpus, the top horizontal is usually, but not in all cases, strongly emphasised ($ŠA_{1c}$). The scribe of KUB 37.55 consistently places the (bottom) *Winkelhaken* into the left vertical while on KUB 37.106 they are always centred between the verticals.

TABLE 3.39 Mittani MA

Am-Mit			O-Mit		As-Mit	
MA_{1a}	MA_{1b}	MA_{1c}	MA_{1a}	MA_{1b}	MA_{1a}	MA_{1c}

Am-Mit (recorded 594 times): EA 28, obverse, line 5; EA 19, obverse line 28, second instance; EA 26, reverse, line 25, second instance. **O-Mit** (recorded 88 times): TB 8001, reverse, line 2; KBo 1.2, reverse, line 26, second instance. **As-Mit** (recorded 95 times): KBo 36.29, fragment 399d, reverse, column 4, line 13; KUB 37.43, reverse, column 4, line 17.

TABLE 3.40 Mittani DA

Am-Mit		O-Mit	As-Mit
DA_{1a}	DA_{1b}	DA_{1b}	DA_{1a}

Am-Mit (recorded 27 times): EA 19, reverse, line 10; EA 25, reverse, column 3, line 62. **O-Mit** (recorded 1 time): KBo 28.66, obverse, line 7. **As-Mit** (recorded 23 times): KUB 37.43, reverse, column 4, line 16.

Horizontals of ŠU (567)

Am-Mit ŠU generally has four horizontal wedges (ŠU_{1a}), apart from a few instances from EA 22, 24, and 25, and more consistently EA 26 and 29, which have five wedges (ŠU_{1b}) (**Table 3.42**). Sometimes the upper horizontal is more emphasised than the middle two. O-Mit ŠU on KBo 1.2, KBo 28.65, KUB 3.80, TB 11021, and probably SMN 1000, consistently occurs with five rather than four wedges (ŠU_{1b}). From the As-Mit tablets ŠU was recorded only with four wedges (ŠU_{1b}), continuing to illustrate a preference for impressing more wedges than common in the Am-Mit and O-Mit documents.

TABLE 3.41 Mittani ŠA

Am-Mit		O-Mit		As-Mit	
ŠA$_{1a}$	ŠA$_{1b}$	ŠA$_{1a}$	ŠA$_{2?}$	ŠA$_{1c}$	ŠA$_{1b}$

Am-Mit (recorded 489 times): EA 19, obverse, line 14; EA 27, obverse, line 41. **O-Mit** (recorded 59 times): AlT 108, obverse, line 4, second instance; KBo 1.2, obverse, line 32, second instance. **As-Mit** (recorded 82 times): KUB 37.106, fragment 640b, obverse, column 2, line 19; KUB 37.55, fragment 423c, column 5, line 25.

TABLE 3.42 Mittani ŠU

Am-Mit		O-Mit		As-Mit
ŠU$_{1a}$	ŠU$_{1b}$	ŠU$_{1a}$	ŠU$_{1b}$	ŠU$_{1b}$

Am-Mit (recorded 488 times): EA 19, obverse, line 13; EA 25, reverse, column 4, line 37. **O-Mit** (recorded 97 times): MS 1848 1, obverse, line 6; KBo 1.2, obverse, line 14. **As-Mit** (recorded 68 times): KBO 36.29, fragment 73b, reverse, column 3, line 52.

Winkelhaken *of ŠE (579), TE (589) and Similar Signs*

In these corpora the ŠE component in, for example, BU and TE can occur in two different subtle varieties; sometimes hard to distinguish from one another and at other times very clear. The first variant of ŠE has a large initial *Winkelhaken* and three consecutive *Winkelhaken* below it; a triangular cluster (1a) (**Table 3.43**). The second is turned a little more on its left and has (almost) equally sized *Winkelhaken*; a square cluster (1b). A very large number of instances of Am-Mit ŠE (579), BU (580) and TE (589) were collected for thorough comparison. However, in the case of the Amarna tablets there is no consistent variation between tablets and occurrences of 1b seem accidental (e.g. more often on

TABLE 3.43 Mittani ŠE and TE

Am-Mit		O-Mit			As-Mit
TE$_{1a}$	**TE$_{1b}$**	**TE$_{1a}$**	**TE$_{1b}$**	**ŠE$_{1b}$**	**TE$_{1a}$**

Am-Mit (TE recorded 123 times): EA 23, obverse, line 7; EA 26, reverse, line 54. **O-Mit** (TE recorded 41 times, ŠE recorded 16 times): KBo 28.66, obverse, line 10; KBo 1.2, obverse, line 21; KBo 1.2, obverse, line 20. **As-Mit** (TE recorded 26 times): KBo 36.29, fragment 1017c, obverse, column 1.

EA 24 where the script is more crowded to start with). The differences in the O-Mit documents are not as clear as on the Amarna tablets. Most scribes follow a 1a impression but either with the upper-left *Winkelhaken* less emphasised or the bottom row of *Winkelhaken* less diagonal – although KBo 1.2 shows a preference for 1b across all three signs (also compare to MU, **Paragraph 3.3.2**). The more even cluster of *Winkelhaken* is also common in Babylonian forms of the sign (see Labat 1988: 168, 172). On the As-Mit tablets the scribes all clearly use 1a forms, with only a few tablets where it can be drawn into question (KUB 37.52, one instance of BU and also one instance of US).

Number of Wedges in Ḫ̮I (631) and Similar Signs

ḪI was recorded from the Am-Mit letters almost always with five *Winkelhaken* (ḪI$_{1b}$), apart from EA 27, where it has four (ḪI$_{1a}$) (**Table 3.44**). This preference is also visible across other signs with 'ḪI' components such as 'A (635) and IM (641), as well as AM (309) which is discussed below. From the O-Mit tablets ḪI was also only recorded only with four or five *Winkelhaken*. However, in the collected As-Mit instances of ḪI often the number of *Winkelhaken* exceeds four – also where the 'ḪI' formation occurs in other signs – particularly on KBo 36.29, KBo 36.34, KUB 37.100a, 37.100b and KUB 37.106 where it is as many as six, seven or even eight *Winkelhaken* (ḪI$_{1c}$).

Am-Mit AM is very regular, occurring with only two small variations: nearly always four *Winkelhaken* on EA 17, 25, 26, 27, 28 and 30 (AM$_{1a}$) and generally five *Winkelhaken* on EA 19, 22 and 29 (AM$_{1b}$). The instances from EA 20, 21 and 24 are unclear due to damage. From the O-Mit tablets AM was also

TABLE 3.44 Mittani ḪI, ʻA, IM and AM

Amarna Mittani Letters			
ḪI$_{1a}$	ʻA$_{1a}$	IM$_{1a}$	AM$_{1a}$

O-Mit		Assyro-Mittanian			
ḪI$_{1a}$	AM$_{1a}$	ḪI$_{1a}$	ḪI$_{1b}$	AM$_{1a}$	AM$_{1b}$
				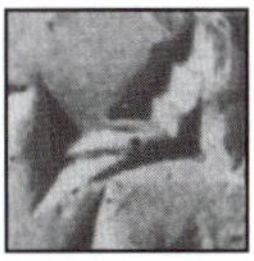	

Am-Mit ḪI (recorded 80 times): EA 30, obverse, line 7. **Am-Mit ʻA** (recorded 61 times): EA 27, obverse, line 39, second instance. **Am-Mit IM** (recorded 117 times): EA 27, obverse, line 28. **Am-Mit AM** (recorded 70 times): EA 26, obverse, line 22. **O-Mit ḪI** (recorded 13 times): KBo 28.66 obverse, line 18. **O-Mit AM** (recorded 16 times): MS 1848 1, obverse, line 3, edge. **As-Mit ḪI** (recorded 22 times): KUB 37.43, reverse, column 4, line 15; KBo 36.34, fragment 829c, obverse, column 1, line 16. **As-Mit AM** (recorded 29 times): KUB 37.55, fragment 373b, reverse, column 6, line 2; KBo 36.29, fragment 1017c, obverse, column 1, line 29.

recorded alternatively with 4 or 5 *Winkelhaken*. The form which stands out most here is from MS 1848 1 which is angled differently (AM$_{1d}$) – the way it is sometimes also impressed on the tablets from Nuzi (**Chapter 5**). The As-Mit corpus has AM$_{1a}$ on KUB 37.43 and 37.55, AM$_{1b}$ on KUB 37.9, and a variant with six *Winkelhaken* on KBo 36.29, KBo 36.34, KUB 37.65 and probably KUB 37.72 (AM$_{1c}$).

The Order of EŠ (711)

EŠ is variously impressed with *Winkelhaken* (EŠ$_1$) or horizontals (EŠ$_2$) and some scribes differentiate between the two, depending on the value of the sign (one numerical, one syllabic) (**Table 3.45**). From the corpora under consideration, each only yielded one tablet on which both forms co-occur. Particularly

TABLE 3.45 Mittani EŠ

Am-Mit		O-Mit		As-Mit	
EŠ$_1$	**EŠ$_2$**	**EŠ$_2$**	**EŠ$_1$**	**EŠ$_2$**	**EŠ$_1$**
			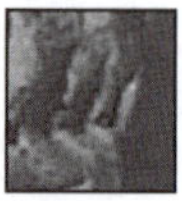		

Am-Mit (recorded 60 times): EA 19, reverse, line 43; EA 19, obverse, line 26. **O-Mit** (recorded 9 times): KBo 1.2, reverse, line 30, second instance; KBo 1.2, obverse, line 13. **As-Mit** (recorded 8 times): KBo 36.29, fragment 399d, reverse, column 4, line 14; KBo 36.29, fragment 743c, obverse, column 1, line 40.

from the Amarna letters it is clear not all scribes differentiated: for example, on EA 25 EŠ occurs only in one form (EŠ$_1$), regardless of the value of the sign. While it makes sense to interpret a numerical EŠ with *Winkelhaken* as 3 × U, between scribes the value of EŠ$_1$ and EŠ$_2$ also differs. In the example from the Amarna letters it is the *Winkelhaken* form which represents numbers, but in the examples on the Am-Mit tablets and the As-Mit documents it is the other way around.

3.4 Comments

3.4.1 *Summary*

Before considering the data from the following chapters, some conclusions can already be drawn about the three corpora under discussion in this chapter. As has been the case for studies of Middle Assyrian previously, the more tablets are discussed and compared, the more sign-forms can be established for the script-group. When sign-forms dependent on the unique shape or placement of a single wedge (divergent wedges for As-Mit and diagonals for KBo 1.2) are eliminated, the other tablets only differ from the Am-Mit documents by circa 3 sign-forms each (**Figure 3.12**). None of the remaining sign-forms are unique to Mittani (i.e. never seen before in any other cuneiform writing).

It is clear that all significant sign-forms between Am-Mit and O-Mit are the same, which means that, besides their contexts and contents, it can be

FIGURE 3.12 Stacked comparison of key Mittani signs
The data to the left of the white sections indicate signs with differently impressed wedges, the data to the right of the white sections indicate different sign-forms independent of wedge impression. Signs included here are ZU, SU, KA, TI, RI, SAG, TA, ŠA, AḪ, MU, GAB, IL, LÚ, ŠAR, ID, and UGU.

said that the O-Mit tablets are indeed palaeographically Mittanian. The only sign-form which occurs in the O-Mit documents which does not occur in the Am-Mit letters is the RU with two initial *Winkelhaken*; this can therefore be considered an addition to the 'standard Mittani' sign-list. Accordingly, ways in which to identify Mittanian writing are:

- BAL (5) with bottom *Winkelhaken*, centred underneath the vertical.
- BA (14) and similar signs almost always occur with straight, unemphasised, horizontal wedges. Rarely are the wedges diagonal, or divergent.
- KA (24) with a horizontal followed by a *Winkelhaken*. Often this *Winkelhaken* can occur a little bit lower than the horizontal but it is rarely centred exactly between the upper and bottom horizontal. KA does not occur in any other forms.
- LI (85) composed only with *Winkelhaken*, not a ŠA component with horizontal wedges. LI was recorded like this over 200 times; if the other form ever does turn up it could potentially be seen as much less common.
- RU (111) with three *Winkelhaken* (two *Winkelhaken*, then two verticals, then another *Winkelhaken*, then a final vertical). RU also occurs with two *Winkelhaken* impressed lightly between the first verticals, and with two *Winkelhaken* preceeding the verticals.
- TI (118) most commonly occurs in the 'small' and 'square' form, with a *Winkelhaken* centred underneath the vertical (like BAL). A 'long' form with five wedges occurs almost exclusively on EA 24 with a horizontal, followed by a *Winkelhaken*, then the vertical, another horizontal, and a final *Winkelhaken*. The 'small' TI was recorded over 250 times, again indicating this is the most common form of the sign for Mittani.
- TA (248) is found impressed with *Winkelhaken* lightly placed between the verticals, or clearly visible between the final verticals. The *Winkelhaken* are never placed in front of the verticals (the same applies to ŠA, 566).
- ŠAR (541) only occurs with an initial cluster of *Winkelhaken*, not with horizontal wedges.
- ḪI (631) and related signs are almost always impressed with four of five wedges. The number of wedges and the angle at which the sign is impressed differs very rarely.
- MEŠ (754) occurs with a row of consecutive *Winkelhaken* or horizontals, but also with a horizontal impressed into the vertical, followed by *Winkelhaken*.

In comparison, the features of Assyro-Mittanian are:

- BAL (5) with a divergent wedge, placed under the horizontal (rather than vertical) and even extending through the horizontal.

- BA (14) and other signs with heavily emphasised or divergent initial wedges.
- Various forms of KA (24). The most common of which consists of a divergent wedge, accompanied by two horizontal wedges. Other forms include the version found with a horizontal followed by *Winkelhaken*, and one with a horizontal wedge, with a *Winkelhaken* above and below it.
- QA (99) is nearly always impressed with a very short upper diagonal or *Winkelhaken* and a bottom horizontal, rather than two diagonal wedges.
- RU (111) occurs with 'small' middle verticals, compared to a 'long' final vertical, where one *Winkelhaken* is impressed before the verticals, and one above. RU also occurs with two *Winkelhaken* impressed more centrally between 'average' sized verticals.
- TI (118) can occur, like BAL, with a bottom divergent wedge which extends through the horizontal. TI can also be found in the 'short' version with a *Winkelhaken* impressed centrally below the vertical, and in a 'long' form, with four wedges, consisting of horizontal, *Winkelhaken*, vertical, and another *Winkelhaken*.
- TA (248) can, like RU, occur with 'small' verticals. The sign also sometimes occurs with at least one *Winkelhaken* in front of ('average' length) verticals, and, as before, with space for the *Winkelhaken* left clearly between the final two verticals.
- ŠAR (541) and similar signs such as LÚ and IN sometimes occur with an initial cluster of *Winkelhaken* – but notably also with horizontal wedges.
- ḪI (631) and related signs almost always occur with five wedges or more; regularly six or seven.

3.4.2 *Tablet Format*

What remains to be reviewed, are the differences between individual scribal hands. Signs with obscured versus those with more obvious *Winkelhaken* agree almost exactly between the tablets, and are present more in Mittanian than Assyro-Mittanian (e.g. TA, RU). As described, it is typical for Assyro-Mittanian to have more component wedges than Mittanian signs (e.g. ḪI, ŠU). While the larger labels may no longer be relevant, there is at least a clear difference between the corpora discussed in this chapter. It is also possible to compare between overall appearance of the tablet and tablet size – particularly in the case of the Amarna letters (**Figure 3.13**). Most Assyro-Mittani tablets are broken or fragmentary and the Other Mittani tablets are all small, apart from KBo 1.2 which is also broken (**Figure 3.14**). However, especially EA 24 and EA 25 stand out for their large size; EA 29 can be added to this group too, and potentially EA 22. EA 24 and EA 25 have certain less or uncommon sign-forms and

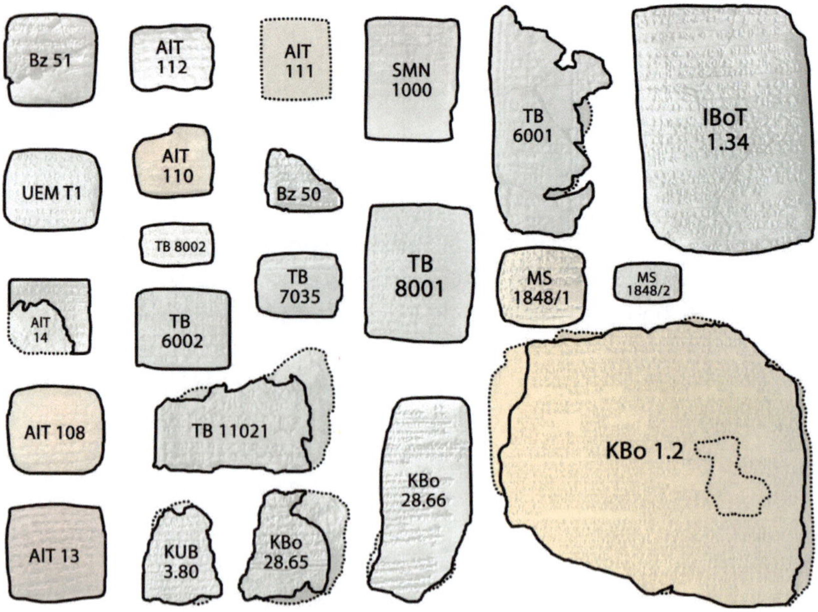

FIGURE 3.13 Size-comparison of all other Mittani documents
Scale 1:3.

variants in common, namely RU, AK, TA, and MEŠ. The same applies to EA 22 and EA 29, although these tablets show a larger number of sign-forms and variants, particularly EA 22. All four tablets use the same variant of NU (112). Moreover, the impression of signs is similar: all tablets have a high frequency of middle- to low placed wedges, strong emphasis on signs such as BA, ZU, SU, and deeply impressed U and DIŠ. All of these characteristics apply less firmly to EA 22 however, which is also the smallest tablet of the four. In addition, EA 30, the smallest tablet overall, stands out with *only* common sign-forms and variants.

This information is important in determining whether differences in forms and variants can be related to the shape, size or content of the tablet, whether there are significant differences between letters and gift-lists, and also whether it would be useful to create a larger tablet-shape-genre typology. The described group encompasses all the very large tablets in the Amarna Mittani collection, with EA 22 and EA 25 being the long gift-lists. Statistically the number of sign-forms and variants can be explained simply by the fact that the large tablets yielded much more instances than the smaller tablets. However, since it has been established that the large tablets have many

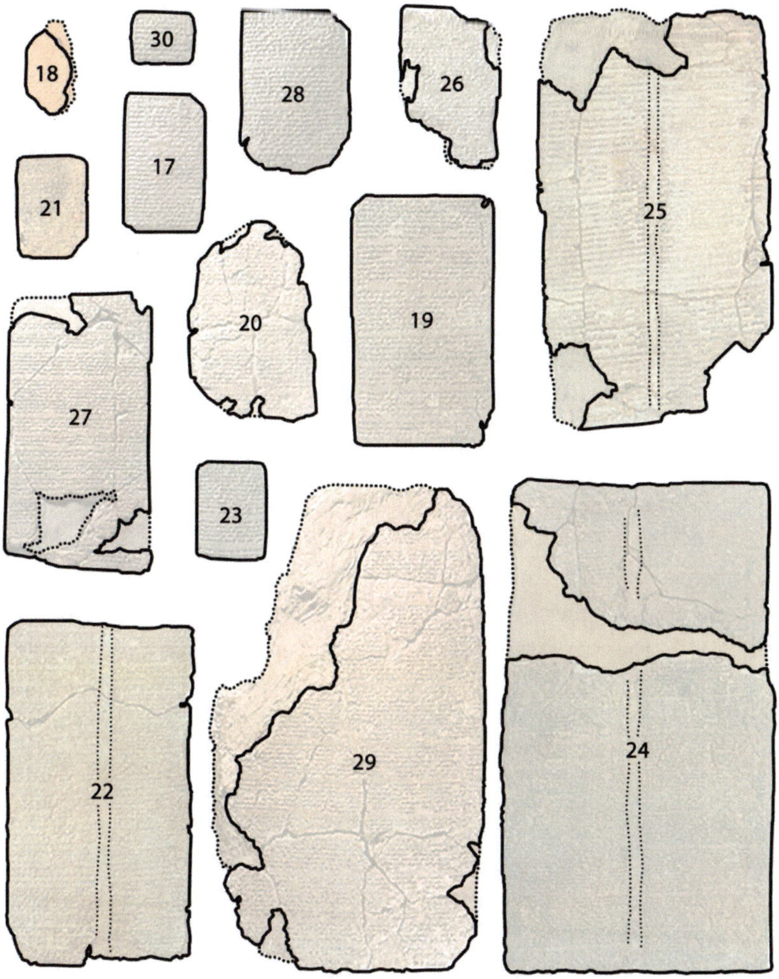

FIGURE 3.14 Size-comparison of all Mittani Amarna tablets
Scale 1:6.

sign-forms and variants in common – in other words, the variety is not random – it is unlikely that the difference can be attributed to standard deviation only. It looks like it was possibly a specific set of scribes who were assigned to work on longer or more important texts. This theory is strengthened particularly by the appearance of EA 26. The style of writing on this tablet differs most clearly from the other documents (use of primary sign-forms only, straight wedges, the 'high' impressions discussed before). The recipient of this letter is not the Pharaoh, but Queen Tiye. While it is impossible to say why a different scribe was chosen to write to the Queen, the odds of it being a coincidence seem be to decreasing because the scribal hand clearly deviates from those who composed the large tablets (see **Paragraph 3.3.3**).

For a potential typology it is also interesting to consider the provenance study discussed previously (**Paragraph 3.2.1**): a neutron activation analysis conducted in 1977 by Doble *et al.* showed that EA 22, 24, 25 and 29 are remarkably homogeneous compared to the other Amarna Mittani tablets. This analysis matches the two established groups perfectly. However, the study has been subject to critique by Goren *et al.*, who point out the different chemical compositions have not been published accurately and the examined samples were statistically invalid (2004: 38). Instead, they concluded that two distinctive clay types were used by the Mittanian scribes: a marly type (including EA 17, 20, 22, 23, 24, 25, 26, 28, 29, and 30) and a clayey type (including EA 18, 19, 21, and 27) (Goren *et al.* 2004: 44). Furthermore, they establish that the two fabrics include similar types of clastic components (silt and sand), indicating a related depositional environment: despite the difference in clay or composition it is still unclear whether the tablets came from different locations (albeit not far apart), or whether two slightly different types of clay were used in the same location. However, since the petrographic analysis proves that the tablets cannot have been written in hugely dissimilar locations, this eliminates the possibility that the tablets were copied or composed in other cities under different powers.

3.4.3 *Relevance of Hurrian*

In addition to its size it is also crucial to consider how the Hurrian letter (EA 24) differs from the Akkadian documents. As has been discussed, the sign-forms do deviate compared to the other tablets, and this cannot be attributed simply to the number of instances recorded. As the tablet is written in Hurrian, it seems that language is a key factor. The question is how the language is of any influence. The options vary between copying mistakes and scribal education. TB 11021 (the Hurrian fragment from Tell Brak) does have the same form of RU as EA 24, but no other significant signs were recorded (e.g. not a single instance of TI). Some of the Other Mittani documents did have a 'long' TI however (KBo 1.2, KBo 28.66, and AlT 13), indicating that, while uncommon, it is not isolated to Hurrian-Mittani.

Although a comparison of orthography has not been made for this corpus, some consideration is necessary in thinking about the identity of the scribes: the Akkadian tablets show substantial Hurrian influence in lexicon and grammar (Adler 1976: 1; Wilhelm 2008: 83). This raises the question how well Hurrian was known throughout the Middle East during the period under discussion. How did the Pharaoh read EA 24? Did the Hurrian messenger read it to him or did his own court officials understand the language? For example, KBo 18.54 suggests that Babylonian messengers were able to read Hittite cuneiform (Weeden 2014: 46). There is also evidence for the presence of foreign scribes at el-Amarna (Izre'el 1997: 10). However, since Akkadian was one of the primary diplomatic languages, it was a bold statement to send such a large document in the 'national' language. Its purpose was not only to be read, but also to send a political message. If appearance was a key purpose, then it is not surprising if the script was purposefully different. Particularly when looking at EA 24 in the context of belonging to a group with EA 25, and possibly EA 22 and 29, it is plausible that a particular (class of?) scribe[41] was selected to compose the tablet (see **Paragraph 7.4**). Other contemporary documents show Hurrian influence in orthography and personal names too, including other Amarna letters but also particularly tablets from Nuzi.

Even if not linguistic, Hurrian exercised cultural influence on script development. The factor which all Assyro-Mittani tablets have in common, is that they were found at Boğazköy. The Hittite dynasty adopted cultural traditions from the Hurrian-speaking parts of Anatolia, and as mentioned previously it eventually became a cult language, used in incantations (Wilhelm 2008: 82). Indeed, many of the available Boğazköy tablets are of a different genre – not diplomatic correspondence like the Amarna Mittani letters – so there was potentially less reason to maintain any similarities or differences to 'standard' Mittanian, whether consciously or unconsciously. In the development of cuneiform as a whole, new script groups or styles were often bound to a specific genre, and new ways of writing have been found *especially* in relation to divination (Veldhuis 2012a: 7). It may therefore be possible that a version of Mittanian script developed separately at or for Boğazköy.

That said, while estimates can be made, it is unclear how to date many of the Boğazköy tablets, and deviation or change in the signs could possibly be attributed to the period and time-span they cover. The 13th–14th centuries include both the 'golden age' and the downfall of the Mittani Empire. For a start, Hurrian was never to be a 'national' language again, (also see **Paragraph 6.3** for a comparison to Ugarit). If politics played any role in the appearance of the script, it is also possible that the scribes writing to or at Ḫattuša were no longer (wanting to be, trying to be, or allowed to be) affiliated with anything Mittanian. The scribal environment in Ḫattuša was dominated by foreign scribes. Tablets found there could have been copied, and they might have originated from

41 In addition, if the scribe of EA 24 composed more of these tablets, he or she was doing it in a different style.

different places. The Assyro-Mittanian scribes may have moved to or been associated with Ḫattuša more permanently, and they may have been writing from an emerging Assyria. These are all factors which complicate any theory of a unified Boğazköy school.

This leaves KBo 1.2. It is, also, difficult to say exactly where and by whom this tablet was written. However, considering the subject of the tablet, its approximate date, and where it eventually ended up, it is clear that Ḫattuša is the factor which sets it apart from the other Mittanian tablets. At the same time, KBo 1.2 is a different genre from the Assyro-Mittanian tablets, which potentially explains why its signs look more Mittanian. Although all of these tablets have Boğazköy in common as a find-place, KBo 1.2 is currently the only tablet which really qualifies as possible 'Ḫattuša-Mittanian' script.

3.5 Final Remarks

As discussed in **Paragraph 2.5**, signs pre-suppose some form of meaning and it is impossible to interpret them without contextual knowledge. In order to successfully interpret icons, indexes and symbols the observer must be aware of the respective producer, time, and place of the sign. In this way, signs (be it clothing, speech, behaviour or indeed written marks) reflect methods of communication and indicate or help create social identity.

Semiotic approaches are most useful when we possess large amounts of data about social and cultural context, as well as the history of the script and the perception of that history (Weeden 2011: 41). However, in the case of ancient societies, such as Mittani, this kind of information is not always available. When experiences or contextual aspects are unknown, or guessed, a line is crossed into phenomenology (imagining the interpretations of people of the past; also see Singer (1980) 'semiotic conception of self'). Archaeologists are not always comfortable with this, preferring to deal with the unambiguous reality of material objects rather than a continually shifting world of individual and collective meanings – while of course both are of interest (Mertz 2007). In the approach taken here, readily accessible information was used to see whether this pieces together part of the puzzle. This information does not include elusive pieces such as cognitive psychology, but it does comprise of corner pieces such as influence of culture and international politics. They are the segments of context where relationships and interaction with cuneiform signs can realistically be identified.

Questions posed in the introduction of this and the previous chapter, which were directed specifically at writing, included how many sign-forms were used in contemporary scripts, how they differ, how they changed; what the boundaries between script-groups are, why variation might occur and how it is possible to assign responsibility for that variation. So far, it has been derived that Mittanian has a limited amount of different sign-forms and variants, whereas so-called Assyro-Mittanian has more. Possible reasons for variation include document genre (diplomatic correspondence versus omens), period (the Amarna Age and earlier, versus possibly but not certainly later), place (the Mittani heartland, versus other or unknown locations) and language (Hurrian versus Akkadian).

All of these factors are not encapsulated in a Mittani bubble but involve interaction with other societies and other script-groups. There is continuous overlap and exchange which blurs boundaries. Therefore, in order to gain a better understanding of Mittanian script, the following chapter will consider writing at nearby Aššur. Cultures are highly complex yet unified structures; so, where does one end and the other begin?

CHAPTER 4

Middle Assyrian

4.1 Introduction

It is now time to turn to Aššur; once a vassal of Mittani but later the heart of one of the most significant Empires the Middle East has ever seen. The following chapter will address a collection of early Middle Assyrian documents of the 15th–14th century BCE, in comparison to later Middle Assyrian documents of the 13th century BCE. These tablets are roughly contemporary and geographically similar to the Mittani texts discussed previously. By pointing out what they have in common and how they differ, particularly with regard to palaeography, it should be possible to gain a better understanding of the choices made by the scribes in each society. However, in order to compare palaeographies of different scribal cultures, the individual palaeography of Middle Assyrian must be understood first. It is necessary to be able to make accurate statements in this regard, if Middle Assyrian, Mittanian and Assyro-Mittanian are to be separated; whether they are altogether one script-group; or whether they are different parts of one overarching script-group.

4.2 The Selected Middle Assyrian Corpus

It is difficult to reconstruct reigns and dates for the early Middle Assyrian period. Manuscripts of the Assyrian King Lists (Khorsabad List, Nassouhi List) differ significantly when it comes to Kings who reigned prior to the 12th century BCE (**Table 4.1**). What is more, there is considerable uncertainty with regard to the structure of the Assyrian calendar during the 15th–12th centuries (Bloch 2012: 24). While Eriba-adad I and Aššur-uballit I can be held responsible for the transformation of Aššur from a vassal state to independence (Koliński 2015: 9), the history of the four preceding rulers is much less clear.

These four early rulers of Aššur were contemporaries of Šauštatar II, Parattarna II and Artatama I of the Mittani Empire (Maidman 2010: xx). While the Hittites dealt with Anatolian affairs in the 15th century, Šauštatar saw his chance to assert power over the south-east, sacking and looting Aššur (Wilhelm 1989: 27). However, Aššur had previously been a prosperous city with a significant international trading network, reaching as far as the Zagros, the Taurus and Babylonia (Postgate 2013: 6) – and Aššur was keen to re-gain its glory. While

 | DOI:10.1163/9789004417243_005

TABLE 4.1 Directory of Middle Assyrian Kings

Ruler	Reign
Aššur-nirari II	1424–1418 BCE
Aššur-bel-nišešu	1417–1409 BCE
Aššur-rim-nišešu	1408–1401 BCE
Aššur-nadin-aḫḫe	1400–1391 BCE
Eriba-adad I	1390–1364 BCE
Aššur-uballiṭ I	1363–1328 BCE
Ellil-nirari	1327–1318 BCE
Arik-den-ili	1317–1306 BCE
Adad-nirari I	1305–1274 BCE
Salmanassar I	1273–1244 BCE
Tukulti-ninurta I	1243–1207 BCE
Aššur-nadin-apli	1206–1203 BCE
Aššur-nirari III	1202–1197 BCE

From Freydank (1991: 188) and Postgate (2013: 429). A 10-year earlier date range has also been suggested, as the length of the reign of 12th century Ninurta-apil-ekur is uncertain – in two copies of the King List it is 3 years, and in the Nassouhi version it is 13 years; as it looks like more than 3 eponyms were used during his reign (Cancik-Kirschbaum 1999) scholars have recently preferred to interpret the length of his reign as 13 years.

it took some years to recover from the looting, excavations have shown that the old palace of Aššur was re-built under Aššur-nadin-aḫḫe (Pedde 2012: 854). It was not long before they convinced the Pharaoh to send over gold – and soon the Assyrian ruler daringly claims to be the equal of the Mittani King (EA 16, lines 19–22). In the meantime, the Hittites had stabilised their Kingdom, and Šuppiluliuma I went on to defeat his Mittanian rivals (Wilhelm 1989: 35). While Šuppiluliuma was left to deal with various complicated Mittani succession issues, and trying to turn it into a vassal state, Aššur quickly moved in to loot the region and claim part of its lands.

In order to stabilise their newly gained domination the Assyrians were willing to adapt to local conditions and they employed a variety of different strategies to achieve this (Tenu 2015: 82). While 'Romanisation' ('to conquer and assimilate', Haverfield 1912) has long been deconstructed (Gardner 2013: 1; Mattingly 2011: 42) the idea that Assyria did not instantly pursue 'Assyrianisation' is relatively new (Jakob 2015: 177; Mühl 2015: 55). Multiple types of settlement change took place during the 14th century (Brown 2014: 95; Koliński 2015: 11), and at least two different styles of provincial administration were adopted (Kühne 2015: 59). While some sites show continuation from Mittani to Middle Assyrian (Tell al-Hamidiye, Tell Fekheriye), others suffered destruction (Tell Brak), or were abandoned entirely (Yorghan Tepe). In a few cases, local dynasties were allowed to hold on to their ancestral territories, while in other cases Assyrians acted as governors in newly founded districts. Perhaps the only significant cohesive change was the move from countryside to city: surveys have shown that after the fall of the Mittani Empire the settled area within the Khabur Valley remained stable – but that the ratio of rural-urban sites shifted from 3:1 to 2:9 (Koliński 2015: 17; Lyon 2000: 89). Particularly attractive in this respect were the existing provincial administrative capitals.

This means that, potentially, there was a degree of continuity between the Mittani and Assyrian administrative systems (Tenu 2015: 78).[1] While most elements are speculative or indirect, they are worth summing up: it is possible that the Assyrians copied their provincial system from either Mittani or Mari (Koliński 2015: 20); if the interpretation of the '*dunnu*' system is correct (fortified agricultural production centres), these may have been modelled from the Mittani '*dimtu*' system (Bonatz & Bartl 2013: 264); there is a continuation of Mittanian to Middle Assyrian pottery, at least in the Balikh Valley (Duistermaat 2015: 143); there is the possibility that 'Mittani buildings' remained in use at Tell Chuera (Jakob 2015: 180); and 'consignment' and 'deficit' documents used at Nuzi closely resemble the system used by the Assyrian scribes at Dur-Katlimmu (Postgate 2013: 350). On the other hand, it has been rightly noted that there are no similarities between Aššur and the Mittani-period administration at Alalaḫ (Postgate 2013: 427). However, in turn, this could be due to distance (for example, Tell Chuera and Yorghan Tepe are both considerably closer to Aššur than Atchana) (see **Maps**), or part of the Assyrian selective strategy of adopting that which was useful to them and abandoning that which was not.

4.2.1 *Aššur 14446*

For the database tablets were selected from the private archive 'Aššur 14446' (or 'Ass. 14446') (see **Appendix**). The tablets were found east of the '*Haus des Beschwörungspriesters*' in Aššur, and date primarily to Eriba-adad and his son Aššur-uballiṭ (Saporetti 1979a: 8). This makes it, currently, the only known collection of Middle Assyrian documents dating earlier than the 13th century

1 Some have argued for an altogether direct Babylonian origin of Assyrian writing and administration (Veldhuis 2012a: 14).

(also see Pedersén 1998: 86, M89). According to the excavation records it is composed of 130 cuneiform tablets, of which 6 copies were originally published by Schröder (KAV, 1920) and another 88 by Ebeling (KAJ, 1927). Saporetti notes that a few others were added to this in volumes of ARu, AfO and MARV (1979a: 3).[2] Transcriptions of all the tablets can be found in Saporetti 1979a and 1982, and also sometimes on CDLI (Jared Wolfe). The high-resolution images used in this database were likewise taken from CDLI, primarily via the Vorderasiatisches Museum, Berlin.

In his 1979a and 1982 *'Famiglia'* editions, Saporetti published as full an overview as possible, piecing together relationships between the various contributors.[3] The documents can be attributed to different families, who were in contact with each other. Saporetti (1979a) divides them into two categories: the families whose members feature as purchasers of goods or creditors in loan contracts; and the families whose members are the sellers of goods, or debtors in loan contracts. Saporetti does not want to attribute the archive to one single family, although he proposes it is possible the archive represents the unification of transactions between several families across generations (1979a: 9). Based on seals, Nissen (1967) determined most scribes came from urban backgrounds (the families from Aššur who were creditors and purchasers of land) while witnesses came from rural settlements (where the land was located). Scribes sometimes belonged to the same family (Saporetti 1979a: 11; 1982: 3) indicating the craft could have been a family profession.[4]

Pedersen already suggested some tablets from Ass. 14446 might date before the Middle Assyrian period and determines the oldest may be from circa 1650 BCE (1988: 86). So far three Old Assyrian tablets have actually been identified, all regarding the purchase of land. About VAT 19852 (otherwise unpublished, and not included in the database) Freydank wrote its eponym is *"untypisch"* and *"lassen keinen anschluß an eine der Generationen des Archivs"* (1991: 177). Donbaz later dates this eponym – Urad-šerua son of Aššur-bani – to

2 Since Saporetti does not directly cite the papers these are difficult to trace back.

3 A further 31 dated tablets were added to this in 2012 by Reculeau & Feller. However, the images are on a scale 1.5:1, which was not high enough to include in the database, and furthermore the interest of the authors was to capture seals (not text), which means many pictures are upside-down or incomplete. In addition, most of these tablets are severely damaged or broken and none can be securely dated before Eriba-adad I (pre-14th century) which would be the most interesting period to expand on. The tablets will therefore be discussed in this chapter only when relevant.

4 There are (as of yet) no Middle Assyrian tablets which describe how or where scribes were trained (Postgate 2013: 49).

the "late 17th or early 16th centuries BC." (2001: 55). This tablet features the scribe Nabium-qarrad, who also occurs in MAH 15962 (not included in the present database) (Gelb & Sollberger 1957: 163). Donbaz further singled out VAT 19864 (or now KAM 10, 1, likewise not included in the database) (1985: 1), which has also been discussed by Reculeau and Feller (2012: 3) and De Ridder (2013: 55). It is likely the owners saved these tablets for such a long time because the long-lasting validity of a sale of real estate remained relevant, proving ownership (De Ridder 2013: 56).

It is difficult to be entirely certain of the dates of the '15th-century' tablets. KAJ 177 could be dated to the reign of Aššur-nirari II, as the name $^{1.d}$A-šur-ni-ra-ri (obverse, line 10) occurs on the tablet in association with $^{1.d}$A-šur-GAL (obverse, line 8), who may be his grandfather, Aššur-rabi I (Fine 1952: 189; Saporetti 1979b: 157).[5] Furthermore, Beran (1957: 143) finds several connections with Mittani in the seal – particularly figures similar to those in the Šauštatar seal from Nuzi.

Other tablets which could potentially be dated to the 15th century are KAJ 22, KAJ 162, KAJ 50, KAJ 174 and KAJ 139. According to the transcription, and readings by Fine (1952: 190) and Saporetti (1979a: 47; 1979b: 157), KAJ 162 bears the name Aššur-bel-nišešu. However, the lines which mention him are both damaged and it is difficult to see how they were transcribed in this way. The scribe, Šamaš-kidinnu son of Adad-da'iq, is listed under Aššur-bel-nišešu by Jakob (2003: 249) but under Aššur-uballiṭ I by Freydank (1991: 193) (both without further explanation). Fine (1952: 192) argues that, because KAJ 162 and KAJ 22 have the names Urad-šerua son of Aššur-iqiša and Ilu-tišmar son of Apuḫija in common, they must be contemporary. The scribe is named Bel-qarrad, possibly the son of Ašamša, according to Saporetti (1979a: 44). In the case of Ašamša, Jakob dates him to Aššur-bel-nišešu (2003: 243). However, Freydank argues the name Ašamša was read incorrectly and dates the tablet to Aššur-uballiṭ I (2003: 245) – again, neither author offering arguments for these dates. This line is likewise damaged and difficult to read. For KAJ 50, Fine also compares names to KAJ 162 and KAJ 22 (Urad-šerua son of Aššur-iqiša, Ilu-tišmar son of Apuḫija, Išme-adad son of Apiḫija and Mar-idigla son of Kubi-eriš). Although the name of a scribe or ruler has not been preserved, Saporetti likewise compares KAJ 50 to KAJ 22 based on these other names (1979a: 46).

5 The eponym is Aššur-mutakkil, son of Adad-eriš, which Freydank (1991: 192) lists as associated with Aššur-nirari II; however, it is unclear what he has based this on (e.g. the publications by Fine and Saporetti).

On KAJ 172 Aššur-bel-nišešu is named more clearly (obverse, line 3: $^{1.d}$A-šur-EN-ni-še-šu). However, Freydank lists the scribe, Mannu-bal Aššur, as dated to Eriba-adad or Aššur-uballiṭ, without explanation (1991: 193). Finally, KAJ 174 has been dated to the reign of either Aššur-nirari or Aššur-bel-nišešu, based on the name Ber-nadin-aḫḫe son of Aššur-nirari ($^{1.d}$Be-er-na-din.ŠEŠ.MEŠ DUMU ^{d}A-šur-ni-ra-ri, reverse edge) (Fine 1952: 190). Fine relates KAJ 132 and KAJ 139 to KAJ 174 based on four names: Dugul-ili, Abu-ṭab, Ibašši-ilu and Eriš-kubi. The Dugul-ili and Abu-ṭab from KAJ 139 are both sons of Mar-šamaš in KAJ 132. Also, Ibašši-ilu occurs as a son of Mar-šamaš in KAJ 174. In addition, KAJ 132 and KAJ 174 both name the scribe as Šumu-libši. However, while Saporetti also notes the co-occurrence of Abu-ṭab (son of Mar-šamaš) on KAJ 132 and KAJ 139 (1979: 31), he did not include KAJ 132 in his '*Famiglia*' publications. Since the dating is so tangential KAJ 132 was not included in the database, but it has been used for comparison in the conclusions at the end of the chapter.

The 14th century documents of Ass. 14446 can be dated with more certainty, based on reading the tablets together with publications by Jakob (2003), Fine (1952), Freydank (1991, 2003) and Saporetti (1979a, 1979b, 1982). The vast majority belong to the reign of Aššur-uballiṭ (53%): KAJ 152, KAJ 153, KAJ 155, KAJ 6, KAJ 58, KAJ 151, KAJ 79, KAJ 154, KAJ 8, KAJ 11, KAJ 12, KAJ 13, KAJ 17, KAJ 19, KAJ 26, KAJ 29, KAJ 36, KAJ 53, KAJ 60, KAJ 61, KAJ 63, KAJ 70, KAJ 96, KAJ 99, KAJ 149, KAJ 150, KAJ 157, KAJ 161, KAJ 163, KAJ 165, KAJ 176, KAJ 229, KAV 211, KAV 212, probably KAJ 21 (very damaged), KAJ 28 (names less clear) and KAJ 170 (names not preserved), as well as KAJ 23, KAJ 24 and KAJ 65 (possibly from different archives according to the CDLI records). The remainder can be dated to either Eriba-adad or Aššur-uballiṭ (36%): KAJ 25, KAJ 43, KAJ 34, KAJ 41, KAJ 33, KAJ 4, KAJ 7, KAJ 18, KAJ 35, KAJ 39, KAJ 40, KAJ 42, KAJ 44, KAJ 45, KAJ 47, KAJ 52, KAJ 66, KAJ 87, KAJ 135, KAJ 143, KAJ 146, KAJ 167, KAJ 236, KAJ 309, KAJ 173 / KAV 210, KAJ 233 and probably KAJ 9 (names not preserved), KAJ 246 (very damaged). Finally, a few tablets can be dated exactly to Eriba-adad (11%): KAJ 209, KAJ 148, KAJ 64 / 68, KAJ 1, KAJ 183 / KAV 93, KAJ 3, KAJ 20, KAJ 160, KAJ 179 and probably KAJ 14 (Freydank (1991: 193) dates it later) and KAJ 147 (names broken).

4.2.2 *Aššur 14410*

For comparison to later Middle Assyrian, the small 13th century private archive of Babu-aḫa-iddina (primarily 'Aššur 14410' or 'Ass. 14410') was included in the database as well (Pedersén 1998: 87, M11) (see **Appendix**). The tablets were found near what was probably his grave (Campo dell'Orto 2004). Babu-aḫa-iddina was an important figure, placed highly in the Assyrian state (Postgate 2013: 201). He turns up in a letter from the Hittite King (KUB 23, 103; reverse, line 8: ᴵBa-ba-ŠEŠ.SUM) as representative of Tukulti-ninurta I (Otten 1959). His archive contains tablets with administrative correspondence, covering a period of circa 35 years.[6] About half of the documents were sent or written by Babu-aḫa-iddina himself, while away on business; the others were written by his subordinates. They cover subjects such as textile production, carpentry and metal-working. Transcriptions have been published in Schröder (1920) and Ebeling (1927) and the images used came from CDLI, again primarily via the Vorderasiatisches Museum, Berlin.

Since the majority of documents can be attributed to one scribe and scribes in his close proximity, existing sign-lists were used as a control. *Die mittelassyrischen Briefe aus Tall Šēḫ Ḥamad* (Cancik-Kirschbaum 1996) includes circa 30 letters (and fragments) from ancient Dur-Katlimmu. These were found in a building on the acropolis, in the vicinity of workshops and storerooms. The letters are not necessarily administrative, or concerned with crafts – instead they concern logistic, military and judiciary matters. These documents are dated by eponyms to the latter half of Tukulti-ninurta's reign. The addressee in most cases is one Aššur-iddin, whose father was a first cousin of Tukulti-ninurta. He is known by the title *sukkallu rabiu* but also *šar mât Ḫanigalbat* – used by the governors of Dur-Katlimmu after taking control of the Mittani lands (Liverani 1999: 141).The letters reflect on script from across Assyria, having been sent from several different places including, possibly, Waššukanni (Cancik-Kirschbaum 1996: 30). This publication was joined more recently by *Die mittelassyrischen Personen- und Rationenlisten aus Tall Šēḫ Ḥamad* (Salah 2013). These are 81 documents, spanning 52 years between Salmanassar I and Tukulti-ninurta I. The tablets were found in 'Building P', on the western slope of the citadel, in a burnt layer filled with ashes. The lists are concerned with regular people working the fields and they name products such as wool and chickpeas. Last, *Die mittelassyrischen Texte aus Tell Chuēra* (Jakob 2003) covers almost 100 tablets from ancient Ḫarbe, a smaller settlement than Dur-Katlimmu. Eponyms likewise date the texts to Tukulti-ninurta I. Instructions were sent from Dur-Katlimmu to Ḫarbe (Postgate 2013: 278), and one Sin-mudammeq occurs in documents at both sites (De Ridder 2011: 124). Besides letters this archive also contains administrative texts about shipments of food, harvesting, rations and property, as well as various lists. All three sign-lists show variations in the sign-forms. Particularly the list by Jakob often has up to ten copies per sign, including minor variations and uncommon occurrences.

6 See Postgate (2013: 201) for an extensive overview of the contents of the entire archive.

Most other Middle Assyrian sign-lists date much later than Babu-aḫa-iddina:[7] for the 12th–11th centuries there are *Die Inschriften von Tall Bderi* (Maul 1992); *Die Inschriften von Tall Ṭābān* (Maul 2005); and *Die Bibliothek Tiglatpilesers I* (Weidner 1952). For the 11th–10th centuries *Das mittelassyrische Tontafelarchiv von Giricano/Dunnu-Ša-Uzibi* (Radner 2004). Tall Taban signs are similar to Tall Bderi and are chronologically contemporary to sign-forms found for the 12th century (Maul 2005: 20, 83)[8] – although, Tall Taban also yielded some "peculiar" sign-forms, "possibly pointing to local differences" (Panayotov 2015).

4.3 Middle Assyrian Tablet Format

As shown in **Paragraph 3.4.2**, it is possible that sign-forms could be related to tablet arrangement, size and / or genre. EA 24, EA 25 and EA 29 all have less common sign-forms in common and at the same time they are (by some margin) the largest documents in the Mittani Amarna collection. This collection of 15th–14th century Middle Assyrian documents is not directly comparable: the documents are not diplomatic correspondence between Kings (apart from the one available Middle Assyrian Amarna letter, EA 15). Nevertheless, because the database includes almost a hundred Middle Assyrian tablets, and less than forty Mittanian tablets, the opportunity can be used for more general comments on the relationship between sign-forms and tablet-size in the 14th century.

Tablet format (paragraph spacing, indentation and dividing lines) usually depends on the nature of the text (Taylor 2011: 8). For instance, official Neo-Assyrian (7th century BCE) texts, such as legal documents, letters and scientific reports to the King adhered to strict rules (Radner 1995: 63). Less official tablets such as administrative lists were not standardised but can still be classified according to the arrangement of the text. Size was not an important factor – the tablets were adapted to their contents and columns were used to divide texts into more easily write-able and read-able lines (Radner 1995: 64). However, Neo-Assyrian contracts generally measure 3.5–4.5 cm horizontally, and 2.5–3.5 cm vertically, resulting in a rectangular cushion shape suitable for envelopes.

---

7 A list for 13th–12th century Sabi Abyad is currently in progress, but it has not yet been published at the time of writing.

8 'The library of Tiglath-pileser I' was previously thought to be a collection of tablets dated to the 11th century but has now been proven to include Middle Assyrian documents, particularly tablets composed by the brothers Marduk-balassu-eriš and Bel-aḫa-iddina, active circa 30–40 years prior to the reign of Tiglath-pileser (Pedersén 1998: 83).

On the other hand, tablets in the archive of Aššur-aḫa-iddina (Ass. 14327), which are 13th century Middle Assyrian, were not usually encased in envelopes, did not have the same tiny cushion-format (albeit still rectangular) and were sealed differently (Postgate 2014). The scribe would leave a blank space at the top of the obverse for the seal, and only officially began the text underneath that space. The left edges of the tablets are sometimes divided into fields (by vertical strokes) to be filled with seals as well. These features (paragraph spacing, indentation and dividing lines) also occur on some of the 15th–13th century tablets included in this chapter, but it is not consistent.[9]

There are two tablets in Ass. 14446 which have a round shape: KAJ 229 (Aššur-uballiṭ) and KAJ 236 (Eriba-adad or Aššur-uballiṭ). The smallest tablet overall is KAJ 209 (Eriba-adad), followed by KAJ 309 (Eriba-adad or Aššur-uballiṭ) – while two of the largest tablets are KAJ 8 (Aššur-uballiṭ) and KAJ 66 (Eriba-adad or Aššur-uballiṭ). None of the tablets – round, small, or large – can be securely dated to the same ruler. On the tiny tablets, paragraph features are absent (possibly due to the spatial limitation). Both of the round tablets have the small paragraph indentation at the beginning of the document. The two large tablets have the indentation, as well as double dividing lines on the left edge. Other large tablets such as KAJ 162 and KAJ 6 are also more clearly formatted. In the context of the large Amarna letters, it would be interesting if formatting could be connected to other factors, such as tablet size and sign-forms. In the archive Ass. 14446 it does appear that larger tablets were formatted more clearly.

In general, it was preferable for both writers and readers to minimise the length of lines on tablets (Radner 1995: 65). For Ass. 14446, to calculate the average amount of signs per line, lines which were damaged or broken were not included. Where this resulted in too few lines on a tablet to come to a fair average, the tablet was excluded from the results. On average most tablets have 7 or 8 sign instances per line. The most common deviations are sets of lines of either 5 or 9 instances. The three-sign phrase "KIŠIB DUB.SAR" occurs on nearly all tablets as well, but not often does a scribe attempt to fit more than 12 instances onto a line. Like the repertoire of signs used, this average does not vary extremely with tablet size and remains relatively stable. While smaller tablets more often have an average of 6 sign instances per line and larger tablets more often an average of 9 instances per line, both categories consist primarily of tablets with 7–8 instances per line. The small Mittani-period documents from the Schøyen Collection and from Tell Brak do not appear immensely different: MS 1848/1 has 10 lines with 7 instances per line; MS 1848/2 has 13 lines

9 A clear example is 14th century (Aššur-uballiṭ) KAJ 163.

with 6 instances per line; TB 7035 has 9 lines with 5 instances per line; TB 6002 has 11 lines with 8 instances per line.

The number or variety of Middle Assyrian sign-forms does not increase with tablet-size and differences cannot be attributed simply to quantity. However, there is no mixing of different sign-forms within any of these tablets, there is no majority of uncommon sign-forms on any of these tablets, and none of the tablets have specific sign-forms in common. If particular scribes were ever in charge of larger documents, then this was either specific to international diplomatic correspondence, or Mittani; not administration at Aššur. In conclusion, from these observations, at Aššur size can only be connected to formatting, not to scribe. Hopefully this 'negative evidence' can serve as a stepping-stone for further study of the relationship between sign-forms and tablet format.

4.4 Comparative Palaeography of Middle Assyrian

The database compiled for this chapter has 13,837 sign instances for Middle Assyrian in total. From the 15th–14th century Middle Assyrian tablets 10,636 instances were collected (9,482 of which 14th century and 1,154 possibly 15th century, as discussed above). The total number of different signs used, recorded from this corpus, was 204 – but with broken instances and signs which were only recorded once or twice left out, the average of frequently used signs was 170. For the 13th century 3,565 instances were collected for the database. The total number of different signs attested was 184, but again, with broken signs, and those recorded once or twice left out, the average of frequently used signs here was 130. The sign-lists from Tell Chuera and Tall Šeḫ Ḥamad likewise do not cross the 200-mark: from Tell Chuera 166 signs are attested and Tall Šeḫ Ḥamad 175 signs (the authors do not state frequency of occurrence). From the outset it is therefore clear that the repertoire of signs in the 13th century had been significantly reduced compared to the preceding centuries.

Winkelhaken *of BAL* (*5*)

Early Middle Assyrian (EMA) BAL occurs both with the *Winkelhaken* following the broken horizontal (BAL_{1a}), and the *Winkelhaken* placed beneath the broken horizontal (BAL_2) (**Table 4.2**). This second form has a variant where it is centred (BAL_{2b}), and one where it is not (BAL_{2a}). Later Middle Assyrian (LMA) BAL was recorded only in the form BAL_1, even showing some preference to impress the *Winkelhaken* above the broken horizontal (BAL_{1b}). Although relatively few, and mostly damaged, instances were recorded from the LMA tablets under consideration, sign-lists of the Middle Assyrian tablets

TABLE 4.2 Middle Assyrian BAL

EMA			LMA
BAL$_{1a}$	BAL$_{2a}$	BAL$_{2b}$	BAL$_{1b}$

EMA (10 instances recorded): KAJ 7, obverse, line 12; KAJ 33, reverse, line 1; KAJ 37, reverse, line 7. LMA (4 instances recorded): KAJ 223, obverse, line 5.

by Jakob (2009: 27), Cancik-Kirschbaum (1996: 73) and Salah (2013: 387) also all show only BAL$_{1b}$.

Divergent Wedges in BA (14), ZU (15) and SU (16)

The Ass. 14446 forms of BA, ZU and SU occur variously with *Winkelhaken* (1a) or horizontals (2) (**Table 4.3**). On a few tablets, the difference is difficult to tell (short horizontals or extended *Winkelhaken*); however, the majority have the forms with *Winkelhaken*, and only 5–10 tablets can be said to have the forms with horizontals. In addition, the Middle Assyrian Amarna letter EA 15 also has the form with *Winkelhaken*. The initial horizontal is in all cases divergent, or otherwise heavily emphasised. The form with *Winkelhaken* is even more common in the LMA documents. Here, in a few cases, all usually horizontal wedges are divergent (1b), such as KAV 203 and KAV 205. Although it is not completely absent from all Middle Assyrian archives, from the corpus under consideration no LMA instances with plain horizontals were recorded.

ARAD (18)

As with BA, ZU and SU, EMA has two distinct forms of ARAD (18) (often with the value ÌR), the first with *Winkelhaken* (ARAD$_{1a}$) or diagonals (ARAD$_{1b}$), the second with horizontals (ARAD$_{2a}$) sometimes even three consecutively (ARAD$_{2b}$) (**Table 4.4**). The sign was not recorded from the Ass. 14410 corpus but it is possible to find it on other 13th century tablets (e.g. KAJ 101, **Table 4.4**), and the documents from Tell Chuera (Jakob 2009: 27) and Tall Šeḫ Ḥamad (Cancik-Kirschbaum 1996: 387; Salah 2013) suggest that preference was for the form with horizontals.

TABLE 4.3 Middle Assyrian BA and ZU

Early Middle Assyrian			
BA$_{1a}$	**ZU$_{1a}$**	**BA$_{2}$**	**ZU$_{2}$**

Later Middle Assyrian			
BA$_{1a}$	**ZU$_{1a}$**	**BA$_{1b}$**	**ZU$_{1b}$**

EMA (101 and 26 instances recorded): KAJ 20, obverse, line 6; KAJ 20, obverse, line 10; KAJ 236, obverse, line 5; KAJ 236, obverse, line 6. **LMA** (20 and 8 instances recorded): KAV 96, reverse, line 1; KAV 103, obverse, line 4; KAV 203, obverse, line 6; KAV 203, obverse, line 3.

TABLE 4.4 Middle Assyrian ARAD

EMA				**LMA**
ARAD$_{1a}$	**ARAD$_{1b}$**	**ARAD$_{2a}$**	**ARAD$_{2b}$**	**ARAD$_{2}$**

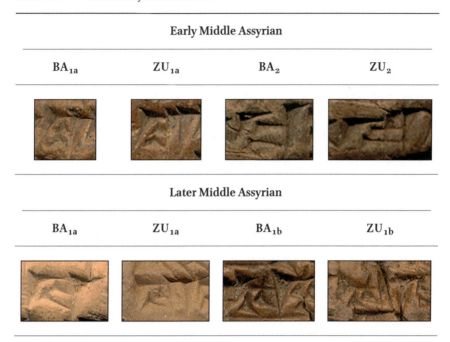

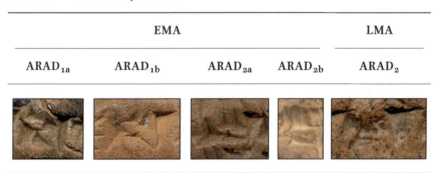

EMA (45 instances recorded): KAJ 236, obverse, line 4; KAJ 148, obverse edge, line 17; KAJ 7, reverse, line 13; KAJ 160, reverse edge, line 12. **LMA** (not recorded in database): KAJ 101, reverse, line 8.

TABLE 4.5 Middle Assyrian ITI

EMA			LMA
ITI$_{1a}$	**ITI$_{1b}$**	**ITI$_{2}$**	**ITI$_{2}$**

EMA (76 instances recorded): KAJ 39, reverse edge, line 13; KAJ 176, reverse, line 3: KAJ 66, reverse edge, line 20. **LMA** (17 instances recorded): KAJ 233, reverse, line 6.

ITI (20)
In EMA there are two forms of ITI: one with an upper broken horizontal (ITI$_{2}$) and one where it is central (ITI$_{1a}$) (**Table 4.5**). Many instances are damaged, but ITI$_{1a}$ was recorded clearly from KAJ 14, KAJ 25, KAJ 33, KAJ 39, KAJ 229, and KAJ 79 (at least 12 out of 76 recorded instances). On KAJ 176 with *Winkelhaken* rather than horizontal (ITI$_{1b}$). From the LMA tablets ITI was recorded 17 times, only with the broken upper horizontal (ITI$_{2}$).

KA (24)
EMA has three different forms of KA: primarily a form with a large, emphasised or divergent initial horizontal with two horizontals underneath (KA$_{1}$); but also a form with a less prominent initial broken horizontal (KA$_{2}$); and a form with an initial horizontal followed by a *Winkelhaken* (KA$_{3}$) (**Table 4.6**). None of these forms co-occur with one another. The first form also has a variant where the bottom horizontals are replaced by *Winkelhaken* (KA$_{1b}$). In the LMA documents the initial horizontal is no longer divergent, occurring either as a centralised or broken horizontal (KA$_{2a}$, KA$_{2b}$). AfO 19 t 5 is the only tablet (an instance from AfO 19 t 6 is unclear) which has a form that differs from the other instances (KA$_{3b}$).

LI (85)
LI has two forms in EMA, one without horizontal impressions (LI$_{1}$), and one with (ŠE+ŠA) (LI$_{2}$) (**Table 4.7**). The second form occurs clearly on KAJ 47, KAJ 79, KAJ 96, and KAJ 155 – and possibly others, but the instances are broken. For example, although the instances are all damaged, it looks like KAJ 6 has one instance of LI$_{2}$ and five instances of LI$_{1}$. This would be the only EMA tablet in the corpus on which the forms co-occur. On the LMA tablets, LI$_{2}$ is more

TABLE 4.6 Middle Assyrian KA

Early Middle Assyrian			
KA$_{1a}$	KA$_{1b}$	KA$_{2b}$	KA$_{3a}$

Later Middle Assyrian		
KA$_{2a}$	KA$_{2b}$	KA$_{3b}$

EMA (64 instances recorded): KAJ 148, reverse, line 5; KAJ 14, obverse, line 12; KAJ 7, reverse, line 10; KAJ 149, reverse, line 1. LMA (36 instances recorded): KAV 109, obverse, line 13; KAV 109, reverlse, line 7; AfO 19 t 5, obverse, line 4.

TABLE 4.7 Middle Assyrian LI

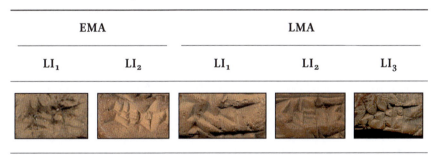

EMA		LMA		
LI$_1$	LI$_2$	LI$_1$	LI$_2$	LI$_3$

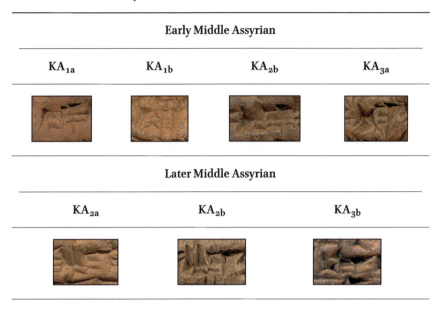

EMA (86 instances recorded): KAJ 151, obverse, line 4; KAJ 47, side, line 2. LMA (40 instances recorded): KAV 104, reverse, line 11; KAV 100, obverse, line 6; KAJ 253, reverse, line 4.

common than LI$_1$, which occurs only on KAV 104 and KAJ 227 (possibly KAV 105). A new form with straight wedges also appears (LI$_3$) on KAJ 353 (possibly RIAA 314, KAV 107). Of the three instances recorded from KAV 205, one is LI$_1$ and two are LI$_2$; and the same seems to apply to the three instances from KAV 105. Again, the instances have suffered mild damage, so it would be misleading to judge that the scribes commonly mixed forms.

QA (99) and NA4 (385)

In EMA the sign QA sometimes occurs with a *Winkelhaken* rather than a more extended diagonal. This is also the only variant of QA recorded from the LMA tablets under consideration. In EMA, this variant matches forms of NA_4 recorded from the same tablets ($NA_{4\text{-}1}$) (**Table 4.10**). The LMA documents on the other hand have a very different form of NA_4 than the EMA tablets: all recorded instances have two additional verticals ($NA_{4\text{-}2.}$). Salah (2013) and Jakob (2009) did not record NA_4, but Cancik-Kirschbaum (1996: 79) also shows $NA_{4\text{-}2.}$

RU (111)

Although many EMA instances of RU are damaged, they either have two *Winkelhaken* between the verticals (RU_2), two initial *Winkelhaken* (RU_{1a}), or smaller verticals and large *Winkelhaken* impressed over them (RU_3) (**Table 4.9**). In addition, a few tablets appear to have only one *Winkelhaken* – but on closer inspection it seems likely that it only appears this way because the second is obscured by another wedge. Middle Assyrian EA 15 is a particularly good example of this – in the image made available by the Metropolitan Museum in 2015, despite being extremely high quality, the angle and light is such that the second *Winkelhaken* is not visible (**Table 4.8**). In an older, lower resolution image, a small mark is visible underneath the vertical. While the older copies of the tablet are particularly unreliable, they were made based on seeing the actual artefact, and both copyists found a second *Winkelhaken* as well. From the LMA tablets, the only instances recorded are in the form RU_{1a} – with the second *Winkelhaken* sometimes crossing into the first vertical (RU_{1b}). All variants recorded by Jakob (2009: 28) and Cancik-Kirschbaum (1996: 74) likewise do not have *Winkelhaken* between the verticals. From the eight instances illustrated by Salah (2013: 388) two have a *Winkelhaken* following the first vertical, but the composition of the sign is crowded and it may have been accidental.

TI (118)

Freydank chose to study the Assyrian forms of TI because they are 'relatively common' and 'obviously changed shape' (1988: 75). However, he rightly wonders whether the way in which a scribe wrote may have changed over the course of their lifetime, and whether different scribes may have come from different scribal traditions; not to mention the difference between everyday writing and writing at court (1988: 76). Regardless, Freydank distinguishes between an 'older' and 'younger' form of TI and then attempts to match these forms to the dates of selected Middle Assyrian tablets. However, he quickly admits that the 'older' form of TI may appear later, the 'younger' form of TI may appear

TABLE 4.8 Comparison of RU from EA 15

EA 15 RU			

All obverse, line 10. Images provided by the Metropolitan Museum, New York.[10] The copies are both after scans from CDLI (nr. P271024).

earlier, and that both the 'older' and 'younger' forms of TI can be found mixed *within* other documents (1988: 78).

Freydank writes that he studied sixty Middle Assyrian tablets, but only records copies of eleven examples of TI (1988: 84) – all (according to him) 15th century. For the data presented here, ninety-two Middle Assyrian tablets from the 15th–14th century were studied. What Freydank calls the 'older' form can be split into two variants; one with a bottom horizontal wedge (here TI_{2b}) and one with a bottom *Winkelhaken* (TI_{2a}) (**Table 4.11**). What Freydank calls the 'younger' form can likewise be split into variants; one with an initial broken horizontal wedge (TI_{2b}) and one with a horizontal impression followed by a *Winkelhaken* (TI_{2a}). To add to the confusion, all forms have the ability to resemble one another, depending on the placement and angle of the middle / bottom *Winkelhaken*, calling into question what Freydank deemed 'obvious' (1988: 75). The labels 'older' and 'younger' clearly need re-defining. TI_2 is not absent from Babylonian and can be found in both Middle Babylonian and Late Old Babylonian documents; it is not 'young', it is only used more recently than TI_1, which is simply less common.

In the corpus considered here, the primary form on the 15th–14th century tablets, TI_1, occurs 105 out of 190 times (55%). The secondary form, TI_2, occurs 85 out of 190 times (45%). It is very difficult to find tablets of the 15th–14th century where TI_1 and TI_2 occur mixed within the same document (as suggested by Freydank); contenders are KAJ 11, KAJ 20, KAJ 26, and KAJ 39 – but all instances are unclear. It is essential to compare this result to the 13th century.

10 The image now falls under 'Public Domain' (March 2019), which means there is no copyright attached to it and the person who associated a work with this deed has waived all of his or her rights to the work worldwide under copyright law, including all related and neighboring rights, to the extent allowed by law. It is allowed to copy, modify, distribute and perform the work, even for commercial purposes.

TABLE 4.9 Middle Assyrian QA and NA4

EMA		LMA	
QA	NA$_{4-1}$	QA	NA$_{4-2}$

EMA QA (24 instances recorded): KAJ 14, reverse, line 6, second instance. **EMA NA$_4$** (27 instances recorded): KAJ 14, obverse, line 3. **LMA QA** (16 instances recorded): KAJ 226, reverse, line 2. **LMA NA$_4$** (26 instances recorded): KAV 109, reverse, line 6.

TABLE 4.10 Middle Assyrian RU

EMA			LMA	
RU$_{1a}$	RU$_2$	RU$_3$	RU$_{1a}$	RU$_{1b}$

EMA (74 instances recorded): KAJ 161, reverse, line 4; KAJ 28, obverse edge, line 14; KAJ 61, obverse, line 5. **LMA** (9 instances recorded): KAV 108, obverse edge, line 13; KAV 200, obverse, line 8.

TABLE 4.11 Middle Assyrian TI

EMA				LMA	
TI$_{1a}$	TI$_{1b}$	TI$_{2a}$	TI$_{2b}$	TI$_{1a}$	TI$_{1b}$

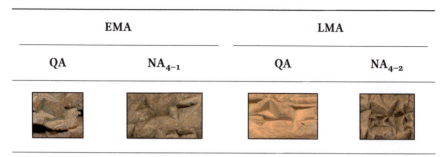

EMA TI$_1$: KAJ 173, obverse, line 5; KAJ 12, obverse edge, line 13. **EMA TI$_2$:** KAJ 1, reverse, line 4; KAJ 147, obverse, line 8. **LMA TI$_1$:** KAV 98, obverse, line 12; KAV 99, reverse, line 19.

Of 37 tablets, 28 instances of TI were recorded, all in the form of TI_2 (also commonly recorded with the second *Winkelhaken* placed above the horizontal, rather than attached to it). The same applies to sign-lists from Šeḫ Ḥamad (Cancik-Kirschbaum 1996: 74; Salah 2013: 389) and Tell Chuera (Jakob 2009: 28). In this perhaps rather artificial situation, it does appear that the 'older' form was more popular during the 15th–14th centuries, changing to the 'younger' form in the 13th century. While this may hardly seem a surprising conclusion, it previously seemed like these forms were used simultaneously during the early Middle Assyrian period without any obvious pattern of change. Rather, an evolution did take place, but it may have been dependent on gradual adaptation of individual education or habit rather than linear and direct overall change. The 13th century form of TI is much more consistent. Instead of attempting to determine whether the 'older' or 'younger' form of TI was characteristic for a specific scribe, school or century, it may have to become more acceptable to consider 15th–14th century Middle Assyrian as characteristically mixed, and 13th century Middle Assyrian as more standardised.

SA (172)

The EMA form of SA has two variants, one with even and consecutive verticals (SA_{1a}), and, less common, one with a more leftward initial vertical and bottom horizontal (SA_{1b}) (also see **Paragraph 3.3.4**) (**Table 4.12**). In LMA, the leftward vertical of SA_{1b} disappears altogether. Salah (2014: 387) still shows it for 5 out of 19 illustrated instances, but it is unclear which instance belongs to which tablet or scribe and how consistent this was.

SAG (184)

Middle Assyrian SAG (EMA and LMA) sometimes occurs with a bottom horizontal (SAG_{1b}), but it is most frequently composed with a *Winkelhaken* (SAG_{1a}) (**Table 4.13**). It is also another sign with obviously divergent wedges, like BA and KA, particularly in LMA.

UM (238), DUB (242) and KIŠIB (486)

Some of the complications encountered when discussing the signs UM (238) and DUB (242) together with KIŠIB (or MES, 486) were already introduced earlier. The same numbering is applied to the sign-forms discussed here, with **Table 4.14** essentially showing the same sign and its sign-forms twice in the case of UM and DUB, and **Figure 4.1** artificially assumes three forms of KIŠIB in order to indicate co-occurrence.

From the EMA tablets UM was recorded primarily with extended verticals (UM_2), but also at least once with verticals 'boxed in' by the horizontals (UM_1).

TABLE 4.12 Middle Assyrian SA

EMA		LMA
SA_{1b}	SA_{1a}	SA_{1a}

EMA (22 instances recorded): KAJ 14, obverse, line 11; KAJ 143, obverse, line 9. **LMA** (13 instances recorded): KAV 105, reverse, line 13.

TABLE 4.13 Middle Assyrian SAG

EMA		LMA
SAG_{1a}	SAG_{1b}	SAG_{1a}

EMA (47 instances recorded): KAJ 165, obverse, line 8; KAJ 17, obverse, line 5, edge. **LMA** (2 instances recorded): KAV 203, reverse edge, line 19.

From the LMA tablets however, UM was recorded only as UM_2. EMA DUB was also primarily collected with long verticals (DUB_2), but on occasion with small impressions surrounded by the horizontals (DUB_1). The occurrences of the latter are not accidental: for example, all three instances of DUB on KAJ 151 and both instances on KAJ 1 are DUB_1. The LMA instances were, again, all DUB_2.

From the Middle Assyrian tablets, the values MIŠ, MEŠ, and so forth, were not recorded, only KIŠIB and $KIŠIB_3$, which is in line with the genre of the tablets.[11] This sign was (potentially) recorded over a hundred times from the EMA tablets. It is meant to be distinguished from UM and DUB by being impressed with three rather than four initial horizontal wedges. Indeed, most

11 Saporetti (1979a, 1982) transliterates KIŠIB (*sigillo*), where the CDLI transliteration by Englund sometimes shows $KIŠIB_3$ (2013 update, the 2010 update likewise shows KIŠIB). Either way, the sign-form is almost always one with three horizontals, i.e. MZ 486.

TABLE 4.14 Middle Assyrian UM, DUB and KIŠIB

Early Middle Assyrian				
UM$_1$	**UM$_2$**	**DUB$_1$**	**DUB$_2$**	**KIŠIB**

Later Middle Assyrian		
UM$_2$	**DUB$_2$**	**KIŠIB**

EMA UM: KAJ 66, obverse, line 6: KAJ 147, obverse edge, line 15. **EMA DUB:** KAJ 151, reverse, line 3; KAJ 165, obverse, line 11. **EMA KIŠIB:** KAJ 88, side, line 1. **LMA UM:** KAV 103, obverse, line 4. **LMA DUB:** AfO 19 t5, obverse, line 9. **LMA KIŠIB:** KAV 99, reverse, line 1.

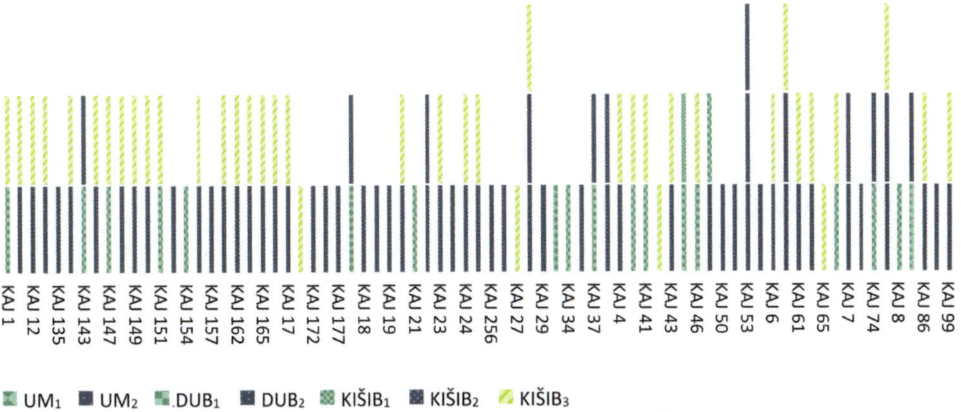

FIGURE 4.1 Comparison of Early Middle Assyrian UM, DUB and KIŠIB
In most cases the scribe differentiates between DUB (242) and KIŠIB (486), but not all. The most common is 'form 2', but 'form 1' is not absent from the corpus.

EMA scribes differentiate between DUB and KIŠIB, with the majority using DUB_2, and KIŠIB as described. However, the scribe of KAJ 22 impresses identical forms (DUB_2), with the values KIŠIB, DUB and ṬUP, and the scribe of KAJ 7 impresses KIŠIB and ṬUP (both reverse line 8) the same (also DUB_2) (**Figure 4.1**). Other tablets which may deviate from the norm are KAJ 179, KAJ 22, KAJ 37, KAJ 39, KAJ 44, KAJ 53, and KAJ 70; but these cases are less easy to determine due to damage. LMA KIŠIB was recorded with extended verticals and without an upper horizontal.

TA (248) DA (561) and ŠA (566)

On the EMA tablets TA occurs with *Winkelhaken* obscured by the verticals (TA_{1a}) or more clearly placed between or over the final two verticals (TA_{1b}) (**Table 4.15**). In LMA however, the *Winkelhaken* are placed in front of the verticals (TA_{2a}) and on a few tablets extended into diagonals (TA_{2b}). No instances of TA_1 were recorded, and it was not listed in Jakob (2009: 30) or Cancik-Kirschbaum (1996: 76) either. From the 25 copies provided by Salah (2013: 391) one has the *Winkelhaken* squeezed into the verticals, but considering the other evidence this was probably accidental.

Differences in DA and ŠA between EMA and LMA are less obvious, but still present. On the EMA tablets, there is a clear preference for DA_{1b} and $ŠA_{1b}$. On the LMA tablets however, these variants are virtually absent, and the *Winkelhaken* are placed consistently before the verticals (with incidental exceptions: e.g. on KAV 105 the upper *Winkelhaken* is placed more to the right). The tablets from Dur-Katlimmu (Cancik-Kirschbaum 1996: 82; Salah 2013: 396) illustrate how, often, these two *Winkelhaken* are both written near the top of the sign – one following the other, rather than one beneath the other. This could be transitional, because the same tablets also, less frequently, show a ŠA composed with only one upper *Winkelhaken* in front of the verticals – which is the common form for Neo-Assyrian (Labat 1988: 162).

DUMU (255)

DUMU illustrates 15th–14th century scribal preference, and it is possibly also a good example of standardisation in 13th century Middle Assyrian. In the database used here, only one variant of DUMU was recorded from the LMA tablets (vertical centred inbetween horizontals: $DUMU_{1a}$) (**Table 4.16**). Cancik-Kirschbaum (1996: 74) shows the same for Tall Šeḫ Ḥamad. Salah (2013: 392) records 24 copies, but they all fit the description of $DUMU_{1a}$. Jakob (2009: 28) shows more variation for Tell Chuera however (also see Labat 1988: 101). From the EMA tablets in this database, DUMU was recorded either with separate initial horizontals or broken horizontals ($DUMU_{1b}$); as well as the vertical crossing-through over the top of the horizontals ($DUMU_{1c}$), or the vertical crossing only barely over the bottom horizontal ($DUMU_{1d}$). Despite the very large number of instances recorded, these variations are relatively consistent per tablet; for example, all three instances of DUMU on KAJ 146 are $DUMU_{1b}$ with broken horizontals; on KAJ 161 five out of seven instances are $DUMU_{1c}$ and two out of seven $DUMU_{1a}$, all with separate initial horizontals; on KAJ 177 all four instances are $DUMU_{1d}$, with separate initial horizontals.

IN (261) and Similar Signs

The EMA forms of IN in the database are few in number and primarily damaged, making it challenging to see whether they might be composed with a 'ŠE' cluster. In LUGAL it looks like in some instances *Winkelhaken* are dominant, as with forms of BA, ZU and SU; it is difficult to judge whether any instances might be composed with horizontal impressions. However, ŠAR (541) was recorded in much greater numbers – clearly both with *Winkelhaken* ($ŠAR_1$) and with horizontals ($ŠAR_2$) (**Table 4.17**). From the LMA tablets, IN occurs only in one form; LUGAL likewise occurs in only one form, but, different from EMA, always with three consecutive upper *Winkelhaken*. ŠAR again occurs in two forms, as in EMA; however, the *Winkelhaken* are less obvious and all instances could potentially be considered $ŠAR_2$. Comparable patterns are distinguishable in, for example, LÚ (514) and ŠEŠ (535).

IL (348)

IL is one of the signs which is clearly different between EMA and LMA. Most instances from the EMA tablets are damaged or broken, but they indicate IL generally has two or three consecutive impressions in the diagonal (IL_1) (**Table 4.18**). In LMA however the diagonal has obviously become a straight broken horizontal (IL2). Notably, this is the case only for the corpus studied here. For Dur-Katlimmu both Cancik-Kirschbaum (1996: 78) and Salah (2013: 393) also show the 'diagonal' form of IL.

RA (511)

On the EMA tablets most instances of RA have three initial horizontal wedges, followed by two slightly wider spaced horizontals, and then two verticals (RA_{1a}) (**Table 4.19**). In a few cases the initial horizontal looks like a broken horizontal instead (RA_{1b}). On the LMA tablets the balance is the other way around: the initial horizontal is almost always broken, and very often there are four or five rather than three initial horizontal wedges. From a handful of tablets (KAJ 14 and KAJ 20 most prominently) the sign was also recorded with a smaller initial vertical (RA_2).

TABLE 4.15 Middle Assyrian TA, DA and ŠA

Early Middle Assyrian			
TA$_{1a}$	TA$_{1b}$	DA$_{1b}$	ŠA$_{1b}$

Later Middle Assyrian			
TA$_{2a}$	TA$_{2b}$	DA$_{2a}$	ŠA$_{2a}$

EMA TA (53 instances recorded): KAJ 167, reverse, line 6; KAJ 170, reverse, line 6. **LMA TA** (51 instances recorded): KAV 105, reverse, line 3, second instance; KAV 98, obverse, line 20. **EMA DA** (109 instances recorded): KAJ 12, obverse, line 6. **LMA DA** (12 instances recorded): AfO 19 t5, obverse, line 9. **EMA ŠA** (213 instances recorded): KAJ 146, obverse, line 10. **LMA ŠA** (102 instances recorded): KAV 100, obverse, line 17.

TABLE 4.16 Middle Assyrian DUMU

EMA				LMA
DUMU$_{1a}$	DUMU$_{1b}$	DUMU$_{1c}$	DUMU$_{1d}$	DUMU$_{1a}$

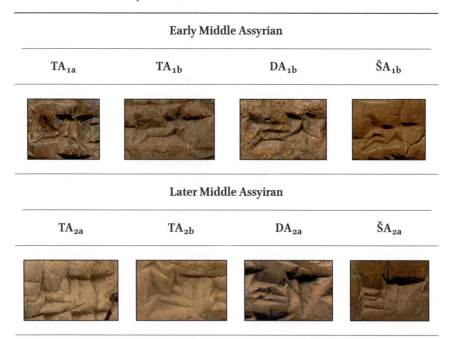

EMA (419 instances recorded): KAJ 161, obverse, line 4; KAJ 161, obverse line 10; KAJ 146, reverse, line 6; KAJ 177, obverse, line 7. **LMA** (14 instances recorded): KAJ 158, reverse, line 6.

TABLE 4.17 Middle Assyrian IN, LUGAL and ŠAR

Early Middle Assyrian					
IN$_{1a}$	**IN$_{1b}$**	**LUGAL$_{1a}$**	**LUGAL$_{1b}$**	**ŠAR$_{1}$**	**ŠAR$_{2}$**

Later Middle Assyrian			
IN$_{1b}$	**LUGAL$_{2}$**	**ŠAR$_{1}$**	**ŠAR$_{2}$**

EMA IN (7 instances recorded): KAJ 146, reverse, line 5; KAJ 35, obverse, line 6. **EMA LUGAL** (25 instances recorded): KAJ 148, reverse, line 8; KAJ 151, reverse, line 4. **EMA ŠAR** (73 instances recorded): KAJ 148, reverse, line 13; KAJ 29, reverse, line 10. **LMA IN** (9 instances recorded): AfO 19 t5, obverse, line 4. **LMA LUGAL** (9 instances recorded): KAV 100, obverse, line 7. **LMA ŠAR** (6 instances recorded): KAV 104, reverse, line 4; KAV 99, obverse, line 7.

TABLE 4.18 Middle Assyrian IL

EMA	**LMA**
IL1	**IL$_{2}$**

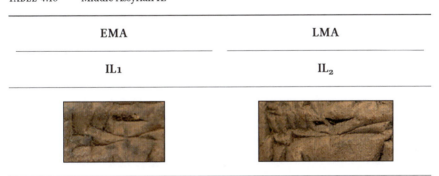

EMA (16 instances recorded): KAJ 7, obverse, line 9. **LMA** (11 instances recorded): KAV 109, reverse, line 10. Note that more forms of LMA IL occur in other corpora.

ḪI (631) and Similar Signs

In the EMA documents there is a mixture of variants of ḪI with 4–5 wedges (1a), and 5+ (1b) (**Table 4.20**) while in the LMA documents nearly all instances have a high number of impressions. These variants are consistent per scribe (also see Nuzi, **Chapter 5**); for example, on EMA KAJ 14 all instances across all signs have a low number of wedges. Similar observations may be made for KAM (253) and ID (560).

UGU (663)

The instances of UGU recorded from the Middle Assyrian corpora under consideration do not differ. From the EMA and LMA tablets UGU was always recorded with horizontal wedges. The same is shown by the sign-lists in Jakob (2009: 37), Cancik-Kirschbaum (1996: 84) and Salah (2014: 98). The spacing of the impressions can differ in such a way that sometimes the upper horizontal seems broken (**Table 4.21**), while other times it looks more separate, with the initial horizontal centred between the following two wedges.

EŠ (711)

The Middle Assyrian tablets provide a second opportunity to consider the sign EŠ (see **Paragraph 3.3.4**). From the EMA tablets the sign was recorded only numerical not syllabic, with the value 30 and the value 3. On KAJ 146, the form with *Winkelhaken* logically has the value 30 (3 × U; $EŠ_2$) and the form with horizontals has the value 3 (3 × AŠ; $EŠ_1$) (**Table 4.22**). No undamaged instances of the sign co-occur on other tablets. However, according to the transcriptions, the form with *Winkelhaken* occurs on other tablets with the value 3, and the form with horizontals occurs on other tablets with the value 30. From the LMA tablets EŠ was recorded solely with the value 30; however, only one instance clearly has *Winkelhaken*. In Babylonian and at Nuzi the sign exclusively occurs with *Winkelhaken* (with very rare exceptions), with the value EŠ, 3 and 30. Since instances with horizontals are rare and present more in Middle Assyrian, especially Later Middle Assyrian, it could be indicative of a preference for using straighter wedges, like in LÚ and ŠAR. For example, from thirteen copies, Salah (2013: 399) shows ten with horizontal impressions and only three with obvious *Winkelhaken*.

MEŠ (754)

From the EMA tablets MEŠ was recorded primarily with a horizontal wedge, separate from the vertical, followed by three or four consecutive *Winkelhaken* ($MEŠ_1$) (**Table 4.23**). On several tablets the horizontal is difficult to see, but it is present regardless (KAJ 13). In a few cases it looks like the horizontal is

TABLE 4.19 Middle Assyrian RA

EMA			LMA	
RA$_{1a}$	RA$_{1b}$	RA$_{2}$	RA$_{1b}$	RA$_{1a}$

EMA (69 instances recorded): KAJ 167, obverse, line 13; KAJ 44, obverse edge, line 12; KAJ 14, reverse, line 7. **LMA** (39 instances recorded): KAV 109, obverse, line 7, edge; KAV 194, obverse, line 6.

TABLE 4.20 Middle Assyrian ḪI, AM, AḪ and IM

Early Middle Assyrian			
ḪI$_{1a}$	ḪI$_{1b}$	AM$_{1a}$	AM$_{1b}$

AḪ$_{1a}$	AḪ$_{1b}$	IM$_{1a}$	IM$_{1b}$

Later Middle Assyrian			
ḪI$_{1b}$	AM$_{1b}$	AḪ$_{1b}$	IM$_{1b}$

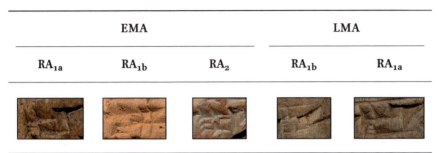

EMA ḪI (143 instances recorded): KAJ 14, obverse, line 13; KAJ 167, obverse, line 10. **EMA AM** (12 instances recorded): KAJ 14, reverse, line 7; KAJ 53, obverse, line 9. **EMA AḪ** (11 instances recorded): KAJ 177, obverse, line 9; KAJ 19, obverse, line 6, edge. **EMA IM** (106 instances recorded): KAJ 150, obverse, line 8; KAJ 61, obverse, line 8. **LMA ḪI** (24 instances recorded): KAV 99, obverse, line 18. **LMA AM** (8 instances recorded): KAV 98, obverse, line 22. **LMA AḪ** (3 instances recorded): KAV 98, obverse, line 9. **LMA IM** (7 instances recorded): KAV 99, obverse, line 20.

TABLE 4.21 Middle Assyrian UGU

EMA	LMA
UGU$_{1}$	**UGU$_{1}$**

EMA (4 instances recorded): KAJ 44, obverse, line 10. **LMA** (17 instances recorded): KAV 105, reverse, line 8.

TABLE 4.22 Middle Assyrian EŠ

EMA		LMA	
EŠ$_{1}$	**EŠ$_{2}$**	**EŠ$_{1}$**	**EŠ$_{2}$**

EMA (23 instances recorded): KAJ 146, obverse, line 8; KAJ 146, obverse, line 2. **LMA** (4 instances recorded): KAV 104, reverse, line 10; KAJ 159, obverse, line 2.

TABLE 4.23 Middle Assyrian MEŠ

EMA		LMA
MEŠ$_{1}$	**MEŠ$_{2}$**	**MEŠ$_{2}$**

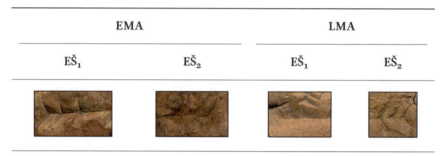

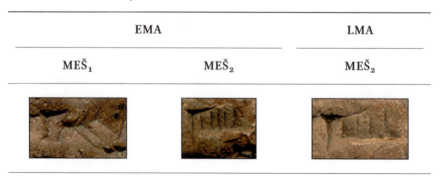

EMA (84 instances recorded): KAJ 157, obverse, line 8; KAJ 309, obverse, line 3. **LMA** (30 instances recorded): KAV 98, reverse, line 13.

pressed into the vertical (KAJ 13, but also KAJ 309, KAJ 79) but never clearly or consistently. Some scribes have angled the *Winkelhaken* so that they have become horizontal impressions – and in a few cases the distance between the first horizontal and the following impressions is so small it looks like one row (MEŠ$_2$). This becomes the primary form on the LMA tablets. Much less variation occurs in the recorded instances, and they practically always have a row of consecutive horizontal impressions. Labat (1988: 218), Jakob (2009: 38), Cancik-Kirschbaum (1996: 86) and Salah (2013: 400) likewise show the 'pause' after the first horizontal disappears in later Assyrian.

4.5 Comparison of Key Signs between Scribes

As mentioned, the dating on some of the so-called 15th century tablets has been heavily debated, and many of the 13th century tablets included here were written by the same scribe. In order to see how this affects the level of representation of the database, a comparison of the key signs follows below. For the 13th century, the different scribal hands are clear, but they all use the same sign-forms (**Table 4.24**). This in combination with the sign-lists by Cancik-Kirschbaum (1996) and Jakob (2009) ensures that the standardised appearance cannot be attributed simply to Babu-aḫa-iddina. For the 15th century a lot more variation is visible (**Table 4.25**). Also interesting is that the 15th century forms of BA and ITI tend to match the 13th century forms, meaning that if these tablets are indeed earlier, there is not a progression from, for example, straight wedges in BA during the Mittani Empire to *Winkelhaken* in BA under the Assyrian Empire.

TABLE 4.24 Comparison of sign-forms between different scribes from Ass. 14410

	KAV 96 (Babu-aḫa-iddina)	AfO 19 t5 (Kidin-gula)	KAV 104 (Mušallim-aššur)	KAV 106 (Aššur-šallimanni)
BA				
ITI				

TABLE 4.25 Comparison of sign-forms between possible 15th century tablets from Ass. 14446

	KAJ 177	KAJ 22	KAJ 162	KAJ 50	KAJ 174	KAJ 139
BA						
ITI			–			–
TI						–
RU						–

4.6 Comments

4.6.1 *Summary*

Aššur had been a prosperous city with a significant international trading network. Memories of this glorious past clearly resonated with the inhabitants of Aššur: the archaeological record shows the old palace was rebuilt, and it was not long before Aššur wrote its way into the Amarna correspondence. Many of the 15th–14th century tablets found at Aššur show a mixture of sign-forms – of which some are eliminated by the 13th century, and others persist, resulting in a quite different script. The most prominent examples of this process are:

- BAL (5) which in EMA often has a bottom *Winkelhaken*, but in LMA always has its *Winkelhaken* above or aligned with the broken horizontal; ITI (20) which in EMA often has a central sequence of *Winkelhaken* and in LMA always an upper broken horizontal; KA (24), which in EMA occurs in various forms, one of which with an upper or central *Winkelhaken*, whereas in LMA the sign only occurs with an upper broken horizontal; IL (348), which in EMA has a broken diagonal, but in LMA a straight broken upper horizontal; signs such as IN (261) and ŠAR (541), which in EMA often have a cluster of *Winkelhaken* but in LMA less impressions, or horizontal impressions; and MEŠ (754), which in EMA often has a horizontal followed by *Winkelhaken*, but in LMA only a straight sequence of horizontals.

- Signs such as BA (14), which are increasingly impressed with *Winkelhaken* in EMA and only with *Winkelhaken* in LMA; SAG (184), which in EMA is impressed either with horizontals or *Winkelhaken* and in LMA only with a bottom *Winkelhaken*.
- LI (85), which in EMA is generally impressed only with *Winkelhaken* rather than also with horizontals, and in LMA this balance is vice versa; RU (111), which has at least three different forms in EMA and only one, with some variation, in LMA; TI (118), which in EMA has two distinct forms and many variants, but in LMA only one of these forms persists; signs such as UM (238), which in EMA occur with small boxed verticals, and in LMA only ever with extended verticals.
- Signs such as TA (248) and DA (561), which in EMA generally have the *Winkelhaken* impressed inbetween the verticals, and in LMA always in front of the verticals.

Overall, there is an obvious difference in sign-forms between Early Middle Assyrian and Later Middle Assyrian. By the 13th century the script is clearly recognisable by the length of the tails of the wedges, and a general straightening out or flattening of impressions. Nearly all forms overlap, but throughout the two centuries one increasingly replaces the other (albeit not chronologically, as proven above). Whereas in EMA the balance between key 'primary' and 'secondary' forms is 55% versus 45%, in LMA this becomes 30% versus 70% (**Figure 4.2**). In addition, much less variation occurs in Later Middle Assyrian (larger blocks versus smaller blocks, **Figure 4.2**). In isolation, this looks like a clear relationship and progression from EMA to LMA, as would make sense for the time during which and the place where the tablets were written.

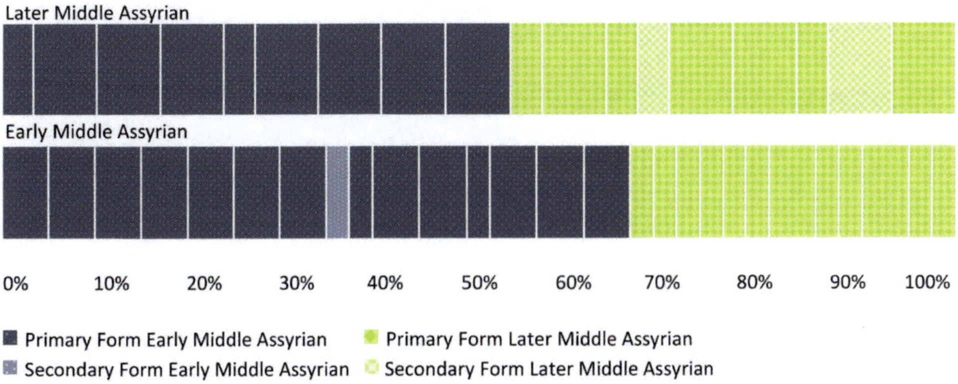

FIGURE 4.2 Comparison of key Middle Assyrian sign-forms
Signs included are BAL, BA, ZU, SU, ITI, LI, RU, TI, UM, DUB, DA, ŠA, IL, and MEŠ.

4.6.2 *Assyrian Amarna Correspondence*

At this point, it is important to return to EA 15. This is a relatively short letter from Aššur-uballiṭ I, 'King of the Land of Aššur', to the Egyptian Pharaoh. Although it is impossible to know if any correspondence preceded this document, it looks like this letter is a kind of greeting or introduction, to establish a diplomatic relationship. The letter was followed by EA 16, of which presently only a copy (Knudtzon 1915) is available for comparison (CDLI nr. P270976). In this letter Aššur-uballiṭ daringly refers to the Pharaoh as 'my brother'. He points out an equal status means equal sharing and urges the Pharaoh to send gold. While this equal relationship is clearly desired by Aššur-uballiṭ, it seems it is not yet fully accomplished at this point in time. The language in both letters is influenced by the 'peripheral Akkadian dialect of Mittani' (Rainey 2015: 1374) and shows selective borrowing from the Mittani-Akkadian/Hurrian 'Northern' thesaurus (Artzi 1997: 324). Artzi even suggests this might be evidence that a Mittanian scribe was working in Aššur (1997: 326).

Key signs recorded from EA 15 include BA (14) and KA (24) with divergent wedges, LI (85) without ŠA component, RU (111) with two *Winkelhaken* (although the second is very difficult to see), a 'long' TI (118), TA (248) and ŠA (566) with *Winkelhaken* impressed between verticals, the bottom *Winkelhaken* through or in front of the first vertical, ḪI (631) with six wedges, MEŠ (754) with consecutive horizontals rather than horizontal pressed into the vertical, and possibly UM (238) only with extended verticals (**Table 4.26**). These are practically all forms which are typically Middle Assyrian rather than Mittanian. Considering the dating of the tablet (late in the Amarna Age) it could be taken as evidence of changes that were beginning to be introduced at Aššur. EA 15 does not yet show a typical straightening of wedges, or, for example, additional horizontals in LI. However, there is no trace of Mittanian KA, MEŠ or TI; no straight wedges in signs like BA, SU and ZU, and the *Winkelhaken* in TA and ŠA are beginning to move towards the front of the composition.

In **Paragraph** 3.4.3 the relevance of Hurrian was addressed already. Just as Hurrian is inseparable from Mittani, Akkadian is entwined with Assyrian identity. At Aššur it is (understandably) possible to find traces of Old Assyrian, not only in the Aššur 14446 archive, but also in various other documents (see Postgate 2013: 57), as well as vocabulary in general, and the Aššur calendar. There are surviving instructions for the training of horses, recipes for preparation of scented oils, laws, royal edicts, and fragments of annual chronicles, all in an Assyrian dialect and intended for use inside Assyria, rather than borrowed from Babylonia (2013: 60). At the same time, there was not an absence of knowledge of Babylonian scholarship (Veldhuis 2012a). It is known that at least one Babylonian scribe was active in 14th century Aššur. However, Wiggerman (2008) suggests that this scribe (Marduk-nadin-aḫḫe) had left his home country

TABLE 4.26 Key sign-forms from EA 15

BA (14)	KA (24)	LI (85)	RU (111)	TI (118)

TA (248)	ŠA (566)	ḪI (631)	MEŠ (754)	UM (238)

BA: obverse, line 13. **KA**: obverse, line 9. **ḪI**: obverse, line 4. **LI**: reverse, line 3. **MEŠ**: reverse, line 4. **RU**: obverse, line 5. **ŠA**: obverse, line 10. **TA**: obverse, line 9. **TI**: reverse, line 5. **UM**: Obverse, line 3.

amidst a power dispute and declared his loyalty to the King of Aššur. This indicates he had not travelled to, been brought to, or invited to Aššur specifically to share the art of Babylonian writing or to impose Babylonian influence on Assyrian writing. Aššur had a strong identity of its own.

As described, the last period in the region of Aššur during which sign-forms were limited in number and standardised across tablets was during Mittani rule. According to the principles of cultural psychology, political economic institutions which dominate social structures, organise other institutions; and thus, organise knowledge. This would explain why Aššur would look to or be influenced by its overlord Mittani, rather than, for example, its closest neighbour Nuzi. It has furthermore been suggested that one of the ways in which the Assyrian Empire was able to become so successful, is because it based itself on existing Mittani structures (Postgate 2015). Improving upon this, the Assyrians tried to introduce homogenous administration from the outset, creating provinces rather than vassals, and introducing an imperial recording system (Düring 2015: 301). This ties in with group-identification and social representation; whereas Aššur had previously been dominated by Mittani, Aššur itself now became the primary source of power and influence. Although the scribes had been exposed to Mittanian writing and begun using it for themselves, the change in group-membership also changed the organisation of knowledge. There was a period where there was no longer a centrally organised Mittanian school of writing, but also not yet an Assyrian school to replace it. Change is closely related to identity-construction – whether the Assyrians simply no longer *had* to follow Mittani ways, or whether they did not *want* to, during the 14th century there was both a shift in power and a shift in writing. Creating a direct link between the two processes without unambiguous evidence is a leap too far, but social identity theory suggests that these developments possess some degree of interrelation.

4.7 Final Remarks

This chapter promised to elaborate further on boundaries between similar script-groups. Early Middle Assyrian showed many more different sign-forms than Mittanian, while Later Middle Assyrian showed only slightly more or a similar number of different sign-forms compared to Mittanian. Mittanian, Assyro-Mittanian and Early Middle Assyrian share some of these forms (as will be shown further later on), as do Early Middle Assyrian and Later Middle Assyrian. However, none of the sign-forms particular to 13th century Middle Assyrian are represented in Mittanian. Thus, the beginning of a boundary is starting to materialise.

So far, a considerable part of the analysis has been quantitative rather than qualitative. Yet signs are more than statistics and also bear relationship to their context. Some factors considered here were social (private versus diplomatic correspondence) and even personal (individual scribal hands). However, particularly the historical and political situation is of interest. When considering the 15th–14th centuries, the Mittani state was relatively well-established while Aššur was a (re-)emerging power. By the 13th century Mittani had fallen and the Assyrian Empire was a fact. This could potentially explain why there is less variation in Mittani as well as Later Middle Assyrian signs and more variation in Early Middle Assyrian signs. This situation reflects the difference between a central and organised way of scribal training and something more loose, varied or scattered. It is therefore possible to identify a relationship between organisation and script, highlighting the condition in which signs which are taught or learned (also see Danesi 2010 'edusemiotics').

At the same time, it has been proposed that this uniform Mittanian and diverse Early Middle Assyrian could belong to the same over-arching script-group. Despite any differences amongst Mittanian and Early Middle Assyrian, it is also clear that there is a boundary between those script-groups which were used in the 15th–14th centuries and the Later Middle Assyrian script which was used in the 13th century (and after). Of course, so far, all comments have been limited to Mittanian and Middle Assyrian, which are evidently closely related either way. The following chapter will move on to neighbouring Nuzi, in search for stronger contrasts.

CHAPTER 5

Nuzi and Tigunanum

As a consequence of post-colonial theory, attention has increased for topics such as resistance, appropriation and 'modes of contact'. Rather than seeing the development of writing methods as the direct outcome of new management structures, it should be seen as the continuous transformation of communication. That is why this chapter will begin by considering the regional centre of Nuzi – located in Arrapḫa (see **Maps**) and one of the most eastern vassals of the Mittani Empire. It was a Hurrian speaking entity, incorporated into the Mittani sphere of influence, near Aššur. Yet, the development of its writing and, as far as it is known, outward communication differed notably. Next, we will go back in time a few centuries, to the mysterious northern city of Tigunanum. Again, a probably Hurrian entity – with a script that no one has quite been able to classify as (Late) Old Babylonian. So where did the people of cities like Nuzi and Tigunanum come from, and who did they identify with? What is the significance of the Hurrian identity in their communication, and what do their scripts look like from a Mittanian point of view?

5.1 Introduction to Nuzi

The available socio-economic information on Nuzi from its tablets makes the settlement an appropriate case-study for comparative palaeography. Where it is traditionally assumed that writing habits were imposed from above (by large Imperial powers), it is likewise possible they arose through other contacts (smaller neighbours, trade, immigration) (Van de Mieroop 1999: 37). The scribes at Nuzi had a unique style, featuring elements borrowed from other areas, and potentially carried across their own influence elsewhere. The world system as well as the acculturation model (Binford & Binford 1968) wrongly view peripheries or recipient cultures as passive groups, lacking in agency or the capacity to act in pursuit of their own goals or interests. Local systems of power and authority coexisted with, and often resisted, centralised governments, allowing room for the expression of individual identity (Yoffee 2005).[1] Especially with regard to the Hurrians, it has been suggested that smaller communities selectively borrowed elements from other cultures, by their own choice, rather than being dominated by a larger power (Stein 2002).

1 Also see Goody (1986) on connections between literacy and state formation.

 | DOI:10.1163/9789004417243_006

Notably, in his PhD thesis on Hurrian orthographic interference in Nuzi Akkadian, Smith concluded that the situation in Nuzi shifted *towards* Hurrian: second generation scribes show more Hurrian tendencies than their predecessors (2007: 209). In the past, it was believed that the native Nuzi language was a relative of Elamite (Oppenheim 1936: 63), but it was quickly recognised as Hurrian instead (Speiser 1936: 136). However, the texts found at Nuzi are composed in a special form of Akkadian (Berkooz 1937: 5). As in the Mittanian heartland, Akkadian was used for official purposes, while Hurrian was used in everyday conversation (Wilhelm 1989). The majority of Nuzi personal names are Hurrian and Hurrian elements appear in many of the documents (Gelb *et al.* 1943).[2] Hurrian influence shines through in vocabulary, morphology, syntax, and orthography and phonology, and language at Nuzi has tentatively been called a 'third Akkadian dialect' (Goetze 1938: 143) or 'Peripheral Akkadian' (Morrison *et al.* 1993: 3).[3]

Because of the availability of so many interconnected personal names, emphasis in Nuzi studies has been on reconstructing family trees. For instance, Purves highlighted the need to classify Nuzi texts by chronological order and scribal group as early as 1940 (although this task still awaits completion today). Since the tablets were discovered in structures ranging from administrative buildings to private houses, personal names have also been analysed to trace a variety of backgrounds (Jankowska 1969). Furthermore, the density of documentation in space and time at Nuzi (circa 7,000 tablets, circa 100 years) allows us to view local phenomena from different perspectives. Notably, Nuzi's legal formulary differs from its Babylonian, Assyrian and Hittite neighbours (Maidman 2010). It is possible to reconstruct socio-economic life by taking into account the distribution of scribes and archives, and the composition of different areas of the town (Negri Scafa 2005: 134). As Starr writes in the introduction to his excavation report "the Nuzians may be seen as human beings, rather than as ciphers in a chronological list" (R. F. S. Starr, August 31, 1938). This is also where questions about palaeography arise. It is significant to consider the extent to which writing at Nuzi differed from its contemporary neighbours; how Nuzi tablets compare to those considered in the previous chapters; whether this helps to find boundaries between larger script-groups; what the difference is between early and later writing at Nuzi; and what the boundaries are between individual scribal hands.

---

2 A name is considered Hurrian when it is composed of one or more elements that have no obvious Semitic etymology but are clearly attested in continuous Hurrian texts, Hurrianisms in Akkadian texts, Hurrian entries in cuneiform vocabularies, or elements in characteristically Hurrian personal and geographical names (Astour 1987: 3).

3 Of particular interest are signs with syllabic values consisting of a CV (stop consonant plus vowel). Hurrian did not distinguish voice and voiceless stops, and the scribes tended to use one set of signs for any CV value, especially *pa/ba* and *pe/be* (Smith 2007).

5.1.1 *Archaeological Context*

Excavations at Nuzi (Yorghan Tepe), took place almost a century ago. In fact, some of the Nuzi tablets appeared on the antiquities market as early as 1890 (Millard 1981: 433). "Twenty donkeys, so the story goes, were needed to carry them [the clay tablets] to Baghdad so that they might be sold" (Starr 1939: xxix). At the suggestion of Gertrude Bell, between 1925 and 1931 expeditions were led by E. Chiera, R. H. Pfeiffer, and R. F. S. Starr, sponsored by the American School of Oriental Research in Baghdad, the Semitic Museum of Harvard University and the Iraq Museum in Baghdad (see the AASOR series).

A large area was uncovered and excavated to virgin soil in a mere 5 seasons, and due to the recording methods used it can be difficult to retrieve data from the reports and field records. This in turn leads to difficulties in reconstructing the archives: it is not always noted that a tablet originated from a particular room, and room as well as museum numbers in the publications contain many errors (Morrison *et al.* 1993: 6). That said, this was the recording convention at the time (see, for instance, Woolley (1948; 1955) on Alalaḫ VII) and fortunately miss-assigned or stray tablets can often be matched to archives according to their contents (see Von Dassow 2005).

The central citadel of Nuzi measures a little over 200 × 200 meters. In the original excavation report, Starr divides the area as follows: Temple, Palace, North-Western Ridge, South-Western Section, North-Eastern Section, City Wall and Related Buildings, and Suburban Buildings. There were eight archives found in the palace, one in the arsenal, one in the temple area and fourteen in various private houses (Pedersén 1998: 17). Most tablets found in the palace are administrative. Administrative archives were mainly concerned with tracing goods, resulting in a limited life-span.[4] One of the palace collections also comprises the personal archive of Tulpunnaya (see **Paragraph 5.2**). Personal archives focussed on only one or a few family members, while family archives were a repository for all tablets relating to the whole family, maintained primarily for their legal value (e.g. proof of ownership) and therefore included records from previous generations. Examples are the archive of Zike, his son Artimi and his grandson Šar-teššup (a house north-west of the palace), and the family of Teḫip-tilla which spans five generations (a house in the suburban area) (Pedersén 1998: 24).

5.1.2 *Social Context*

Nearly all tablets found at Nuzi are concerned with economic and legal matters. The texts rarely hint at religious cults such as those of the Hittites, nor do they document international royal correspondence such as those of Amarna.

4 See Bernbeck (2009: 56) and Proust (2010: 262) on discard practice.

Instead, the tablets engage with everyday activities such as manufacture and land sales. For example, SMN 855 (translation from Maidman 2010: 85): [*Thus Ḫutiya: "I most certainly*] *gave to Kuššši-ḫarpe* [*two*] *sheep as a purchase price / gift, and the two sheep – which he took – and the land together with its seed, he gave to Qîsteya".* The Nuzi legal practices show many similarities with other Mesopotamian legal systems (Liebesny 1941: 142). However, they are unique in some ways, such as the 'adoption' procedures.[5] This is likely due to blending of Babylonian, Assyrian and Hurrian legal elements (Paulissian 1999).

While the archaeological record often allows for a relatively neutral bottom-up approach to known history, documents can fill gaps in the record and enhance our understanding. For example, the Eastern Archive (Group 18A) is located across the street from the palace, in an area where the quality of construction work is inferior to, for instance, the south-western section (Morrison 1987); it is described as "less desirable for private homes", "of lesser wealth" and "of humbler class" (Starr 1939: 321). Although Starr's interpretation of the architecture and finds may be questioned, it is significant to take into account either way. He writes that the width of the main courtyard is much larger than that of private houses and that it was probably shared between several residences. Furthermore, Starr suggests that the space was used by flocks as well as people (Starr 1939: 313). More certain is that the doorways and entryways were poorly preserved, making it difficult to reconstruct how the rooms related to each other. Four steps descend down about 30 cm to a corridor in which a pot-stand and 65 scattered tablets were found – probably thrown out of a room (S307) during the looting of the building. Morrison (1993: 21) notes that tablet registers only record 42 tablets however; in addition, some of the texts belong to other archives, while in other archives texts belonging to this group have been found too.

Group 18A, the archive of the Ḫuya family, seems to contain the personal documents of a palace official, who developed his own estate in the course of his career (Morrison *et al.* 1993: 46). Tarmiya and Šeḫal-teššup were irrigation officers, Puḫi-šenni and Pula-ḫali were bankers. All of them also owned real estate, land, or both (Morrison *et al.* 1993: 123). They were hardly the poorer members of society, as Starr suggested in his description of the architecture. Instead, the neighbourhood was associated with the administrative and commercial sectors of the population, which prospered especially in the later period of Nuzi (Morrison *et al.* 1993: 129). The buildings that show most reconstruction and variation in the plan are those that produced the tablets. This could be related to increased activity, as the wealth of the archive-owners

5 For example, where the adoption focusses on real-estate and the status of the person as an heir (a 'son' who can be either male or female) (see Fincke 2012; Paradise 1987).

expanded and reconstruction was necessary to meet the growth of commerce and bureaucracy. Morrison (*ibid.*) also suggests that renovations took place in order to attract more outsiders to Nuzi, when the threat of Assyria started to come closer. The overall picture of Arrapḫean commerce, combining texts and architecture, is that of a complex network of financial interests in which the private sectors co-exist and overlap (Morrison *et al.* 1993: 108).

The inter-related character of the Nuzi documents brings out the different social relations that existed in Nuzi. Individual identity is often complicated to detect and understand, but, needless to say, investigation of common characteristics has allowed insight into different social phenomena. For instance, it has been possible to identify scribes who worked with palace administration but were not part of the palace personnel (Negri Scafa 1995: 63). Also, it has been possible to reconstruct the roles of people in the entire production process and circulation of weapons (in which the palace played only a passive role) (Negri Scafa 1995: 69). The 'important role of women' at Nuzi has been pointed out on several occasions as well – such as women as the sole representatives of their families (Morrison 1987: 196) and daughters being adopted as 'sons' in relation to property claims (Paradise 1987: 213). However, 'important' remains largely undefined. More significant is the information the documents provide, detailing the different roles of women in Nuzi, the various roles that existed in Nuzi society in general, and especially the relationships between them (also see below, the archive of Tulpunnaya).

Various arguments exist for Babylonian, Assyrian and Mittanian influence on writing at Nuzi. For example, a popular suggestion is that the earliest Nuzi scribes were Babylonian (e.g. Cooper 1999: 70). Within this argument, it remains speculative whether these were sent there by the Babylonians or imported by the Nuzians. Later generations of scribes may therefore have been Babylonian descendants. Alternatively, it is possible that Nuzians travelled to Babylonia to obtain scribal education or requested that Babylonians teach them – in which case the scribes would have been Hurrians *using* Babylonian.[6]

At the time Nuzi blossomed, Aššur was a minor power – but trading connections and its close proximity to Nuzi should not be ignored. While relations between Aššur and Nuzi were hostile at times, there were at least two generations of peaceful diplomatic contact (Maidman 2010: 15). There is evidence that Nuzi chariots were exported to Assyria (SMN 2056), and there is evidence for Assyrian labourers and scribes in Nuzi (JEN V, 446; JEN V, 458; JEN VI, 613). That said, Aššur in turn borrowed cultural heritage from Babylonia (Veldhuis 2012b: 12) – and it is difficult to separate such layers of influence. In addition,

6 Additionally, see Negri Scafa (1999) on scribal education and Van Soldt (1989) on language interference in the Tušratta letters.

Chapter 3 and **Chapter 4** have shown how closely Mittanian and Early Middle Assyrian resemble one another. Considering that both Aššur and Nuzi were Mittanian vassals in the period under consideration, and the primary spoken language was Hurrian, it could make more sense to speak of Mittanian influence rather than Assyrian.

5.2 The Selected Nuzi Corpus

One of the interesting features of the Nuzi archives is the generations over which they are divided. In this chapter generations of different families are used to investigate whether there are chronological ramifications to sign-use. In fact, this chapter should have probably been named 'experimenting with Nuzi palaeography', so please bear that in mind whilst reading. What follows is a particularly preliminary study, to be understood primarily in the context of Mittani standardisation. It is not a complete palaeography of Nuzi; it could not hope to be so considering the database only includes 67 out of circa 7,000 Nuzi tablets.

As things stand at the moment, there is no absolute dating for the Nuzi tablets. Very few documents were impressed with date formulae, and those that were bear little reference to external chronology (Friedmann 1987: 109). Approximates have been based on Šauštatar's seal (also see **Paragraph 3.2.2**), in combination with a battle between Assyria and Arrapḫa (Maidman 2011). The entire corpus has been estimated to cover as little as 60 to as much as 150 years (Friedmann 1987: 113). The scribal generations of Nuzi are roughly parallel, but understandably cover different ranges, as not every scribe naturally reached the same age, or was active equally long.

For generation II most tablets used here are from the archive of Tulpunnaya, a prominent businesswoman (Abrahami & Lion 2012; Pfeiffer & Speiser 1936: texts 15–45). This is an archive of 37 tablets and fragments (see **Appendix**), from room 120 in the palace (where the excavation records indicate provenience).[7] Tulpunnaya was the daughter of Irwi-šarri and Šeltunnaya, and she was married to Ḫašuar. Tulpunnaya and her mother built a considerable fortune and seemingly managed it as well. The entire archive has been dated through SMN 2036, which names Teḫip-tilla as judiciary. His parents, Puḫi-šenni and Winnirgi, also feature in the archive. Teḫip-tilla in turn has been named as a potential contemporary of Šauštatar (Friedmann 1987: 109). The tablets concern adoptions ('sale adoptions'), security and lawsuits. Very useful is that named scribes occur on all but three tablets and several produced multiple texts: Nabu-naṣir SMN 2038 and SMN 2044, Sin-iqiša SMN 2043, SMN 2045 and SMN 2206, and

7 Only the 31 tablets originally published by Speiser in AASOR 16 are included here.

Urḫiya SMN 2018, SMN 2023, SMN 2031 and SMN 2037. This means it is possible to compare differences in scribal hand. The tablets are currently all in the Semitic Museum, Harvard, United States, and high-resolution images were taken from CDLI.[8] The database also includes two second generation tablets from the Šilwa-teššup archive and one (broken) second generation tablet from the British Museum (see **Appendix**). For this generation, 5,835 instances were collected.

For generation III, 5 tablets dated to Šurki-tilla, the son of Teḫip-tilla, were included in the database (see **Appendix**). These are also currently in the British Museum and photographs were taken in the tablet room by the author (see **Paragraph 5.3.1** for further comments). 422 instances were collected from these tablets. For generation IV, British museum tablets dated to Zike, the son of Šurki-tilla, were used – as well as Wištanzu, the wife of Zike, and possible brothers and sisters of Zike (13 tablets in total) (see **Appendix**). In addition, 16 tablets dated to Šilwa-Teššup, the son of Šarri, from the Harvard collection were included. These tablets are primarily (but not all) lists and catalogues and therefore less comparable to the legal and real-estate dealings of Tulpunnaya. They were added to cover as large a variety of genres as possible in the database, and they were selected based on quality of the tablet rather than full coverage of the archive. This resulted in 1,953 instances. Tablets from generation I and generation V are more elusive, but for the latter two tablets dated to Puḫi-šenni, the son of Zike, from the British Museum, were added as well (see **Appendix**). Only 154 instances were collected. As a result, the primary comparison in this chapter will be between Tulpunnaya, generation II, and Zike and Šilwa-teššup, generation IV. Transcriptions of the Harvard tablets were published in Pfeiffer (1942, HSS XIII) and Lacheman (1950, HSS XIV). Transcriptions and copies of the British Museum tablets can be found in Müller (1998).

5.3 Comparative Palaeography of Nuzi

5.3.1 *Note on the Old Copies*

Besides forming a contrast with contemporary script-groups, this chapter will also review Contenau's sign-list. Sometimes Contenau made judgements which are understandable only when studying the tablet from a different angle, or under different lighting. A few tablets were photographed from different angles at the British Museum to illustrate this. For example, Contenau drew the primary

8 The images presented in the joint database of the Semitic Museum (SM) at Harvard University and CDLI are freely available for scholarly use, including publication (personal communication March 2019).

form of ḪÉ (253) with a straight central horizontal, rather than broken horizontal. However, when the angle and lighting are adjusted, a broken horizontal appears in all recorded cases (**Table 5.1**). Another example is BAL (5). Contenau drew the sign with *Winkelhaken* attached to the horizontal, while in reality it is nearly always placed slightly below it (also see the following paragraph). The same applies to detecting spacing in signs like BA and NA (whether the horizontals are broken or not).

BAL (5)
Contenau's list shows two forms of BAL (**Table 5.2**). The first cannot be found anywhere in the database used here and the second has a central *Winkelhaken* which compares to Babylonian (BAL_{1b}). The variant which occurs most frequently however is one with a slightly lower *Winkelhaken* (BAL_{1a}). Since BAL was not recorded many times it was not possible to observe differences in scribal hand.

LI (85)
Contenau failed to record LI altogether. All instances collected from Nuzi in this database are a form with only *Winkelhaken*. It looks like the scribes of generation II may have had a preference for a more even 'ŠE' cluster of *Winkelhaken* (1a), and the scribes of generation IV preferred a triangular shape to the composition (1b) (**Table 5.3**). Since only one instance was recorded for both Nabu-naṣir and Sin-iqiša it is difficult to tell what the individual differences are; however, Urḫiya clearly preferred to impress LI with slightly flatter or longer wedges (**Table 5.4**).

TABLE 5.1 Nuzi signs photographed from different angles

Contenau	BM 26278, obverse, line 11	BM 26283, reverse, line 4
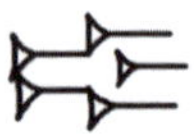		
Contenau	**BM 102355, reverse, line 3**	

Top ḪÉ (253), bottom BAL (5).

RU (111)

Contenau's list suggests three forms of RU, one with a vertical wedge followed by a second *Winkelhaken* and one with a vertical followed by a second diagonal, as well as one with a second *Winkelhaken* after two verticals at the very end of the composition (**Table 5.5**). This last form has not been found in the database created for this project. While there are several cases where it is difficult to see the second *Winkelhaken* at all (also see **Paragraph 4.4**), it is usually possible to detect it and it is unlikely that it was common at Nuzi to only impress one

TABLE 5.2 Nuzi BAL: comparison between generations

Generation II	Generation IV	Contenau
BAL$_{1a}$	BAL$_{1b}$	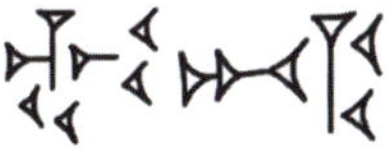

II (6 instances recorded): SMN 2044, obverse, line 11. IV (4 instances recorded): BM 102355, reverse, line 3.

TABLE 5.3 Nuzi LI: comparison between generations

Generation II	Generation IV	Contenau
LI$_{1a}$	LI$_{1b}$	–

II (39 instances recorded): SMN 2109, obverse, line 7. IV ZU (7 instances recorded): BM 26240, obverse, line 9.

TABLE 5.4 Nuzi LI: comparison between scribes

Nabu-naṣir	Sin-iqiša	Urḫiya			

NN: SMN 2044, reverse, line 4. **SI:** SMN 2045, obverse edge. **U:** SMN 2018, obverse, line 1; SMN 2023, obverse, line 8; SMN 2031, obverse, line 10.

as is typical for Babylonian. In addition, although more instances with clearly visible *Winkelhaken* were collected for generation IV, there is no striking difference between the generations. Finally, as Contenau hinted, there are many variants of RU at Nuzi. Most common are instances composed of W-v-W-v-v (RU$_{1a}$), alternatively with this second *Winkelhaken* obscured by the vertical (RU$_{1b}$). A form with three *Winkelhaken* is present too (RU$_{2}$). At Nuzi this form follows an order of W-v-W-v-W-v. Any form with two initial *Winkelhaken* seems absent from the Nuzi archives considered here. Variants with only two verticals, as indicated by Contenau, were not found either. As for individual hands: in Nabu-naṣir's instances the second *Winkelhaken* is obscured, in Urḫiya's instances this second *Winkelhaken* is either quite extended or a diagonal, and in Sin-iqiša's instances both *Winkelhaken* are extended or diagonals (**Table 5.6**). This is reminiscent of KBo 1.2, whose scribe also preferred to impress signs with diagonals (n.b. a connection is unlikely).

AK (*127*)

AK varies little across all corpora, and even between individual Nuzi scribes (**Table 5.8**). However, it is worth pointing out that Contenau recorded a version with an initial broken horizontal wedge (**Table 5.9**). It is possible to see how he reached this conclusion: some instances are highly condensed, and it

TABLE 5.5 Nuzi RU: comparison between generations

Generation II			**Contenau**
RU$_{1a}$	**RU$_{1b}$**	**RU$_{2}$**	

Generation IV			
RU$_{1a}$	**RU$_{1b}$**	**RU$_{2}$**	

II (57 instances recorded): HSS 13410, obverse, line 8, edge; SMN 2044, obverse, line 5; SMN 2017, reverse, line 15. IV (17 instances recorded): HSS 13480, reverse, line 6; VM 26240, obverse, line 7; BM 26283, reverse, line 3

is difficult to see where the initial horizontal ends, and the broken horizontal begins. However, these are all clearly variations of one primary form.

UM (238), DUB (242), and the Absence of KIŠIB (486)

As mentioned several times now, it is not always possible to distinguish the signs UM, DUB and KIŠIB (or MES) from one another. Contenau did not record UM or KIŠIB and his version of DUB cannot be found in the Nuzi

TABLE 5.6 Nuzi RU: comparison between scribes

Nabu-naṣir		**Sin-iqiša**			**Urḫiya**		

NN: SMN 2038, obverse, line 8; SMN 2044, obverse, line 5. **SI:** SMN 2043, obverse, line 12; SMN 2045, obverse, line 10; SMN 2206, obverse, line 5. **U:** SMN 2018, obverse, line 14; SMN 2023, reverse, line 4; SMN 2031, reverse, line 5.

TABLE 5.7 Nuzi AK: comparison between generations

Generation II		**Generation IV**	**Contenau**
AK$_1$		**AK$_1$**	
			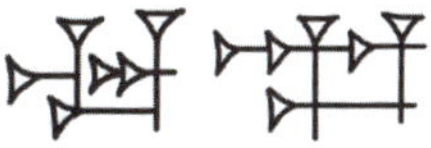

II (23 instances recorded): SMN 2021, obverse, line 11; SMN 2118, obverse, line 4. IV (7 instances recorded): HSS 13422, reverse, line 13.

TABLE 5.8 Nuzi AK: comparison between scribes

Nabu-naṣir		**Sin-iqiša**		**Urḫiya**

NN: SMN 2038, obverse edge; SMN 2044, obverse, line 10, edge. **SI:** SMN 2045, reverse, line 6; SMN 2206,reverse, line 7. **U:** SMN 2037, reverse, line 15.

documents under consideration. For UM and DUB a form with shorter verticals inside the horizontals and a form with verticals extended above the upper horizontal occur on the studied Nuzi tablets, demonstrated with particular clarity by the generation II tablets. Less instances were collected for generation IV, but DUB indicates that it is the case there too (**Table 5.9**). Nabu-naṣir uses extended or long verticals for UM as well as DUB, while Sin-iqiša and Urḫiya use small verticals.

The value MES (MIŠ, etc.) itself was not recorded from the Nuzi tablets considered here, only KIŠIB (seal). While KIŠIB can be described as a sign with extended verticals and three horizontal wedges – generally classified as 486 MES – this form does not occur on the Nuzi tablets included in the database. Instead, the value KIŠIB is composed identical to UM and DUB (see particularly Nabu-naṣir and Urḫiya, **Table 5.10**). From generation IV only one instance with the value KIŠIB was recorded, and this has small verticals 'boxed in' by four horizontals ('form 1') (**Figure 5.1**). There are a few tablets where it is possible the scribe used 'form 1' for UM and DUB and 'form 2' for KIŠIB – in particular SMN 2036 – but this could be co-incidental. As illustrated by the instances collected for Urḫiya wedges were not always placed in exactly the same position each and every time.

TABLE 5.9 Nuzi UM and DUB: comparison between generations

Generation II		**Generation IV**		**Contenau**
UM$_1$	**UM$_2$**	**UM$_1$**		
				–
DUB$_1$	**DUB$_2$**	**DUB$_1$**	**DUB$_2$**	

II **UM** (16 instances recorded): SMN 2028, obverse, line 14; SMN 2017, obverse, line 17. II **DUB** (38 instances recorded): SMN 2109, obverse edge; SMN 2021, obverse, line 17. II **KIŠIB** (52 instances recorded): SMN 1714, side; SMN 2254, reverse, line 2. IV **UM** (9 instances recorded): HSS 13422, obverse, line 16. IV **DUB** (4 instances recorded): BM 26283, reverse, line 3, edge; BM 26240, obverse, line 10.

TABLE 5.10 Nuzi UM, DUB and KIŠIB: comparison between scribes

	Nabu-naṣir	Sin-iqiša	Urḫiya
UM			
DUB	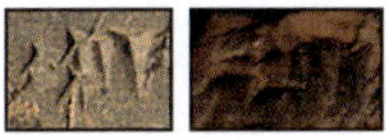		
KIŠIB		–	

NN UM: SMN 2044, obverse, line 15. **NN DUB**: SMN 2038, obverse edge; SMN 2044, obverse, line 1. **NN KIŠIB**: SMN 2044, side. **SI UM**: SMN 2206, side. **SI DUB**: SMN 2043, obverse edge; SMN 2045, obverse edge; SMN 2206, reverse, line 4. **U UM**: SMN 2037, obverse, line 16. **U DUB**: SMN 2018, reverse, line 2; SMN 2023, side; SMN 2031, obverse, line 1; SMN 2037, side. **U KIŠIB**: SMN 2018, reverse, line 4; SMN 2023, reverse, line 4; SMN 2031, reverse, line 10.

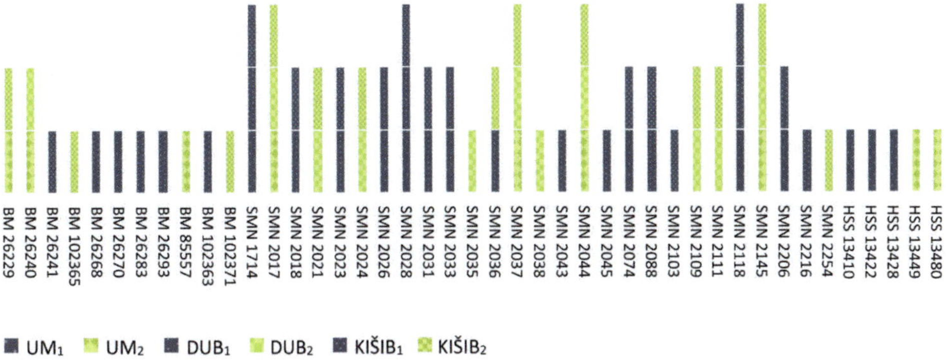

FIGURE 5.1 Comparison of Nuzi UM, DUB and KIŠIB
Tablets from Generation II, III, IV and V included in the figure. Note that nearly all scribes use identical forms for all sign values, with 'form 1' as the most common form overall.

5.3.2 *Differences between the Corpora*

BA (14), ZU (15) and SU (16)

From the archive of Teḫip-tilla, only BA was recorded, and only once, impressed with slightly diagonal top and bottom wedges and a small central horizontal, most comparable to Babylonian (BA_2) (**Table 5.11**). In the archive of Tulpunnaya, the signs are most commonly impressed with a broken horizontal (BA_1); for example, on both tablets written by Sin-iqiša (**Table 5.12**). The form with a more central impression occurs as well, but on fewer tablets. It is also important to consider the two instances shown for Urḫiya: the difference between broken horizontal and central horizontal is minimal in the instance from SMN 2031, line 15. This shows how essential it is to compare multiple instances, when trying to understand the way in which a certain scribe wrote. The handful of generation III instances recorded of ZU all have a central horizontal; as does the one instance of SU. For generation IV, the signs all have a separate rather than broken middle horizontal wedge – both in the archive of Zike and the archive of Šilwa-teššup. None of the signs were recorded from the two generation V tablets. Contenau only recorded the forms with small, separate middle horizontal impressions; and no diagonal upper or lower wedges.

KA (24)

No instances of KA were collected from generation II or V, but a few instances were collected from two generation III tablets (Šurki-tilla, and his wife Allai-turaḫe), with a broken horizontal (KA_1) (**Table 5.13**). For generation IV, some more instances were collected. In the archive of Šilwa-teššup the initial horizontal is also broken, but in the archive of Zike, the initial horizontal is followed by a (centred) *Winkelhaken* (KA_2). Contenau's list does not show the first form, and instead suggests a different one altogether, with a highly placed

TABLE 5.11 Nuzi BA and ZU: comparison between generations

Generation II		Generation IV	Contenau
BA_1	**BA_2**	**ZU_2**	

II **BA** (19 instances recorded): SMN 2206, obverse, line 9; HSS 13410, obverse edge. IV **ZU** (7 instances recorded): BM 26240, obverse, line 9.

TABLE 5.12 Nuzi BA and ZU: comparison between scribes

Nabu-naṣir	Sin-iqiša		Urḫiya	

NN: SMN 2038, obverse, line 16. **SI:** SMN 2043, obverse, line 5; SMN 2206, obverse, line 16. **U:** SMN 2031,obverse, line 15; SMN 2037, obverse, line 14.

TABLE 5.13 Nuzi KA: comparison between generations

Generation III	Generation IV		Contenau
KA_1	KA_1	KA_2	

III (3 instances recorded): BM 85607, obverse, line 4. IV (8 instances recorded): HSS 13409, obverse, line 7; BM 26240, obverse, line 9.

Winkelhaken followed by a horizontal. This was not recorded in the database created for this project. Since KA occurs on none of the tablets written by the three selected Tulpunnaya scribes it cannot be compared for individual differences.

DUMU (255)
Contenau did not demonstrate how far the horizontals cross through the vertical, which is a feature nearly all recorded instances of DUMU have (**Table 5.14**). He also does not show the differing length of the vertical; although it seems to be the general intention to impress it above the horizontals. He does however illustrate how the final two horizontal wedges can occur both behind and in front of the vertical. These two wedges are normally distinct at Nuzi. The individual scribes from generation II all place a lot of emphasis on the horizontals, nearly obscuring the vertical (**Table 5.15**). As with other signs, Nabu-naṣir's compositions are condensed and those of the other two scribes more extended.

TABLE 5.14 Nuzi DUMU: comparison between generations

Generation II		Generation IV		Contenau
DUMU$_{1a}$	DUMU$_{1b}$	DUMU$_{1a}$	DUMU$_{1b}$	

II (180 instances recorded): SMN 2045, obverse edge; SMN 2088, reverse, line 21. IV (43 instances recorded): HSS 14573, obverse, line 5; HSS 13409, obverse, line 5.

TABLE 5.15 Nuzi DUMU: comparison between scribes

Nabu-naṣir		Sin-iqiša			Urḫiya			

NN: SMN 2038, obverse, line 14; SMN 2044, obverse, line 3. **SI:** SMN 2043, obverse, line 12; SMN 2045, obverse, line 4; SMN 2206, obverse, line 1, edge. **U:** SMN 2018, obverse, line 4; SMN 2023, reverse, line 2; SMN 2031, obverse, line 9, edge; SMN 2037, reverse, line 15.

IN (261) and Similar Signs

At Nuzi these signs are always composed with a rectangular cluster of six (or more) *Winkelhaken*. There are a few instances where the *Winkelhaken* appear more like horizontals. However, as will be discussed for NA (**Paragraph 5.3.3**), at Nuzi this should probably be attributed to scribe and stylus rather than identifying a new sign-form (see Sin-iqiša, **Table 5.17**). Contenau also drew a ŠAR with a single bottom horizontal wedge, which was not found in the database used here (**Table 5.16**).

LUGAL (266) and LÚ (514)

As with some other signs, Contenau illustrated all forms of LUGAL and LÚ with diagonals. While some instances from the database resemble this (see generation IV, **Table 4.18**), mostly they are composed with obvious *Winkelhaken*. Otherwise, all suggestions made by Contenau are also attested in the corpora considered here: variation in number of verticals, and number

TABLE 5.16 Nuzi IN, ŠAR and SUM: comparison between generations

Generation II		Generation IV		Contenau
IN$_{1a}$	IN$_{1b}$	IN$_{1a}$		

ŠAR$_{1a}$	ŠAR$_{1b}$	ŠAR$_{1a}$	ŠAR$_{1b}$	

SUM$_{1a}$	SUM$_{1b}$	SUM		
		–		

II IN (11 instances recorded): SMN 2216, obverse, line 7; SMN 2103, obverse, line 11, edge. II ŠAR (41 instances recorded): SMN 2088, reverse, line 22; SMN 2036, obverse, line 15. II SUM (4 instances recorded): SMN 2033, obverse, line 10; SMN 2043, obverse, line 11. IV IN (4 instances recorded): HSS 13421, obverse, line 4. IV ŠAR (13 instances recorded): HSS 13422, obverse, line 14; HSS 13422, reverse, line 9.

and composition of *Winkelhaken*. The *Winkelhaken* are generally arranged in a cluster of three or a row of three.

IL (348)

IL is one of the few signs for which Contenau included many different forms, most of which can be found in the database created here as well. These include a form with a large central *Winkelhaken*, one with a small cluster of three to four *Winkelhaken*, one with a broken or diagonal row of *Winkelhaken*, one with an even, straight row of *Winkelhaken*, and one with verticals. There is certainly a lot more variation in this sign than in any of the other considered corpora as well as completely different forms. As demonstrated by the individual scribes, a range of forms was used at the same time; Sin-iqiša used a form with verticals, while the other two use the small clusters (**Table 5.19**). The 'straighter'

TABLE 5.17 Nuzi IN, ŠAR and SUM: comparison between scribes

	Nabu-naṣir	Sin-iqiša	Urḫiya
IN			–
ŠAR	 	  	  
SUM			

NN IN: SMN 2044, obverse, line 8, edge. **NN ŠAR**: SMN 2038, obverse edge; SMN 2044, obverse, line 10. **NN SUM**: SMN 2038, obverse, line 4. **SI IN**: SMN 2043, obverse, line 17. **SI ŠAR**: SMN 2043, obverse edge; SMN 2045, reverse, line 2; SMN 2206, obverse, line 10. **SI SUM**: SMN 2043, obverse, line 11. **U ŠAR**: SMN 2018, obverse, line 6; SMN 2023, side; SMN 2037, side. **U SUM**: SMN 2037, obverse, line 11.

TABLE 5.18 Nuzi LUGAL and LÚ: comparison between generations

Generation II		Generation IV		Contenau
LUGAL$_{1a}$	LUGAL$_{1b}$	LUGAL$_{1a}$		

LÚ$_{1a}$	LÚ$_{1b}$	LÚ$_{1a}$	LÚ$_{1b}$	

II LUGAL (16 instances recorded): SMN 2109, obverse, line 2; SMN 2017, obverse, line 14. **II LÚ** (24 instances recorded): SMN 1714, obverse, line 8; SMN 2028, obverse, line 19, edge (continued on reverse). **IV LUGAL** (6 instances recorded): HSS 13441, side. **IV LÚ** (10 instances recorded): HSS 13409, obverse, line 13; HSS 13422, obverse, line 6.

TABLE 5.19 Nuzi IL: comparison between generations

Generation II				Contenau
IL$_1$		IL$_2$		
				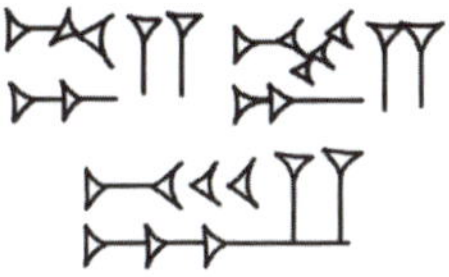
Generation IV				
IL$_3$	IL$_4$	IL$_5$		

II (27 instances recorded): SMN 2088, reverse, line 12; SMN 2037, reverse, line 8; SMN 1714, obverse, line 8; SMN 2109, reverse, line 3. IV (21 instances recorded): HSS 13422, obverse, line 2; HSS 13472, reverse, line 1; HSS 13409, obverse, line 12.

TABLE 5.20 Nuzi IL: comparison between scribes

Nabu-naṣir	Sin-iqiša	Urḫiya		

NN: SMN 2038, obverse, line 6. **SI**: SMN 2206, obverse edge. **U**: SMN 2023, obverse, line 8; SMN 2031, reverse, line 4; SMN 2037, reverse, line 8.

forms are absent from generation II at Nuzi and seem limited to the archive of Šilwa-teššup (**Table 5.20**).

ḪI (631) and Similar Signs

ḪI and some signs with a 'ḪI' element clearly stand out at Nuzi. ḪI is often impressed with more than three initial wedges, at varying uncommon angles

(**Table 5.21**). In addition, the final bottom wedge, which is normally cause of the triangular shape of the sign, is sometimes added into the sequence of initial wedges. Contenau made no note of this whatsoever. In other corpora (**Chapter 3, Chapter 4**), the way ḪI is impressed is also reflected in other signs, such as AḪ and AM. At Nuzi some of this can be seen, but generally these signs are composed with a more 'regular' triangular ḪI element. This is particularly

TABLE 5.21 Nuzi ḪI: comparison between generations

Generation II			**Generation IV**		**Contenau**
ḪI$_{1a}$	**ḪI**$_{2}$	**ḪI**$_{3}$	**ḪI**$_{1b}$	**ḪI**$_{2}$	
				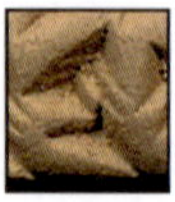	
AḪ$_{1}$		**AḪ**$_{2}$	**AḪ**$_{3}$		
					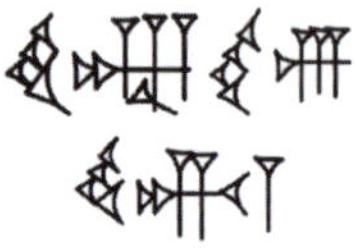
IM$_{2}$		**IM**$_{3}$	**IM**$_{2}$		

AM$_{2}$		**AM**$_{3}$	**AM**$_{2}$		
			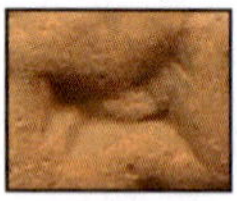		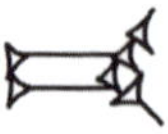

II **ḪI** (47 instances recorded): SMN 2043, obverse, line 9, edge; HSS 13438, obverse, line 12; SMN 2023, side. II **AḪ** (9 instances recorded): SMN 2045, obverse edge; SMN 2017, reverse, line 15. II **IM** (20 instances recorded): SMN 2036, obverse, line 11; SMN 2017, obverse, line 10. II **AM** (19 instances recorded): SMN 2109, obverse, line 3; SMN 2017, reverse, line 19. IV **ḪI** (9 instances recorded): BM 26240, reverse, line 1; HSS 13451, obverse edge. IV **AḪ** (3 instances recorded): BM 102352, obverse, line 10. IV **IM** (4 instances recorded): BM 26240, obverse, line 6. IV **AM** (2 instances recorded): BM 85557, obverse, line 6.

obvious when looking at the individual scribes (**Table 5.22**). While the expectation might be that a scribe would impress this element similarly in different sign compositions, in reality this is not the case. Urḫiya's signs all show a degree of difference; while one instance of ḪI and the instance of AM consist of multiple angled *Winkelhaken*, the other signs have more triangular clusters. In Sin-iqiša's signs the ḪI element is more consistent, but impressed with less wedges when part of other signs. If anything, this degree of variation illustrates the less standardised style of writing at Nuzi.

In this collection of signs, AḪ stands out as well. Contenau recorded two forms with an additional *Winkelhaken* inbetween the verticals. Although it was difficult to find an example as clear as the illustration, it does occur (see e.g. SMN 2017, **Table 5.21**).

Contenau did not record GI (141), which is why it is especially important to include it here. This is likewise a sign with a ḪI element, which occurs with varying wedges and angles. Matching the other instances, Nabu-naṣir impresses the sign with a more triangular element, while Urḫiya impresses it with the flatter and more even sequence of *Winkelhaken* (**Table 5.24**).

TABLE 5.22 Nuzi ḪI: comparison between scribes

	Nabu-naṣir	Sin-iqiša	Urḫiya
ḪI	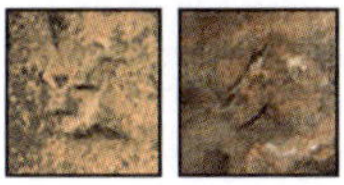	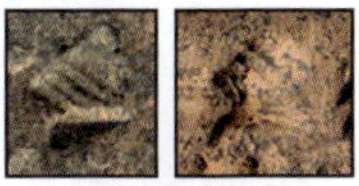	
AḪ	n/a		
IM			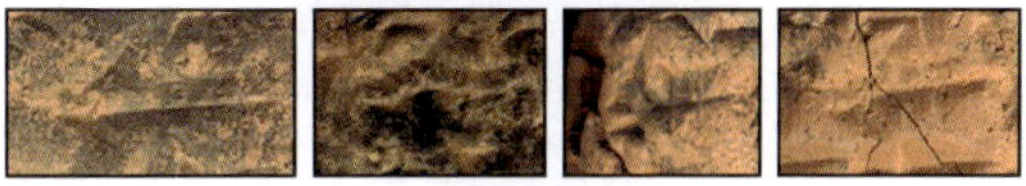
AM	n/a		

NN ḪI: SMN 2038, obverse, line 10; SMN 2044, obverse, line 7, edge. **NN IM:** SMN 2044, obverse, line 6, edge. **SI ḪI:** SMN 2043, obverse, line 9, edge; SMN 2206, obverse edge. **SI AḪ:** SMN 2045, obverse edge. **SI IM:** SMN 2045, obverse, line 7. **SI AM:** SMN 2045, obverse edge. **U ḪI:** SMN 2018, obverse edge; SMN 2023, side; SMN 2037, reverse, line 8. **U AḪ:** SMN 2023, obverse, line 3; SMN 2037, reverse, line 8. **U IM:** SMN 2018, obverse, line 7; SMN 2023, obverse, line 5; SMN 2031, obverse, line 6, edge; SMN 2037, obverse, line 18. **U AM:** SMN 2018, obverse, line 9.

TABLE 5.23 Nuzi QA: co.mparison between scribes

Nabu-naṣir	Sin-iqiša	Urḫiya

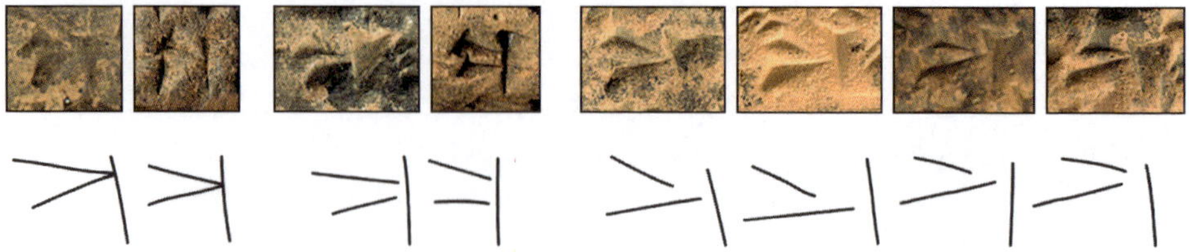

NN: SMN 2038, obverse, line 19; SMN 2044, obverse edge. SI: SMN 2043, obverse, line 12; SMN 2045, obverse edge; SMN 2206, obverse, line 10. U: SMN 2018, obverse, line 17; SMN 2023, reverse, line 5; SMN 2031, obverse, line 8; SMN 2037, obverse, line 14. The lines were drawn at the visibly deepest point of the wedges, as the CuneiformAnalyser would do.

TABLE 5.24 Nuzi comparison between scribes

Nabu-naṣir	Sin-iqiša	Urḫiya

NN: SMN 2038, obverse, line 12; SMN 2044, side. SI: SMN 2206, obverse, line 5, second instance. U: SMN 2018, obverse edge; SMN 2023, obverse, line 16; SMN 2031, obverse, line 10.

MEŠ (754)
Contenau only illustrated Nuzi MEŠ with an initial horizontal. This version does occur; particularly in the archive of Tulpunnaya, although the horizontal is impressed into the vertical. However, forms with only *Winkelhaken*, detached from the vertical, are more common in the corpora included here. The number of *Winkelhaken* recorded varies between five and two (**Table 5.25**). MEŠ is one the few signs where, in the database compiled here, there is a difference between generation II and IV. At the same time, the signs differ little between the individual generation II scribes (**Table 5.26**).

5.3.3 *Differences between Scribes*

QA (99) and NA (110)
Forms of QA very rarely differ between any script-group. However, as discussed in **Paragraph 3.3.4**, the angle can vary between scribes. At Nuzi this can be

TABLE 5.25 Nuzi MEŠ: comparison between generations

Generation II				Contenau
MEŠ$_{1a}$	MEŠ$_{1b}$	MEŠ$_{2a}$	MEŠ$_{2b}$	

Generation IV				
MEŠ$_{2a}$		MEŠ$_{2b}$		

II (81 instances recorded): SMN 2023, obverse, line 15; SMN 2017, obverse, line 10, second instance; HSS 13438, obverse, line 13; SMN 2145, obverse, line 7. IV (47 instances recorded): HSS 14508, obverse, line 3; HSS 13381, obverse, line 5; HSS 13094, obverse, line 13.

TABLE 5.26 Nuzi MEŠ: comparison between scribes

Nabu-naṣir	Sin-iqiša	Urḫiya
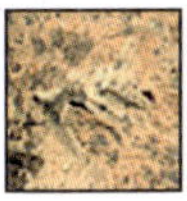 		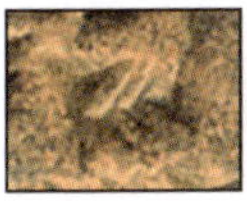   

NN: SMN 2038, obverse, line 6, edge; SMN 2044, obverse, line 9. **SI:** SMN 2045, obverse, line 8. **U:** SMN 2018, obverse, line 9; SMN 2023, obverse, line 9 SMN 2031, obverse, line 7; SMN 2037, obverse, line 12.

measured as well (**Table 5.23**). The angle on Nabu-naṣir's and Urḫiya's QA is circa 30°, while on Sin-iqiša's QA the angle is 20°. In addition, Urḫiya, as has already been seen in signs such as LI, created comparatively longer wedges and 'flatter' compositions. Here also with an upper wedge which is often shorter than the lower wedge (whereas with the other two scribes this is the other way around).

The same can be said for NA (**Table 5.27**). Several images show that the collected instances are all variants rather than forms. By switching the angle of the stylus slightly, the horizontals can become *Winkelhaken* (or vice versa) and by placing the initial impression slightly higher (or upper impression slightly lower) it can become a broken horizontal. It is necessary to study several instances per scribe or tablet for this to be clear; for example, on SMN 2038 some instances are much more obvious than others. All variants also occur on the generation III and V tablets included; however, the instances with straight horizontals are most common for generation II. **Table 5.28** shows how these are specific to scribal hand: Nabu-naṣir is one of the few scribes to impress NA with *Winkelhaken*; Sin-iqiša shows that impressing the wedges closer together can result in the horizontal appearing broken; while Urḫiya preferred to place the wedges further apart. That said, NA is also one of the most distinctly different signs in the Nuzi corpus, because, regardless of shape or angle, the final horizontal or *Winkelhaken* is generally impressed below the initial horizontal.

TABLE 5.27 Nuzi NA: comparison between generations

Generation II		**Generation IV**		**Contenau**
NA$_1$	**NA$_2$**	**NA$_1$**	**NA$_2$**	

II (242 instances recorded): SMN 2017, obverse, line 3; SMN 2038, obverse edge. IV (41 instances recorded): HSS 13411, obverse, line 9; BM 26283, obverse, line 5.

TABLE 5.28 Nuzi NA: comparison between scribes

Nabu-naṣir		**Sin-iqiša**			**Urḫiya**			

NN: SMN 2038, obverse, line 3; SMN 2044, obverse, line 3. **SI:** SMN 2043, obverse, line 10; SMN 2045, obverse, line 6; SMN 2206, obverse, line 17. **U:** SMN 2018, obverse, line 6; SMN 2023, obverse, line 11; SMN 2031, obverse, line 15; SMN 2037, obverse, line 8.

NU (112)

Like QA and NA, NU shows how much variation can exist between individual scribes (NU$_{1a}$, NU$_{1b}$) (**Table 5.29, Table 5.30**), rather than script-groups. Some scribes (e.g. Tilammu, SMN 2017) impress the diagonal and horizontal lines into one another (instead of crossing more clearly) (NU$_{2}$). Since these instances are repeated in all cases (e.g. SMN 2017, obverse line 1 as well as 2) this variation cannot be attributed to an accidentally high impression of the diagonal, or a mistake.

TI (118)

Nuzi TI is an excellent example of the fine line between 'short' and 'long' forms which differ clearly in Assyro-Mittanian and Early Middle Assyrian. Comparing the way in which Urḫiya impresses TI across all his tablets shows that placing the bottom wedge higher up can be accidental (**Table 5.31**). Taking this into consideration, the third instance shown for generation II and IV (**Table 5.32**) is not so clearly different. However, the reason these can still be

TABLE 5.29 Nuzi NU: comparison between generations

Generation II			Generation IV		Contenau
NU$_{1a}$	NU$_{1b}$	NU$_{2}$	NU$_{1a}$	NU$_{2}$	
					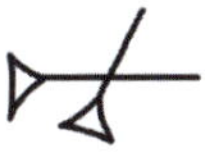

II (57 instances recorded): SMN 2028, obverse, line 14; SMN 2088 obverse, line 7; SMN 2017, obverse, line 2. IV (28 instances recorded): HSS 13475, obverse, line 4, edge; HSS 13499, obverse, line 9.

TABLE 5.30 Nuzi NU: comparison between scribes

Nabu-naṣir	Sin-iqiša		Urḫiya	
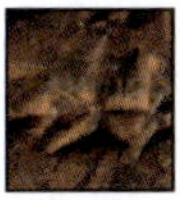		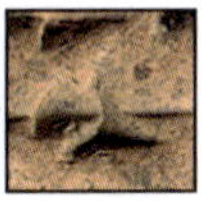		

NN: SMN 2044, reverse, line 4. SI: SN 2045, obverse, line 5, edge; SMN 2206, obverse, line 11. U: SMN 2031, obverse, line 20; SMN 2037, reverse, line 15.

TABLE 5.31 Nuzi TI: comparison between generations

Generation II			Generation IV			Contenau
TI$_{1a}$	TI$_{1b}$	TI$_{2}$	TI$_{1a}$	TI$_{1b}$	TI$_{2}$	
						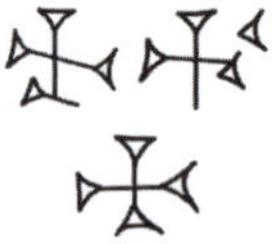

II (117 instances recorded): SMN 2103, obverse, line 15; SMN 2028, obverse, line 27, edge; SMN 2037, obverse, line 9. IV (30 instances recorded): BM 94448, obverse, line 4; HSS 13441, reverse, line 11; BM 26278, obverse, line 9, second instance.

TABLE 5.32 Nuzi TI: comparison between scribes

Nabu-naṣir		Sin-iqiša			Urḫiya			

NN: SMN 2038, obverse, line 14; SMN 2044, obverse, line 5. **SI:** SMN 2043, reverse, line 2; SMN 2045, obverse, line 5, edge; SMN 2206, obverse, line 3. **U:** SMN 2018, obverse, line 2; SMN 2023, obverse, line 3; SMN 2031, obverse, line 1; SMN 2037, obverse, line 9.

considered different forms is the differences in scribal hand. From the other instances it is clear that Urḫiya normally impresses this wedge lower down. In addition, while Nabu-naṣir prefers a horizontal bottom wedge, Sin-iqiša opts for a *Winkelhaken*. Contenau did not record the 'long' form, and instead draws one with two final *Winkelhaken* which is not attested anywhere in the database compiled for this project.

RI (*142*)

Contenau included one form of RI, with a diagonal wedge. Although there is some variation in the way the second wedge is impressed, this is not the most common version found in this Nuzi database. However, individual scribes illustrate how much this can differ per person. Sin-iqiša tends to impress the wedge before or through the second vertical, and Urḫiya extends it into a horizontal (**Table 5.33**). All three scribes impress the final vertical relatively evenly, at the same size as the other verticals.

TABLE 5.33 Nuzi RI: comparison between scribes

Nabu-naṣir		Sin-iqiša		Urḫiya		

NN: SMN 2038, obverse, line 11, second instance; SMN 2044, obverse edge. **SI:** SMN 2043, obverse, line 1; SMN 2045, reverse edge. **U:** SMN 2018, obverse, line 10; SMN 2031, obverse, line 11; SMN 2037, reverse, line 14.

TABLE 5.34 Nuzi TA and ŠA: comparison between generations

Generation II		Generation IV	Contenau
TA$_{1a}$	TA$_{1b}$	TA$_{1a}$	

ŠA$_{1a}$	ŠA$_{1c}$	ŠA$_{1b}$	

II **TA** (101 instances recorded): HSS 13410, reverse, line 4; SMN 2033, reverse, line 6. IV **TA** (36 instances recorded): HSS 13497, obverse, line 5. II **ŠA** (102 instances recorded): HSS 13438, obverse, line 18; SMN 2033, reverse, line 5. IV **ŠA** (57 instances recorded): HSS 14573, obverse, line 4.

TA (248) and ŠA (566)

Contenau had a preference to illustrate both TA and ŠA with small or low initial verticals, possibly because this was more common in Babylonian. This is much less obvious when studying photographs or scans of the Nuzi tablets however. In some cases, the verticals in TA indeed occur like this (TA$_{1b}$, **Table 5.34**), but not in most.

The verticals of both TA and ŠA are spaced apart. Occasionally the *Winkelhaken* are less clear because they are impressed into the verticals, but they never vanish altogether. Differences between individual scribes are centred on the shape of the wedges and number of horizontals. Nabu-naṣir's signs are more condensed with obvious *Winkelhaken*, whereas Sin-iqiša and Urḫiya extend the wedges more and they become horizontally shaped. In addition, Urḫiya is one of the scribes who impressed slightly shorter verticals. In Urḫiya's ŠA on SMN 2031 (**Table 5.35**) it is also possible to see why Contenau would illustrate the signs with diagonals rather than *Winkelhaken* or horizontals.

NA4 (385)
Like IL, Nuzi NA_4 also in some cases has additional verticals (**Table 5.36**). Contenau's list further suggests the final vertical is not always broken, but it is possible this is down to the lighting in the images, or, when studying the tablets in person, the angle (see **Paragraph 5.3.1**). The movement of the *Winkelhaken* is not a trick of the light however. As illustrated by the individual scribes, there were a lot of unique variants of this sign at Nuzi; for example, while Sin-iqiša places the *Winkelhaken* more horizontally, Urḫiya's occur at an angle (**Table 5.37**).

MUNUS (883)
Of course, the sign MUNUS (*sinništu*, woman) is abundant in the Tulpunnaya archive, which allows for detailed comparison. There are not any different forms between the various corpora considered in this project thus far, or between generation II and IV (**Table 5.38**). However, the placement of wedges around

TABLE 5.35 Nuzi TA and ŠA: comparison between scribes

	Nabu-naṣir	Sin-iqiša	Urḫiya
TA	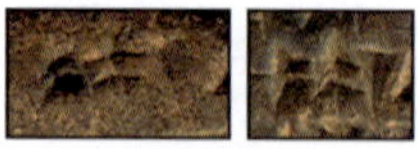		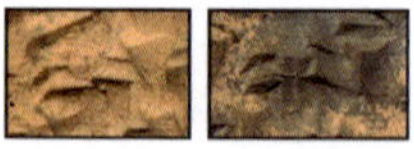
ŠA			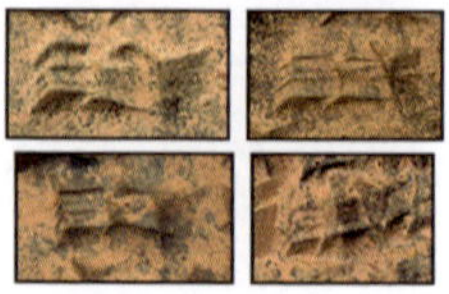

NN TA: SMN 2038, reverse, line 1; SMN 2044, obverse edge. **SI TA:** SMN 2043, obverse, line 8; SMN 2045, obverse, line 3. **U TA:** SMN 2023, reverse, line 1; SMN 2031, obverse, line 15. **NN ŠA:** SMN 2044, obverse, line 7. **SI ŠA:** SMN 2043, obverse, line 5; SMN 2045, obverse, line 1; SMN 2206, reverse, line 1. **U ŠA:** SMN 2018, obverse, line 12; SMN 2023, obverse, line 13, second instance; SMN 2031, obverse, line 11; SMN 2037, obverse, line 15.

TABLE 5.36 Nuzi NA4: comparison between generations

Generation II	Generation IV		Contenau
NA_{4-1}	NA_{4-1}	NA_{4-2}	
	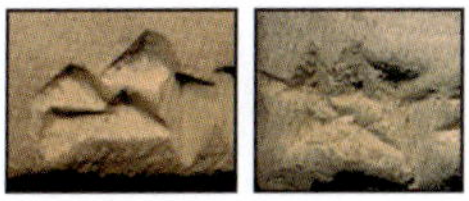		

II (88 instances recorded): SMN 2028, side; SMN 1714, side. IV (27 instances recorded): HSS 14506, reverse, line 6; HSS 14573, reverse, line 1; HSS 13409, reverse, line 4.

TABLE 5.37 Nuzi NA4: comparison between scribes

Nabu-naṣir	Sin-iqiša	Urḫiya
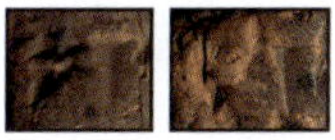		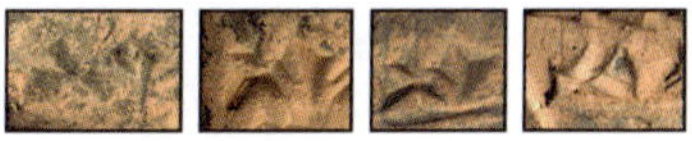

NN: SMN 2038, reverse, line 2; SMN 2044, side. **SI:** SMN 2043, reverse, line 3; SMN 2045, reverse, line 10; SMN 2206, side. **U:** SMN 2018, side; SMN 2023, reverse, line 6; SMN 2031, reverse, line 9; SMN 2037, side.

TABLE 5.38 Nuzi MUNUS: comparison between generations

Generation II		Generation IV		Contenau
$MUNUS_{1a}$	$MUNUS_{1b}$	$MUNUS_{1a}$	$MUNUS_{1b}$	

II (108 instances recorded): SMN 2088, obverse, line 14; SMN 2023, obverse, line 4; SMN 2028, obverse, line 16; SMN 2038, obverse, line 5. IV (18 instances recorded): HSS 14508, obverse, line 4; HSS 14506, obverse, line 4.

TABLE 5.39 Nuzi MUNUS: comparison between scribes

Nabu-naṣir	**Sin-iqiša**	**Urḫiya**
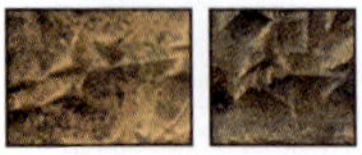		

NN: SMN 2038, obverse, line 5; SMN 2044, obverse, line 12. **SI:** SMN 2045, obverse, line 1; SMN 2043, obverse, line 7: SMN 2206, obverse, line 7. **U:** SMN 2018, obverse, line 9; SMN 2023, obverse, line 11; SMN 2031, obverse, line 8; SMN 2037, obverse, line 20.

the vertical differs strongly between scribes. For example, Nabu-naṣir consistently impressed the *Winkelhaken* before the vertical, while Urḫiya crossed them through the vertical, and Sin-iqiša composed the sign with three more even and 'flat' impressions (**Table 5.39**). Contenau made no note of this kind of variation. In fact, the variant he illustrated is relatively rare in the database created for this project, as the bottom and upper *Winkelhaken* generally align.

5.4 Comments

5.4.1 *Summary*

Because of the extent of individual differences between scribes, the ways in which to recognise Nuzi script differ slightly from the previous two chapters. On one hand, it is recognisable by the degree of variation; on the other hand, the degree of variation makes it more difficult to pin down when found in isolation. In addition, as emphasised, this list is based on a limited corpus and should be considered a step forward rather than definitive. Nevertheless, some characteristics are:

- BA (14) and similar signs are often impressed with diagonally angled wedges, or with the central wedge placed high up in the composition, making the initial wedge appear broken.
- LI (85) occurs without horizontal wedges.
- RU (111) can occur with three *Winkelhaken*, but in the order W-v-W-v-W-v. Most common however is a version with two *Winkelhaken* (W-v-W-v-v). The sign does not seem to occur with only one or two initial *Winkelhaken*.
- KA (24) was not recorded many times, but generally it occurs with an initial horizontal, either broken, or followed by a *Winkelhaken*. This *Winkelhaken* can also be impressed more centrally between the horizontals.
- NA (110) most commonly occurs with a horizontal followed by another two horizontals (one above, one below), or a horizontal followed by two

Winkelhaken (clearly one above, one below). The sign very rarely occurs with a horizontal followed by a *Winkelhaken* and another *Winkelhaken* above it.
- TI (118) is difficult to distinguish at Nuzi, because the density of the script means the 'short' and 'long' forms can look very similar. However, it is clear that most scribes had a preference for the 'short' form; and if it is 'long', it has four rather than five wedges.
- ḪI (631) is found impressed at a variety of uncommon angles, with more than four impressions. The 'standard' form of ḪI impressed as a triangle with four wedges is not absent from the corpus however. Signs with ḪI elements are less likely to be impressed at different angles, although this does occur.
- At least five different forms of IL (348) were attested from the data collected here. These are a form with a large central *Winkelhaken*, one with a small cluster of three or four *Winkelhaken*, one with a broken or diagonal row of *Winkelhaken*, one with an even, straight row of *Winkelhaken*, and one with verticals.
- MEŠ (754) occurs with a sequence of *Winkelhaken* or horizontal impressions, as well as with a horizontal wedge pressed into the vertical, which is then followed by *Winkelhaken*.

5.4.2 *Individual Scribal Hands*

Based on the analysis in this chapter it is possible to describe three clearly separate and identifiable scribal hands (**Table 5.40**). Illustrating how and how strongly variations in the signs may occur has helped with establishing differences between the broader script-groups (see **Paragraph 6.2.1**). For instance, Nabu-naṣir creates quite sharp wedges and therefore many of his signs feature very clear *Winkelhaken*. Good examples are the way in which he impresses ŠAR and NA. Sin-iqiša on the other hand extends the wedges much more, into flat horizontals. In MUNUS, for instance, the two *Winkelhaken* and the horizontal are equal and can barely be distinguished from one another. Urḫiya likewise impressed straighter wedges, but not so flat that *Winkelhaken* become horizontals; in ŠAR it is, for example, still possible to tell the difference. Urḫiya is also the scribe for which most tablets were available and therefore naturally shows the most variation in writing. He does not consistently impress ḪI the same way across all tablets and signs, signifying how much less standardised even individual scribal hands were at Nuzi.

The only signs which were found to differ slightly between the generation II and IV tablets considered here are MEŠ, BAL, LI, NA, IL, LÚ, and NA_4; however, nearly all forms or variants overlap between the generations and from the limited number of tablets studied it is also unclear how much difference should be attributed to the generation, how much to the scribal family and how much to the archive. The NA_4 with two additional central verticals has

TABLE 5.40 Comparison between Nuzi scribal hands

Value	Nabu-naṣir	Sin-iqiša	Urḫiya
LI			
BA			
DUMU			
ŠAR			
SUM			
ḪI			
IM			
IL			
MEŠ			
QA			
NA			
TI			
RI			
TA			
ŠA			
MUNUS			

been attested for both Zike (son of Šurki-tilla) and Šilwa-teššup (son of Šarri); but this is the only sign which in the present database occurs consistently for generation IV only. Two instances of NA_4 were collected for generation V as well (Puḫi-šenni son of Zike), both without verticals; so even in the event that, theorethically, the form with verticals became more prominent, it continued to overlap, also within the same family.

5.4.3 *Historical Background*

Whereas the era of the Nuzi tablets has been a popular topic of discussion, the stratigraphy of Yorghan Tepe goes much deeper. During the Early Dynastic period (late 3rd millennium BCE) a city named Gasur existed in the same location. Around 220 Old Akkadian documents have been found there, recording agricultural activity and land management (Foster 1982: 39). The names in these documents are primarily Akkadian; some Sumerian; apparently no Hurrian (Gelb 1944: 7). While the Hurrians were present in the region (Astour 1987: 17), they did not materialise at Yorghan Tepe until much later (the details of which are unclear). The Hurrians then take over the site and are the ones to re-name it Nuzi.[9]

Nuzi maintained close connections with settlements south of the Lower Zab and east of the Tigris (Postgate 2013: 343), and there is evidence in the archives for well-established families with Kassite names as well as pure Babylonian names (Postgate 2013: 347). As mentioned in **Paragraph 5.1.2**, it has been suggested that the earliest scribes of Nuzi were in fact of Babylonian origin (also see Negri Scafa 1999: 68). Considering the size of Nuzi relative to Aššur (small) and the amount of documents found there (large), the tablets are a "fairly representative sample" of written culture (Postgate 2013: 370). By the contents of the documents it seems likely most towns had resident scribes in addition to scribes who travelled around Arrapḫa, suggesting a dense and uniform scribal culture (Postgate 2013: 372). In addition, the Mittani state preferred to rule indirectly, its territory consisting of vassals and provinces, with different Kings, councils, and institutions (Düring 2015: 301). It is therefore not surprising that writing at Nuzi differed from its Mittanian overlord and bears more similarity to its Babylonian precedent (see **Chapter 6** for comparative comments). Most of the documents relate to the internal economy of Nuzi, rather than affairs of state or international diplomacy, which perhaps explains the development of Nuzi's own tradition as opposed to being a subject to strong Mittanian (or Assyrian) influence.

9 See *The Routledge Handbook of the Peoples and Places of Ancient Western Asia* (2009: 68) for a concise overview of the history of the Kingdom of Arrapḫa as a whole.

A few Old Assyrian tablets have been found at Nuzi (see for instance Owen 1995: 65), and at least in the two generations before its downfall Nuzi maintained normal diplomatic and commercial relations with Aššur (Maidman 2011: 210). Approaching Aššur from Nuzi, more Assyrian influence becomes evident, and in the bordering towns 10–20% Akkadian names can be found (Müller 1999: 85). Linguistically, Nuzi texts show evidence of Old and Middle Babylonian features, as well as Middle Assyrian (Negri Scafa 1999: 70). However, some time during the 14th century Aššur launches a (possibly unexpected) attack on the Arrapḫan town of Turša. Mittani sends help (Maidman 2011: 215), but eventually Arrapḫa is annihilated. Arrapḫa apparently did not try to compete with Aššur's international ambitions; it only controlled a small area; and it was economically successful. In theory, it could have been incorporated into the new Assyrian Empire as a useful and supportive vassal. However, clearly, the Arrapḫans were loyal to Mittani; and, apparently, amidst its attempt to overthrow its Mittani overlord combined with its large-scale international ambitions, Assyria had no desire to preserve Nuzi.

5.5 Introduction to Tigunanum

As hinted in the previous paragraph, having considered various contemporary archives, it is necessary to take a small step back into history. Standardisation is a process and Mittanian writing was not invented instantaneously. Then, where (and who) did it come from? This is a complicated question with, currently, no clear answer; particularly because it concerns a period (the 17th–15th centuries BCE) about which comparatively little is known and from which very few tablets are available for study.

Recently, more and more scholars have been turning to Tigunanum (also Tikunani or Tikunan) to find answers. The exact location of the circa 17th–16th century BCE (city-)state is still unknown, but based on the places mentioned in the texts – such as Niḫriya, Ḫaḫḫum, Zalba(r) and Ašnakkum (which can all potentially be identified with sites in the upper Balikh area) – it would have been on an Assyrian trade-route somewhere (north-)east of the Euphrates, on the Tigris (Salvini 1996: 12; Miller 2001: 419; Charpin 2006: 225; George 2017: 99).[10] This corresponds to the western territory of the later Mittani Empire (see **Maps**). In fact, Miller (2001: 424) suggests it is possible that the Mittani entity already existed at this time but had not yet expanded northward. Tigunanum's currently only known King was Tunip-Teššup, who was, as follows from the

10 For discussions on many of the specific ancient cities and their potential locations, see *A Historical Geography of Anatolia in the Old Assyrian Colony Period* by Barjamovic (2011).

documents, a contemporary of Ḫattušili I of the Hittites. Since Tunip-Teššup is a Hurrian name, several of the tablets contain Hurrian names, and at least one document was written entirely in Hurrian, it is possible that Tigunanum was a Hurro-Akkadian political predecessor of Mittani (Salvini 1996: 13).[11]

5.6 The Tigunanum Corpus

Comparable to the Mittani corpus, currently less than fourty tablets from Tigunanum have been published. However, to complicate matters further, these are all in private collections, which means that few are personally accessible and only around a dozen photographs are widely available at the time of writing. As with Mittanian, this means that any statements on the palaeography of Tigunanum must be made with caution; however, playing the waiting game until more tablets surface should not be used as an excuse to avoid investigation at present.

In 1996 Salvini published four documents from Tigunanum (see **Appendix**). To begin with, this includes a prism listing the personnel of King Tunip-Teššup. The datation formula is Babylonian, while two officers are named according to the Assyrian *līmu* system. The names of the workers are divided into three groups, each headed by an overseer which Salvini connects to the later Assyrian *rab ešerte* and Nuzian *emantuḫlu* (1996: 9). Next in line is an Akkadian letter sent by Labarna (Ḫattušili I) to his vassal Tuniya (Tunip-Teššup) asking for help with a military operation (also see Salvini 1994). On their relationship, Ḫattušili writes "you are my servant, protect me <…> and I will protect you" (obverse, lines 4 and 5), indicating that if Tigunanum was not a vassal then at least it ought to act like one (Hoffner 2009: 76; Miller 2001: 424). The salutation is also typically found in Mari letters (Durand & Charpin 2006: 221), and at the same time the tablet does not have any lines dividing between paragraphs as would have been found in later Hittite letters (Hoffner 2009: 75). Salvini's publication also discusses a tablet containing anomalous canine birth omens, which says "the Ḫabiru will be there" (obverse, line 7). Salvini comments that the grammar and language used are Old Babylonian, but there are also "elements of Old Assyrian grammar" and "traces of a peripheral syllabary" (1996: 117). Finally, Salvini identifies a fragmentary Hurrian document. It talks of a "Kuzzi" (obverse, line 5), a name also found at Mari, Alalaḫ and Nuzi; and Salvini thinks he recognises a word which reminds of Šubartum (reverse, line 12) (1996: 126).

11 For further discussion see Freu 2007: 92 and Miller 2001: 422.

On the palaeography of the documents, Salvini states that the texts were written "towards the end of the Old Babylonian period" (1996: 9). He identifies 109 signs from the prism, versus 87 signs from the letter, with 15 sign-forms differing. This suggests that the tablets were composed in the same period or sphere of influence but by different scribes (*ibid*). Salvini's sign-list is accurate and refers to the locations on the tablets the copies were based on. It is an excellent reference guide, and rather than suggesting corrections, as was done for Nuzi, it will be used to accompany the analysis below. Close-up black and white photographs and transcriptions of these four texts, as well as the comparative sign-list can all be found in Salvini 1996.

Joining these documents are a number of tablets published from the Schøyen Collection (CUSAS 12, 18 and 34 thus far). These were recognised as "tablets that do not derive from Babylonia but belong together as products of a palace scriptorium in the far north of Mesopotamia" (George 2013: 101). CUSAS 12, 3.3.4, or MS 2798, is a bilingual Sumerian and Hurrian fragment, which Civil originally identified as "the first of its kind" and "Middle Babylonian period, most likely from Emar" (2010: 127). A transcription and images are available in CUSAS 12 and images can also be found on CDLI via the Schøyen Collection (last checked in August 2019).

The documents in CUSAS 18 are all omens and their script matches the sign-list found in Salvini's publication. CUSAS 18, 17 or MS 2796 is an omen of the gallbladder. It is a small, 12-line, fragment from the upper left corner for a much larger, ruled, tablet. George (2013: 110) suggests it is a well-made copy of a "southern" text, either created in Tigunanum or imported from a different site in Northern Mesopotamia. CUSAS 18, 19 or MS 1807 is an omen of 38 surviving lines, about a bird's heart being dropped in water. It is also the upper section of a larger tablet, but in this case about two thirds has survived. The content and style can be compared to, but do not match, Old Babylonian oil omens (George 2013: 113). CUSAS 18, 19 or MS 1805 is the lower section of a teratomantic tablet, with 50 surviving lines. It has some notes in the margins, which include several unintelligible sign instances which George (2013: 117) suggests could be Hurrian. CUSAS 18, 20 or MS 1806 is the top third of a teratomantic tablet, consisting of 25 remaining lines. The subscript says it was originally meant to hold 39 omens, but only 7 survive. Lastly, CUSAS 18, 21 or MS 2797 is again the bottom section of a teratomantic tablet, with 39 consecutive surviving lines. One of the omens is composed with particularly heavy logographic spelling, which George (2013: 126) takes as evidence that the omens were collected from disparate sources. The language on all five tablets is "Old Babylonian" but "with significant intrusions of north Mesopotamian dialects" (George 2013: 106). Transcriptions can be found in CUSAS 18 (George 2013) and photographs have been released on CDLI via the Schøyen Collection.

CUSAS 34 has an additional five tablets, which "bear further witness to the palace's economic activities" (George 2018: 100). CUSAS 34, 59 or MS 1812 is a fragment accounting for food (lentils, beans, barley, and so forth). One of the personal names mentioned, Ariya, has also been attested by Salvini (1996:38), and been found at Alalaḫ, Tell al-Rimah and Nuzi (George 2018: 102), firmly establishing the described activities in Northern Mesopotamia. CUSAS 34, 60 or MS 1856/1 is a complete tablet about the flocks under control of the palace. Again, one of the personal names, Kuzzi in this case, has also been found on the prism (Salvini 1996: 43) and at Alalaḫ as well as Nuzi (George 2018: 103). CUSAS 34, 61 or MS 1856/2 is a second complete tablet on the flocks under control of the palace. CUSAS 34, 61 or MS 2799 is the top left-hand corner of an accounting tablet, once more on the flocks under control of the palace. Finally, CUSAS 34, 63 or MS 4995 records the disbursement of silver for luxury goods.

What remains are a handful of stand-alone publications. In 2010 Akdoğan & Wilhelm published a tablet with a register of grain rations for nineteen men with non-Akkadian, mostly Hurrian, names. It belongs to a Turkish private collector, Mr Erdal Erkakan, and holds the inventory number 121. Its provenance is unknown but "probably Syria" (Akdoğan & Wilhelm 2010: 159). The 20-line tablet is lined, and both the obverse and reverse contain two columns of text. They determine, amongst other features, "*weitgehende Übereinstimmungen*" in sign-forms with tablets published by Salvini, particularly the prism, and determine they might be dealing with another tablet from the still unidentified site of Tigunanum (Akdoğan & Wilhelm 2010: 160). A low-quality black and white photograph, a copy, and the transcription of this tablet can be found in Akdoğan & Wilhelm 2010.

Zorzi has recently picked up the study of teratomantic tablets (2016) from Tigunanum, classifying them as Old Babylonian – albeit a distinctive peripheral form – and identified a new fragment from an anonymous private collection (2017). It appears that the majority of Tigunanum omen tablets have a Syro-Anatolian social and religious character, mentioning the storm god Adad and Hurrian earth goddess Alluntum or Alani, plus they often have indentions after the first line and poor-quality writing and language (Zorzi 2016: 127). Zorzi also found that the corpus' imagery is that of Middle and Late Bronze Age Anatolia and Northern Mesopotamia, even edging toward what is known from the Middle Assyrian period (2016: 143). A copy and transcription of the fragment Zorzi describes can both be found in her 2017 publication.

Finally, not considered in this chapter are at least fifteen known unpublished tablets in the Hirayama Ikuyo Silkroad Museum collection, under analysis by Akio Tsukimoto. These are also all omen tablets, of which half anomalous birth omens (George 2013: 102). Notes left by Lambert suggest that there are hundreds more Tigunanum tablets in circulation (George 2013: 102), most likely currently in the hands of anonymous private collectors and on the illegal anqitities market. If these are ever offered to museums for study, they would surely provide a significant addition to the comments made here.

5.7 Comparative Palaeography of Tigunanum

Tigunanum is often discussed in relation to the origins of Hittite cuneiform script (see e.g. Weeden 2011: 70; van den Hout 2009: 26; Klinger 1998: 371). The currently dominant theory is that Hittite came from Old Babylonian (or even older) and developed through a general Northern Syrian tradition of writing (Wilhelm 2010). Here, the only tablet which can definitely be attributed to the time of Hittite King Ḫattušili I is the Labarna letter. About this letter, Klinger wrote that it is "*ganz offensichtlich*" not related to Old-Hittite (2003: 240) and Archi adds that Ḫattušili "when campaigning northern Syria, had to entrust a local scribe with the task of drawing up this message" (2010: 39). In addition, Weeden (2016: 162) writes that both a text concerning Uršum (KBo 1.11) and the Labarna letter "do not belong to regular Hittite cuneiform", and they "do not fit into the developmental framework of Hittite cuneiform" (also see Klinger 2003); with van den Hout labelling the cuneiform on the Labarna tablet "Syrian" (2012: 152). As such, despite period and geographical position, a connection between writing at Tigunanum and writing at Ḫattuša is less than certain.

A detailed comparison between sign-forms from Tigunanum and Hittite would be welcome here, but that was not within the scope of this project. The same can be said for composing a contrast with Old Assyrian, or a comparison to Old or Middle Babylonian. What follows will only be an examination of writing at Tigunanum in relation to fellow Hurrian and Northern Mesopotamian Mittani, with references to other sign-lists in the comments section (**Paragraph 5.8**).

To join Salvini's existing sign-list, 2,480 instances were extracted from the tablets described above.[12] These included 158 signs, of which 17 recorded only once. Most instances were recorded from MS 1805 (96 signs, 730 instances); less than the prism but more than the letter. Around 20 different sign-forms can be identified, as well as some variation, including variation between documents from the same collection (i.e. the Schøyen collection). The available Tigunanum corpus overall does not show the same amount of standardisation as the Mittani corpus.

12 The images shown here will primarily be those from the Schøyen collection. They allow use and publication of their images in relation to research projects (Press Office, May 2019).

BAL (*5*)

Salvini finds two forms of BAL, one with a broken initial horizontal, and one with a regular initial horizontal (**Table 5.41**). All instances recorded in this case were from MS 1806 so it is not unlikely that a different scribe might have used a different form or variant. In none of the documents surveyed from Tigunanum thus far does the initial *Winkelhaken* move down to occur centrally underneath or across the vertical wedge.

TABLE 5.41 Tigunanum BAL

Database	Salvini
BAL	

MS 1806, obverse, line 14 (4 instances recorded).

TABLE 5.42 Tigunanum BA, ZU and SU

Database			
BA	ZU_1	ZU_2	SU

Salvini			

BA: MS 1856/2, reverse, line 6 (40 instances recorded). **ZU:** MS 1856/1, reverse, line 6; MS 1805, obverse, line 22 (22 instances recorded). **SU:** MS 2797, reverse, line 12 (3 instances recorded).

BA (14), ZU (15) and SU (16)
Tigunanum BA is a notably 'Babylonian' edition of the sign, with emphasised upper and lower horizontal wedges which can also be found placed at a more diagonal angle (**Table 5.42**). There is little variation in this form. While this is different but comparable to the script-groups discussed before, ZU and SU deviate completely, following much 'older' forms of the signs where multiple verticals are still incorporated as well. Salvini finds a fair amount of variation in ZU. The two different forms shown here are from different tablets.

ITI (20)
The form of ITI which Salvini has found has a slightly 'diagonal' composition, where it is almost encompassed by a diagonal or large *Winkelhaken*, like the sign DI (see below). In the Schøyen collection two very distinct forms can be found, on two different tablets (**Table 5.43**). The first consists of two horizontals separated by a row of *Winkelhaken* and followed by a broken vertical. The second bears more similarity to the form found by Salvini, with a large *Winkelhaken* or diagonal and a small cluster of *Winkelhaken* (even if not ascending, as in Salvini's version).

KA (24)
KA has thus far only been recorded in one form from the Tigunanum documents, albeit with some variation (**Table 5.44**). The form consists of two horizontals separated by a central *Winkelhaken*, followed by a vertical, two horizontal wedges, and another vertical. The initial *Winkelhaken* can also be seen moving upward slightly in some of the collected instances, but in none of the cases does it align exactly with the upper horizontal. In addition, it is variation which cannot be attributed to scribal hand, because the scribe of MS 1805 variously impressed either KA_{1a} or KA_{1b}. While the number of wedges used in Tigunanum sign-forms appears relatively flexible (additional horizontals, verticals, *Winkelhaken*) KA is only ever impressed with the same number of wedges.

LI (85)
LI occurs in multiple forms at Tigunanum (**Table 5.45**). Salvini has found two of these (one variant), which can also be seen in the collection studied here. The first (LI_1), and most frequent, is a form with a small cluster of four *Winkelhaken*, followed by two horizontal wedges attached to another two *Winkelhaken*, crossed by two verticals – the first of which is sometimes smaller, or difficult to see (Salvini did not copy it, or found a different form). The second form (LI_2) consists only of *Winkelhaken*, and no horizontal wedges. On finding the first form in the Labarna letter, van den Hout comments that the

TABLE 5.43 Tigunanum ITI

Database		Salvini
ITI$_1$	ITI$_2$	

MS 1807, reverse edge, line 2; MS 1812, obverse, column 2, line 7 (10 instances recorded).

TABLE 5.44 Tigunanum KA

Database		Salvini
KA$_{1a}$	KA$_{1b}$	

MS 2799, obverse, line 6; MS 1805, obverse, line 6 (31 instances recorded).

TABLE 5.45 Tigunanum LI

Database		Salvini
LI$_1$	LI$_2$	
		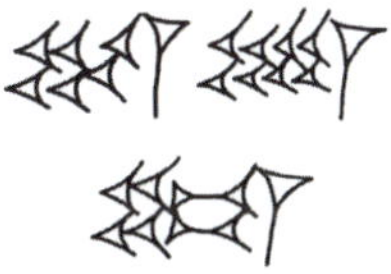

MS 1807, obverse, line 1; MS 1806, obverse, line 13 (22 instances recorded).

horizontals are impressed at a slight angle, which also occurred at Alalaḫ (VII) (2012: 157).

TU (68), MU (98) and Similar Signs

There are several signs which can be found in the Tigunanum documents which will either have a 'triangular' cluster of four *Winkelhaken* (1a), a 'square' cluster of four *Winkelhaken* (1b) or a cluster of 6 *Winkelhaken* (1c). TU and MU are some of these signs (**Table 5.46**), and, having been recorded several times from a number of tablets, it shows that the choice in cluster of *Winkelhaken* was down to scribal preference. The clusters do not mix on individual tablets, but instead differ between tablets. The same applies to ZI (140), IN (261), and of course ŠE (579), BU (580), US (583) and TE (589).

LA (89)

LA is an interesting sign for the palaeography of Tigunanum, because it is quite distinct (**Table 5.47**). Either the upper or the lower horizontal wedge is longer and more emphasised than the remaining horizontal wedges. Salvini's version reflects the first, but the Schøyen collection also revealed the latter. There is still an extended upper horizontal wedge, but the bottom wedge is impressed even more strongly or deeply, capping the end of the vertical wedge and creating a more 'square' shape. Although it is difficult to see from the instances collected (damage), it is also possible that there is a second vertical in this form. Whilst illustrated this still looks similar to the LA found in other corpora, impressed in clay the emphasis of these wedges gives the sign a rather different appearance, particularly the second form.

QA (99)

QA is another distinct sign from Tigunanum (**Table 5.48**). Whereas all later Bronze Age corpora discussed up until now, including Mittani, have moved on to a QA impressed with two initial wedges followed by a vertical, Tigunanum only has the one. It can be found variously as a short diagonal, more like a *Winkelhaken*, or almost horizontal, but in all recorded instances, as well as Salvini's list, this wedge is on its own. That said, Van den Hout (2012: 157) records the Labarna QA with two crossing diagonal wedges (which he calls the 'later' shape); he does not however note where in the letter he found this instance.

NA (110)

Salvini records the Tigunanum NA as one with an initial horizontal wedge, with a *Winkelhaken* centrally above and below, and a final vertical. The documents studied here show a few subtle variants, indicating that actually the version copied by Salvini is relatively less common in these texts (**Table 5.49**). Instead, the first *Winkelhaken* is usually found attached to, or floating slightly above

TABLE 5.46 Tigunanum TU and MU

Database			
TU_{1a}	TU_{1c}	MU_{1a}	MU_{1b}

Salvini			

TU: MS 1812, obverse, column 2, line 7; MS 1856/1, obverse, line 4 (20 instances recorded). **MU:** MS 1856/2, obverse, line 8, edge; MS 2799, obverse, line 2 (16 instances recorded).

TABLE 5.47 Tigunanum LA

Database		Salvini
LA_1	LA_2	

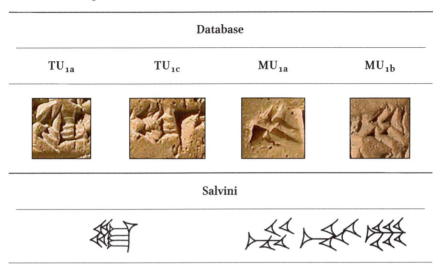

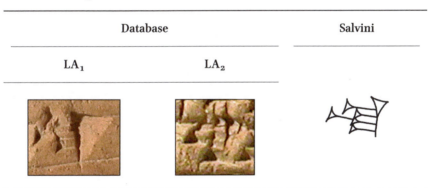

MS 2799, obverse, line 6; MS 1805, reverse, line 18 (21 instances recorded).

the horizontal, and the second *Winkelhaken* edges toward the right above this, often encountering the vertical. In fact, the first *Winkelhaken* is stretched so far, crossing the vertical, that it may be fair to label it a diagonal wedge instead. This is, again, a quite distinct way to impress NA in comparison to the later Bronze Age corpora discussed thus far.

RU (111)

Salvini found two forms of RU in the four documents he studied, one with a second horizontal wedge, crossing through the centre of the composition, and

TABLE 5.48 Tigunanum QA

Database	Salvini
QA	

MS 2797, reverse, line 8 (25 instances recorded).

TABLE 5.49 Tigunanum NA

Database		Salvini
NA$_{1a}$	NA$_{1b}$	

MS 1812, obverse, column 2, line 11; MS 2796, reverse, line 4 (65 instances recorded).

TABLE 5.50 Tigunanum RU

Database		Salvini
RU$_1$	RU$_2$	

MS 1805, obverse, line 16; MS 4995, reverse, line 2 (14 instances recorded).

one without (**Table 5.50**). On the tablets studied here, the form with an additional horizontal wedge does not occur; instead, the *Winkelhaken* can again be seen to be stretched out, like a diagonal impression, crossing through the verticals. This occurs on multiple tablets, so it cannot necessarily be attributed to a single scribe deviating. More importantly, a second form of RU can be found on MS 4995, where it is clearly composed with three *Winkelhaken*: two preceeding the first vertical, and one before the final vertical – as on EA 24, EA 25 and EA 29.

NU (112)

The NU found at Tigunanum belongs to the more 'pressed together' type (**Table 5.51**). The two wedges are not distinctly separated, and instead the diagonal is both impressed in and through the horizontal. Whilst in some script-groups the horizontal is also impressed at a diagonal angle, the wedge is normally found straight at Tigunanum. Like QA, it is only ever composed with two wedges, not more.

TI (118)

Having spent some time analysing TI in the previous chapters, especially **Chapter 3**, it is of course interesting to see what sign-forms Tigunanum delivers. Salvini records two forms ('long' and 'short'), and one variant ('short' with a decentralised *Winkelhaken*) (**Table 5.52**). The same versions have all been recorded during this study as well. The dominant form is TI_1 ('long') with *four* impressions (rather than *five* found in Mittanian). The twelve instances found on MS 1805 are all TI_1, as are those on the fragment published by Zorzi (2017); while MS 4995 has only TI_2. Significantly, the forms can also be found mixed on the same tablet (see for example MS 1806, reverse, line 2; versus MS 1806, reverse, line 3). In fact, all three images in the table below were extracted from the same tablet. This reminds of the Hurrian Mittani letter, EA 24. While it is tempting to jump to conclusions, no direct connection should be made at this point. However, it is certainly a feature to keep in mind for future research.

AK (127)

Like LA, Tigunanum AK has a relatively unique shape when it is seen impressed in clay. Salvini found two forms, one with additional vertical wedges (AK_1), and one without (AK_2) (**Table 5.53**). Due to the crowdedness of the script it can be difficult to differentiate between the two, but in the end the same can be said for the documents from the Schøyen collection. In fact, because the verticals obscure the horizontals, they sometimes disappear altogether. In his analysis of Alalaḫ VII script, van den Hout differentiates between an 'older' form with many horizontals, and a 'later' form with a reduced number of wedges, some

TABLE 5.51 Tigunanum NU

Database	Salvini
NU	
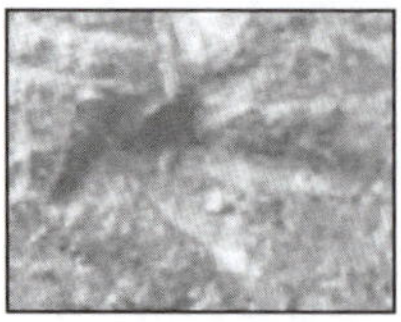	

Erkakan 121, reverse, column 3, line 2 (40 instances recorded).

TABLE 5.52 Tigunanum TI

Database			Salvini
TI_1	TI_{2a}	TI_{2b}	

MS 1806, reverse, line 2; MS 1806, reverse, line 3; MS 1806, obverse, line 8 (31 instances recorded).

TABLE 5.53 Tigunanum AK

Database		Salvini
AK_1	AK_2	

MS 1805, reverse, line 7; MS 1812, obverse, column 1, line 10; MS 1856/1, reverse, line 11 (33 instances recorded).

of which vertical. He comments that the shape he encountered in the Labarna letter belongs to the former category, which was also the most common in Alalaḫ VII texts (as opposed to later Hittite documents) (2012: 159). Because later forms of the sign (e.g. Mittani) usually allocate more space between the wedges these instances can look considerably different when studying a tablet in person.

IG (136)

Salvini records a large variety of IG, distinguishing between a form with two verticals crossed by a horizontal wedge, and two variants of a form without the vertical which instead has a number of additional horizontal wedges, with an extended and emphasised central and/or horizontal wedge. Due to the movement of the clay, it is difficult to determine, from images, whether the first form found in the Schøyen documents could have this additional central horizontal (**Table 5.54**). Perhaps more interesting is the additional form found here, which has three or four horizontal wedges, but also two vertical wedges, as well as three *Winkelhaken*. While this is related to the forms or variants illustrated by Salvini, it does not quite match them. None of the undamaged instances recorded from the documents under consideration were from the same tablet, so it is also impossible to establish whether the placement or number of wedges could be attributed to scribal hand or not.

GI (141)

Whereas the clusters of *Winkelhaken* in signs such as TU and ZI can be found to differ, Tigunanum GI only occurs with a distinct diagonal sequence of impressions (**Table 5.55**). It can also be found in other script-groups (e.g. Nuzi), but never in Mittanian or Middle Assyrian. Significantly, Mittanian GI does occur

TABLE 5.54 Tigunanum IG

Database		**Salvini**
IG$_1$	**IG$_2$**	

MS 1806, obverse, line 11; MS 1807, obverse, line 2 (6 instances recorded).

TABLE 5.55 Tigunanum GI

Database	Salvini
GI	
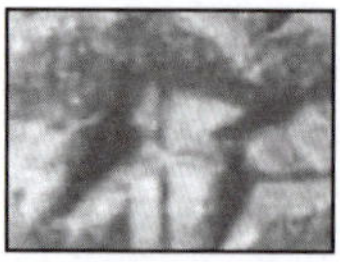	

Erkakan 121, obverse, column 1, line 4 (10 instances recorded).

TABLE 5.56 Tigunanum EN

Database	Salvini
EN	

MS 2799, obverse, line 4 (7 instances recorded).

TABLE 5.57 Tigunanum TIM

Database	Salvini
TIM	

MS 2799, obverse, line 3 (5 instances recorded).

in two variants, with both the 'triangular' and 'square' cluster, so, considering the standardised nature of that script-group, it is perhaps surprising not to see more variation at Tigunanum.

EN (164)

Tigunanum EN stands out for the slightly diagonal alignment of its bottom *Winkelhaken* (**Table 5.56**). Whilst this seems like a small thing to pick up on when studying a new tablet, it was the same on each tablet considered here, including the fragment published by Zorzi (2017), and Salvini also reflects it in his copy. There are no different forms, and otherwise very little variation.

TIM (167)

There is only one form of TIM in the Tigunanum texts, which has an initial horizontal followed by two *Winkelhaken*, then a short vertical, and two final diagonal wedges, creating a 'diamond'-like shape (**Table 5.57**). As with AK, this is more obvious in the clay, than in copies. TIM posed somewhat of a mystery in **Paragraph 3.3.3**, as EA 19 was the only tablet in the entire Mittani corpus to indicate a different sign-form might exist. The form found at Tigunanum is one which matches neither Mittani form, but it does closely resemble the more general form, found on all tablets except for EA 19. The Mittani form has 'lost' the central vertical, and is usually impressed allowing more space, making it seem 'longer', but it is otherwise the same.

SA (172)

In previous chapters, the distance between the vertical wedges in SA was discussed. When studying the instances very carefully, sometimes a small section of extra space could be detected between the initial and following vertical wedges (which also varied in number), plus the initial vertical may have been slightly larger. However, the SA observed both by Salvini and in the documents studied here is one with three equally spaced and sized verticals (**Table 5.58**). The horizontal wedges are not always parallel, with the bottom also occurring longer and sometimes at a slightly more diagonal angle, but this is the only variation found.

ŠUM (221)

The form of ŠUM attested from the Tigunanum texts is a relatively simple one, compared to older script-groups. Whereas later forms occur with a central horizontal wedge rather than a vertical wedge as seen here, it has 'lost' many other wedges traditionally used to compose the sign. Most instances recorded were found on the edges of tablets, which can make wedges seem impressed at

TABLE 5.58 Tigunanum SA

Database	Salvini
SA	

MS 1812, obverse, column 2, line 12 (8 instances recorded).

a distorted diagonal angle, but actually the form consists of two double horizontals, followed by two diagonals with the central vertical wedge – sometimes inside the 'box' and sometimes crossing through the other wedges (**Table 5.59**).

UM (238)
The difference (or lack thereof) between UM, DUB and KIŠIB has been addressed several times now. However, from the Tigunanum documents only UM (the value, and the sign) was recorded, so no such comparison can be made here. Salvini provides a copy with a small initial or central vertical wedge, whereas the initial verticals found in the documents considered here are generally a little longer, on par with the second vertical (**Table 5.60**). As far as it is possible to tell (some instances are damaged, or the tablet has cracks) no additional verticals occur at Tigunanum.

TA (248)
In contrast to UM, the TA recorded from the Schøyen collection is one with a shorter and / or more central initial vertical wedge (TA_1) (**Table 5.61**). In some cases it is so difficult to detect that Salvini has copied it as a different sign-form, with only one vertical wedge (perhaps TA_2). The instance shown in the table is from MS 1805; from this tablet seven other instances were collected, of which at least three with lightly impressed or faint central vertical wedges. On the other hand, Salvini has also found a form with three vertical wedges ($TA_{3?}$), not attested in the corpus considered here. This is significant, because it is the form with three verticals which becomes popular during the Mittanian and Middle Assyrian periods.

TABLE 5.59 Tigunanum ŠUM

Database	Salvini
ŠUM	

MS 1807, obverse, line 9 (15 instances recorded).

TABLE 5.60 Tigunanum UM

Database	Salvini
UM	

MS 1805, obverse, line 18 (18 instances recorded).

TABLE 5.61 Tigunanum TA

Database		Salvini
TA$_1$	TA$_2$	

MS 2796, reverse, line 9; MS 1805, obverse, line 7 (23 instances recorded).

ḪÉ (253)
Despite a small number of instances recorded, two forms of ḪÉ can be found at Tigunanum (seen in both Salvini's documents and the corpus considered here) (**Table 5.62**). The first is an interesting one with, instead of a central horizontal wedge, two crossing diagonals. The second is more complicated, with a small sequence of *Winkelhaken* at the bottom of the sign composition. The form found in the Schøyen collection differs from the form found by Salvini, as it is also preceded by a *Winkelhaken.*

LUGAL (266)
LUGAL is one of the signs which actually became less simplified over time. Older version can be found composed of as little as four wedges (also see the form found by Salvini), whereas more typically, in Mittanian, but also at Nuzi, LUGAL will occur with at least some horizontal wedges as well – as attested in the Schøyen collection (**Table 5.63**). Notably, at Tigunanum, there is one form which is joined by an additional central vertical wedge, and one form where this has disappeared.

IL (348)
Only one form of IL was recorded from the Tigunanum corpus. It is a version with a small cluster of *Winkelhaken* (**Table 5.64**), interestingly also seen at Nuzi, but not in Mittanian. More significantly, this sign-form occurs with very little variation, whereas in all other corpora considered there are two or more forms and many variants. However, all later forms of the sign occur with two final verticals, whereas at Tigunanum IL has one broken vertical wedge.

DU (350), IŠ (357) and Similar Signs
Instances of DU from the Tigunanum corpus only ever occur with the *Winkelhaken* placed firmly at the end of the upper horizontal wedge (**Table 5.65**). In other corpora it can be seen to be placed more central in the composition, but neither Salvini nor the tablets considered here show this form or variant. There is even one less common instance (MS 1805, obverse, line 19) where the *Winkelhaken* has taken on the appearance of a horizontal instead (like the sign AB, 223). However, the sign IŠ does occur with a slightly lower *Winkelhaken*, indicating that the apparent lack of variation in DU may have to be attributed to the limited number of tablets available for study. The same can be said for UŠ (381), which in the Tigunanum corpus is difficult to distinguish from DU because it only has one vertical wedge (as opposed to multiple).

TABLE 5.62 Tigunanum ḪÉ

Database		Salvini
ḪÉ$_1$	ḪÉ$_2$	
		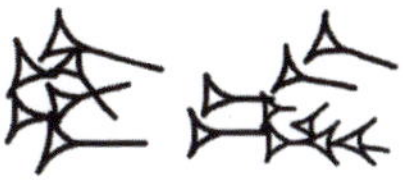

MS 1812, obverse, column 1, line 6; MS 1806, obverse, line 10 (4 instances recorded).

TABLE 5.63 Tigunanum LUGAL

Database		Salvini
LUGAL$_1$	LUGAL$_2$	

MS 1807, obverse, line 9; MS 1806, obverse, line 6 (14 instances recorded).

TABLE 5.64 Tigunanum IL

Database	Salvini
IL	

MS 1856/1, obverse, line 6 (19 instances recorded).

TABLE 5.65 Tigunanum DU and IŠ

Database			Salvini	
DU$_{1b}$	**IŠ$_{1a}$**	**IŠ$_{1b}$**	**DU**	**IŠ**

DU: MS 1856/1, reverse, line 12 (12 instances recorded). **IŠ**: MS 2799, obverse, line 4 (16 instances recorded).

TABLE 5.66 Tigunanum AL

Database		Salvini
AL$_1$	**AL$_2$**	

MS 1806, obverse, line 8, edge; MS 2797, obverse edge, line 1 (13 instances recorded).

AL (474)

Salvini presented three forms of AL: one with a central *Winkelhaken* and vertical, one without the vertical, and one without the *Winkelhaken* or the vertical (**Table 5.66**). The first and the second have also been found in the corpus under consideration here, but not the third. It is possible that the form Salvini copied without *Winkelhaken* is perhaps one where the script was condensed, and one wedge obscured another – but this is difficult to confirm without seeing the original tablet. In addition, Van den Hout, in his comparison between Alalaḫ VII, the Labarna letter and the Uršu text, likewise records the third form – which he labels 'older shape' – but it is not clear whether he based his illustration on the original tablet or on Salvini's publication. Either way, another feature to note is that the bottom horizontal wedge is consistently impressed at an angle (thus possibly better referred to as a diagonal wedge). This gives the form a somewhat triangular shape when it is viewed on the tablet, as opposed to the copy.

UN (501)

Tigunanum UN is composed of a large number of wedges, impressed closely together, and thus difficult to analyse. Salvini recorded at least four different forms or variants, but it is almost impossible to identify whether these correlate with the documents considered here. In the most clear instances from the Schøyen collection as well as Erkakan 121, UN is composed of three initial horizontal wedges, an 'A' formation, two more vertical wedges crossed by a horizontal, and a final broken vertical wedge (**Table 5.67**).

RA (511), ŠA (566) and Similar Signs

Several forms of RA can be found in the Tigunanum documents (**Table 5.68**). In the Schøyen texts it is possible to see a form which begins with four horizontals, and then has two verticals encased by another two horizontal wedges, usually with the first of the two verticals impressed shorter than the second. The second form begins with three horizontal wedges, and then has two taller verticals joined by a bottom horizontal wedge, either obscuring a fourth upper horizontal wedge, or lacking one altogether. These forms are also reflected in Salvini's sign-list, albeit in slightly different editions.

Similarly, the shorter initial vertical wedge also features in the sign ŠA (566), giving it a distinct appearance. Salvini records one form, but in the Schøyen collection it occurs in a couple of variants, one where the *Winkelhaken* are impressed into the first vertical wedge, and one in which the *Winkelhaken* are given more space.

MA (552)

MA is an important sign to make note of for the Tigunanum corpus, as it follows the 'older' Babylonian form of the sign. That is, with an emphasised top

TABLE 5.67 Tigunanum UN

Database	Salvini
UN	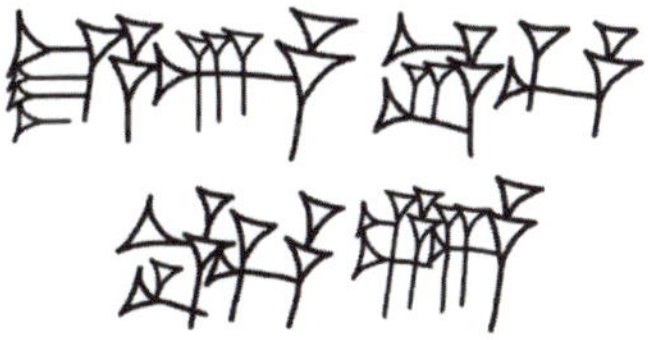

MS 2796, reverse, line 2 (8 instances recorded).

TABLE 5.68 Tigunanum RA

Database			Salvini
RA$_{1}$	RA$_{2}$		

ŠA$_{1a}$	ŠA$_{1b}$	ŠA$_{1c}$	

RA: MS 1856/2, obverse, line 9; MS 1805, obverse, line 20 (11 instances recorded). **ŠA:** MS 1856/1, reverse, line 11; MS 2799, reverse, line 5, second instance; MS 2797, reverse, line 12.

and bottom horizontal wedge, very similar to BA (14). At Tigunanum it is possible to distinguish between BA and MA because the first was impressed with slanted or diagonal wedges and the second with straight horizontal wedges. There is also a significant variant, not represented in Salvini's sign-list (where it has a slightly longer or more extended upper horizontal wedge) (**Table 5.69**).

ID (560) and DA (561)
Salvini has found four different forms of ID, not all of which occur in the corpus studied here. In particular, the form which misses the cluster of *Winkelhaken* could be recognised in a slightly damaged and distorted instance from MS 2797 (**Table 5.70**) but due to the condition it is difficult to establish with certainty. The dominant form in this corpus is one with three or four horizontal wedges followed by a cluster of *Winkelhaken* and then a broken vertical wedge. Later Mittanian has a regular vertical wedge (which Salvini has found), but also a broken central horizontal wedge. Similarly, the sign DA only ever occurs with one final vertical wedge, while in Mittanian and at Nuzi it is found with two verticals. In these corpora DA normally has a broken central horizontal wedge as well, which is absent at Tigunanum.

ŠÀ (599)
Tigunanum's ŠÀ is a form with a small upward-diagonal cluster of three *Winkelhaken* followed by a vertical wedge (**Table 5.71**). This is quite different

TABLE 5.69 Tigunanum MA

Database		Salvini
MA_{1a}	MA_{1b}	

MS 1807, obverse, line 7; MS 1805, obverse, line 20 (106 instances recorded).

TABLE 5.70 Tigunanum ID and DA

Database			
ID_{1a}	ID_{1b}	$ID_{2?}$	DA_1

Salvini			

ID: MS 1807, obverse, line 8; MS 1856/1, obverse, line 8, edge; MS 2797, obverse edge, line 3 (17 instances recorded). **DA**: MS 1856/1, obverse, line 10 (18 instances recorded).

from some of the later Bronze Age forms discussed in this chapter and the previous chapters, where the *Winkelhaken* have migrated to sit between three vertical wedges. Despite the intricate cluster of *Winkelhaken* Tigunanum ŠÀ does not appear to have significant variants.

ḪI (631), AḪ (636) and Similar Signs

Comparable to Mittanian ḪI, this sign does not vary at Tigunanum. It is made up of three small upper *Winkelhaken* and one larger bottom *Winkelhaken* (**Table 5.72**). It is not usually placed at an interesting angle, for example, more diagonally; and it is never composed with more impressions. This forms a strong contrast with ḪI at Nuzi, where it is hugely varied. The same unchanging 'ḪI'

TABLE 5.71 Tigunanum ŠÀ

Database	Salvini
ŠÀ	

MS 1812, obverse, column 1, line 12 (13 instances recorded).

TABLE 5.72 Tigunanum ḪI and AḪ

Database		Salvini
ḪI	AḪ	

ḪI: MS 1805, reverse, line 21 (45 instances recorded). **AḪ**: MS 2796, reverse, line 4 (9 instances recorded).

formation is also found in Tigunanum signs such as AḪ (636) and IM (641). The sign AḪ is composed of only a 'ḪI' element and a broken horizontal wedge (although, most instances collected were damaged, and it is possible some may have been composed with a regular horizontal wedge). In other script-groups the horizontal of AḪ is often joined by a set of vertical wedges as well.

AR (725)

Tigunanum AR is composed with a large *Winkelhaken*, followed by a broken horizontal wedge crossed by three verticals, and another *Winkelhaken* inbetween the last two verticals (**Table 5.73**). The final *Winkelhaken* is generally given a lot of space, resulting in a rather 'long' or large sign-form. Whilst the *Winkelhaken* usually occurs centrally, it can also be found lower in the

TABLE 5.73 Tigunanum AR

Database		Salvini
AR_{1a}	AR_{1b}	

MS 1805, obverse, line 20; MS 1812, obverse, column 2, line 8 (8 instances recorded).

composition, crossing through the final vertical. This is especially the case on tablets with more condensed signs (e.g. MS 1812).

DI (736) and KI (737)

DI and KI are classic 'diamond' shaped signs at Tigunanum (**Table 5.74**). DI is composed of a large *Winkelhaken* with a smaller *Winkelhaken* at the top, or according to Salvini, a *Winkelhaken* and tiny horizontal wedge at the top. KI is likewise made up of a large initial *Winkelhaken*, but, as reflected by Salvini's sign-list, the upper *Winkelhaken* sometimes matches this in size. KI can also be found with an additional vertical wedge.

MEŠ (754)

Tigunanum MEŠ has only been found in one sign-form, the ME + EŠ formation (**Table 5.75**). There is always a horizontal wedge, which is sometimes found impressed into the vertical. The number of *Winkelhaken* is only ever three, and this does not vary.

KU (808) and LU (812)

KU at Tigunanum is often impressed with three even horizontal wedges followed by a vertical, similar to MA found in other script-groups. It does also occur with a vertical, but this is usually impressed so that, when copied, it looks like it is 'hiding' behind the other wedges (**Table 5.76**).

The same applies to LU, although each instance collected from this corpus – and Salvini's sign-list shows the same – is always composed with three verticals. Some scribes place more emphasis, or impress more deeply, the vertical wedges (MS 1805), others the horizontal wedges (MS 4995). The number of wedges varies quite little, or possibly not at all; because they are impressed closely together the displacement of the clay could easily obscure another

TABLE 5.74 Tigunanum DI and KI

Database		
DI	**KI$_1$**	**KI$_2$**

Salvini		

DI: MS 1812, obverse, column 1, line 3 (17 instances recorded). **KI**: MS 1856/1, obverse, line 10; MS 1805, reverse, line 3 (46 instances recorded).

TABLE 5.75 Tigunanum MEŠ

Database		**Salvini**
MEŠ$_{1a}$	**MEŠ$_{1b}$**	

MS 1812, obverse, column 2, line 2; MS 2797, obverse edge, line 4 (12 instances recorded).

horizontal. In addition, some scribes space the verticals evenly while others place the final two more closely together.

ḪA (856)

Tigunanum's ḪA is a form composed of ZA plus two *Winkelhalen*, rather than one *Winkelhaken* (**Table 5.77**). Not many instances were collected however. In the small database composed from CUSAS and other fragments it is difficult to detect the second *Winkelhaken* in damaged instances and perhaps this sign does also exist with one *Winkelhaken* at Tigunanum.

TABLE 5.76 Tigunanum KU and LU

Database		
KU$_1$	KU$_2$	LU

Salvini		

KU: MS 1805, reverse, line 14; MS 1806, obverse, line 8, edge (30 instances recorded). LU: MS 1806, reverse, line 1 (26 instances recorded).

TABLE 5.77 Tigunanum ḪA

Database	Salvini
ḪA	

MS 1812, obverse, column 1, line 13 (10 instances recorded).

Numerals at Tigunanum

Numbers recorded from Tigunanum appear in quite specific formations (**Table 5.78**). The numbers 1 and 10, 2 and 20 and 3 and 30 are differentiated as 'DIŠ' and 'U' formations at Tigunanum. Whereas in the Mittani corpus the number 4 could be composed like 'ZA' or 'ŠE' at Tigunanum this is always 'GAR'. For the number 40 this gets turned onto its side like 'ḪI'. Some of the higher multiples were not recorded from the documents under consideration, which is where

TABLE 5.78 Tigunanum numerals

Database								
1	2	3	4	5	6	7	8	9

10	20	30	40	50	60	70	80	90
					–	–	–	

1: MS 1856/1, obverse, line 6. **2**: MS 2799, obverse, line 3. **3**: MS 1856/1, obverse, line 9. **4**: MS 1856/2, reverse, line 1. **5**: MS 4995, obverse, line 2. **6**: MS 2799, obverse, line 2. **7**: MS 1812, obverse, column 1, line 12. **8**: MS 1856/2, reverse, line 2. **9**: MS 1856/2, obverse, line 1. **10**: MS 27 99, reverse, line 4. **20**: MS 2799, obverse, line 2. **30**: MS 1856/2, obverse, line 1. **40**: MS 2799, obverse, line 1. **50**: MS 2799, obverse, line 1. **90**: MS 2799, obverse, line 1.

things get interesting in a sexagesimal system, but the number 90 actually follows a DIŠ × EŠ formula, which translates into 60 + 10 + 10 + 10 (= 90).

5.8 Comments

5.8.1 *Summary*

Recognising Tigunanum texts is a comparatively easy task in relation to the preceeding script-groups and sub-groups, as it is not contemporary and closer to Old Babylonian than Middle Assyrian. However, it has consistently been labeled as 'some form of' Babylonian, or 'peripheral' Babylonian, and so forth, setting it apart as a yet-to-be classified, different, script-group. Tigunanum was introduced in this book, because it is possibly an early neighbour or predecessor to the Mittani state, with Hurrian documents containing Hurrian names and quite probably lead by a Hurrian ruler. The script is much more varied than Mittanian, with signs often occurring in two forms; yet it is also not as varied as the writing of the family-educated Nuzi scribes. Scribal transmission at Tigunanum can barely be speculated about at the moment, so this has to be left to the future. However, some characteristics of script at Tigunanum are:

- BA (14) will occur with emphasised top and bottom wedges, which may also be placed at a more diagonal angle. In comparison, MA (551) occurs with straight horizontal wedges, but also the top and bottom wedge clearly emphasised. ZU (15) and SU (16) are typically impressed with at least three vertical wedges, of which some are smaller or shorter wedges, crossing the horizontal impressions. Whereas this is not a-typical in the context of Old Babylonian or Old Assyrian this is also not observed in any of the script-groups discussed thus far, and therefore a significant and noteable difference in the context of Mittani palaeography.
- KA (24) is only ever found composed with a *Winkelhaken* centred between the two initial horizontal wedges. This sign does not occur in any other forms at Tigunanum. Similarly, DU (350) and IŠ (357) vary little, DU composed with a top horizontal followed by a *Winkelhaken*, and IŠ again also with a more central *Winkelhaken*; neither with any additional wedges that can be found in other script-groups, e.g. an extra vertical wedge or an initial *Winkelhaken*.
- LI (85) is not found in a ŠE+ŠA form – at least not the way in which ŠA occurs at Tigunanum – instead the dominant form is a composition consisting of *Winkelhaken* followed by double parallel horizontals and *Winkelhaken* and then a vertical; and a second form consists only of *Winkelhaken*, which can vary in number and formation.
- LA (89) is composed with either an emphasised top horizontal wedge, or emphasised top and bottom horizontal wedge, also found in Babylonian (Labat 1978: 59).
- QA (99) consists of just one small diagonal wedge or *Winkelhaken* followed by a vertical.
- Wedge placement in NA (110) and EN (164). NA is made up of a horizontal wedge and two *Winkelhaken*, usually placed quite high in the composition; the upper *Winkelhaken* hovering above and sometimes going through the vertical. EN consists of a horizontal, two verticals and two *Winkelhaken*, the second placed lower than the first creating a diagonal line of impression.
- LUGAL (266) occurs in two or three simple forms at Tigunanum; for instance, if there is a vertical incorporated it is only one wedge, not more. In one form LUGAL has four initial horizontal wedges (but not two portruding as seen in later forms of the sign), in another form found by Salvini these are absent altogether and LUGAL is made up of only a diagonal and three *Winkelhaken*.
- IL (348) only ever occurs with a small cluster of *Winkelhaken*. No other forms of this sign have been recorded for Tigunanum, even though previously discussed corpora had multiple, most notably transforming the *Winkelhaken*

into a broken diagonal. The form with the cluster of *Winkelhaken* also persists in Nuzi and Assyro-Mittanian writing.
- ŠA (566) is impressed with four initial horizontal wedges, and a short vertical, two *Winkelhaken*, and finally a longer vertical wedge. The short vertical wedge gives it a distinct appearance in the clay.
- DI (736) and to a lesser extent KI (373) are dominated by an initial large *Winkelhaken* giving a 'diamond' shape to the sign-forms, which is clearer at Tigunanum than in later script-groups, (where the verticals and horizontals usually dominate).
- MEŠ (754) varies little at Tigunanum. It is impressed with a vertical followed by a small horizontal wedge, sometimes pressed into the vertical (but not in front of it), and always followed by exactly three *Winkelhaken* in the instances attested thus far.
- ḪA (856) is composed of a ZA plus two *Winkelhaken* (as opposed to one).

5.8.2 *Comparing Tigunanum to Other Script-groups*

The focus of this book has not been on older traditions of the Middle Bronze Age and thus it cannot be determined precisely how Tigunanum compares or differs (although some comments can be found in the following paragraphs). However, a detailed comparison to Mittanian is both called for and possible here.

When sign-forms differ at Tigunanum (see **Table 5.79** and also the **Appendix**) this is contradictively because either they have additional (vertical) wedges, compared to Mittanian (for example SU but also ŠUM); or, because the form actually has less wedges than the one found in Mittanian (especially LUGAL but also IL). Only a few forms differ entirely, such as QA and ŠÀ. The great majority of key-sign forms (i.e. not relatively unchanging signs such as AŠ or AN) are comparable between Tigunanum and Mittanian: they are almost the same but not an exact match (examples in **Table 5.80**). For instance, in the case of AL and AS Tigunanum has one form which matches Mittanian, but also one that does not. In other forms, the number of wedges may match, but not the emphasis placed on them, or their length; for example, LA and ŠA. Finally, there are some forms which could be said to match when considering more variable script-groups than Mittanian, such as Nuzi; but in this case, dozens if not hundreds of Mittanian instances have been collected, thus the sign-forms of KA cannot quite be said to be *exactly* the same. However, some sign-forms found at Tigunanum do match Mittanian (**Table 5.81**). Most notably, the forms found of ('short') TI and MEŠ. A few less significant signs such as ŠU and BI

TABLE 5.79 Sign forms which differ between Mittani and Tigunanum

	Mittani	Tigunanum
	Different sign-forms	
BA		
ZU		
SU		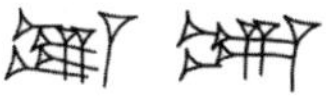
QA		
ŠUM		
UM		
LUGAL		
IL		
ŠÀ		
AḪ		
ḪA		

TABLE 5.80 Sign-forms which are comparable between Mittani and Tigunanum

	Mittani	Tigunanum
	Comparable sign-forms	
BAL		
LI		
KA	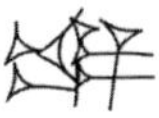	

TABLE 5.80 Sign-forms which are comparable between Mittani and Tigunanum (*cont.*)

	Mittani	Tigunanum
	Comparable sign-forms	
LA		
MU		
NA		
RU		
NU		
DIN		
AK		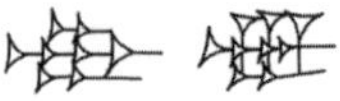
GI		
TA		
IŠ		
AL	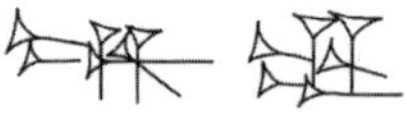	
AS	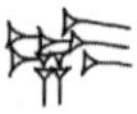	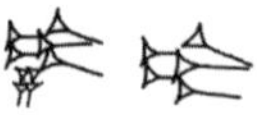
GA		
DA		
ŠA		
US		

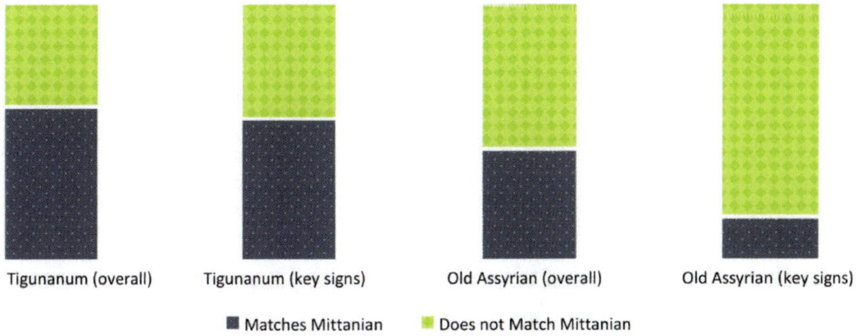

FIGURE 5.2 Comparison of Old Assyrian and Tigunanum sign-forms with Mittanian
The overall comparison is based on all signs in the Appendix; for the 'key signs' a selection of 40 signs was made, excluding less relevant signs (those which are the same across periods, script-groups) such as AŠ (1) and including more relevant signs (those which differ across periods, script-groups) such as KA (24).

could be considered comparable as well, because they can differ quite strongly in older script-groups, especially Old Assyrian.[13]

It is interesting that the sign-forms from the prism (see Salvini 1996) are slightly closer to later Mittanian than the same forms found in the other documents; and the writing at Tigunanum in general is closer to Mittanian than Old Assyrian (**Figure 5.2**). Tigunanum and Mittani scribes used the same or very similar forms of at least KA (24), LA (89), NA (110), TI (118), ZI (140), EN (164), SAG (184), IN (261), AM (309), DU (350) IŠ (357), BI (358) and MEŠ (754) – and more.

For contrast, copies of the Old Assyrian tablets from Aššur 14446 (VAT 19852, VAT 19864 (KAM 10, 1) and MAH 15962) as well as copies from CCT 1 were studied together with Labat's *Manuel*.[14] Of the Old Assyrian signs, circa 50% matches Mittanian and 50% does not (**Figure 5.2**). These are generally sign-forms which occur similarly in many script-groups, across many periods, such as I (252) and A (839). When only key signs are considered, around 25% of the Old Assyrian signs match Mittanian and 75% does not. The Old Assyrian sign-forms are considerably more Archaic than Tigunanum forms, which are comparatively paired down. What is more, there seem to be few similarities between the Old Assyrian from Ass. 14446, and the Early Middle Assyrian from the same archive. From the mentioned Tigunanum tablets around 65%

13 For detailed comments on Tigunanum NI, AḪ, ŠA, Ú, E, SU and LI in the context of Hittite cuneiform, see Weeden 2011: 70–76.

14 Old Assyrian palaeography is still poorly understood and a sample is used here purely to show a potential degree of difference between script-groups not because it has any relationship to Tigunanum or Mittanian.

TABLE 5.81 Sign-forms which match between Mittani and Tigunanum

	Mittani	Tigunanum
	Matching sign-forms	
TU		
TI		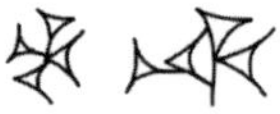
RI		
EN		
AT		
IN		
AM		
DU		
BI		
GEŠ		
Ú		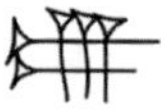
BUR		
ŠU		
ḪI		
MEŠ		

matches Mittanian, and 35% does not (**Figure 5.2**). This does not change drastically when only key signs are considered: around 60% still matches Mittanian, and 40% does not. Thus far, only Later Middle Assyrian and Nuzi have been compared to Mittanian as being different script-groups. When key signs were considered, these script-groups differed around 30%, which in fact means Tigunanum comes close to falling into the same category.

Since Nuzi has been used as a corpus to find boundaries, and contrast with Mittanian, it is of interest to place these sign-forms next to Tigunanum as well. When really narrowing in on palaeographic detail, there are a couple of sign-forms from Tigunanum which are a slightly closer match with Nuzi than Mittani – namely due to more 'Babylonian' features. For example, both Nuzi and Tigunanum scribes have a tendency to shorten the middle wedge of MA, or to place the upper and lower horizontal of signs such as BA at a more diagonal than straight angle (albeit not as diagonal as even older forms of the sign!). In addition, where in Mittani signs such as KA the *Winkelhaken* noticeably moved up, to touch the horizontal wedge, at Tigunanum and Nuzi the *Winkelhaken* still hovers more in the middle of the composition. Finally, Tigunanum IL more obviously matches the 'Babylonian' form found at Nuzi rather than Mittani, and the same can be said for the sequence of horizontal wedges found in RA. It is certainly possible that this bias is coincidental, due to the extremely limited number of presently accessible Tigunanum texts as well as the necessarily limited Nuzi corpus used for comparison. However, logically it would not be odd for some older Babylonian influence to be visible in Tigunanum (whose script has repeatedly been classified as 'Old Babylonian', see **Paragraph 5.5**). For one, Tigunanum UM and DUB are more similar to Middle Babylonian than either Mittani or Nuzi (Fossey 1926: 319; Labat 1988: 98).

5.9 Final Remarks

Following on from the analysis of Middle Assyrian and Mittanian, Nuzi was introduced to highlight more universal script-boundaries (such as differences between contemporary neighbours) but also internal script-boundaries (individual variation). The Nuzi tablets were written in short timespan and in many cases by related people. They are more varied and more personal than Mittanian or Middle Assyrian. The texts also present a much higher density and availability of data than Mittanian: the location of Nuzi is known, thousands of documents survive and the documents reveal details about everyday life including the names and relationships of particular scribes. This has allowed for a critical look at differences between sign-forms and variants. For example, not all Nuzi scribes impress the *Winkelhaken* clusters of AḪ or AM with as many wedges or even at the same angle as they impress ḪI. Therefore – in the context of the uniform script found in the Mittani Amarna letters – while it is tempting to differentiate, for example, a ḪI with five impressions and a ḪI with seven impressions as distinct sign-forms, the number of wedges is not always indicative of script-group, scribal school or even individual hand. This does not mean the variation is not significant, or equally diverse and numerous in other script-groups; it simply reveals the human element of the sign. In particular, it reveals a strong contrast between the degree of variation in writing at Nuzi and in Mittanian.

It almost goes without saying that signs are not only produced or recognised as part of a particular script-group, but also specifically as different from other script-groups (also see Buccellati (2010) about the semiotics of Hurrian ethnicity at Urkeš). Script at Nuzi varies as much as or more than Early Middle Assyrian, it was used at the same time as Early Middle Assyrian, it was found not all that far from Aššur, and it was written under the hegemony of the same Empire; yet it differs from Early Middle Assyrian – and it also differs from Mittanian and Later Middle Assyrian. Thus, if a scribe learned to write in a particular way in a particular place, then the scribe's writing will reflect that. It apparently does not require the organisation of an Empire to set apart a script-group; as Nuzi illustrates, a single family may be enough. The Nuzi scribes learned how to write at home in Nuzi and not in the Mittani heartland. In addition, it looks like the Mittani ruler was not in the business of setting up schools across Mittani lands or imposing a Mittani writing system on its subjects. If scribes wanted to use the same system, maybe transmission worked along the lines of asking for permission, or to be invited, to come learn it.

Expanding into the recent past of Northern Mesopotamia, Tigunanum entered the scene in this chapter as well. Although older, and likened to Old Babylonian, a distinct link to Mittanian sign-forms could be made. Significantly, Tigunanum does not follow Old Assyrian, not even the Old Assyrian found in Ass. 14446. Whereas it is impossible to take away the label of 'Old Babylonian' without conducting thorough and detailed palaeographic analysis with contemporary script-groups, especially from the same or a nearby region, an argument may, cautiously, be made to think of this script-group as 'Old Mittanian'.

So, now it is time to compare all data from Mittanian, Middle Assyrian, Nuzi and even some Tigunanum, and see how they fit in the broader Late Bronze Age writing traditions of Northern Mesopotamia. On one hand, the following chapter will indicate similarities and overlap. On the other hand, it will discuss, where possible, how the individual script-groups were learned and used, and offer comments on their geographical and historical context.

CHAPTER 6

Comparative Palaeography

6.1 Introduction

This chapter will compare all the data collected and analysed up until now, to correlate the internal characteristics of each discussed corpus. In order to gain a better understanding of their regional and historical context, this chapter will include comparisons to Babylonian sign-lists, later joined by references to contemporary Late Bronze Age cuneiform from other sites. It remains unclear how and why the different powers emerging in the 15th century based their writing on old or new methods, their own or others'. Considering all these different script-groups together will provide a basis for making statements both about the internal aspect of Mittani script (how it was learned and used) but also about the geographical and historical aspect (the lines of transmission resulting in its presence in Northern Mesopotamia). Accordingly, the aim of this chapter is to create a more cohesive narrative of Mittanian writing.

It should be (and has been) noted that it was not in the aim and scope of this project to also compile a palaeography of Babylonian. In the comparative tables which will follow, the discussion will be based on the exhaustive research conducted by Fossey (1926),[1] Labat (1988)[2] and Mittermayer (2006).[3] While these forms may not be representative of Babylonian as a whole nor of specific corpora, they are used here as a contrast to Mittanian and as a broad reflection on wider cuneiform writing practices such as the disparity between larger southern and northern writing traditions.

In this context, it is of note that during the Amarna Age the Mittani ruler and the Babylonian ruler seem equal in most respects. It is difficult to say which appears more powerful from the Amarna correspondence. On one hand, the

1 Fossey (1926: viii–xi) does not provide an index with works used per period or script, but he refers to a bibliography which includes previously composed overviews (e.g. P. Haupt (1881) *Akkadische und sumerische Keilschrifttexte*), miscellaneous museum collections (e.g. H. V. Hilprecht (1893) *The Babylonian expedition of the university of Pennsylvania*), and private collections (e.g. Th. G. Pinches (1908) *The Amherst Tablets*).

2 Labat's list is based primarily on Howardy (1904), Deimel (1922), Thureau-Dangin (1926) and Fossey (1926).

3 Mittermayer's list is based on a restricted corpus of Sumerian literary texts. The inventory of signs refers exclusively to Old Babylonian texts from Nippur and Ur, as well as tablets kept in the collections of the University Museum (Philadelphia), the British Museum (London) and the Hilprecht-Sammlung (Jena).

 | DOI:10.1163/9789004417243_007

Mittani-Egyptian relationship carried on for longer – but on the other hand, Babylonia seems to be at equal or even better footing by the time these letters are written; plus, the Mittanian and Babylonian letters express equal amounts of concern about their relative status and hierarchy (Avruch 2000: 161). It is obvious that although the Pharaoh and the King of Mittani, and the King of Babylonia, address one another as brothers – the first acts as the big brother, and the other two as little brothers. Mittani tries to break this pattern once in EA 23 by reminding Amenhotep that Tušratta is also his father-in-law; but Egypt does not respond. The only other ruler who comments on the Pharaoh's status is Šuppiluliuma, who is indignant about the fact that the Egyptian ruler's name is placed above his (EA 42). Babylonia never brings up such matters (in the preserved correspondence). Perhaps, considering this, Mittani has a slight edge over Babylonia; but it is also clear that Egypt likes to appear as if it is towering over both.

6.2 Complete Comparison

The tables below only show the most representative forms from each corpus considered or forms particularly relevant to the discussion (i.e. the categories displayed may differ per sign). For a detailed overview of each sign and all its variants, please refer to the tables presented previously. The top lines of the graphs in this chapter show data from individual tablets, while the large stacked columns show percentual averages.

BAL (5)

Mittani BAL is a relatively stable sign, with only one slight variation (bottom *Winkelhaken*, or horizontal), whereas Assyro-Mittanian BAL may occur with a bottom divergent wedge. In Middle Assyrian BAL, the *Winkelhaken* usually occurs impressed through or above the broken horizontal, rather than lower down. This most resembles the Assyro-Mittanian variant but does not match it exactly (e.g. EMA KAJ 7, obverse, line 12) (**Table 6.1**). Nuzi BAL is comparable to both Mittani and Early Middle Assyrian and thus not indicative of differences between those two contemporary script-groups.

In Old Babylonian the *Winkelhaken* is usually placed centrally, or occasionally below the horizontal (Fossey 1926: 18; Labat 1988: 44; Mittermayer 2006: 3), which can likewise be seen in Middle Babylonian. In Neo-Assyrian on the other hand, BAL is generally composed with the *Winkelhaken* (or a horizontal) above the broken horizontal (Borger 2004: 47; Labat 1988: 44). Whereas it is only a minute difference in wedge placement (in reality often several

TABLE 6.1 Comparison of BAL

BAL			5
Tigunanum	Nuzi	Am-Mit	As-Mit

Early Middle Assyrian			LMA

Tigunanum: MS 1806, obverse, line 14. **Nuzi:** SMN 2044, obverse, line 11. **Am-Mit:** EA 24, reverse, column 2, line 23. **As-Mit:** KBo 36.34, fragment 829c, obverse, column 2, line 16. **EMA:** KAJ 7, obverse, line 12; KAJ 33, reverse, line 1; KAJ 37, reverse, line 7. **LMA:** KAJ 223, obverse, line 5.

TABLE 6.2 Comparison of ARAD

ARAD					18
Tigunanum	Nuzi		Am-Mit	EMA	

Tigunanum: MS 2797, reverse, line 6. **Nuzi:** SMN 2028, obverse, line 13; HSS 14508, obverse, line 2. **Am-Mit:** EA 30, obverse, line 2. **EMA:** KAJ 1, reverse, line 12; KAJ 7, reverse, line 13.

millimetres) it could be considered a difference between older and younger forms of the sign. In the case of the database created for this project, it is certainly an observable difference between Mittanian and Later Middle Assyrian. That said, the few Tigunanum instances of BAL that were collected also have a *Winkelhaken* following the broken horizontal, as opposed to a *Winkelhaken* at the bottom of the vertical wedge.

TABLE 6.3 Comparison of ITI

ITI		20
Am-Mit	EMA	LMA

Am-Mit: EA 29, obverse, line 26. **EMA:** KAJ 176, reverse, line 3; KAJ 37, obverse, line 6. **LMA:** KAJ 223, reverse, line 6.

TABLE 6.4 Comparison of BA, ZU and SU

BA / ZU / SU		14 / 15 / 16
Tigunanum	Nuzi	Amarna Mittani Letters

Assyro-Mittanian		Middle Assyrian

Tigunanum: MS 1806, obverse, line 15. **Nuzi:** SMN 2206, obverse, line 9; HSS 13410, obverse edge. **Am-Mit:** EA 19, obverse, line 9 (second instance); EA 26, obverse, line 27. **As-Mit:** KBo 36.29, fragment 285a, obverse, column 2, line 10; KUB 37.55, fragment 373b, reverse, column 6, line 5. **MA:** EA 15, obverse, line 9; KAV 203, obverse, line 6.

BA (14), ZU (15), SU (16)

The (later) Middle Assyrian form of BA, ZU and SU with *Winkelhaken* was not recorded from any of the Mittani tablets (**Table 6.4**). However, some of the Middle Assyrian and Assyro-Mittanian tablets have the divergent initial wedge in common (**Figure 6.1**). The tendency to either impress the central *Winkelhaken* quite high up in the composition, or to use a broken horizontal,

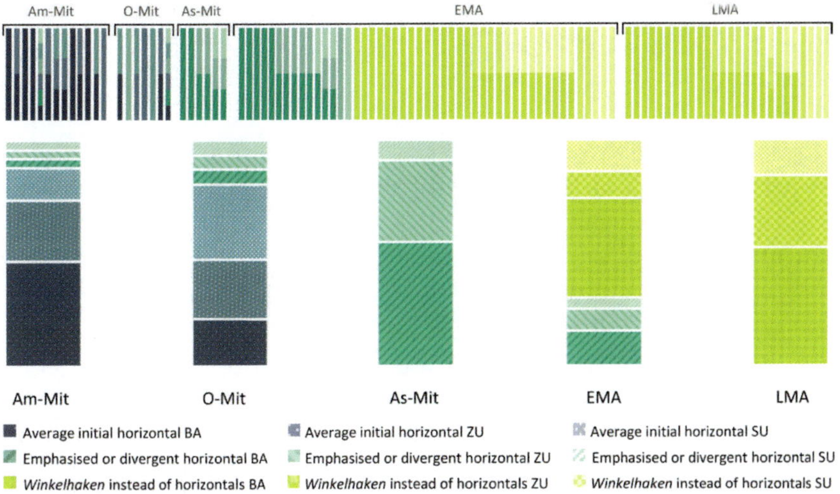

FIGURE 6.1 Comparison of BA, ZU and SU

is much more common at Nuzi than in Mittanian, Assyro-Mittanian or Early Middle Assyrian.

It is characteristic for Babylonian to use slightly more slanted or diagonal wedges (Fossey 1926: 3; Labat 1988: 42; Mittermayer 2006: 121), which is one of the features that sets Babylonian and Babylonian-like scripts apart from Mittanian and Middle Assyrian. Certainly not all Middle Babylonian BA, ZU or SU occur with diagonal wedges, but it is common. In addition, older forms of these signs, especially ZU and SU may occur with more wedges, as illustrated by Tigunanum (see **Paragraph 5.7**). In Neo-Assyrian wedges were always impressed straight (Borger 2004: 50; Labat 1988: 42), likely the result of a general trend of straightening out wedges over time.

ARAD (*18*)

The handful of Mittani instances which were collected of ARAD all have *Winkelhaken*, while Early Middle Assyrian ARAD is often also made up of broken horizontal impressions. At Nuzi it looks like both forms can be found – although, it is the older generation II tablets of Tulpunnaya which favour *Winkelhaken*, and a generation IV tablet from Šilwa-teššup which shows straighter wedges (**Table 6.2**). No instances were collected for Assyro-Mittanian or Later Middle Assyrian for comparison.

In Late Old Babylonian ARAD was composed with diagonals or *Winkelhaken* (Fossey 1926: 66; Labat 1988: 58; Mittermayer 2006: 8) and the same can be said for Middle Babylonian – whereas the instances collected from Tigunanum were again made up solely of *Winkelhaken*. Forms with straighter wedges only become common later on, and prevalent during the Neo-Assyrian period (Borger 2004: 51; Labat 1988: 58).

ITI (20)

ITI was recorded only once for Mittani, making it less useful for comparative purposes. However, notably, (later) Middle Assyrian has a different form altogether (**Table 6.3**). In Early Middle Assyrian ITI often has a central row of *Winkelhaken*, but less horizontals; in Later Middle Assyrian the central row has moved up into a broken horizontal. ITI was not recorded from the studied Assyro-Mittani or Nuzi tablets.

In Old and Middle Babylonian ITI was composed with *Winkelhaken* inside the initial two wedges. Fossey (1926: 70) and Labat (1988: 58) show the sign with outer diagonal wedges, Mittermayer (2006: 133) shows straight horizontals. These wedges move upward and become a broken horizontal in Neo-Assyrian (Borger 2004: 52; Labat 1988: 58), which fits in with the pattern set thus far by BAL and ARAD.

KA (24)

Mittani KA is much more standardised than Middle Assyrian. Only one form of the sign was found across all Mittani Amarna letters, one or perhaps two forms in Assyro-Mittanian, but at least four forms were collected from the Early Middle Assyrian tablets. KA is also a distinguishing sign between the three groups (**Table 6.5**). The Mittani form is the one with horizontal followed by *Winkelhaken*; in Assyro-Mittanian this is often replaced by a divergent wedge; and in Middle Assyrian sometimes the bottom horizontals are replaced by *Winkelhaken*. There is some overlap however, especially between Assyro-Mittanian and Middle Assyrian (**Figure 6.2**). Furthermore, Middle Assyrian KAJ 4 has an instance of KA which matches 'Mittani' KUB 37.55; however, rather than concluding there is therefore an overlap between Mittanian and Middle Assyrian, considering the other sign-forms from KUB 37.55 (see **Paragraph 6.2.2**) it is more likely that this tablet was composed by an Assyrian scribe.

In Old Babylonian KA is generally composed with the initial diagonal wedges, with a collection of horizontals and occasionally an additional small vertical inside – followed by a taller vertical, two horizontals and another vertical (Fossey 1926: 37; Labat 1988: 47; Mittermayer 2006: 123). In Middle Babylonian this is simplified slightly, and it is more common to only find one central *Winkelhaken* inside the diagonals (Labat 1988: 48). This is a form which can be found in many other script-groups, as shown for Tigunanum, Nuzi and also Ugarit, Qaṭna and Emar to name a few. In Neo-Assyrian it becomes the standard to use a horizontal wedge rather than the *Winkelhaken*

TABLE 6.5 Comparison of KA

KA					24
Tigunanum	**Nuzi**		**Am-Mit**	**As-Mit**	

Early Middle Assyrian				**Later Middle Assyrian**	

Tigunanum: MS 2799, obverse, line 6. **Nuzi:** BM 85607, obverse, line 4; BM 26240, obverse, line 9. **Am-Mit:** EA 19, obverse, line 18. **As-Mit:** KBo 36.34, fragment 254e, obverse, column 2, line 5. **EMA:** KAJ 148, reverse, line 5; KAJ 149, reverse, line 1; KAJ 7, reverse, line 10; KAJ 14, obverse, line 12. **LMA:** KAV 109, obverse, line 13; AfO 19 t 5, obverse, line 4.

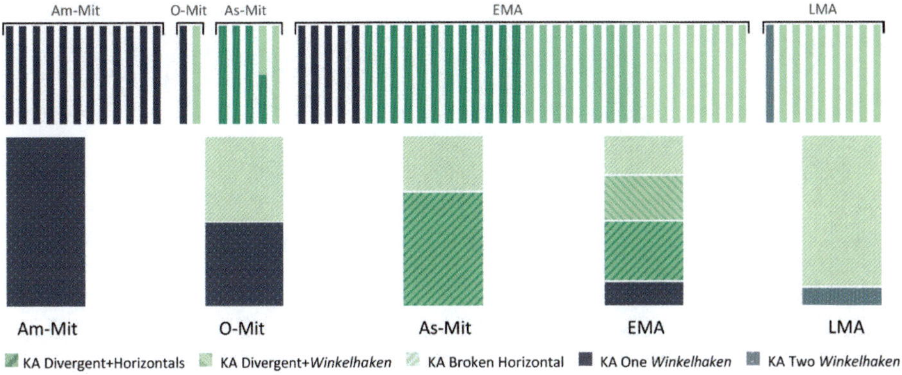

FIGURE 6.2 Comparison of KA
Note only two tablets included from 'Other Mittani'.

(Borger 2004: 53; Labat 1988: 48) although a form with a horizontal followed by two *Winkelhaken* also persists (Fossey 1926: 43).

LI (85)

Mittani and Nuzi LI never have horizontal wedges (with one possible exception, see **Paragraph 3.3.4**), whereas in Early Middle Assyrian this form occurs sometimes, and in Later Middle Assyrian more frequently **(Figure 6.3)**. It is

TABLE 6.6 Comparison of LI

LI					85
Tigunanum		**Nuzi**	**Am-Mit**	**As-Mit**	

Early Middle Assyrian		**Later Middle Assyrian**		

Tigunanum: MS 1807, obverse, line 1; MS 1806, obverse, line 13. **Nuzi:** HSS 13480, reverse, line 9. **Am-Mit:** EA 19, obverse, line 15. **As-Mit:** KUB 37.106, fragment 640b, obverse, column 2, line 13. **EMA:** KAJ 151, obverse, line 4; KAJ 47, side, line 2. **LMA:** KAV 104, reverse, line 11; KAV 100, obverse, line 6; KAJ 253, reverse, line 4.

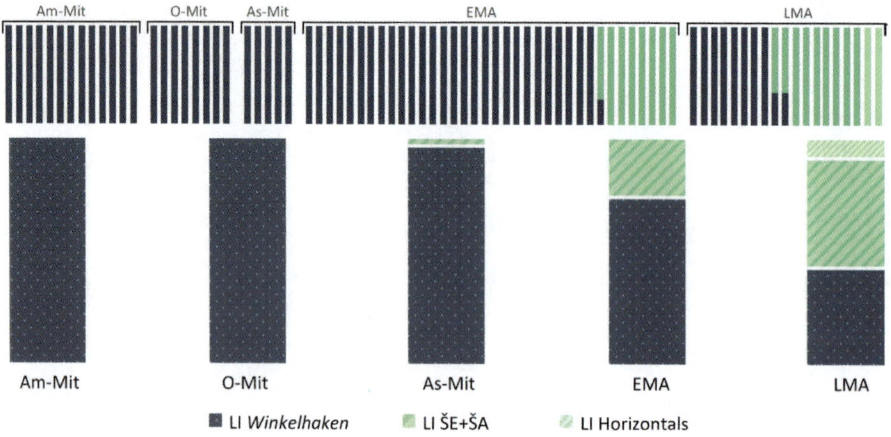

FIGURE 6.3 Comparison of LI

also notable that this is one of the few signs at Nuzi which bears more resemblance to Mittanian than Assyrian or Babylonian forms (**Table 6.6**). The ŠE+ŠA form is also attested in Old Babylonian (Fossey 1926: 113; Labat 1988: 60; Mittermayer 2006: 149), as well as Middle Babylonian, and again in Neo-Assyrian (Borger 2004: 62; Fossey 1926: 120; Labat 1988: 60). Plus, some horizontal wedges appear in one of the Tigunanum forms of LI. Therefore,

TABLE 6.7 Comparison of NA

NA		110
Tigunanum	Nuzi	Am-Mit

O-Mit	As-Mit	MA
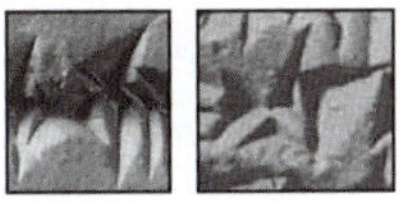	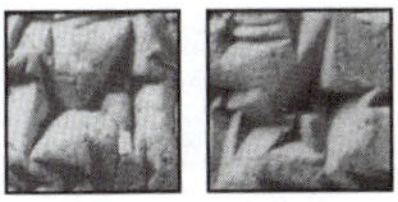	

Tigunanum: MS 1807, reverse edge. **Nuzi:** HSS 13411, obverse, line 9; BM 26283, obverse, line 5. **Am-Mit:** EA 29, obverse line 15. **O-Mit:** KBo 28.66, obverse, line 15; KBo 1.2, obverse, line 34. **As-Mit:** KBo 36.29, fragment 1017c, obverse, column 1, line 24; KUB 37.42, reverse, column 4, line 19. **MA:** KAJ 155, obverse, line 9; KAJ 179, obverse edge, line 14.

the horizontals (or ŠA part) are not necessarily a mark of sign progression or evolution (also see Weeden 2012: 240). Rather, their relative absence could be considered characteristic for this period inbetween, in Northern Mesopotamia in the Late Bronze Age (also see **Paragraph 6.4**).

QA (99) and NA$_4$ (385)

QA shows how big differences can be between individuals (see **Paragraph 5.3.3**), and therefore also helps in determining the border between form and variant. Assyro-Mittanian QA is generally impressed with a *Winkelhaken* rather than diagonal; the same can be said for Early Middle Assyrian and Later Middle Assyrian; although there it is less obvious (**Table 6.8**). Either way, while this version of QA might look quite different from Mittanian, this does not make it a different sign-form straight away. The individual Nuzi scribes impress the sign at a wide variety of different angles and with different wedge shapes and lengths.

Schwemer (1998: 27) records a single instance of NA$_4$ from the Assyro-Mittani tablets, with a question mark, with two extra, small, verticals inserted on the left-hand side ('NA$_4$? Mir-šú-ma'). From the tablets studied here this was confirmed for Assyro-Mittanian, and also found in Later Middle Assyrian. It is not a special kind of innovation and forms with one or two

TABLE 6.8 Comparison of NA$_4$

NA$_4$		385
Nuzi		**Am-Mit**
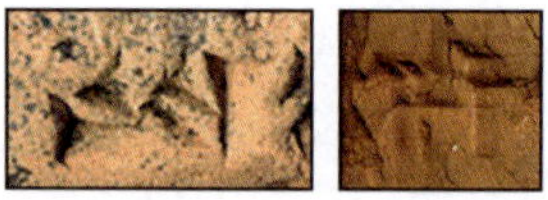		
As-Mit	**EMA**	**LMA**

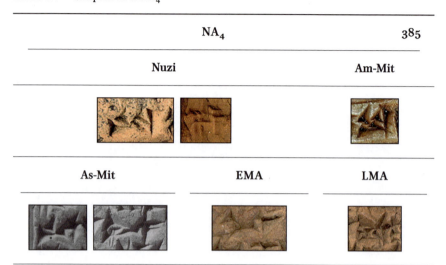

Nuzi: SMN 2028, side; HSS 13409, reverse, line 4. **Am-Mit:** EA 25, obverse, column 1, line 62. **As-Mit:** KUB 37.52, obverse, line 8; KBo 36.29, fragment 510d, column 3, line 22. **EMA:** KAJ 14, obverse, line 3. **LMA:** KAV 109, reverse, line 6.

superfluous initial verticals can be found across all periods, from Archaic to Neo-Assyrian, including Nuzi (Fossey 1926: 507–509; Labat 1988: 125). Forms without initial left-hand side verticals occur across all periods as well (demonstrated particularly well by the use of both forms at Nuzi), but, in the context of the database discussed here, the exclusive use of this form was particular to Mittani and Early Middle Assyrian.

NA (110)
The Nuzi variant or form of NA with straight wedges does not occur in Mittannian, Assyro-Mittanian or Middle Assyrian; and none of those three show as much drastic variation in the sign either, despite collecting an extremely large number of instances (**Table 6.7**). This makes NA one of the clearer markers of Nuzi script and differentiates it from the other corpora considered. What is more, Tigunanum NA is generally found with its two *Winkelhaken* floating above the horizontal, and the upper *Winkelhaken* of those even cutting through the top of the horizontal wedge. This also differs from all other corpora considered, including Nuzi, and it can be considered a marker of the Tigunanum script-group.

In much of Old Babylonian and Old Assyrian NA was composed with diagonals enclosing a row of horizontals attached to the vertical, but already during this period the diagonals changed into two *Winkelhaken* and the additional horizontals vanished (Fossey 1926: 143; Labat 1988: 68; Mittermayer 2006: 11). Late Old Babylonian generally only includes the latter form of NA, which remains the same into the Neo-Assyrian period (Borger 2004: 67; Fossey 1926: 149).

RU (*111*)

From the Middle Assyrian tablets no instances of RU were recorded where there were clearly more than two *Winkelhaken*, like the form on the large Mittani Amarna tablets (**Figure 6.4**). However, at Nuzi a form with more *Winkelhaken* does occur. It is not the same as Mittanian: the Nuzi form follows an order of W-v-W-v-W-v (**Table 6.9**). There are also several cases across all corpora where it is difficult to see a second *Winkelhaken* (see **Paragraph 4.4**). However, it is usually possible to detect it and unlikely that it was common to only impress one.

TABLE 6.9 Comparison of RU

RU		111
Tigunanum	**Nuzi**	**Am-Mit**
		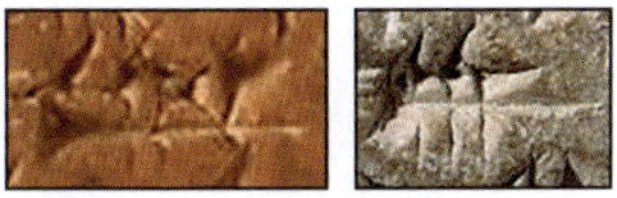
Other Mittani Documents	**Assyro-Mittanian**	
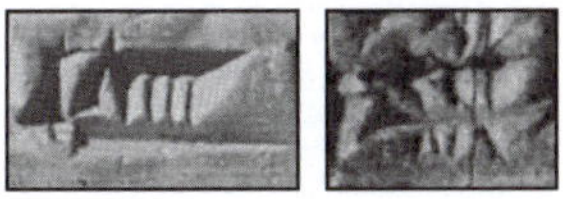		
Early Middle Assyrian	**LMA**	

Tigunanum: MS 1805, obverse, line 8; MS 4995, reverse, line 2. **Nuzi:** HSS 13410, obverse, line 8, edge; SMN 2017, reverse, line 15. **Am-Mit:** EA 29, obverse, line 33. EA 26, obverse, line 24. **O-Mit:** KBo 1.2, obverse, line 5; TB 11021, obverse, line 5. **As-Mit:** KUB 37.65, obverse, line 6; KUB 4.16, obverse, line 6; KUB 37.43, reverse, column 4, line 9. **LMA:** KAV 200, obverse, line 8. **EMA:** KAJ 1, reverse, line 12; KAJ 28, obverse edge, line 14; KAJ 209, reverse, line 3; KAJ 61, obverse, line 5.

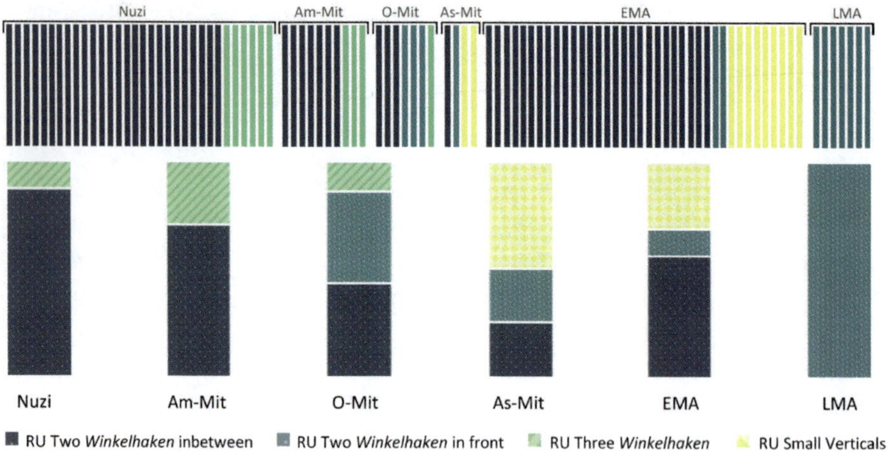

FIGURE 6.4 Comparison of RU

In Old Babylonian most of the described forms can be found as well – often with two *Winkelhaken* somewhere between the verticals (Fossey 1926: 137; Mittermayer 2006: 25) – although most common is a RU with only one initial *Winkelhaken* (Labat 1988: 66). This is also the primary form that can be found for Middle Babylonian and Tigunanum. In Neo-Assyrian the RU composition usually starts with two *Winkelhaken* (Borger 2004: 67; Labat 1988: 66). It is worth noting that Labat records a version of RU for Middle Babylonian with two preceding *Winkelhaken* and one inbetween the verticals – which must be the form from EA 24 (and thus not necessarily representative of Middle Babylonian at all). Fossey shows the form as well (1926: 138, nr. 4439), citing that it was traced from the Amarna tablets. However, significantly, one instance following this pattern was also collected from the studied Tigunanum texts.

NU (112)

NU has been discussed as a marker of scribal hand, beginning with differences between the Mittani Amarna letters (**Paragraph 3.3.4**, also Nuzi, **Paragraph 5.3.3**). There, the larger documents have a more 'angled' NU than the others; and the angle of NU matches the overall appearance of the script on each tablet. For example, all signs on EA 17 and EA 19 have straighter rather than more diagonal wedges. It seemed peculiar for the scribe(s) of KBo 28.66 and KBo 28.65 to impress the diagonal into the horizontal, but now it is clear that some scribes at Nuzi did this too, and it also occurs in the Middle Assyrian as well as the Tigunanum database (**Table 6.10**). This calls into question whether to call that version a different sign-form, or whether it is another variant. It is notable at least that it is completely absent from Amarna Mittanian.

TABLE 6.10 Comparison of NU

NU			112
Tigunanum	**Nuzi**	**Am-Mit**	
	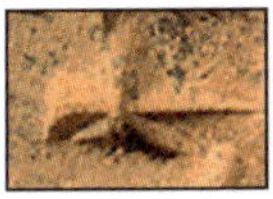 	 	
O-Mit	**As-Mit**	**MA**	

Tigunanum: MS 1806, obverse, line 13. **Nuzi:** SMN 2028, obverse, line 14; SMN 2017, obverse, line 2. **Am-Mit:** EA 25, obverse, column 1, line 36; EA 19, obverse, line 32 **O-Mit:** AlT 108, obverse, line 5; KBo 28.66, obverse, line 11. **As-Mit:** KUB 37.9, reverse, column 3, line 1; KUB 4.16, reverse, line 8. **MA:** KAJ 12, obverse, line 6; KAJ 60, reverse, line 4.

TABLE 6.11 Comparison of AK

AK			127
Tigunanum	**Nuzi**	**Am-Mit**	

As-Mit		**MA**	

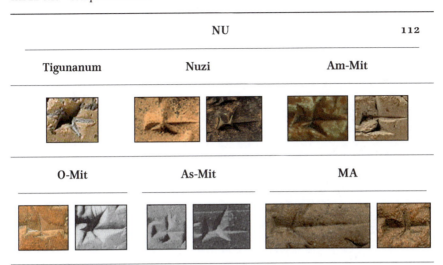

Tigunanum: MS 1856 2, obverse, line 9. **Nuzi:** SMN 2118, obverse, line 4. **Mittani:** EA 19, obverse, line 30; EA 25, obverse, column 2, line 26. **As-Mit:** KBo 36.29, fragment 2533c, reverse, column 3, line 26. **MA:** KAJ 14, obverse, line 11; KAV 200, obverse, line 6.

TABLE 6.12 Comparison of SA

SA		172
Tigunanum	**Mittani**	**Assyro-Mittanian**

Early Middle Assyrian		**LMA**

Tigunanum: MS 1806, obverse, line 10. **Mittani:** EA 22, reverse, column 1, line 38. **As-Mit:** KUB 37.55, fragment 423c, reverse, column 5, line 19; KUB 37.100a, fragment 656c, obverse, column 1, line 28. **EMA:** KAJ 14, obverse, line 11; KAJ 143, obverse, line 9. **LMA:** KAV 105, reverse, line 13.

In the Archaic period NU was impressed with three wedges, forming a triangular shape (Fossey 1926: 160) and in Old Babylonian the sign was still often impressed with two diagonals or *Winkelhaken* pressed into the horizontal (Mittermayer 2006: 9). The number of wedges eventually reduced to just two, but the diagonal did not make a permanent change into an upside down vertical. Labat (1988: 70) and Borger (2004: 66) insinuate Neo-Assyrian NU was almost always impressed with a diagonal rather than vertical. However, glancing at a selection of original tablets on CDLI, this does not necessarily prove consistent, and primary preference was probably for straighter wedges, with the overall form of the sign remaining dependent on scribal hand.

TI (118)

Nuzi TI is an excellent example of the fine line between 'short' and 'long' forms so clearly present in Assyro-Mittanian and Early Middle Assyrian (**Table 6.13**). Overall, Nuzi shows as much variation in TI as Early Middle Assyrian and the balance is similar: mostly the 'short, square' form, but also occurrences of the 'long, rectangular' form. In the more standardised later Middle Assyrian the form becomes limited to just one ('long'). In the Akkadian letters of the Tušratta correspondence from Amarna (circa 1370–1350 BCE) only the first form of TI occurs. The second is completely absent, with one fundamental

TABLE 6.13 Comparison of TI

TI		118
Tigunanum	**Nuzi**	**Am-Mit**
	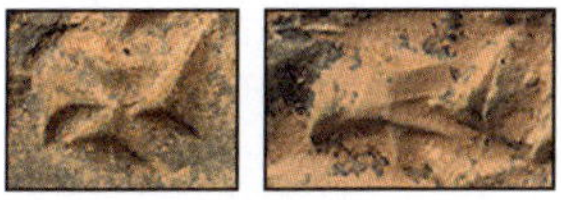	
O-Mit	**As-Mit**	

Early Middle Assyrian	**Later Middle Assyrian**	
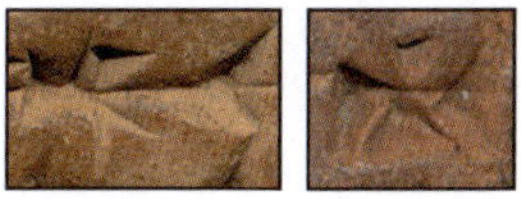		

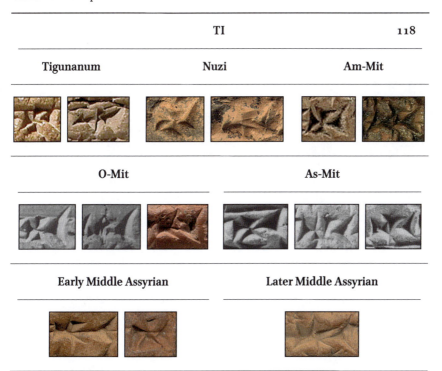

Tigunanum: MS 1812, obverse, column 1, line 2; MS1807, obverse, line 4. **Nuzi:** SMN 2103, obverse, line 15; SMN 2037, obverse, line 9. **Am-Mit:** EA 19, reverse, line 34, second instance; EA 24, reverse, column 2, line 32. **O-Mit:** KBo 1.2, obverse, line 40; KBo 1.2, obverse, line 15; AlT 13, reverse, line 1. **As-Mit:** KUB 37.43, reverse, column 4, line 10; KUB 37.106, fragment 536b, obverse, column 2, line 27; KUB 37.43, obverse, column 1, line 14. **EMA:** KAJ 173, obverse, line 5; KAJ 1, reverse, line 4. **LMA:** KAV 98, obverse, line 12.

exception: the Hurrian letter, EA 24. It is the only tablet in the Mittani Amarna collection which displays this form of TI. It is also the most frequently used form of TI on EA 24 (85% of all occurrences). There are at least two more tablets in the Tušratta correspondence which rival EA 24 in size and sign-variety (EA 25 and EA 29), but neither demonstrates this form of TI. What is more, this form of TI turns up on Akkadian-language KBo 1.2 as well; likewise mixed with the first form. Significantly, the 'long, rectangular' form of TI found only on EA 24 and KBo 1.2 has *five* wedges rather than four, distinguishing itself from the 'long, rectangular' TI recorded from the Assyro-Mittani and Middle Assyrian tablets under consideration **(Figure 6.5)**. In addition, although a few Middle Assyrian instances approximate the highly emphasised Assyro-Mittani TI, none match it exactly.

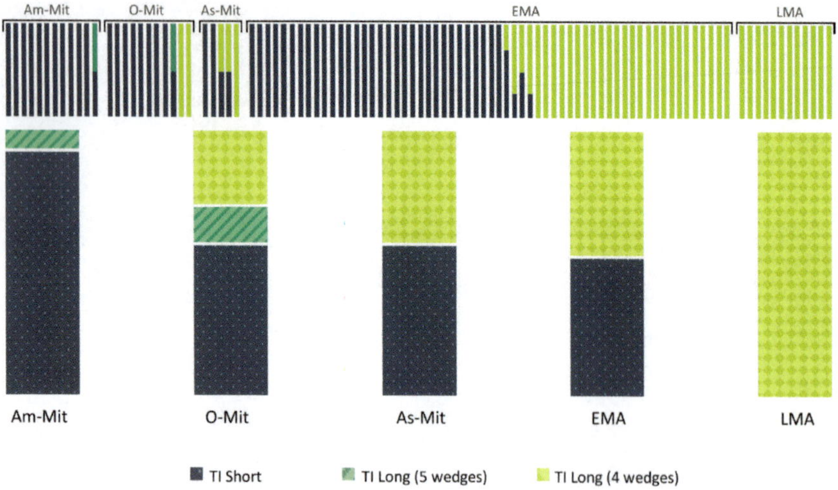

FIGURE 6.5 Comparison of TI

The only 'problem' which remains is AlT 13. This is dated one of the oldest Mittani tablets due to its seal. However, it looks like it has the 'long, rectangular' TI with four impressions (rather than five like EA 24 and KBo 1.2, both dated later). It is, thus far, the only Mittani tablet with this form (three instances were recorded). The two other Alalaḫ tablets both have the 'small, square' form. No other key signs were recorded from AlT 13 to determine whether it might be a different script-type such as EMA (and only sealed by a Mittani King). It could be possible that the second horizontal is very lightly impressed and obscured by a different wedge. However, it is more likely that this sign-form emphasises the close resemblance of Mittani to Middle Assyrian; the exceptional degree of standardisation amongst the Amarna letters (as opposed to other letters or administration); and the use of a mix of forms of TI throughout the 15th–14th centuries. That said, the long form of TI found at Tigunanum is also one with four impressions.

Freydank briefly questions whether some forms of TI could be attributed to different geographic origins, such as "*den älteren hurritischen*" or "*einen jüngeren babylonischen Einfluß*" (1988: 76). The Tušratta letters were written within such a short period, and so similarly, that one sign is unlikely to have gone through large changes because of time or place alone. All described forms of TI can already be found in Old Babylonian (Fossey 1926: 154; Labat 1988: 68; Mittermayer 2006: 11) – particularly the 'long' form, which goes back to the sign's development in the Archaic period. Possibly, the centring and lowering of its initial *Winkelhaken* could be compared to signs such as BAL, as something which was more common in Babylonian; and the *Winkelhaken* moving back up, or the horizontal simply becoming a straightened out broken horizontal, is more common for Neo-Assyrian (Borger 2004: 69; Labat 1988: 68). Since the 'long' form does return to popularity in Later Middle Assyrian and Neo-Assyrian, it cannot be assigned to a specific place or period.

AK (127)

Density of composition is not necessarily a reason to classify something as a different sign-form. However, in some of the Mittani Amarna letters, the broken horizontal of AK so clearly receives more space that it affects the overall appearance of the tablets. This is something which can be found across many script-groups and it is also especially prominent on the Middle Assyrian tablets included in the database (**Table 6.11**).

In Archaic forms of the sign the horizontals were placed clearly inside a 'box' (Fossey 1926: 224), and in some Old Babylonian texts forms occur with many additional horizontal wedges (Labat 1988: 82; Mittermayer 2006: 22; see also Tigunanum). The space given to the horizontals understandably seems largely dependent on the size of the tablets involved. For example, at Nuzi writing is a lot more condensed, and this 'spacious' AK is completely absent.

SA (172)

Schwemer (1998: 22) commented that the variant of SA with a more leftward initial lower horizontal was particularly 'Mittanian'. Schwemer's argument that this form (which often also has a more separate initial vertical) is more Mittanian is strengthened by KAJ 177 (the most securely dated 15th century Middle Assyrian tablet), where this form clearly occurs. However, Weeden (2012: 241) has shown that this variant also occurs at Boğazköy and in other Middle Assyrian texts, and the same can be seen in the database created for this project (**Table 6.12**). The difference in Middle Assyrian is also much less obvious than in the Mittani and Assyro-Mittanian documents – for example, on KAJ 170 two instances could be the first form as described, and two instances could be a more balanced second form. Because this even second form is the only recorded form of the Later Middle Assyrian tablets under consideration, this could be indicative of progression in the usage of the sign-forms, from the 15th century to the 13th century (also see Labat 1988: 86).

The larger and more separate initial vertical impression of SA hints back to the Archaic angular form of the sign () (see Fossey 1926: 248; Labat 1988: 86). However, as with TI, any progression visible here would be limited to Middle Assyrian. The more even second form occurs already in Old Babylonian as well (Mittermayer 2006: 58); the handful of Tigunanum instances collected all have three even verticals; and the Archaic form makes the occasional come-back much later on in deliberately archaeising writing, such as the cylinder of Antiochus (BM 36377, see also Fossey 1926: 252).

SAG (184)

In **Paragraph 3.3.1** the divergent wedge in SAG was discussed; where the use of this impression is not necessarily clear in Amarna Mittanian, it is very obvious in Assyro-Mittanian. In addition, **Paragraph 4.4** shows how, while Mittanian SAG always has a bottom horizontal, in Middle Assyrian this is often replaced by a *Winkelhaken*. Only one instance was recorded from Nuzi, apparently a different form with three (short) horizontals (**Table 6.14**).

In Late Old Babylonian SAG is almost always composed of two diagonals with a small vertical in the middle, followed by a tall vertical, two horizontals and another vertical (Labat 1988: 90; Mittermayer 2006: 122), although in some cases the small vertical is difficult to see or absent (Fossey 1926: 276). This first form can also be found in Middle Babylonian, but actually not at Tigunanum. In Neo-Assyrian the initial additional vertical is no longer inserted and the wedges are impressed straight rather than diagonally (Borger 2004: 84; Labat 1988: 90), a preference which can also be seen in the Mittanian and Middle Assyrian studied here.

TABLE 6.14 Comparison of SAG

SAG 184		
Tigunanum	Nuzi	Am-Mit

As-Mit	MA	

Tigunanum: MS 1806, obverse, line 13. **Nuzi:** SMN 2088, reverse, line 3. **Am-Mit:** EA 25, obverse, column 1, line 30. **As-Mit:** KBo 36.29, fragment 285a, obverse, column 2, line 12. **MA:** KAJ 165, obverse, line 8; KAJ 17, obverse, line 5, edge.

UM (238), DUB (242) and KIŠIB (486)

UM, DUB and KIŠIB were already discussed extensively in the previous three chapters. Schwemer wrote that it is difficult to distinguish between signs with the value UM, DUB and KIŠIB in Mittanian and Assyro-Mittanian, while in Middle Assyrian KIŠIB was usually composed differently from UM and DUB, as 'MES' (MZ number 486) (1998: 11, 17).

As indicated in **Chapter 2, Table 2.1**, the value of these signs does not necessarily match the form of the signs or vice versa, and they can sometimes all be seen as one and the same. Borger, who uses the Neo-Assyrian sign-forms, encountered similar problems, listing MES also as KIŠIB and DUB (2004: 133); and DUB also as KIŠIB and MES (2004: 93). Labat likewise lists his DUB as MES (1988: 99), adding there is a "*confusion de signe avec* KIŠIB, UM *et* URUDU" (**Table 6.15**). In the database used here all signs were saved according to value first, and given a number next. It was therefore possible to see how many instances occurred with which value, in which form. However, regardless of value, graphically, the discussion revolves around only three forms (**Table 6.16**).

The more instances are studied from these corpora, the less likely it seems that they are a distinguishing factor between Assyrian and Mittanian (Weeden 2016). Most Early Middle Assyrian scribes differentiated between UM / DUB and KIŠIB, but not all; and while the scribes of EA 24 and EA 25 did not differentiate between UM / DUB and KIŠIB, other Mittanian Amarna scribes did. In fact, the most consistent corpus considered has been Nuzi, where scribes rarely differentiated between any of the three and used the same sign-form in all cases (whether 'form 1' or 'form 2') (**Table 6.17**, **Figure 6.6**).

TABLE 6.15 UM, DUB and KIŠIB as recorded by Labat

	Main form	Middle Assyrian	Middle Babylonian
UM	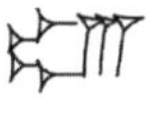	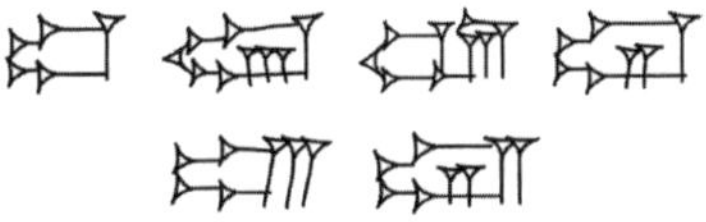	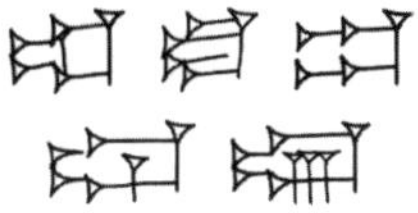
DUB			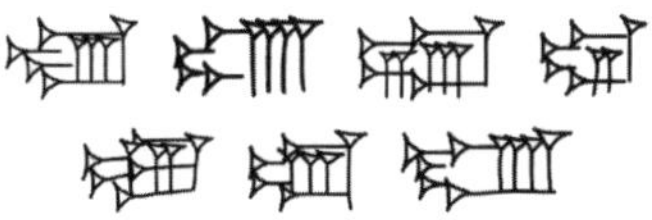
KIŠIB			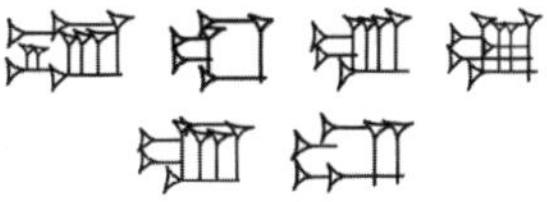

TABLE 6.16 Comparison of values and forms of UM and similar signs in the database

Amarna Mittani			Early Middle Assyrian		
Form 1	Form 2	Form 3	Form 1	Form 2	Form 3

KÌŠIB, UM, TUP, DUP, ṬUP	KÌŠIB, UM	KÌŠIB, MIŠ, MÈŠ	UM, DUB, ṬUP	KÌŠIB, UM, DUB, ṬUP	KIŠIB, KÌŠIB

From published transliterations as listed in **Chapter** 3 and **Chapter** 4; also see the Appendices.

TABLE 6.17 Comparison of UM

	UM	238
Nuzi	**Am-Mit**	
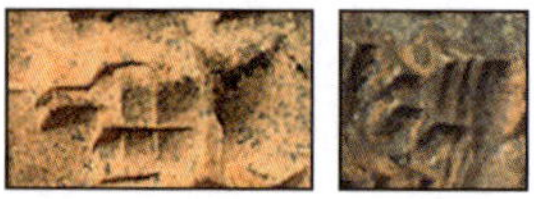		
As-Mit	**EMA**	**LMA**
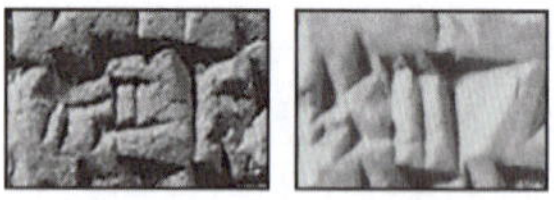		

Nuzi: SMN 2028, obverse, line 14; SMN 2017, obverse, line 17. **Am-Mit:** EA 19, obverse, line 30; EA 25, obverse, column 2, line 26. **As-Mit:** KUB 37.55, fragment 423c, column 2, line 7; KUB 37.62, obverse, line 3. **EMA:** KAJ 147, obverse edge, line 15; KAJ 66, obverse, line 6. **LMA:** KAV 103, obverse, line 4.

A potential change which is visible, is the frequency and variation of 'form 1' versus 'form 2'. In Mittanian and at Nuzi 'form 1' (small, enclosed verticals) was most common for UM and DUB, while in Early Middle Assyrian 'form 2' (extended verticals) became more popular (77% of instances of UM, and 75% of instances of DUB), and it was the only form found for Later Middle Assyrian. In addition, much more variation can be found in the placement of wedges at

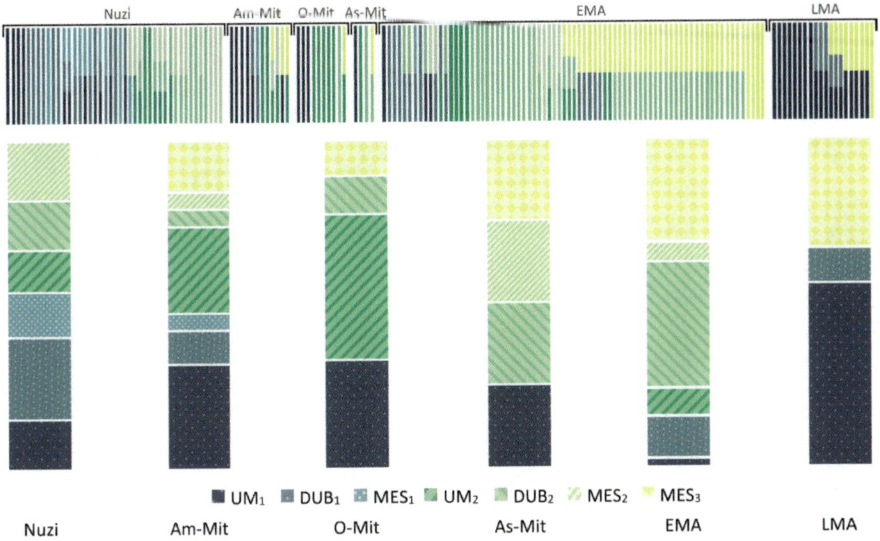

FIGURE 6.6 Comparison of UM, DUB and MES

TABLE 6.18 Comparison of UGU

		UGU		663
Mittani	**As-Mit**		**Middle Assyrian**	

Mittani: EA 27, obverse, line 12. **As-Mit:** KUB 37.43, reverse, column 4, line 19; KBo 36.29, fragment 2533c, reverse, column 3, line 21. **MA:** KAJ 44, obverse, line 10; KAJ 158, obverse, line 8.

Nuzi, and several potential variants were noted for Assyro-Mittanian – while the Later Middle Assyrian instances are all much more consistent.

Throughout time, all of these signs can also be found without any central vertical wedges, particularly in Old Babylonian (Mittermayer 2006: 44–45, numbers 112a MES, 112b DUB and 113, UM), while later Assyrian examples often only have extended verticals (Borger 2004: 92; Fossey 1926: 319; Labat 1988: 98) – both with exceptions. For Tigunanum, no instances with the value DUB or KIŠIB were collected and only a few instances of UM, so it is not possible to provide meaningful comments.

TABLE 6.19 Comparison of TA, DA and ŠA

	TA / DA / ŠA	248 / 561 / 566
	Tigunanum	
TA	**DA**	**ŠA**

	Nuzi	
TA	**DA**	**ŠA**

	Amarna Mittani Letters	
TA	**DA**	**ŠA**

	Assyro-Mittanian	
TA	**DA**	**ŠA**

TABLE 6.19 Comparison of TA, DA and ŠA (*cont.*)

TA / DA / ŠA		248 / 561 / 566
Early Middle Assyrian		
TA	**DA**	**ŠA**

Later Middle Assyrian		
TA	**DA**	**ŠA**
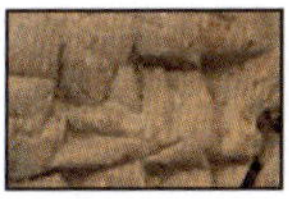 		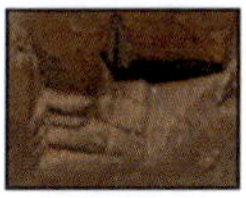

Tigunanum: MS 1805, reverse, line 1. **Tigunanum DA:** MS 1856 2, obverse edge. **Tigunanum ŠA:** MS 1856 1, reverse, line 11. **Nuzi TA:** HSS 13410, reverse, line 4; SMN 2033, reverse, line. **Nuzi DA:** SMN 2043, obverse, line 13. **Nuzi ŠA:** SMN 2033, reverse, line 5. **Am-Mit TA:** EA 19, obverse, line 34; EA 24, reverse, column 1, line 107, second instance. **Am-Mit DA:** EA 19, reverse, line 10; EA 25, reverse, column 3, line 62. **Am-Mit ŠA:** EA 19, obverse, line 14. **As-Mit TA:** KBo 36.29, fragment 2533c, reverse, column 3, line 26; KUB 4.16, reverse, line 5; KUB 37.55, fragment 423c, reverse, column 5, line 8, second instance. **As-Mit DA:** KUB 37.43, reverse, column 4, line 16. **As-Mit ŠA:** KUB 37.55, fragment 423c, column 5, line 25. **EMA TA:** KAJ 167, reverse, line 6; KAJ 170, reverse, line 6. **EMA DA:** KAJ 12, obverse, line 6. **EMA ŠA:** KAJ 146, obverse, line 10. **LMA TA:** KAV 105, reverse, line 3, second instance. **LMA DA:** AfO 19 t5, obverse, line 9. **LMA ŠA:** KAV 100, obverse, line 17.

TA (248), DA (561) and ŠA (566)

TA and similar signs have been discussed because of the differing sign-forms between the 15th–14th and 13th centuries, and it is interesting that the primary difference here is between EMA and LMA, rather than between Mittani and Middle Assyrian (**Figure 6.7**). Another point of attention has been the variants of these signs: the space allocated to the *Winkelhaken* and their placement with regard to the verticals. In the Mittani Amarna letters (see **Paragraph 3.3.4**) there was a clear scribal preference for the placement of the *Winkelhaken* in DA – either in front of the verticals or between; similarly, ŠA only occurs with

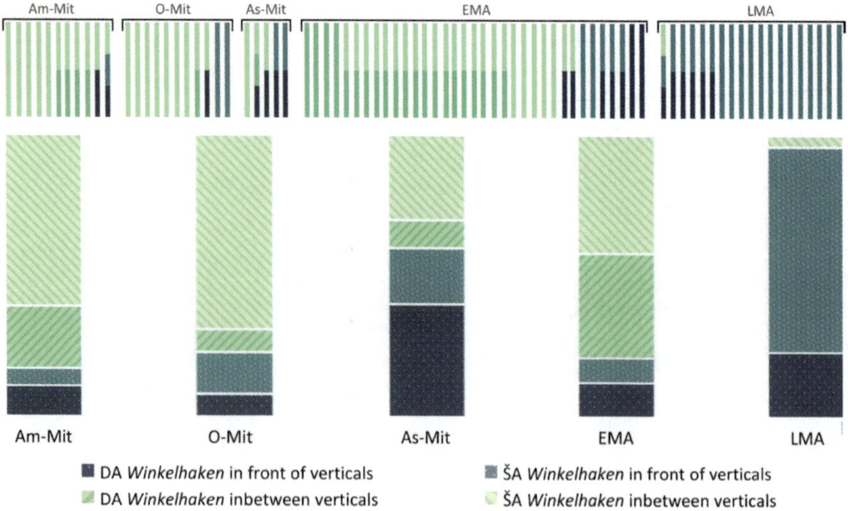

FIGURE 6.7 Comparison of DA and ŠA

Winkelhaken between the verticals in Mittani and Assyro-Mittani. From the Assyro-Mittanian and Nuzi tablets some instances were collected with smaller verticals – but not from the Mittanian and Middle Assyrian tablets (**Table 6.19**). In a few of the corpora there is also a clear difference in the spacing of the verticals on tablets; whereas in some compositions there is plenty of space to show the *Winkelhaken*, in others the verticals are more consecutive and the *Winkelhaken* obscured.

Signs with small verticals (also see the discussion on 'slipping' of verticals in **Paragraph 3.3.4**) can also be found in Old and Neo-Babylonian (Fossey 1926: 325. 330) as well as Tigunanum. In addition, the Babylonian forms do not always have multiple verticals at all, but only one (compare, for example, Labat 1988: 98, 162). In some cases, the only way in which Babylonian TA and ŠA were distinguished from one another was through the length of the horizontal wedges (long for TA, short for ŠA; both one vertical) (compare Mittermayer 2006: 49, 80), and in other cases they were distinguished through the number of horizontals used (two for TA, four for ŠA; both two verticals) (compare Labat 1988: 98, 162; also Tigunanum). Mittanian and Middle Assyrian emphasis on verticals and Babylonian emphasis on horizontals in these signs is a distinguishing difference between the scripts.

DUMU (*255*)

Despite the large number of instances recorded and the number of wedges which could vary, Mittanian DUMU rarely differs, while for Early Middle Assyrian and Nuzi it is possible to detect many variants (**Table 6.20**). In addition, the

TABLE 6.20 Comparison of DUMU

DUMU	255
Tigunanum	**Nuzi**

Mittani	**Assyro-Mittanian**

Early Middle Assyrian	**Later Middle Assyrian**
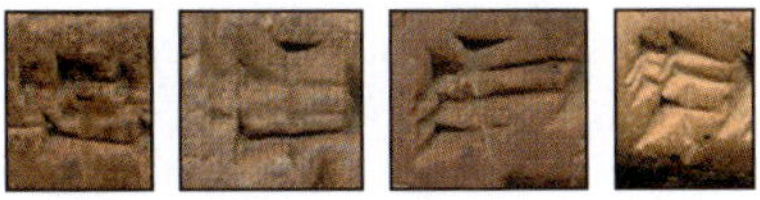	

Tigunanum: MS 1856 1, reverse, line 10. **Nuzi:** SMN 2045, obverse edge; SMN 2088, reverse, line 21; HSS 14573, obverse, line 5; HSS 13409, obverse, line 5. **Mittani:** EA 19, obverse, line 17; EA 25, reverse, column 4, line 57; KBo 1.2, obverse, line 24. **As-Mit:** KUB 37.65, obverse, line 4; KBo 36.29, fragment 97q, obverse, column 2, line 48. **EMA:** KAJ 161, obverse, line 4; KAJ 161, obverse line 10; KAJ 146, reverse, line 6; KAJ 177, obverse, line 7. **LMA:** KAJ 158, reverse, line 6.

initial two wedges of the composition at Nuzi are normally very distinct, while in Mittanian and Middle Assyrian they are less obvious. Scribal preference is seen across all considered corpora: the Amarna scribes generally prefer to impress DUMU with the vertical above the second horizontal, but the scribe of EA 25 impresses the vertical lower down in the composition; and the scribe of KBo 1.2 impresses the vertical below the second horizontal. Only four instances were collected for Assyro-Mittanian, of which three from KBo 36.29 which are likewise all impressed with a vertical low down in the composition.

In Old Babylonian, DUMU occurs in many forms and variants (Mittermayer 2006: 154) and according to published copies often without central vertical (Fossey 1926: 338; Labat 1988: 100). The absence of this wedge has not been observed in any of the studied 15th–13th century corpora, nor Tigunanum.

TABLE 6.21 Comparison of IL

IL **348**

Nuzi

Tigunanum	**Am-Mit**	**O-Mit**	**As-Mit**

Early Middle Assyrian	**Later Middle Assyrian**

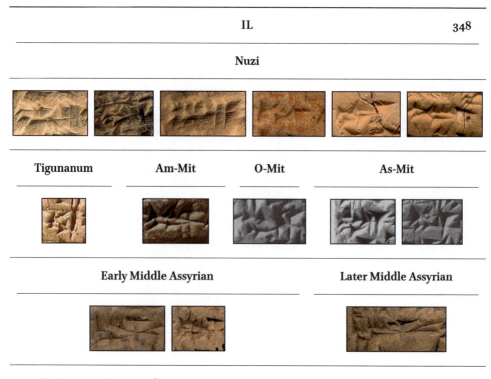

Nuzi: SMN 2088, reverse, line 12; SMN 2037, reverse, line 8; SMN 1714, obverse, line 8; HSS 13422, obverse, line 2; HSS 13472, reverse, line 1; HSS 13409, obverse, line 12. **Tigunanum:** MS 1805, reverse, line 20. **Am-Mit:** EA 28, obverse, line 18. **O-Mit:** KBo 1.2, obverse, line 18. **As-Mit:** KUB 37.43, reverse, column 4, line 6; KBo 36.29, fragment 510d, obverse, column 2, line 20. **EMA:** KAJ 7, obverse, line 9; KAJ 61, obverse, line 11. **LMA:** KAV 109, reverse, line 10.

IL (348)

Early Middle Assyrian IL is comparable to the Assyro-Mittani and Mittani forms – although these can also be found with a more protruding broken diagonal, and with *Winkelhaken* (**Table 6.21**). No instances recorded from Middle Assyrian matched the single instance from KBo 36.29 with a small cluster of *Winkelhaken*. The distribution and limitation of these forms looks specific to the corpora included here, and the instances recorded (**Figure 6.8**). The form with a small cluster of *Winkelhaken* as spotted in Assyro-Mittanian as well as the form with a neat row of upper *Winkelhaken* as in Later Middle Assyrian can both be found at Nuzi. Labat also records almost as wide a variety as the Nuzi forms for all of Middle Assyrian and Middle Babylonian (1988: 116).

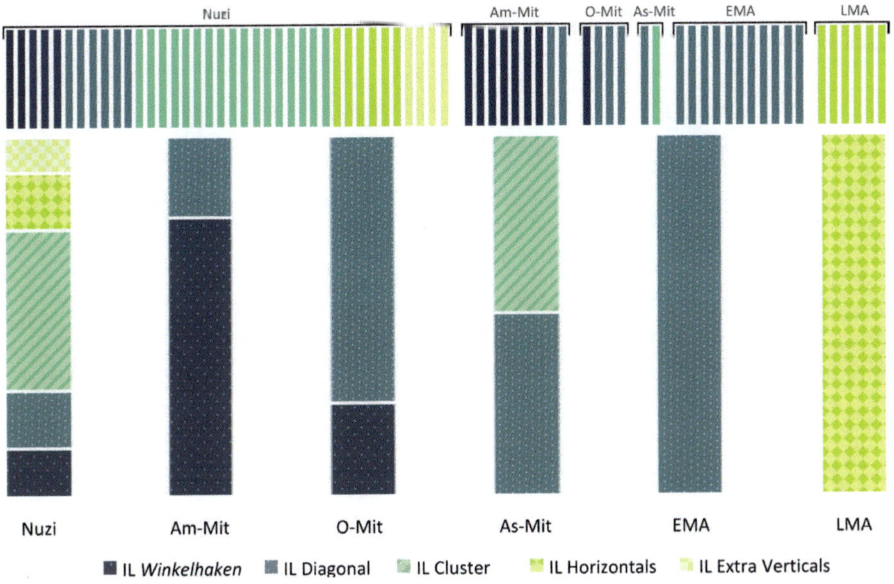

FIGURE 6.8 Comparison of IL
Note, very few instances were collected from the O-Mit and As-Mit corpora.

Old Babylonian IL does not set a clear precedent: Mittermayer (2006: 32) recorded all described forms (broken diagonal, even group of *Winkelhaken*, cluster of *Winkelhaken*, additional initial vertical, and so forth) and Fossey (1926: 454–463) dedicated nearly ten pages to the sign. At the same time, only one form occurs at Tigunanum: the version with a cluster of three *Winkelhaken*, but ending with a broken vertical rather than two vertical wedges.

LÚ (514) and Similar Signs

In **Paragraph 3.3.2** it was described how some Assyro-Mittanian instances of signs such as LÚ occur with horizontal wedges. Weeden (2012: 240) has called this form "distinctly Middle Assyrian", noting that it is rarer on Mittani tablets. Not many instances of these signs were recorded for the Early Middle Assyrian database and it is difficult to judge whether any instances might be composed with horizontal impressions, as in Assyro-Mittanian (although, this does look more likely than compositions with e.g. diagonals as present in Mittanian). At Nuzi the *Winkelhaken* of LÚ are generally arranged in a cluster of three or a row of three, more clearly than in Mittanian or Early Middle Assyrian, and resembling (but not matching) the Babylonian cluster. IN and ŠAR are always composed with a rectangular cluster of six (or more) *Winkelhaken*, which is also more usual for Babylonian (**Table 6.22**).

TABLE 6.22 Comparison of LÚ, ŠAR and IN

LÚ / ŠAR / IN				514 / 541 / 261
Tigunanum			Nuzi	
LÚ	ŠAR	IN	LÚ	IN

Amarna Mittani Letters				
LÚ	ŠAR	IN		

Assyro-Mittanian				
LÚ	ŠAR	IN		

Early Middle Assyrian				
LÚ	ŠAR	IN		

TABLE 6.22 Comparison of LÚ, ŠAR and IN (*cont.*)

	LÚ / ŠAR / IN	514 / 541 / 261
	Later Middle Assyrian	
LÚ	**ŠAR**	**IN**

Tigunanum LÚ: MS 1806, obverse, line 14, second instance. **Tigunanum ŠAR:** MS 1805, obverse, line 7; MS 1856 2, reverse, line 3. **Tigunanum IN:** MS 1805, reverse, line 21; MS 1856 1, reverse, line 11, edge. **Nuzi LÚ:** HSS 13422, obverse, line 6. **Nuzi IN:** SMN 2103, obverse, line 11, edge. **Am-Mit LÚ:** EA 26, reverse, line 19, second instance. **Am-Mit ŠAR:** EA 25, obverse, column 2, line 7; EA 22, obverse, column 1, line 31. **Am-Mit IN:** EA 24, obverse, column 1, line 74; EA 19, reverse, line 39. **As-Mit LÚ:** KBo 9.47, obverse, line 9. **As-Mit ŠAR:** KBo 36.29, fragment 166e, reverse, column 4, line 12. **As-Mit IN:** KBo 36.29, fragment 1017c, obverse, column 1, line 28: KUB 37.43, obverse, column 1, line 10. **EMA LÚ:** KAJ 148, reverse, line 8; KAJ 151, reverse, line 4. **EMA ŠAR:** KAJ 148, reverse, line 13; KAJ 29, reverse, line 10. **EMA IN:** KAJ 35, obverse, line 6. **LMA LÚ:** KAV 100, obverse, line 7. **LMA ŠAR:** KAV 104, reverse, line 4; KAV 99, obverse, line 7. **LMA IN:** AfO 19 t5, obverse, line 4.

In Old Babylonian as well as Tigunanum fewer wedges are used for LÚ (sometimes as few as three), with compositions primarily consisting out of *Winkelhaken* and diagonals, and occasionally with a row of additional verticals (Labat 1988: 150; Mittermayer 2006: 102). IN is always composed with a large cluster of *Winkelhaken* and generally with only one vertical, either centred, or placed more to the left of the composition (Fossey 1926: 354; Labat 1988: 102; Mittermayer 2006: 152). In Neo-Assyrian these signs are both less simplified and both occur with straight horizontal wedges (Borger 2004: 96, 142; Labat 1988: 102, 150).

ḪI (631)

ḪI has proven a useful sign to distinguish between the corpora considered. Mittanian and Tigunanum ḪI rarely vary at all, whereas Assyro-Mittanian ḪI and Later Middle Assyrian ḪI are often composed with more than the 'standard' four to five wedges, and Nuzi ḪI is frequently impressed at a different angle (**Table 6.23**). This variation is carried on in signs with a ḪI component, such as AM, IM and AḪ.

TABLE 6.23 Comparison of ḪI

	ḪI	631
Tigunanum	**Nuzi**	**Am-Mit**
		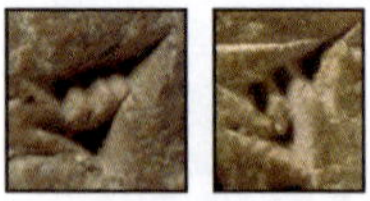
As-Mit	**EMA**	**LMA**
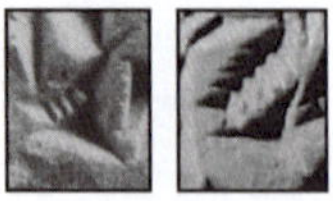		

Tigunanum: MS 1856 2, obverse, line 2, second instance. **Nuzi:** SMN 2043, obverse, line 9, edge; SMN 2023, side; HSS 13451, obverse edge. **Am-Mit:** EA 30, obverse, line 7; EA 27, reverse, line 41. **As-Mit:** KUB 37.43, reverse, column 4, line 15; KBo 36.34, fragment 829c, obverse, column 1, line 16. **EMA:** KAJ 14, obverse, line 13; KAJ 167, obverse, line 10. **LMA:** KAV 99, obverse, line 18.

Old Babylonian ḪI is almost always found in variations with fewer wedges (Fossey 1926: 782; Labat 1988: 180; Mittermayer 2006: 110), and Late Old Babylonian as well as Middle Babylonian generally have a ḪI with only four to five wedges.

UGU (663)

Middle Assyrian UGU (Early and Late) is composed with a *Winkelhaken*, followed by an upper broken horizontal or a trio of horizontals. On the Mittani (and most Assyro-Mittani) tablets, UGU is instead composed with an upper horizontal followed by another *Winkelhaken* (**Table 6.18**). As will be discussed further in **Paragraph 6.2.2**, there are only two exceptions: KUB 3.80 and KUB 4.53. UGU was not recorded for comparison from any of the Nuzi or Tigunanum tablets under consideration.

In Old Babylonian UGU was also composed with a second *Winkelhaken*, often central to the composition (with some variation: two or three small *Winkelhaken*, or additional small horizontals) (Mittermayer 2006: 141). Middle Babylonian usually has a low or central *Winkelhaken* as well. Copies by Fossey (1926: 820–822) and Labat (1988: 190) suggest the *Winkelhaken* moved upwards over time and eventually became a horizontal impression, which matches what is observed for Later Middle Assyrian in the database.

MEŠ (754)

In Mittanian a form of MEŠ with the horizontal impressed into the vertical occurs clearly and consistently on the larger tablets; but not on the other tablets. This form is (largely) absent from Assyro-Mittanian and Middle Assyrian but does also occur at Nuzi and Tigunanum (**Table 6.24**). Between Early and Later Middle Assyrian, the wedges standardise into a neat, straight sequence of horizontals. Notably, the same seems to apply between generation II and IV at Nuzi, although this should probably be interpreted as coincidence due to the limited number of tablets studied.

In Old Babylonian MEŠ the vertical was also followed by a horizontal and then *Winkelhaken*, with the horizontal often impressed into the vertical (Fossey 1926: 955; Labat 1988: 218). Although it is difficult to say based on the evidence available, this, combined with the data from Tigunanum, could be a hint that the scribes who wrote these larger Amarna tablets, and particularly the Hurrian tablet, were either older, were more aware of older Babylonian writing, or received a more old-fashioned form of training.

TABLE 6.24 Comparison MEŠ

		MEŠ		754
Tigunanum		**Nuzi**		

Am-Mit	**O-Mit**	**As-Mit**	**EMA**	**LMA**

Tigunanum: MS 1812, obverse, column 2, line 2; MS 2797, obverse edge, line 4. **Nuzi:** SMN 2023, obverse, line 15; HSS 13438, obverse, line 13; SMN 2145, obverse, line 7; HSS 14508, obverse, line 3; HSS 13381, obverse, line 5. **Am-Mit:** EA 19, obverse, line 6; EA 25, reverse, column 4, line 57. **O-Mit:** KBo 1.2, reverse, line 29. **As-Mit:** KUB 37.55, fragment 423c, reverse, column 5, line 17. **EMA:** KAJ 157, obverse, line 8; KAJ 309, obverse, line 3. **LMA:** KAV 98, reverse, line 13.

TABLE 6.25 Comparison of MUNUS

	MUNUS	883
Tigunanum	**Nuzi**	**Am-Mit**

As-Mit	**EMA**	**LMA**

Tigunanum: MS 1805, reverse, line 2. **Nuzi:** HSS 14508, obverse, line 4; HSS 14506, obverse, line 4. **Am-Mit:** EA 26, obverse, line 6. **As-Mit:** KBo 36.34, fragment 321a, obverse, column 2, line 19. **EMA:** KAJ 170, obverse, line 2. **LMA:** AfO 19 t5, obverse, line 19.

MUNUS (883)

MUNUS was thus far only discussed in **Paragraph 5.3.3** as it rarely occurs in different variants in the other corpora. However, comparing all corpora, there is a notable difference between Mittanian, and Assyro-Mittanian and Middle Assyrian (**Table 6.25**). In Mittanian the vertical stands tall compared to the *Winkelhaken* and reaches above the horizontal, but in Assyro-Mittanian the vertical is significantly shorter. Whereas this reminds of previous notes made about the 'slipping' of the vertical in signs such as RU and TA, Old Babylonian – as well as Tigunanum – MUNUS often occurred without any vertical at all, and when verticals were impressed they could be either short or tall (Fossey 1926: 993; Labat 1988: 228; Mittermayer 2006: 178). Taking all the evidence together, the difference in the placement of verticals with regard to the horizontal as observed by Starke (1985) for Hittite can be observed throughout this database, but it cannot be applied to dating.

6.2.1 *Analysis*

The effect of the comparison across the chapters has been cumulative. **Chapter 3** showed comparisons for Amarna-Mittani, Other Mittani documents and Assyro-Mittani, **Chapter 4** included comparisons between Early and Later Middle Assyrian, and **Chapter 5** had a look at Nuzi and Tigunanum. The main concern throughout has been the relationship between Mittanian,

Assyro-Mittanian and Early Middle Assyrian. There is a lot more variety in sign-forms in both As-Mit and EMA. It could be attributed to the logistics of the corpus: coincidence of genre and number of tablets. However, taking the present evidence for what it is, it can also be said that Mittanian was much more standardised (large blocks versus smaller blocks in **Figure 6.9**). The tablets considered were, after all, probably written by different scribes. They were also written during the reign of an Empire in its heartland; like the LMA tablets. The As-Mit tablets considered were found (although not necessarily written) in a different region which was controlled by a different Empire; the EMA tablets were written during a period of relative turmoil.

A few features which, from a Mittani perspective, seemed 'out of place' in Assyro-Mittanian occur in (early) Middle Assyrian, strengthening the 'Assyro' of 'Assyro-Mittanian'. In particular, the signs which occasionally have smaller verticals (RU and RA) and divergent initial wedges (BA). On the other hand, both of these features were recorded more, and more clearly, from Assyro-Mittanian than from Middle Assyrian. Of the Assyro-Mittanian sign-forms, around 35% match Mittanian, 27.5% match Middle Assyrian, and another 37.5% is particular to Assyro-Mittanian (**Figure 6.9**).

Of the EMA sign-forms 48% matches Mittanian, whereas 52% matches Later Middle Assyrian (**Figure 6.9**). There is a clear overlap, but also a clear difference. Considering the chronological, administrative and geographical setting, it could potentially be considered a transitional script-group. It would fit perfectly if the 15th century tablets had more Mittanian sign-forms and the tablets dated to Aššur-uballiṭ had more LMA sign-forms. However, either the dating of the potential 15th century tablets has to be reconsidered, or this theory is false. It is more likely that scribes at 15th–14th century Aššur wrote with

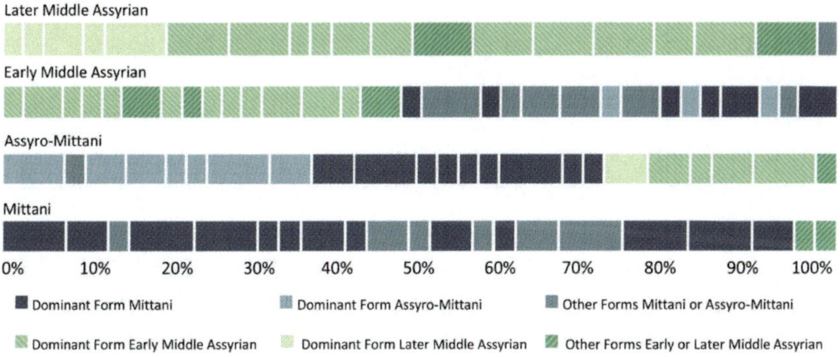

FIGURE 6.9 Abridged comparison of Mittani and Middle Assyrian sign-forms. Signs included are BAL, BA, ZU, SU, KA, ITI, LI, RU, TI, TA, DA, ŠA, IL, MEŠ, ŠAR, LÚ, UGU, UM and DUB. (Refer to individual charts throughout the chapter for a sign by sign comparison.)

a slight regional variation already, which gained the upper hand as the Mittani Empire lost its power.

The analysis here includes only significant sign-forms, which are noted in the table and figure descriptions. Around one hundred signs which change very little and match across places and periods, such as AŠ (1), were not included.[4] When analysing the key sign-forms, borders between the different corpora lie around a 30–50% difference. Most notably, more than fifteen sign-forms differ significantly between Mittanian and Later Middle Assyrian, and both are more standardised than the other two corpora considered, setting them apart altogether.

Therefore, the label 'Assyro-Mittanian' given by Wilhelm may be considered correct, as well as the statement by Weeden (2012) that Assyro-Mittanian *is* Middle Assyrian. As explained in **Chapter 3**, Weeden has suggested a terminological re-calibration, using Assyro-Mittanian as the over-arching category which includes Early Middle Assyrian and Mittanian. Anything that is neither Early Middle Assyrian nor Mittanian, but shares features with both, can be defined as belonging to the larger script group. While it would be tempting to divide sub-groups by location (Aššur, Ḫattuša, etc.) it is not always possible to tell where or by whom tablets were written, or whether they were moved after being written.

In order to shed more light on the subtleties of these differences, **Chapter 5** considered tablets from Nuzi, which are contemporary yet different. This shows how close or extreme the percentual borders between script-groups can be. Signs which can be said to differ between Nuzi and Mittanian, Assyro-Mittanian or Early Middle Assyrian are RU, BA, ZU, SU, KA, DUMU, IN, ŠAR, SUM, LUGAL, LÚ, ḪI, AḪ, IM, AM, GI, IL, MEŠ, NA, and to some extent also TI, NU, NA_4, and MUNUS (**Figure 6.10**). This is comparable to the number of signs that differs between these corpora and Later Middle Assyrian. In addition, as evidenced by, for example, IL, there is much more variation at Nuzi than in Mittanian and Later Middle Assyrian.

Although it has been possible to see how Nuzi script was influenced by Babylonian, its scribes do not use a significantly larger number of Babylonian sign-forms than the other corpora. Classifying Nuzi as a sub-group of Middle Babylonian seems hasty. Berkooz (1937: 9) instead suggests that Nuzi script may be an eastern branch of the 'Amarna-Boğazköy' family or 'Akkado-Hittite syllabary' (also see Gamkrelidze 1961; Thureau-Dangin 1926). Notably, Berkooz bases his comments on the comparison created by Contenau and does not

4 Analyses including less relevant signs such as AŠ (1) make little percentual difference when comparing similar script-groups.

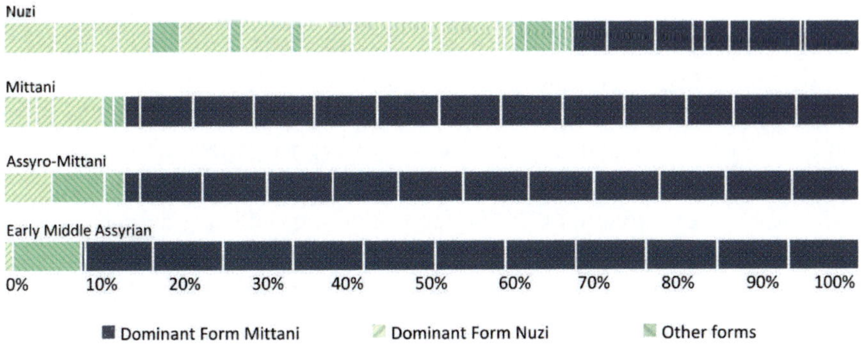

FIGURE 6.10 Abridged comparison of Mittani, Middle Assyrian and Nuzi sign-forms. Signs included are RU, BA, ZU, SU, KA, LUGAL, LÚ, ḪI, AḪ, IM, MEŠ, NA, NA_4, and IL. (Refer to individual charts throughout the chapter for a sign by sign comparison.)

provide his own palaeographic analysis. However, despite not possessing all the information we have today, he might have been on the right track. For example, Van den Hout, from his analysis of the Alalaḫ VII texts, concludes that Alalaḫ was peripheral from a Babylonian perspective and probably "not dictated from above" (2012: 163).[5] Similarly, it is conceivable that at Nuzi signs were borrowed, selected and adapted from both Babylonian and Mittanian, evolving into a more particular 'Nuzi style' by the time the site was destroyed. Moreover, as exemplified by the scribal families, there is evidence that Nuzi scribes were educated in a family setting ('father-to-son'), whether through blood-relations or apprenticeships, and not in a central palace (Fincke 2011). Overall, the Nuzi tablets of course only span around a century, and five generations; used primarily for internal administration. Whatever script we are reading, it was not standardised for Imperial purposes; it was actively changing and developing.

Finally, **Chapter** 5 also introduced a non-contemporary archive: Tigunanum. This has thus far been considered a form of Old Babylonian, and the present chapter also included comparisons to Babylonian sign lists. This has allowed for reflection on signs in their historical and geographical context where relevant. For example, the horizontals in Tigunanum and Babylonian BA (14), ZU (15) and SU (16) are usually slanted or diagonal and signs such

5 This ties in with suggestions made by Purves (1940: 169), who pointed out that the script of early Nuzi scribes is much larger and clearer than that of their successors. However, it is not clear which tablets he compared to reach this conclusion and as shown in **Chapter** 5 the size of the signs can be attributed to scribal hand rather than period.

as ARAD (18) were composed with clusters of *Winkelhaken* – as opposed to straighter wedges and sequences of broken horizontals in some Early Middle Assyrian and Assyro-Mittanian and all Later Middle Assyrian. Most versions observed of both Babylonian and Tigunanum KA (24) were a form with a central *Winkelhaken*; and of course MEŠ (754) with a horizontal pressed into the vertical – both as in many Mittanian instances. On the other hand, Babylonian and Tigunanum LI (85) can be found with horizontals, absent in Mittanian; and Babylonian RU (111) is found with one *Winkelhaken*, not observed in any of the other script-groups considered. (With, notably, one instance collected from Tigunanum which does have three *Winkelhaken*, matching the Mittanian form of the sign.)

The database makes it possible to provide some statistics for comparison.[6] From the Amarna Mittani letters 17,721 instances were collected (most of all corpora), 215 signs, 3 of which had different forms; from the Other Mittani documents 2,812 instances were collected, 158 signs, of which probably also 6 with different forms; from the Assyro-Mittani tablets 3,242 instances were collected, 210 signs, 10 different sign-forms; from Early Middle Assyrian 10,577 instances were collected, 206 signs, of which at least 15 with different forms; from Later Middle Assyrian 3,254 instances were collected, 184 signs, with perhaps 4 different forms; from Nuzi 7,681 instances were collected (generations II–V), 178 signs, at least 15 different forms; and from Tigunanum 2,480 instances were collected, 158 signs, and around 20 different sign-forms. The groups which stand out for their variety in sign-forms are Nuzi and Early Middle Assyrian, whereas the groups with the least variety are (Amarna) Mittanian and Later Middle Assyrian.

6.2.2 *Are They Mittanian?*

After analysis of all Am-Mit, O-Mit and As-Mit tablets there were two tablets which did not fit into the O-Mit corpus introduced previously and were separated from the rest of the data for further reflection.

Thus far, divergent wedges have acted as an identifier of Assyro-Mittanian – and these are clearly present on KUB 4.53. While Wilhelm (1994) classified this tablet as 'Mittanian', a re-classification as 'Assyro-Mittanian' is now more appropriate (**Table 6.26**). As it was found in the same place, it is possible KUB 3.80

6 For comparison, contrast and general understanding a collection of Babylonian tablets and high-quality photographs was also studied, but not included in the analysis. From the Amarna Babylonian letters 2,906 instances were collected, 141 signs, of which approximately 6 had different forms, from Middle Babylonian (not Amarna, University of Pennsylvania, Museum of Archaeology and Anthropology (UM) collection) 2,567 instances were collected, 197 signs, maybe 6 sign-forms; from Late Old Babylonian (the Cornell University (CUNES) corpus) 3,883 instances were collected, 197 signs, with around 13 different forms.

TABLE 6.26 Significant signs from KUB 4.53

KUB 4.53						
BA	ZU	RU	TI	UM	IT	DA

BA, reverse, line 9; **ZU**, obverse, line 2; **RU**, reverse, line 10; **TI**, obverse, line 3; **UM**, reverse, line 10, **IT**, reverse, line 4; **DA**, reverse, line 7.

TABLE 6.27 Comparison of key signs from KUB 4.53 and KUB 3.80

UGU		KA		
KUB 3.80	KUB 4.53	KUB 3.80		KUB 4.53

UGU: KUB 3.80, obverse, line 10; KUB 4.53, reverse, line 6. **KA:** KUB 3.80, obverse, line 2; KUB 3.80, obverse, line 2; KUB 3.80, obverse, line 9; KUB 4.53 obverse, line 1.

may be Assyro-Mittanian as well (although – it was sent from elsewhere). None of the identifying sign-forms occur on this tablet apart from a damaged version of KA. However, the KA (24) and UGU (663) of KUB 4.53 and KUB 3.80 match (**Table 6.27**). In addition, KUB 3.80 also has a (damaged) LUGAL (266) with straight wedges rather than *Winkelhaken*. While this is very little grounds for a definite re-identification, in combination with their provenance there is more basis for the label Assyro-Mittanian than Mittanian.

KUB 37.55 stands out for consistently using shorter verticals in the signs TA (248), ŠA (566) and RU (111) (**Table 6.28**). It also is the only tablet which displays a form of KA with a central horizontal flanked by two *Winkelhaken* – which is a form typical for Middle Assyrian (Weeden 2012: 239). This goes back to the discussion of variant versus sign-form introduced in **Paragraph 2.6**. While wedge deviation was cause to discuss 'Assyro-Mittanian' and KBo 1.2 separately, the differences in this case are smaller (less signs) and less consistent (some but not all of the forms also occur on other tablets). KUB 37.43 likewise has

TABLE 6.28 Comparison of key signs from KUB 37.55 and KUB 37.43

KUB 37.55			
KA	RU	TA	ŠA

KUB 37.43			
KA	RU	TA	ŠA

KUB 37.55: fragment 373b, reverse, column 6, line 4; fragment 423c, obverse, column 2, line 23; fragment 423c, reverse, column 6, line 11; fragment 423c, obverse, column 2, line 22. KUB 37.43: reverse, column 4, line 14; reverse, column 4, line 9; obverse, column 1, line 9; reverse, column 4, line 10.

a RU with small verticals, possibly ŠA, but not TA, and it has a different form of KA (**Table 6.28**). The only other tablet with this form of RU is the abovementioned KUB 4.53. As illustrated, it is possible that its KA is more similar to KUB 37.55 than other tablets, but it is not clear. Few instances of TA and ŠA were collected and while they could have smaller verticals it is again unclear.

KUB 37.43 is notable for exhibiting comparatively many Amarna Mittanian sign-forms (KA, TI, UGU). At the same time, the scribe did emphasise the horizontal wedges in, for example, BA (albeit not as strong as to make them appear like verticals), used small central horizontals in IT and DA, and used the forms of LÚ (514) and LI (85) which match Assyro-Mittanian more than Amarna Mittanian.

As mentioned in **Paragraph 3.2.3**, the HPM identifies at least another thirty fragments as Assyro-Mittanian as well. However, based on the signs discussed in the previous paragraphs, only KUB 37.115 can qualify with some certainty to belong to this category; it has a BA (14) with strongly emphasised initial horizontal and the form of RU with smaller verticals. KUB 37.58 likewise has an emphasised BA, as well as the elongated form of TI (118) found in Assyro-Mittanian (TI_4) and the Middle Assyrian form of KA found only on KUB 37.55 (KA_4).

KUB 37.107 on the other hand has a ZU (15) with *Winkelhaken* rather than horizontals – typical for later Middle Assyrian – found nowhere in the discussed Mittani or Assyro-Mittani documents. Nearly all other fragments have no signs identifying them clearly as Assyro-Mittanian (or Mittanian, or Middle Assyrian for that matter), apart from hints (preference for straight horizontal wedges rather than *Winkelhaken*; retracted middle horizontals; more than the average number or horizontals or *Winkelhaken*). Without these forms, the fragments could equally be Mittanian, Assyro-Mittanian or Middle Assyrian.

KUB *47.41*

KUB 47.41 (Salvini & Wegner 1986: nr. 80) is a Hurrian fragment found at Boğazköy, classified by the HPM (2016) as 'Middle Assyrian'. It is an 'AZU ritual' which has puzzled various authors. Klinger thinks it may relate to a Hittite ritual recorded on KBo 24.43 – in which case probably dictated, translated and/or re-written rather than copied directly (2001: 200). Miller (2004: 536) and Archi (2015: 284) in turn suggest that this ritual could be linked to Kizzuwatna (see **Maps**). However, all (other) compositions found at Boğazköy which might have come through Kizzuwatna are written in a typical Ḫattušan *ductus* (Miller 2004: 536). Miller thus wonders if the tablet may have instead been composed in or imported from Kizzuwatna itself (*ibid*). However, Yakubovich later comments that the content gives no indication of this (2010: 274).

The sign-form which could identify the tablet as Middle Assyrian is LI (85), which occurs here, twice, with horizontal wedges (**Table 6.29**). These were not recorded for Mittanian or Assyro-Mittanian in the database created for this project (with one exception, see **Paragrap 3.3.4**). However, apart from this sign-form, the variations in writing on KUB 47.41 remind more of Assyro-Mittanian; for example, the impression of NA (110), the possibility of a divergent wedge in TI (118), position of the *Winkelhaken* in TA (248) and ŠA (566), and the number of *Winkelhaken* in ḪI (631) and AḪ (636). The Assyro-Mittanian database further yielded very similar instances of KUB 47.41 QA (99), UM (238), UŠ (381), and ḪA (856). A final judgement based on signs alone is difficult to make, as they also deviate very little from Mittanian and only LI (85) is typically Middle Assyrian. However, considering other tablets found at Boğazköy, the genre of the tablet and the question where the tablet was composed and who composed it, Assyro-Mittanian seems like the most fitting category.

Particularly KUB 37.43 proves that Amarna Mittani forms were known and used in the tablets found at Boğazköy; while it also has forms overlapping with KUB 4.53 and KUB 37.55, in turn illustrating how closely the tablets can be linked to Middle Assyrian. Naturally this relates to the question whether these three corpora are all the same script-group to start with, and whether the overall Mittani script is the same as Middle Assyrian.

TABLE 6.29 Comparison of KUB 47.41 to Mittani, Assyro-Mittanian and Middle Assyrian

KUB 47.41	Mittani	As-Mit	EMA
LI (85)			
			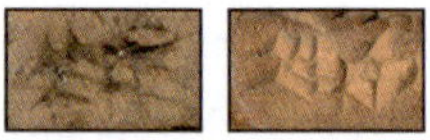
QA (99)			

NA (110)			

TI (118)			
			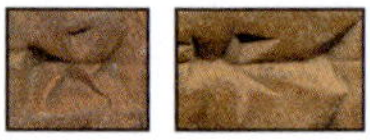
RI (142)			

UM (238)			

TA (248)			
			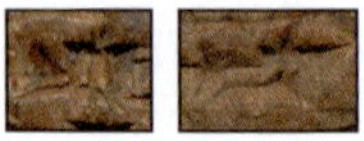

TABLE 6.29 Comparison of KUB 47.41 to Mittani, Assyro-Mittanian and Middle Assyrian (*cont.*)

KUB 47.41	Mittani	As-Mit	EMA
	IŠ (357)		

	UŠ (381)		

	ŠA (566)		
	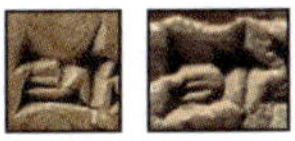		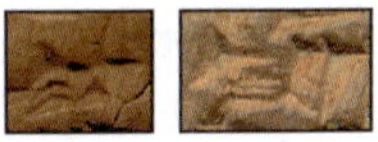
	ḪI (631)		
	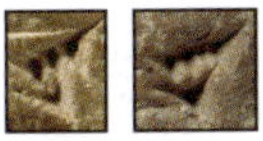		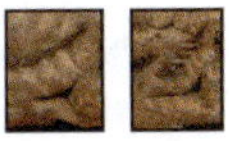
	AḪ (636)		

	AR (726)		

	ḪA (856)		

Image of KUB 47.41 available through the HPM (Bo 2250). All other images as cited in this chapter and the previous chapters.

HMM 86-014

Finally, there is HMM 86-014 from Tell Hammam at-Turkman left to consider. This tablet is not normally included in lists of Mittani documents and van Soldt already commented "the script is Old Babylonian or slightly later" (1995: 277). Nevertheless, since the claim that it may be Mittanian was made, it deserves equal consideration.

The tablet is extremely damaged, so it is nearly impossible to make certain statements about the signs. However, carefully comparing the scan of the slide, a negative image created digitally, and the copy by van Soldt, a few signs can be discussed (**Table 6.30**). The only instance of KI (808) occurs on the edge; nevertheless, besides the curvature caused by this, it looks like the form has more diagonal rather than vertical wedges, which are more common for Babylonian (Labat 1988: 206). Although it can be imagined, there is no obvious *Winkelhaken* present in KA (24) and van Soldt did not draw one either. This KA with two initial horizontals, and possibly a central one as well (as illustrated) is likewise more common in Babylonian (Labat 1988: 48). It is nearly impossible to see the *Winkelhaken* of RU (111) in the image, but van Soldt suggests it is a form with two initial impressions; while this does occur on a few Mittani tablets, it is absent from the Mittani Amarna letters. In Babylonian, RU often only has one *Winkelhaken* (Labat 1988: 66) – which could be a possibility here. There is also a mark above the sign, which could either be a *Winkelhaken* or a crack (according to the reconstruction the sign above it should be LUGAL (266), which would not have e.g. a vertical extending downward). IŠ (357) is the best-preserved sign on the tablet. While this sign differs little between different script-groups, it is notable that the verticals extend very far down, through the dividing line, which is uncommon in Mittani documents. Many of the signs are also very 'condensed' (e.g. RU, but also ŠA (566) in line 1) which is likewise less common in Mittanian and more popular in Late Old Babylonian. According to the copy, LI may occur with horizontal wedges, which are normally absent in Mittanian. These are not visible in the image however. Finally, the image suggests that IL (348) may have a broken diagonal and additional *Winkelhaken* as in Mittanian; although the copy instead shows a broken vertical. On the other hand, the bottom diagonal may also be interpreted as a vertical – which would again be more typical for Babylonian forms of the sign (Labat 1988: 116). Based on the evidence gathered in this chapter, 'Old Babylonian or slightly later' seems like a fair assessment. If the tablet has anything to do with Mittani or a Mittanian King, the script probably does not. Of course it is always possible that this would be a very early version of Mittanian, transitional Mittanian, or previously unseen Babylonian-Mittanian. In fact, a comparison to Tigunanum may be suggested here as well (see **Paragraph 5.7**). Either way, despite the damage, HM 86-014 differs from 'Imperial' Mittanian.

TABLE 6.30 Comparison of signs between the Amarna Mittani Letters and HMM 86 014

	KI (737)	KA (24)	RU (111)
Amarna			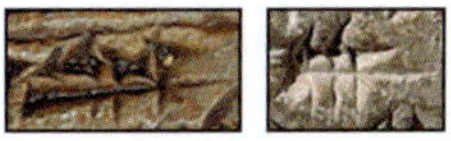
HMM 86-014		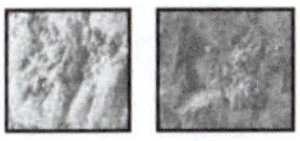	
Negative		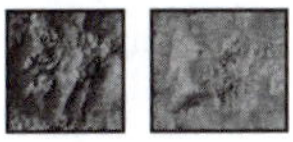	
Copy		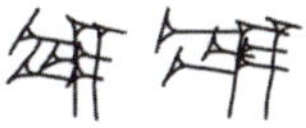	
	IŠ (357)	**LI (85)**	**IL (348)**
Amarna			
HMM 86-014			
Negative			
Copy			

6.3 Other Writing from Northern Mesopotamia

In the first chapter, the idea of a broader northern (peripheral) Mesopotamian script was introduced, with specific reference to Ugarit, Qaṭna and Emar. Having compared and analysed Mittanian, it is worth it to briefly return to this discussion.

About Ugarit, Van Soldt writes "we may assume that Mittannian teachers probably worked in Syria" – explaining the strong Hurrian influence – but also "Assyria slowly took its place ... it is therefore not surprising to find an increasing Assyrian influence" (1999: 45). When the Hittites took over power in Syria, it is likely that the use of written Hurrian gradually declined and became confined primarily to scribes and rituals (Vita 2009: 224). The script itself, of the Hurrian tablets at Ugarit, has been described as 'Middle Babylonian' (Dietrich & Mayer 1999: 58; Postgate 2013), which is a reasonable assessment. A comparison: the same forms of KA are used in Mittanian, at Nuzi and at Ugarit (**Table 6.31**). Ugaritic BA, ZU and SU are more slanted, like the Babylonian, but despite the common Middle Babylonian form of LI with horizontals, at Ugarit LI is found with only *Winkelhaken*. Other relevant signs which match between Mittani and Hurrian at Ugarit are ARAD, SA, UM, UGU, probably MEŠ; a cluster of *Winkelhaken* in signs such as IN; 'space' in signs such as TA; few *Winkelhaken* in signs such as ḪI; the 'short' TI; and possibly even three *Winkelhaken* in RU (less clear) (based on photographs published by Ernst-Pradal 2008; 2015). Overall the signs match rather closely. This is not to say that it is the same script-group, without further in-depth study. For now, the assessment that these tablets are a form of Middle Babylonian may stand. The question is how Mittanian fits into that, often having been described as Middle Assyrian. Combining evidence from (at least) Mittani, Nuzi and Ugarit, it is clear that Hurrian scribes shared a common sphere of influence. This also creates a divide between these three corpora, and Assyro-Mittanian and Middle Assyrian. The signs mentioned above start to differ between Mittanian and Middle Assyrian during the 14th century, and are almost completely different in 13th century Middle Assyrian.

At Qaṭna, it is possible to find a typical Babylonian RU with one *Winkelhaken* and MEŠ with horizontal impressed into the vertical (**Table 6.31**). The SU with more than two verticals reminds of Older Babylonian forms of the sign (Fossey 1926: 6). Whereas a 'long' TI is also used in later Middle Assyrian, the LI without *Winkelhaken* and TA with *Winkelhaken* clearly visible inbetween rather than in front of the verticals become less common in Later Middle Assyrian.

At Emar, Babylonian influence can likewise be seen in the RU with one *Winkelhaken*, although the horizontals of BA, ZU and SU are generally impressed straight rather than slanted (**Table 6.31**). This is another place where evidence has been found for the activity of foreign scribes. Cohen describes how one Kidin-Gula taught at Emar, who likely came from "North Babylonia or the Mid-Euphrates region", adding in a footnote that "Hurrians as intermediaries of Mesopotamian schooling materials ... should not be ignored" (2004: 82). From the selected Emar tablets the KA with *Winkelhaken* matches Mittanian; instances of LI found here occurred without horizontal wedges and only a 'short' TI was recorded.

This section comprises only a brief 'surface' comparison. At first glance, none of the writing at these three sites directly matches the Mittanian script. However, they all differ relatively strongly from (later) Middle Assyrian. The

TABLE 6.31 Comparison between Mittani, Ugarit, Qaṭna and Emar

	Mittani	Ugarit	Qaṭna	Emar
TI				
RU	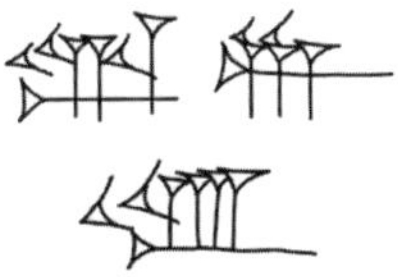	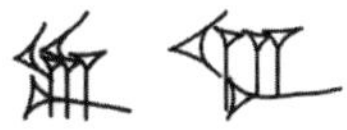		
TA		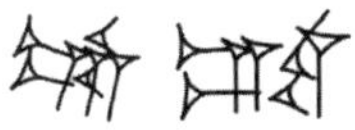		
ZU/SU				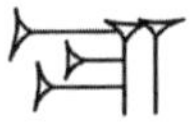
KA	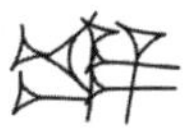			
LI				
ŠAR				
MEŠ				

The Ugarit copies are based on high-quality images provided by Ernst-Pradal (personal communication). The Qaṭna copies are based on the high-quality images of letters in Richter and Lange (2012). The Emar copies are based on low-quality images and copies in Westenholz (2000).

classification 'Middle Babylonian' has thus far been applied without the completion of a thorough palaeographic comparison. This is not the place for such a project either. However, in the context of the palaeography of Mittani, it is possible to see how the script would fit into the same developmental process. Mittani was a significant player on the international scene at the time the considered tablets at all three sites were composed.

6.4 Final Remarks

At this point Mittanian has been compared to the writing of neighbouring cuneiform cultures and it has been possible to show how sign-forms change depending on scribal, cultural and political environment in each case. Understanding signs is dependent on context and interpretation, which in turn are dependent on one another. Adaptations can reveal clues about scribal contacts and the transmission of cuneiform. Variation, or lack thereof, can reflect on scribal education and the way in which scribes learned. During this project, boundaries have been indicated between script-groups, showing, potentially, when a tablet is Mittanian, when it belongs to the broader Mittani script-group, and when it differs altogether. In some cases, sign-forms were found to be unique to a corpus, while in other cases there is overlap all the way from Old Babylonian to Neo-Assyrian.

Besides recognising unity, script-groups are also set apart through contrast. While there is a degree of overlap between Middle Assyrian and Middle Babylonian, within this it is possible to tell the difference between, for example, Nuzi and Mittanian. At the same time, it is possible to distinguish all of these script-groups clearly from Old Assyrian. A focal point of the analysis has been the amount of data collected and the statistical information drawn from it. While standardisation can be shown in numbers, it can also be indicated through social factors. In the cases studied, smaller organisational structures (Tigunanum, Nuzi) have shown more variation than large institutions (Mittani, Later Assyrian). The administration of Mittani, Assyria, but also Babylonia and the Kingdom of Tigunanum is reflected in the writing produced by each. It is clear that there is a relationship between organisational principles, such as learning, training or school, and the conception of script, sign-forms and variation.

There are many possibilities for further research on the topics that have been addressed here, as particularly the comparisons to Babylonian, Tigunanum and other northern Mesopotamian sites have only scratched the surface. These possibilities had to be included, for contrast, comparison and context. However, additional corpus-based studies of any or all of these remain necessary. Such analyses will undoubtedly contribute to the further unravelling of transmission of Late Bronze Age cuneiform.

CHAPTER 7

Conclusions

7.1 Introduction

Having reached the end of the comparison, it is time to return to the initial theories: processual theory considers factors such as political economy, comparative analytical frameworks, and the use of large reliable datasets; postprocessual theory introduced a concern for agency, practice, ideology; the role of material culture and cultural identity. This comes together in studies of interregional interaction and group identification.

One of the leading philosophical issues in this regard, has been that of identity. As proposed by Bourdieu, identity is a social phenomenon, and social agents develop strategies in response to their entire social environment. These responses are not necessarily directly linked to, or reflected by, one another. A social representation is not static: it is co-produced by different groups of people, changing over time as it develops. Terms such as 'acculturation' and 'adaptation' can rarely be applied generally to an entire society, and power-relations involved in group-identification are not necessarily a one-way flow (e.g. from complex states to less developed polities). People build part of their identity on the basis of group membership, divided over several levels (e.g. country versus city; tribe versus family; language versus dialect). People might identify with one group, but compare to other groups, and express themselves based on the relevance of each. Therefore, the definition of identity throughout this book must be understood as performative.

Written signs are a form of social representation: they are shaped through an assortment of scribes working in diverse environments across different periods. Of importance here is the difference between a universally recognised form of a sign (an abstract entity, such as illustrated in Borger's *Zeichenlexikon*), and its unique personal rendition (a particular handwritten instance, such as those found on clay tablets). How individual instances come to be is related to a number of social factors such as significance, perception and motivation. Peirce attempted to compartmentalise this and classified signs according to qualities ('icon'), conventions ('symbol') and facts ('index'). These attributes are not necessarily mutually exclusive (cuneiform covers all three) and they depend on the relationship of the sign with its context. Examples are what the sign resembles and how it is understood; in the case of cuneiform this includes why, when, where and by whom the sign was composed or read. Writing signs

 | DOI:10.1163/9789004417243_008

is an expression of social practice and social networks: it can serve as direct evidence of the conditions under which people were educated and in what kind of institutions they were learning.

Since writing is interactional and transformable it is not easy to divide into categories. This project has used a very specific corpus-based categorisation of signs. Sign-forms were defined as frequently occurring and often, but not always, indicative of overarching school or tradition. The form must either differ in composition entirely, or wedges must be *consistently* placed at a specific angle, in a particular shape, or a unique number. Variants were defined as occurrences which are notably different, but not different enough to constitute their own form-category. Variants can be, but are not always, indicative of individual scribal hands. While variation can be specific to a school or tradition as well, this category has been used when differences in the order, manner, angle or number of the impressions are *inconsistent* on or between tablets.

7.2 Writing as a Marker of Identity

As described above, identity should be seen as performed rather than created. Sign-forms by themselves do not translate directly into identity and it is a combination of characteristics that assigns significance (if any) to their formation. Interpretations and theories aided by sign-context are only attainable when there is sufficient information to build an argument. In the study of cuneiform writing on clay tablets meaningful information can be drawn from archaeological context (e.g. find-spot, condition), medium (e.g. colour, inclusions), layout (e.g. shape, size), language (e.g. formulae and abbreviations) and sealing practices – as well as historical context. Historical context may include broad information about period, culture or political situation, but also more specific information about institutions, social networks and educational systems.

Particularly the Mittani Amarna correspondence has served as a useful case-study on writing and identity, beginning with the languages in which the letters were composed. From a socio-linguistic perspective it is often seen that the use of one language declines in favour of another. For example, a language may lose popularity when the local or native language is considered to have a lower prestige, or to be less useful. On the other hand, languages can flourish when spoken by more high-status people, or simply the surrounding communities. Principally, a social representation such as language will be co-produced by different groups, changing over time as it develops (exposure, acceptance and use). An example of this is the use of Akkadian in Mittani documents, while the Mittani population was made up of native speakers of Hurrian. It is possible to detect Hurrian lexicon and grammar in their Akkadian, and the majority of the population used Hurrian personal names. When a script is allocated the role of an identity marker for a speech community, it strengthens the language, and even helps to preserve minority languages. However, the Hurrians, as far as it is possible to tell at the moment, did not have a unique script, and they rarely wrote in their own language. As the Mittani Empire, the Hurrians only held significant power for a short period of time. After this period, spoken Hurrian and documents produced in Hurrian declined almost simultaneously. This can be compared to most languages which are endangered at present: they either never had their own script, or no longer use it.

A more specific source of information on writing and identity is the person who wrote the document. The preceeding chapters looked at scribes from different points of view: the Mittani tablets were all potentially written by different scribes, or at least in different hands, whereas many of the Later Middle Assyrian tablets under consideration were produced in one scribal hand and the Nuzi tablets were written by a multitude scribes of which three identifiable by name and comparable. While the Mittani tablets are dominated by royal correspondence, the Early Middle Assyrian and Nuzi tablets were concerned primarily with the local economy. Together, these corpora cover a wide range of different people, with different positions and backgrounds.

With regard to Mittani scribal status, a few contemporary cuneiform documents reveal general clues. For example, EA 32 refers to a scribe reading the letter once it has reached its destination. This indicates that, rulers may have been dependent on scribes for the reception of their letters (Van der Toorn 2000: 101, 105). Rather than functioning only as executives, royal secretaries would have been close to the King. Some of the other Amarna letters also refer to 'the scribe of the King' (EA 286–289, 316). Nevertheless, little is currently known about the number of scribes employed in Imperial institutions. In Amarna itself there were possibly several royal workshops, in which groups of an unknown number of employees were active (Mynářová 2014: 380). However, prosopography of the Amarna letters overall suggests that the position of scribe of the King was not rare or held by a single person; 'royal scribe' is attested at least 15 times and 'royal secretary' is attested at least 8 times. It is known from later centuries that Aššur also distinguished at least between common scribes and royal scribes (Wiggerman 2008: 208), with Neo-Assyrian documents referring to the *rab ṭupšarri* (chief scribe) and *ṭupšar ēkalli* (palace scribe) (Luuko 2007: 227). The scribes described in this context were evidently held in high esteem. If the scribes of the large Mittani Amarna letters also held the highest status at the royal court, they would have been the most senior. This seniority could potentially explain why they would have been the last to use more Archaic sign-forms in cases such as MEŠ, which are not encountered again in later (Assyrian) documents.

Another avenue to explore is the context in which the tablets were composed and delivered. Although we know very little about the presentation of royal correspondence, many letters themselves describe grand visual displays of gift-giving ceremonies, involving processions of chariots and containers filled with treasure. It is possible to imagine EA 24 (and its companions) came to Egypt in a similar fashion, as part of the grand display, and that more than one person would have carried such tablets. Moreover, someone would have been needed to read or translate it (as suggested in e.g. EA 32), especially when assuming Hurrian was not a commonly known language at the Egyptian court. In EA 24, Tušratta complains about not receiving impressive gifts from Egypt, so he might well be setting an example with his own gifts. Tušratta is also intent on strengthening unity between the two Empires (emphasising their relationship as 'brothers' in several letters), which means he cannot appear too subservient on this occasion. In all likelihood Tušratta had EA 24 intentionally composed as a marker of national identity.

So how is it possible to tell the difference between scribal hands? Small variations in the way signs were impressed (for example, the angle of NU) show that the Mittani Amarna letters were probably all written by different scribes, or at least in different styles; yet their writing is very similar otherwise. Although it is a limited corpus, the cuneiform used represents a unity. The script gives little indication that it was common to invite scribes from different regions or schools to the Mittani heartland. With only three signs definitively occurring in different sign-forms across the entire Amarna Mittani corpus (RU, TI and MEŠ), there must have been a system in place resembling centrally organised schooling or training. This is discernible in the other Mittani tablets considered too. While found in different places across northern Mesopotamia, and potentially dating outside the Amarna period, they share the same standardised nature of writing. Only one additional sign-form was found during this study (RU), and all other sign-forms as well as variants are consistent. For example, none of the currently known Mittani tablets (as listed in **Chapter 3**, with KUB 4.53 and possibly KUB 3.80 excluded) show any additional forms of KA; whereas nearly all other known contemporary cuneiform script-groups had more than one form.

Even though the corpus is highly standardised, the larger Amarna tablets stand out as comparatively different. These are the tablets on which the three different forms of RU, TI and MEŠ occur most frequently; especially on the largest tablet of all, the Hurrian letter EA 24. The large letters were extremely important and carefully composed documents, with the Egyptian Pharaoh as their recipient. It is therefore dubious that factors such as scribe, language or layout can be attributed simply to coincidence. What is more, Mittani would not have been the only great power to use its own style of writing when corresponding with the Pharaoh. One of the Hittite Amarna letters was written in a "typical Hittite *ductus*", indicating that the Ḫattuša chancellery did not always use a special script for Akkadian diplomatic texts (Devecchi 2012: 149).

Returning to the other corpora under discussion: while it was impossible to establish a clear difference between 15th and 14th century Middle Assyrian, or Generation II and IV at Nuzi, it was possible to establish differences between families and individual scribal hands in the considered Nuzi corpora. For example, the tablets associated with Teḫip-tilla son of Puḫi-šenni have more in common with the tablets from Zike son of Šurki-tilla than with the tablets from the Tulpunnaya archive. This could be interesting for further research. However, as the initial focus of this project was on generations rather than families, it is unrealistic to provide further comments at this time. That said, it was possible to establish clearly the hands of Nabu-naṣir, Sin-iqiša and Urḫiya. They show that the angle of the stylus (or impression of the wedge) was particular to the individual scribe. For example, the short and thick strokes made by Nabu-naṣir result in a significantly different DUMU (255) and ŠAR (541) than the variants impressed by Sin-iqiša and Urḫiya. In addition, each scribe consistently impressed the wedges of QA (99) at the same angle – but at a different angle from one another.

Identifying or dating tablets by sign-form or variant is nearly always unreliable, because only the latest sign, not the oldest, can indicate a boundary. Nevertheless, even when considering a versatile sign such as TI (118), the Nuzi scribes show how the use of select sign-forms may have been an individual choice. As has been previously demonstrated by Freydank (1988), there is no particular historical or political reason for the use of any (Assyrian) form of TI. Mittanian or Middle Assyrian do not have one single form for a single period, and most forms occur from Old Babylonian through to Neo-Assyrian. However, it is possible that differences can be attributed to individual choice, because the different forms of TI rarely occur mixed within documents. This is illustrated not only by the Nuzi scribes, but in fact most tablets considered throughout this project. There are only four Early Middle Assyrian contenders for mixed use, three Mittanian (one of which EA 24), one Tigunanum, and one Assyro-Mittanian.

Commonly, scribes also impress variants of ḪI (631), or signs composed with such an element, with the same number of *Winkelhaken*. For example, EA 29 is the only tablet where all these signs are impressed consistently with more wedges than the other Mittani Amarna letters; and Sin-iqiša almost always impresses the composition at a horizontal angle. However, significantly, this is also where it is especially clear how much less standardised writing was at Nuzi. Urḫiya impresses ḪI and signs with a ḪI element differently on several occasions; and while it was very common for Nuzi scribes to impress ḪI with many wedges, or at a peculiar angle, the 'standard' 4-wedge variant also occurs in the corpus. Therefore, while this is a reasonably good marker of scribal hand, it is less trustworthy than choice in TI.

7.3 Defining Mittani Script

What remains is the task of describing Mittani script and separating it from Middle Assyrian. By creating co-occurrence matrices, it has been possible to show how sign-forms and variants interact on various levels (e.g. between tablets, scribal hands, corpora or script-groups). Graphs can illustrate when, and how frequently, sign-forms overlap and also when they differ (such as forms present in Mittanian and Early Middle Assyrian; or forms present in Early Middle Assyrian and Later Middle Assyrian). In addition, the graphs have shown the amount and degree of variation within and between the corpora under consideration.

The main ways in which the 36–39 tablets currently labelled 'Mittani' can be distinguished from any other contemporary writing are standardisation (few sign-forms) and lack of variation (few variants). As mentioned, the only signs which definitively occur in multiple forms are RU (111), TI (118) and MEŠ (754) (**Table 7.1**); other possibilities are TIM (167) (not attested often enough for conclusions); KA (24) (primarily less clear on tablets other than Amarna); UGU (663); IN (261) (cluster of *Winkelhaken* on EA 24); and ID (560) (differs only on KBo 1.2). Signs with significant variants are TA (248) and ŠA (566) (order of impression or depth of *Winkelhaken* and spacing between verticals), NU (112) (angle of the diagonal) and DA (561) (possibility of *Winkelhaken* impressed before verticals as in e.g. Later Middle Assyrian). Another way to recognise Mittanian is by knowing the combination of the single forms of the signs used, such as KA (24) with an upper *Winkelhaken*, LI (85) without horizontals, and NA_4 (385) without additional verticals. It might also prove significant to keep an eye out for a RU (111) and TI (118) with additional wedges. Furthermore, the Mittani tablets are bound together by an absence of features present in other corpora: divergent wedges and a strong emphasis of initial wedges as seen in Assyro-Mittanian and later Middle Assyrian (only BA and ZU on EA 22 and the Alalaḫ tablets hint at this).

TABLE 7.1 Recognising Mittani

Mittani				
BAL (5)	**KA (24)**	**LI (85)**	**RU (111)**	**TI (118)**
			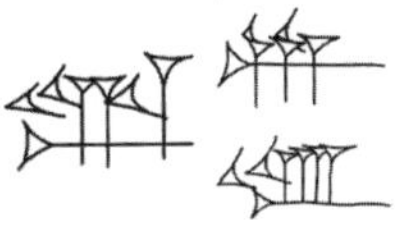	
TA (248)	**ŠAR (541)**	**ḪI (631)**	**MEŠ (754)**	
		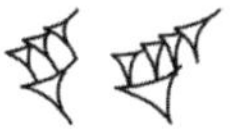		

Significant features include a relative lack of variation and specific forms of signs such as KA and LI. See the **Comparative Sign-List** in the Appendix for a comparative table and **Chapter 3** for discussion of individual instances.

Whether it is due to location, genre of document, or period, it is possible to see why scholars have traditionally distinguished between Mittanian, Assyro-Mittanian and Early Middle Assyrian. As described in **Chapter 3**, Assyro-Mittanian often (but not always) has divergent wedges in signs such as BAL (5), BA (14), KA (24), TI (118) and SAG (184). Assyro-Mittanian also has a few additional sign-forms for signs such as KA (24), RU (111), GAB (148), IL (348), and ŠAR (541) (**Table 7.2**). Finally, Assyro-Mittanian variants of ḪI (631), or signs with such an element, are nearly always composed with more than four wedges.

Wedges may likewise be impressed divergent or with emphasis in Early Middle Assyrian, although generally less strongly than in Assyro-Mittanian. Instead, Middle Assyrian of the 15th–14th centuries primarily stands out because of a degree of overlap with Middle Assyrian of the 13th century and later. This can be seen in the forms of BAL (5), BA (14), ZU (15) and SU (16), ARAD (18), ITI (20), KA (24), LI (85), IL (348), NA_4 (385) as well as TA (248) DA (561) and ŠA (566). TI (118) and MEŠ (754) standardise and it is possible to see a flattening trend of wedges in signs such as IN (261) and LÚ (514). The Later Middle Assyrian forms of the signs never occur on the Mittani tablets, therefore forming a clear divide between at least Mittanian and Later Middle Assyrian.

TABLE 7.2 Recognising Assyro-Mittanian

Assyro-Mittanian				
BAL (5)	**BA (14)**	**KA (24)**	**QA (99)**	**RU (111)**

TI (118)	**TA (248)**	**ŠAR (541)**	**ḪI (631)**	
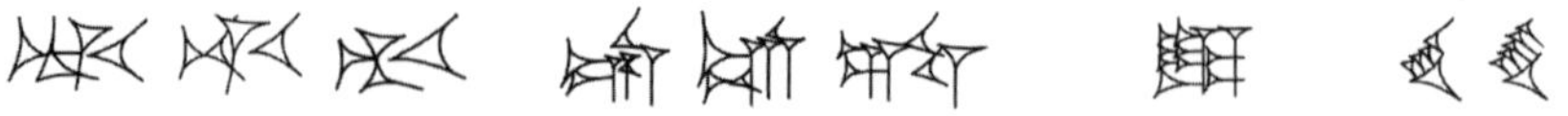				

Significant features include the divergent horizontal and vertical wedges, and number of *Winkelhaken* used. See the **Comparative Sign-List** in the Appendix for a comparative table and **Chapter 3** for discussion of individual instances.

TABLE 7.3 Recognising Early Middle Assyrian

Early Middle Assyrian				
BAL (5)	**BA (14)**	**ITI (20)**	**KA (24)**	**LI (85)**

TI (118)	**TA (248)**	**IL (348)**	**ŠAR (541)**	**MEŠ (754)**
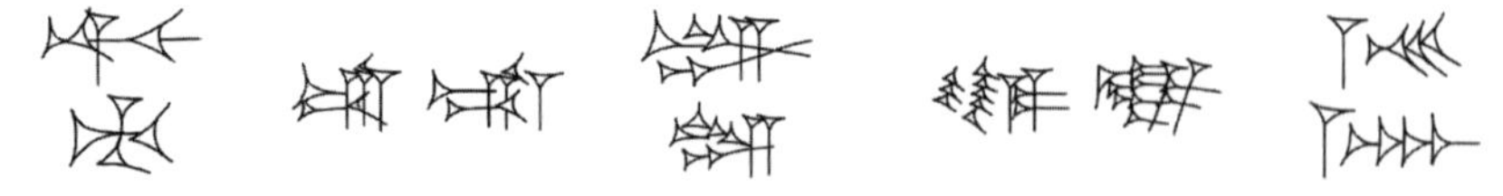				

Significant features include the standardisation of certain forms and at the same time the relatively large amount of variation. See the **Comparative Sign-List** in the Appendix for a comparative table and **Chapter 4** for discussion of individual instances.

TABLE 7.4 Recognising Later Middle Assyrian

Later Middle Assyrian					
BAL (5)	**BA (14)**	**ITI (20)**	**KA (24)**	**LI (85)**	

ŠAR (541)	**TI (118)**	**TA (248)**	**IL (348)**	**LÚ (514)**	**MEŠ (754)**
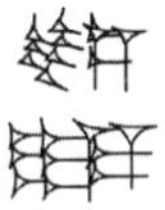					

Significant features include the standardisation of certain forms and specific forms of signs such as KA and LI. See the **Comparative Sign-List** in the Appendix for a comparative table and **Chapter 4** for discussion of individual instances.

Of course, Nuzi (**Table 7.5**) and Tigunanum (**Table 7.6**) fall slightly outside the discussion. It is a risk to determine how to identify these script-groups; first of all because they were chosen as a contrast to Mittanian and Middle Assyrian, and second due to the limited number of tablets studied, and the absence of a detailed expert comparison in this book (to Middle Babylonian or Old Babylonian, amongst others). However, while the data is incomplete, it may still be of use.

Nuzi BA (14) and similar signs are often impressed with diagonally angled wedges. At least five different forms of IL (348) were attested; at the same time, LI (85) only occurs without horizontal wedges. RU (111) can occur with three *Winkelhaken*, but in the order W-v-W-v-W-v, as well as a version with two *Winkelhaken* (W-v-W-v-v). The distinct Nuzi NA (112) most commonly occurs with a horizontal wedge followed by another two horizontals (one above, one below). In addition, ḪI (631) is found impressed at a variety of uncommon angles, with more than four impressions.

Among the documents studied for this book, Tigunanum ZU (15) and SU (16) differ from all other script-groups considered and are typically impressed with at least three vertical wedges. Similarly, QA (99) consists of just one small diagonal wedge or *Winkelhaken* followed by a vertical. Uniquely, LA (89) is composed with either an emphasised top horizontal wedge, or emphasised

TABLE 7.5 Recognising Nuzi

Nuzi				
BA (14)	KA (24)	LI (85)	NA (112)	RU (111)

TI (118)	IL (348)	ḪI (631)	MEŠ (754)	

Significant features include the variation in certain forms and specific variants of signs such as NA and ḪI. See the **Comparative Sign-List** in the Appendix for a comparative table and **Chapter** 5 for discussion of individual instances.

TABLE 7.6 Recognising Tigunanum

Tigunanum					
BA (14)	ZU (16)	KA (24)	LA (89)	QA (99)	RU (111)

TI (118)	AK (127)	HI (631)	NA (252)	ḪA (856)	MEŠ (754)

Significant features include the comparatively more Old Babylonian forms of the signs, and specific variants of LA and NA. See the **Comparative Sign-List** in the Appendix for a comparative table and **Chapter** 5 for discussion of individual instances.

top and bottom horizontal wedge, and NA (112) is made up of a horizontal wedge and two *Winkelhaken*, usually placed quite high in the composition. KA (24) is only ever found composed with a *Winkelhaken* centred between the two initial horizontal wedges, and IL (348) only ever occurs with a small cluster of *Winkelhaken*.

Moving from script-definitions back to sign-definitions, two signs potentially challenging the described definitions of sign-form and variant are ḪI and TA – making this a good point to elaborate on these classifications further. ḪI has been classified as variant because the number of wedges impressed is not consistent. Each individual scribe uses a different number, with, for example, most Mittani scribes using few and most Assyro-Mittani scribes using many. Since this results in many versions of the sign (at least six, not counting more from Nuzi), none of which are truly used consistently per group, these have been referred to as variants rather than forms. However, as mentioned, it is not only sign-forms that differentiate the script-groups: variants can as well. Mittani TA could be considered to have different sign-forms because the overall appearance of the illustrated versions differs, even if the number of wedges does not. However, it has been classified as variant because the spacing between wedges may vary depending on crowdedness of the script on a given tablet, or how clearly / when an individual scribe impresses the *Winkelhaken* (compare to RU and ŠA as well) – while in Later Middle Assyrian the difference is much more obvious, when the *Winkelhaken* move to the front of the composition consistently in the entire corpus under consideration as well as the publications used for comparison. As emphasised in previously, the classifications used here are corpus-based, applicable to the corpora studied for this project.

When defining script-groups there is the amount of available data which cannot be ignored. This project has aimed to find statistically satisfying answers to questions about sign-form occurrence and variation, but there is only a limited number of Mittani tablets available to include in the analysis. Through the available data alone, it is not unlikely that Mittani currently looks different from Assyro-Mittanian and Early Middle Assyrian simply due to the lack of further evidence that they are the same. Note for example the occurrence of 'Middle Assyrian' LI on 'Assyro-Mittanian' KUB 47.41.

The largest and clearest collection of Mittanian tablets are the Amarna letters, and since they are the same genre and written in a close timespan it is not surprising that together they make Mittani script appear standardised. It is of course possible that future excavations may find Mittani tablets with, for instance, divergent wedges or different forms of KA. However, besides these conditions, the Tušratta letters do vary in language, size, clay-type, topic, forms

TABLE 7.7 Mittanian, Assyro-Mittanian or Middle Assyrian?

KUB 37.81						
TE (line 2)	ZI (line 2)	LÚ (line 3)	ŠA (line 4)	UR (line 5)	GI (line 5)	MA (line 6)

and variants. They were probably composed by a group of different, although similarly educated scribes. Significantly, the sign-forms and variants found on Middle Assyrian Amarna letter EA 15 differ from the Mittani Amarna letters (e.g. divergent BA, different KA and RU, 'long' TI, many *Winkelhaken* in ḪI and non-Archaic MEŠ). This means it would be highly unlikely that the Mittanian and Assyrian scribes involved in the Amarna correspondence were educated or writing in the same place.

That said, despite the described limitations and distinctions, so-called Mittanian, Assyro-Mittanian and 15th–14th century Middle Assyrian have enough features in common to consider them together as one larger script-group. When key signs such as RU, TI, and MEŠ and signs with specifically emphasised or angled wedges are absent from a tablet it is nearly impossible to tell which of the three individual groups the document belongs to.

The credibility of this overarching script-group is reflected by many of the fragments found at Boğazköy labelled as potentially, but not certainly, Assyro-Mittanian by the HPM. It can be difficult to assign such small fragments to a specific script-group. It is usually possible to determine that these fragments are not part of an altogether different script-group – such as earlier Tigunanum or later Middle Assyrian – but not whether they are specifically Mittanian, Assyro-Mittanian or Early Middle Assyrian. An example which demonstrates how a tablet fits into the larger, overarching, script-group, and not one of the three other individual script-groups described, is KUB 37.81 (Bo 5885) (**Table** 7.7).[1] This fragment was selected randomly from the list provided in **Paragraph 3.2.3**, and what is explained below is applicable to other documents included in this list as well.

1 A black-and-white photograph of this tablet was downloaded from the HPM via the Vorderasiatisches Museum Berlin and a transcription can be found in Biggs 1967: 50.

The only significant signs which occur on KUB 37.81 are LÚ and ŠA. The form of LÚ used on the tablet occurs in Mittanian, and probably Assyro-Mittanian as well as Early Middle Assyrian. The form of ŠA used on the tablet occurs in Mittanian, Assyro-Mittanian as well as Early Middle Assyrian. However, both are extremely rare for Later Middle Assyrian. There is no obvious flattening of *Winkelhaken* into horizontals, and the clusters of *Winkelhaken* present have a more 'square' than 'triangular' formation which was preferred in Later Middle Assyrian. For a more certain identification of KUB 37.81 as Assyro-Mittanian, as suggested by the HPM, it would be preferable to see divergent wedges, or a large number of *Winkelhaken* in, for instance, GI (qè, line 5).[2] However, since these are not consistent features of Assyro-Mittanian, their absence may be excused. Thus, based on palaeography alone (and not tablet context or content – see also KUB 47.41) the document could be from anywhere in northern Mesopotamia and composed any time during the 15th–14th centuries. Please do note however, that this is not an argument against Assyro-Mittanian identification, and instead, for instance, Mittanian or Middle Assyrian. KUB 37.81 was found at Boğazköy and it is an Akkadian prescription for curing impotence (Schwemer 2013: 154) – so it still has both place and genre in common with most (other) alleged Assyro-Mittanian tablets. However, the proposition here is that cuneiform alone does not necessarily identify this tablet as Assyro-Mittanian and instead it serves as evidence that Mittanian, Assyro-Mittanian and Early Middle Assyrian can be considered one overarching Northern Mesopotamian script-group.

What we currently know about Mittanian, is that it was written in the heartland of the Mittani Empire and it looks as if many surrounding cities and regions used the same or a similar style of writing. Since there are no large sets of tablets to compare for these other locations, it is unclear whether the writing has any notable regional variation. The only place where many contemporary tablets have been found, thus far, is Aššur. The writing of the 15th–14th centuries here is very similar to Mittanian but it shows a few deviations (as described before, *Winkelhaken* and sequences of *Winkelhaken* moving from the centre to the top of the composition, and *Winkelhaken* becoming horizontals; *Winkelhaken* begin to occur in front of rather than inbetween verticals in signs such as DA; more emphasis on initial horizontal wedges in signs such as BA). Since Aššur survived beyond Mittani, the script was able to develop further.

2 While composition of the sign is not useful here, orthography is: GI is almost always used only for the e-vowel, e.g. in EA 24 and at Nuzi (Giorgieri & Wilhelm 1995); this contributes to the argument that the tablet could also be Mittanian rather than Assyrian.

The so-called Assyro-Mittanian found (but not necessarily written) at Boğazköy, has an almost equal amount of sign-forms in common with the Mittani heartland, as with Aššur (around 30% each). Assyro-Mittanian, as an individual script-group, has more variation in signs and sign-forms than Mittanian and it has a few sign-forms (such as KA) in common with Middle Assyrian which have not been attested for Mittanian at all. Those places where Mittani held less influence – in this case apparently Nuzi, and eventually Aššur – is where the contemporary script deviates most. Particularly with regard to potentially later tablets from Ḫattuša and Aššur it is tempting to conclude that changes in the development of the script increased after Mittani's fall from power.

Historically, Mittanian came before Middle Assyrian. This is the power that ruled over the city Aššur, long before it broke free and before Assyria itself became an Empire. The evidence as is suggests that there may have been a central Imperial Mittanian scribal education, and that scribes wrote, if not the same, then very similarly, across the Mittani Empire. At the same time, Nuzi illustrates that it was also possible to either keep or develop writing differently from its overlord (see more below). Nuzi was obliterated around 1350 BCE so we will never know how cuneiform might have evolved further there. However, Aššur had overtaken Mittani by this point. It is plausible that there was an ongoing development in cuneiform there too; starting with the Mittanian style of writing and becoming more Assyrian over time – eventually making Mittanian Middle Assyrian.

7.4 The Organisation of Society

The final two topics left to consider are the motivation to use a certain type of script and how script reflects on the organisation of society and cultural identity. Especially curious in this context is the degree of difference between Aššur and Nuzi. Only around 100 km apart, both dominated by Mittani, their writing was noticeably distinct. The key to this problem lies in Mittani methods of administration. Overall Mittani administration was loose, divergent and dependent on location, people and existing institutions. These institutions were not necessarily identical to those running the Mittani state: power does not automatically extend evenly across the social landscape. While similarities may occur, a polity which exerts ideological power does not necessarily exert economic power, and a polity which exerts political power does not necessarily exert military power (Stein 2002: 907).

At the time of Mittani domination, Aššur was a city state. It only became known as the 'Land of Aššur' from the late 14th century to early 13th century onwards (Harmanşah 2012: 54; Postgate 1992: 247, 251). However, a flourishing society had previously existed at Aššur. It had maintained a large international trading network and produced documents in its 'own' Old Assyrian script. The Akkadian Assyrians did not share a language or ethnicity with their Mittanian overlord nor their Arrapḫan neighbours. According to the documents and evidence for surviving traditions (**Paragraph 4.1**), Assyrians retained memories of past glory and longed to regain their power. They became involved in the Amarna correspondence and later overtook many Mittani administrative centres. Aššur based itself on newer Mittanian customs, considered what surrounding polities were doing, and looked forward.

One the other hand, the 'Land of Arrapḫa' was already well-established by the 14th century. This Kingdom adhered to a policy of non-interference (Jankowska 1969: 233), which is a difference that can also be seen in the genre of the available tablets. At Nuzi private documents (currently) greatly outnumber state documents. Scribal education took place in a family setting and the craft was transferred from parent to child, as opposed to a system where senior or royal scribes taught more centrally. The lands of Arrapḫa were densely settled and it would have been possible to travel between settlements in less than a day, resulting in a strong, active and rapidly developing internal system of administration. There is, at the moment, no evidence of Nuzi scribes visiting foreign courts to transfer their craft. What is more, when war broke out and Aššur attacked, Nuzi needed support from Mittani to defend itself. Nuzi was on good terms with its Mittani overlord (Maidman 2011: 212), but it was also a much more inward looking society than Aššur. Nuzi probably based its writing in part off older Babylonian traditions, paying less conscious attention to international developments.

The search for a connection between writing and organisation is not new. On one hand, scribes have been observed to show more innovation in a fragmented political landscape (Veldhuis 2012a: 22). On the other hand, the development of the 'semi-monumental' Ur III writing style can be considered a reflection of official government practices (Veldhuis 2012a: 12). In a sense, Mittani complies with both situations. As mentioned, the Mittani state preferred to rule indirectly: there was a high degree of internal freedom and the Mittani territory consisted of vassals and provinces, with different Kings, councils, and institutions (Düring 2015: 301). At the same time, there was also a sovereign Mittani King and a central authority.

In palaeography, to discuss organisation is to consider standardisation. Standardisation has a "rather muddied history" in Assyriological research (Veldhuis 2003: 627). It has been suggested that, where script in the Canaanite Amarna letters is very similar, the scribes may have come from the same school, or received similar training (Vita 2015: 142). In addition, known later

Assyrian royal scribes were all involved in the education of one or more other scribes (Wiggerman 2008: 210). However, there are no statistics available to prove these points.

By collecting a very large number of instances of signs for Mittanian and Assyrian it has been possible to provide some statistics with regard to script standardisation. (Noting that while all known Mittani tablets were included, the other corpora such as Nuzi were much more limited.) As shown, in the Nuzi and Early Middle Assyrian corpora under consideration up to 8% of all signs occur in multiple sign-forms, while in Amarna Mittanian and Later Middle Assyrian this is less than 2%. However, one of the most serious problems of Mittani palaeography is still the fact that most available tablets – which are also the most photographed or scanned and most well-preserved – are the high-status, carefully composed, royal Amarna correspondence. Every contemporary power could potentially have spent significant effort on the composition of its diplomatic letters. So how does Mittanian compare? How standardised can we really say it was?

As discussed, it is not possible to create a statistical comparison for Assyrian, as only two Amarna letters survive. However, Devecchi has compared the four Akkadian Amarna letters from Ḫatti (EA 41–44). Her palaeographic analysis shows that three of the examined texts attest a "mixed *ductus*" (EA 41, 42 and 44), while one has a completely Hittite *ductus* (EA 43) (2012: 149). In Devecchi's sign-list (2012: 150), the forms of RU, NI, LÚ, ŠEŠ, AK, LA, and KU can all be said to differ between EA 43 and the other letters. At the same time, forms of RU, NI, LÚ, ŠEŠ, AK, LA, and UM also differ between EA 41, 42 and 44; and she shows two distinct forms of ŠEŠ occur on EA 42. Based on this specific sign-list and the available documents, contemporary diplomatic writing from the Amarna correspondence at Ḫattuša was less standardised than the Mittani Amarna letters.[3] (Which is not to say the same is in any way applicable to Old, Middle or Neo-Hittite more generally, which are comparatively more standardised.)

Studying ten Babylonian letters from the Amarna correspondence (EA 2, 4, 6, 8–14) resulted in 2,906 instances. The same form of KA is used throughout, apart from EA 9 (and Schröder (1915: 76) shows three or four different forms in total); at least three different forms of LI occur (Schröder shows five or more); as well as different forms of LUGAL, IL, UM and AL. EA 9 is the most recent of the Babylonian letters (sent to Tutankhamun) and differs most from the others. However, the other letters amongst themselves also show a larger variety in sign-forms than the fourteen Mittani tablets. Goren *et al.* established

3 Also see e.g. Klinger (1998: 368) on Hittite diplomatic '*Kanzlei-Duktus*'.

that the Babylonian letters chemically form a solid group; they were fired at the same temperature and the clay comes from the same region (2004: 37). Differences can thus not be attributed to variety in location. In addition, a quick survey showed that differences can also not necessarily be attributed to ruler (whether written under Kadašman-Enlil or Burna-Buriaš). In fact, Vita already found that it was possible for a scribe in one location to write letters for multiple Kings (e.g. in Gezer) (2015: 3, 141).

Of course, this brief survey does not completely answer the question whether and to which extent all, several hundred, Amarna letters were standardised.[4] However, the tablets as discussed above at least show that the Mittani Amarna tablets were equally if not more standardised than those of their powerful contemporary neighbours. What is more, Mittanian overall was much more standardised than all other 15th–14th century writing discussed in the preceding chapters.

While it is beyond the scope of this monograph to investigate all cuneiform that came before Mittanian, one of the possibilities considered was Tigunanum. Although its exact location is not known, 17th–16th century Tigunanum was probably located east of the Euphrates but not beyond the Tigris, corresponding to the western territory of what would later be Mittani. The ruler of Tigunanum had a Hurrian name and the Tigunanum tablets show a script with similarities to Mittanian. Signs collected from the available Tigunanum tablets show 60–65% similarity to Mittanian, with 35–40% differing. When the sign-forms differ, it is often because they are more varied or complicated than later Mittanian counterparts, which were pared down and more standardised. This means that in this region it is possible to observe the development from a script with a large number of variants to a script with a reduced number of variants. While a derivation has to remain hypothetical, it could reflect on political developments in the region. There is already evidence that the Hurrians were present in this area prior to the 15th century and that they were unified at least under Kings or as armies. It is possible that their administration, in part, advanced from the modest Kingdom of Tigunanum to the later Mittani polity. In addition, significant sign-forms at Nuzi and from Later Middle Assyrian were also shown to differ around 30% from Mittanian. This brings the percentual boundaries of Tigunanum and these later script-groups very close. For contrast, a small selection of Old Assyrian was investigated, of which only 25–50% matched Mittanian and 50–75% did not. Whereas this was a limited corpus and an experimental survey, it indicated that large historical or geographical breaks between scribal traditions (for example, between Old Assyrian, Middle

4 See the forthcoming publication by Mynářová, *The Amarna Palaeography Project*.

Assyrian and Neo-Assyrian) must be sought at this 50–75% difference in signs (most likely more towards the 70% mark). As a result, Tigunanum serves as supportive evidence for the development of the described broader northern or upper Mesopotamian scribal tradition, in which statistically 30% of significant sign-forms or less differ from one another. As proposed, it will be interesting to find out how writing at sites such as Ugarit, Qaṭna and Emar compares.

Traditionally, the view has been that the Assyrians were the preservers of Babylonian heritage, changing and standardising it from the 13th century BCE onwards (Veldhuis 2012b: 11). It has already been acknowledged that in order to do this the Assyrians likely based themselves on the lexical tradition preserved by their Mittani overlord and that the transmission of this knowledge cannot be "abbreviated in a neat linear stemma" (Veldhuis 2012b: 11, 22). The palaeography of Mittani supports this line of thinking, illustrating that a standardised way of writing already existed before the new Assyrian Empire took hold of the region. As described, writing is an activity which expresses social practice and script is a performative reflection of long-term developments. People might identify with one group, but compare to other groups, and express themselves based on the relevance of each. Due to the large datasets used it was possible to draw percentual boundaries between script-groups and show in which ways they overlap as well as where they differ, reflecting on both similar and unique social practices. This has resulted in the statistical differentiation between Mittanian, Assyro-Mittanian and Early Middle Assyrian individually, but also brought forth evidence that these are all subgroups (circa 30% difference) of one over-arching northern Mesopotamian tradition (Assyro-Mittanian, which includes Mittanian and Early Middle Assyrian).

Within this group, the collection of 'Assyro-Mittanian' tablets found at Boğazköy is probably least cohesive, having likely been written in different places, at different times. It shows, comparatively, a lot of variation between tablets, particularly in the use of different sign-forms. The corpus of early Middle Assyrian documents considered was composed during a period of relative turmoil, when major changes in power were taking place in the region; sign-forms overlap with Mittanian, Assyro-Mittanian as well as Later Middle Assyrian. This is not to mention Nuzi, where, while part of the same Empire, the overall script differs from the other corpora considered and sign-forms regularly differ per scribe. These scripts were all in use during the Late Bronze Age but developed distinctively in part due to differing social and political institutions.

Variety could be attributed to the logistics of the corpus: coincidence of genre and number of tablets. However, it is of considerable significance that the Mittani tablets were written during the reign of an Empire in its heartland;

as were, for example, the Later Assyrian documents. The Mittani Amarna letters do show small variations between individual scribes, but they are also exceptionally homogenous. If it were true that the Mittani palace selected different scribes for specific tasks, it looks like it is possible that they learned their craft in the same place. Most of the other Mittanian tablets are damaged, none of them are large enough to compare to EA 24 and they all come from different sites. However, the Amarna and other Mittani tablets put together share essential sign-forms and there are no substantial differences between them. It is conceivable their scribes were trained together. The excavators of Umm el-Marra and Bazi already suggested that the tablets found there would have been composed in the Mittani capital. Then, considering the Mittani Amarna and other Mittani tablets together, it is possible there was centralised education for Mittani scribes.

Appendices

Appendix A Complete Mittani Corpus (as of 2018)

Publication, collection or excavation Nr.	Museum, inventory or accession Nr.	Size (cm)	Remarks
EA 17	BM 029792	12.3 × 7.7 × 1	Letter from Tušratta to Amenhotep III
EA 18	VAT 01880 + VAT 01879	c. 8.3 × 7.6 × ?	Letter from Tušratta to Amenhotep III
EA 19	BM 029791	22.2 × 12.7	Letter from Tušratta to Amenhotep III
EA 20	VAT 00191	17.8 × 11.5 × ?	Letter from Tušratta to Amenhotep III
EA 21	VAT 00190	9.2 × 7.6 × 1.1	Letter from Tušratta to Amenhotep III
EA 22	VAT 00395	50.5 × 17.5 × 1.8	Gift-list from Tušratta to Amenhotep III
EA 23	BM 029793	8.9 × 6.7 × 0.9	Letter from Tušratta to Amenhotep III
EA 24	VAT 00422	43.5 × 25 × 1.8	Hurrian letter from Tušratta to Amenhotep III
EA 25	VAT 00340 (+) VAT 02191 + fragments	37 × 21.5 × 2.3	Gift-list from Tušratta to Amenhotep III
EA 26	BM 029794 + A 09356	14.7 × 9.5 × 2.4	Letter from Tušratta to Queen Tiye
EA 27	VAT 00233 + VAT 02197 + VAT 02193	24.8 × 13.6 × ?	Letter from Tušratta to Amenhotep IV
EA 28	BM 037645	14.6 × 10.2 × 2.4	Letter from Tušratta to Amenhotep IV
EA 29	VAT 00271 + VAT 01600 + VAT 01618 + VAT 01619 + VAT 01620 + VAT 02192 + VAT 02194 + VAT 02195 + VAT 02196 + VAT 02197	43.2 × 24.9 × ?	Letter from Tušratta to Amenhotep IV
EA 30	BM 029841	4.8 × 6 × ?	Letter from Tušratta to 'the Kings of Canaan'
KBo 1.2	VAT 13024	14.4 × 17.1 × ?	Manuscript B of CTH 51, Treaty between Šuppiluliuma I and Šattiwazza

 | DOI:10.1163/9789004417243_009

Appendix A: Complete Mittani Corpus (as of 2018) (*cont.*)

Publication, collection or excavation Nr.	Museum, inventory or accession Nr.	Size (cm)	Remarks
KBo 28.65	2539/c	5.9 × 4.8 × ?	Seal of the King of Ḫanigalbat
KBo 28.66	1603/c	10.6 × 4.7 × ?	Letter from the Mittani King to the Hittite King / a dignitary
HSS 09, 001	SMN 1000	5.7 × 7.0 × 2.2	Letter about the boundary adjustment of property
AlT 13	ATmB 31.1, BM 131452	5.1 × 5.3 × ?	Judgement from King Saušṭatar
AlT 14	ATmB 31.2	c. 4.3 × 4.4 × ?	Judgement from King Saušṭatar
AlT 108	ATmB 2.5, BM 131497	4.5 × 5.4 × ?	Letter from a King to Utti
AlT 110	BM 131498	5.2 × 4.9 × ?	Letter from Tiriṣ-ra to Niqmepa
AlT 111	ATT/8/9	4.5 × 4 × ?	Letter from Tiriṣ-ra to Niqmepa
AlT 112	n/a	4.8 × 3.8 × ?	Letter from Tiriṣ-ra to Niqmepa
UEM T1	n/a	4.3 × 5.2 × ?	Contract by Kubi
Bz 50	n/a	4.3 × 5.0 × 2.0	Saušatar grants the town Baidali to the people of Baṣiru
Bz 51	n/a	3.2 × 4.1 × 1.7	Grant of a town to the people of Baṣiru
TB 11021	n/a	c. 6.5 × 9.5 × 3.5	Fragmentary Hurrian document
TB 6001	n/a	12.0 × 7.2 × 3.2	Administrative document with Hurrian names
TB 6002	n/a	4.2 × 5.2 × 1.8	Real-estate transaction
TB 7035	n/a	3.3 × 4.5 × 1.8	Private letter
TB 8001	n/a	7.2 × 5.8 × 2.5	Real-estate transaction
TB 8002	n/a	2.4 × 3.6 × 2.1	Issue of reeds or arrows
MS 1848/1	n/a	4.2 × 4.7 × 1.2	Letter about the people of Ašlakka
MS 1848/2	n/a	2.3 × 4.2 × 1.1	Private letter about a debt

Appendix B Selected Assyro-Mittanian Corpus

Publication Nr.	Fragments	Remarks
KUB 37.55+KBo 36.32	323c, 373b, 423c, 450c, 472c, 468c + 2693c	CTH 803, Manuscript A; witchcraft therapies
KUB 37.9	166/d	CTH 812–13, Manuscript B; witchcraft therapies
KUB 37.43	231/g	CTH 804; incantation ritual
KUB 37.52	337/e	CTH 804; ritual instructions
KBo 9.47	212/n	CTH 804; therapeutic ritual
KUB 37.100a + 100b + 103 + 106 / KBo 36.11	1016/c, 656/c + 241/c + 523/b + 536/b, 640/b	CTH 805; Sumerian incantation
KBo 36.29	166/e, 73/b, 285/a, 2533/c, 34/k, 1017/c, 399/d, 2555/c, 97/q, 510/d, 743/c, 1039/c	CTH 812–813, Manuscript A; recipes and rituals
KBo 36.34	829/c, 842/c, 254/e	CTH 812–813, Manuscript B; recipes and rituals
KUB 37.57	359/c	CTH 812–813, Manuscript X1; recipes and rituals
KUB 37.62	626/b	CTH 812–813, Manuscript X2; recipes and rituals
KUB 37.65	1428/c	CTH 812–813, Manuscript X3; recipes and rituals
KUB 37.74	2622/c	CTH 812–813, Manuscript X4; recipes and rituals
KUB 37.66	1402/c	CTH 812–813, Manuscript X5; recipes and rituals
KUB 37.72	38/a	CTH 812–813, Manuscript X6; recipes and rituals
KUB 37.86	1792/c	CTH 812–813, Manuscript X7; recipes and rituals
KUB 37.97	400/b	CTH 812–813, Manuscript X8; recipes and rituals
KUB 4.16	Bo 6345	CTH 812–813; Demon exorcism

Appendix C Selected Early Middle Assyrian Corpus

Documents from Ass. 14446 included in the Database			
Accession Nr.	Museum Nr.	CDLI Nr.	Condition
AfO 20, 122	VAT 08923	P282425	Wide; good condition
AfO 20, 123b	VAT 09034	P282426	Broken and damaged
ARu 16	VAT 08873	P282432	Good condition
KAJ 1	VAT 08947	P282016	Good condition
KAJ 3	VAT 08795	P282018	Wide; broken but otherwise good condition
KAJ 4	VAT 08965	P282019	Broken and damaged
KAJ 6	VAT 08802	P282021	Damaged
KAJ 7	VAT 08758	P282022	Large; corner broken but otherwise good
KAJ 8	VAT 09028	P282023	Some damage
KAJ 9	VAT 08759	P282024	Obverse damaged
KAJ 11	VAT 08793	P282026	Good condition
KAJ 12	VAT 08016	P282027	A little broken but good condition
KAJ 13	VAT 09756	P282028	Good condition
KAJ 14	VAT 08771	P282029	A little broken but good condition
KAJ 17	VAT 08770	P282032	Small; broken but otherwise good condition
KAJ 18	VAT 09135	P282033	Obverse damaged
KAJ 19	VAT 08797	P282034	Good condition
KAJ 20	VAT 08777	P282035	Bottom broken but otherwise good condition
KAJ 21	VAT 08961	P282036	Damaged
KAJ 22	VAT 08902	P282037	Broken but otherwise good condition
KAJ 23	VAT 08933	P282038	Corner broken but otherwise good condition
KAJ 24	VAT 09015	P282039	Corner broken but otherwise good condition
KAJ 25	VAT 08871	P282040	Corner broken but otherwise good condition
KAJ 26	VAT 09023	P282041	Broken but otherwise good condition
KAJ 27	VAT 08620	P282042	Also Ass. 14987; obverse damaged
KAJ 28	VAT 08892	P282043	Broken but otherwise good condition
KAJ 29	VAT 08794	P282044	Some damage
KAJ 33	VAT 08226	P282048	Small; good condition
KAJ 34	VAT 08784	P282049	Small; broken and damage to obverse
KAJ 35	VAT 08922	P282050	Burnt and broken; otherwise good condition
KAJ 36	VAT 08964	P282051	Broken and damaged
KAJ 37	VAT 08713	P282052	Also Ass. 14886; damaged

Appendix C: Selected Early Middle Assyrian Corpus (*cont.*)

Documents from Ass. 14446 included in the Database			
Accession Nr.	**Museum Nr.**	**CDLI Nr.**	**Condition**
KAJ 39	VAT 08994	P282054	Good condition
KAJ 40	VAT 09136	P282055	Good condition
KAJ 41	VAT 08929	P282056	Good condition
KAJ 42	VAT 08982	P282057	Broken and damaged
KAJ 43	VAT 08944	P282058	Small; broken but good condition
KAJ 44	VAT 09134	P282059	Good condition
KAJ 45	VAT 08954	P282060	Reverse damaged
KAJ 46	VAT 08716	P282061	Also Ass. 14886; small; damaged
KAJ 47	VAT 08018	P282062	Broken but otherwise good condition
KAJ 50	VAT 08778	P282065	Corner broken; some damage
KAJ 52	VAT 08963	P282067	Good condition
KAJ 53	VAT 09022	P282068	Some damage
KAJ 58	VAT 08769	P282073	Broken and damaged
KAJ 60	VAT 08958	P282075	A little broken but otherwise good
KAJ 61	VAT 08986	P282076	Broken but otherwise good condition
KAJ 63	VAT 09031	P282078	Good condition
KAJ 64 = 68	VAT 08938	P282079	Broken but otherwise good condition
KAJ 65	VAT 08888	P282080	Good condition
KAJ 66	VAT 08761	P282081	Broken and damaged
KAJ 70	VAT 09036	P282084	Broken and damaged
KAJ 74	VAT 08615	P282088	Also Ass. 14987; very small; good condition
KAJ 79	VAT 08976	P282093	Reverse damaged
KAJ 85	VAT 08730	P282099	Also Ass. 14886; good condition
KAJ 86	VAT 08631	P282100	Also Ass. 14987; small; corner broken
KAJ 87	VAT 08977	P282101	Good condition
KAJ 96	VAT 08227	P282110	Small; corner broken but otherwise good
KAJ 99	VAT 08806	P282113	Obverse damaged
KAJ 135	VAT 08783	P282149	Broken but otherwise good
KAJ 139	VAT 08905	P282152	Broken but otherwise good
KAJ 143	VAT 08927	P282156	Some damage
KAJ 146	VAT 09035	P282159	Broken but good
KAJ 147	VAT 08868	P282160	Good condition
KAJ 148	VAT 08966	P282161	Good condition

Appendix C: Selected Early Middle Assyrian Corpus (*cont.*)

Documents from Ass. 14446 included in the Database			
Accession Nr.	**Museum Nr.**	**CDLI Nr.**	**Condition**
KAJ 149	VAT 08942	P282162	Good condition
KAJ 150	VAT 08959	P282163	Corner broken but otherwise good
KAJ 151	VAT 08017	P282164	Corner broken but otherwise good
KAJ 152	VAT 09020	P282165	Broken but good condition
KAJ 153	VAT 08804 + VAT 19869	P282166	Good condition
KAJ 154	VAT 08023	P282167	Corner damaged but otherwise good
KAJ 155	VAT 08874	P282168	Good condition
KAJ 157	VAT 08894	P282170	Broken, reverse damaged
KAJ 160	VAT 08941	P282173	Corner broken but otherwise good
KAJ 161	VAT 08785	P282174	Bottom broken but otherwise good
KAJ 162	VAT 08245	P282175	Corner broken but otherwise good
KAJ 163	VAT 08774	P282176	Large; good condition
KAJ 165	VAT 08805	P282178	Good condition
KAJ 167	VAT 09011	P282180	Good condition
KAJ 170	VAT 08999	P282183	Broken but otherwise good condition
KAJ 172	VAT 08627	P282185	Also Ass. 14987; damaged
KAJ 173 = KAV 210	VAT 08995	P282186	Small; corner broken but otherwise good
KAJ 174	VAT 08799	P282187	Broken but otherwise good condition
KAJ 176	VAT 08904	P282189	Very small; broken but otherwise good
KAJ 177	VAT 08951	P282190	Good condition
KAJ 179	VAT 08952	P282192	Good condition
KAJ 183 = KAV 93	VAT 08921	P282196	Very small; good condition
KAJ 209	VAT 09395	P282222	Also Ass. 06096; very small; good condition
KAJ 229	VAT 08998	P282241	Very small; good condition
KAJ 233	VAT 08950	P282245	Very small; damaged
KAJ 236	VAT 08974	P282248	Very small; good condition
KAJ 246	VAT 08796	P282258	Very small; damaged
KAJ 309	VAT 08956	P282323	Tiny; good condition
KAV 211	VAT 08945	P281763	Small; broken but otherwise good
KAV 212	VAT 08790	P281753	Small; good condition

Appendix D Selected Later Middle Assyrian Corpus

Documents from Ass. 14410 included in the Database

Accession Nr.	Museum Nr.	CDLI Nr.	Condition
AfO 19 T.5	VAT 08851	P282421	Good condition
AfO 19 T.6	VAT 08236	P282422	Broken but otherwise good condition
AfO 19 T.7 2	VAT 09017	P282424	Broken but otherwise good condition
KAJ 125	VAT 08844	P282139	Broken and damaged
KAJ 138 = 312	VAT 09037	P282098	Broken but otherwise good condition
KAJ 158	VAT 09754	P282171	Also Ass. 14445; bottom broken
KAJ 159	VAT 09760	P282172	Also Ass. 14445; broken and damaged
KAJ 223	VAT 08839	P282236	Small; good condition
KAJ 226	VAT 08019	P282238	Small; good condition
KAJ 231	VAT 08985	P282243	Small; broken; good condition
KAJ 242	VAT 08858	P282254	Broken; reverse damaged
KAJ 253	VAT 09012	P282265	Small; damaged
KAJ 256	VAT 08015	P282268	Corner broken; good condition
KAJ 277	VAT 09039	P282289	Broken but otherwise good condition
KAJ 279	VAT 09040	P282291	Also Ass. 14445; small; broken
KAJ 317	VAT 08837	P282331	Small; damaged
KAV 96	VAT 08013	P281733	Corner broken; good condition
KAV 98	VAT 08231	P281741	Large; corner broken; good condition
KAV 99	VAT 08011	P281732	Large; good condition
KAV 100	VAT 08024	P281734	Broken but otherwise good condition
KAV 102	VAT 08032	P281738	Small; good condition
KAV 103	VAT 08033	P281739	Good condition
KAV 104	VAT 08225	P281740	Corner broken; good condition
KAV 105	VAT 08028	P281735	Broken but otherwise good condition
KAV 107	VAT 08842	P281756	Top broken but otherwise good condition
KAV 108	VAT 08861	P281758	Broken; reverse damaged
KAV 109	VAT 08030	P281737	Good condition
KAV 110 = KAJ 227	VAT 08031	P282239	Tiny; good condition
KAV 158 = KAJ 232	VAT 08857	P282244	Tiny; damaged
KAV 194	VAT 08862	P281759	Broken; some damage
KAV 200	VAT 08993	P281764	Bottom broken but otherwise good condition
KAV 203	VAT 09033	P281768	Broken but otherwise good condition

Appendix D: Selected Later Middle Assyrian Corpus (*cont.*)

Documents from Ass. 14410 included in the Database			
Accession Nr.	**Museum Nr.**	**CDLI Nr.**	**Condition**
KAV 205	VAT 08259	P281742	Large; broken; good condition
MARV 39	VAT 18003	P281876	Also Ass. 16008; broken; damaged
RIAA 314	MRAH O.0504	P282528	Small; damaged

Appendix E Selected Nuzi Corpus

Documents from Nuzi Generation II included in the Database				
Accession or Museum Nr.	**CDLI Nr.**	**Significant Names**	**Size (cm)**	**Condition**
BM 95344	n/a	Teḫip-tilla son of Puḫi-šenni	2.4 × 4.0 × 1.2	Broken
HSS 13 410	P408577	Teḫip-tilla son of Puḫi-šenni	7.2 × 6.3 × 2.8	Broken & damaged
HSS 13 438	P408599	Teḫip-tilla; Ariqani son of Arusari	10.9 × 7.8 × 3.2	Broken but good
SMN 2109	P388494	Tulpunnaya wife of Ḫašuar; Nabu-ilu	9.0 × 6.7 × 3.1	Good
SMN 2021	P388495	Tulpunnsya wife of Ḫašuar; Nabu-ilu	9.6 × 6.8 × 2.8	Good
SMN 2036	P388496	Teḫip-tilla son of Puḫi-šenni; Tulpunnaya	8.2 × 6.8 × 2.3	Good
SMN 2044	P388497	Tulpunnaya daughter of Šeltunnaya; Ḫapurši son of Puḫi-šenni; Itḫapiḫe; Nabu-naṣir	9.6 × 7.1 × 3.2	Good
SMN 2254	P388498	Tulpunnaya; Yalampa	10.0 × 6.7 × 3.0	Broken but good
SMN 2035	P388499	Ḫiupapu son of Šurakka; Sin-iqiša?; Tulpunnaya daughter of Šeltunnaya	10.2 × 7.1 × 3.6	Good
SMN 2206	P388500	Tulpunnaya daughter of Šeltunnaya; Sin-iqiša	12.7 × 9.1 × 4.0	Broken but good

Appendix E: Selected Nuzi Corpus (*cont.*)

Documents from Nuzi Generation II included in the Database

Accession or Museum Nr.	CDLI Nr.	Significant Names	Size (cm)	Condition
SMN 2216	P388501	Šitanki daughter of Ḫabildamqu; Ḫanatu son of Habildamqu; Šeršiya; Tulpunnaya daughter of Irwišarri	11.4 × 8.9 × 3.7	Broken but good
SMN 2038	P388503	Ḫanatu son of Ḫabildamqu; Nabu-naṣir; Tulpunnaya daughter of Šeltunnaya	10.5 × 7.9 × 3.4	Good
SMN 2017	P388504	Tulpunnaya daughter of Šeltunnaya; Tilammu	13.0 × 8.5 × 3.6	Good
SMN 2020	P388505	Puḫi-šenni son of Waradgini; Tulpunnaya	11.6 × 7.3 × 3.4	Good
SMN 2031	P388506	Taena son of Ukari; Tulpunnaya; Urḫiya	10.5 × 7.1 × 3.5	Good
SMN 2045	P388507	Tulpunnaya daughter of Šeltunnaya; Taya son of Artamuzi; Sin-iqiša; Artirwa son of Taya	12.2 × 8.6 × 3.6	Broken but good
SMN 2118	P388508	Tulpunnaya; Urḫiya	10.6 × 6.8 × 3.0	Broken but good
SMN 2103	P388510	Arteya son of Awiškipa; Kisaya wife of Arteya; Šeršiya; Tulpunnaya	10.0 × 7.6 × 3.4	Broken but good
SMN 2026	P388511	Kisaya daughter of Ariya, wife of Arteya; Inzi-teššup son of Arteya; Tulpunnaya; Sin-iddin	10.7 × 7.5 × 3.2	Good
SMN 2028	P388513	Ḫanaya son of Tenteya; Urḫiya?; Tulpunnaya daughter of Šeltunnaya; Ḫašunnaya	13.2 × 7.7 × 3.7	Good
SMN 2018	P388514	Tulpunnaya; Urḫiya	11.2 × 7.0 × 3.5	Broken but good
SMN 1714	P388516	Tulpunnaya	7.1 × 7.4 × 3.6	Broken but good
SMN 2111	P388516	Mušteya son of Arillumti; Arpiḫe son of Mušteya; Tulpunnaya daughter of Šeltunnaya; Šamaš-ilu-reštu	9.6 × 6.0 × 3.5	Good

Appendix E: Selected Nuzi Corpus (*cont.*)

Documents from Nuzi Generation II included in the Database

Accession or Museum Nr.	CDLI Nr.	Significant Names	Size (cm)	Condition
SMN 2033	P388517	Tulpunnaya; Utḫapše son of Kaliya; Tawe son of Aqawatil	9.5 × 6.1 × 2.8	Broken but good
SMN 2074	P388518	Tulpunnaya daughter of Šeltunnaya; Zammini daughter of Ilabriya; Wantiya son of Ilabriya; Arteia son of Puitae; Ḫais-teššup son of Puḫi-šenni	13.4 × 8.4 × 3.6	Broken but good
SMN 2145	P388519	Tulpunnaya; Šumu-libši	11.5 × 8.2 × 3.3	Good
SMN 2023	P388520	Tulpunnaya daughter of Šeltunnaya; Killi son of Eḫliya; Urḫiya	10.3 × 6.9 × 2.9	Good
SMN 2037	P388521	Ḫalpapuša daughter of Šukrapu; Šukrapu son of Arnamar; Ḫiyarelli wife of Šukrapu; Urḫiya	10.6 × 6.8 × 3.4	Broken but good
SMN 2024	P388522	Tulpunnaya; Amurriya: III; Kari son of Akap-šenni; Ḫanatu son of Kutanni; Šimikari son of Nirpiya	10.1 × 7.4 × 2.9	Good
SMN 2043	P388523	Tulpunnaya; Sin-iqiša	10.2 × 7.4 × 3.1	Good
SMN 2088	P388524	Awišnaya wife of Arzizza; Tulpunnaya; Šešwaya son of Arzizza; Šeršiya; Muštešup son of the King	n/a	Broken but good

Documents from Nuzi Generation III included in the Database

Museum Nr.	Significant Names	Size (cm)	Condition
BM 26262	fAllai-turaḫe wife of Šurki-tilla	5.3 × 5.3 × 1.4	Good
BM 26229	Šurki-tilla son of Teḫip-tilla	9.4 × 6.7 × 1.9	Worn but good
BM 102365	Šurki-tilla son of Teḫip-tilla	6.5 × 7.5 × 3.5	Broken but good
BM 102371	Šurki-tilla son of Teḫip-tilla	6.8 × 5.4 × 3.1	Broken but good
BM 85607	fAllai-turaḫe wife of Šurki-tilla	3.8 × 4.2 × 1.8	Broken but good

Appendix E: Selected Nuzi Corpus (*cont.*)

Documents from Nuzi Generation IV included in the Database

Accession or Museum Nr.	CDLI Nr.	Significant Names	Size (cm)	Condition
BM 26240	n/a	Zike son of Šurki-tilla	5.5 × 6.6 × 1.7	Good
BM 26241	n/a	Zike son of Šurki-tilla	5.9 × 7.6 × 1.2	Damaged but good
BM 26249	n/a	Zike son of Šurki-tilla	7.7 × 6.1 × 1.8	Good
BM 26270	n/a	*about* Zike son of Šurki-tilla	4.8 × 4.5 × 1.3	Good
BM 26273	n/a	fWištanzu wife of Zike	6.3 × 5.7 × 1.6	Good
BM 26278	n/a	*about* Zike son of Šurki-tilla	5.8 × 4.7 × 1.7	Good
BM 26283	n/a	*about* Zike son of Šurki-tilla	5.8 × 4.8 × 1.5	Broken but good
BM 85534	n/a	fWištanzu wife of Zike	1.4.3 × 5.1 × 1.3	Good
BM 85557	n/a	*brothers* of Zike	5.1 × 4.4 × 1.3	Good
BM 94448	n/a	Zike son of Šurki-tilla	5.9 × 6.0 × 2.5	Broken
BM 102352	n/a	*sister* of Zike son of Šurki-tilla	12.7 × 7.0 × 1.5	Good
BM 102355	n/a	*brother* of Zike son of Šurki-tilla	9.1 × 7.6 × 1.7	Broken but good
BM 102363	n/a	Zike son of Šurki-tilla	10.7 × 4.3 × 2.9	Broken
HSS 13 371	P408545	Šilwa-teššup; Ḫutip-tilla son of Tayuka	4.9 × 5.6 × 2.1	Broken but good
HSS 13 381	P408551	Šilwa-teššup	5.6 × 6.0 × 2.4	Broken but good
HSS 13 409	P408576	Šilwa-teššup; Tašeniwa	6.6 × 5.6 × 2.4	Broken but good
HSS 13 421	P408585	Šilwa-teššup	3.5 × 4.0 × 2.0	Good
HSS 13 422	P408586	Šilwa-teššup	9.4 × 6.7 × 3.6	Good
HSS 13 441	P408601	Šilwa-teššup; Ani Daisnu?	11.7 × 7.5 × 3.4	Broken but good
HSS 13 449	P408608	Šilwa-teššup son of Šarri; Ilimaḫi son of Sepilišu	5.5 × 4.6 × 2.2	Good
HSS 13 451	P408609	Šilwa-teššup	7.4 × 5.3 × 2.1	Broken but good
HSS 13 472	P408629	Killi son of Arrazari; Šilwa-teššup	5.6 × 4.3 × 2.1	Some damage
HSS 13 475	P408632	Šilwa-teššup	5.2 × 5.3 × 2.1	Reverse damaged
HSS 13 480	P408635	Šilwa-teššup	6.3 × 7.0 × 2.6	Good
HSS 13 495	P408646	Šilwa-teššup	5.0 × 4.6 × 2.2	Cracked but good
HSS 13 497	P408648	Šilwa-teššup	5.8 × 6.6 × 2.5	Good
HSS 14 506	P408797	Šilwa-teššup	4.5 × 4.8 × 2.2	Good
HSS 14 508	P408799	Šilwa-teššup	5.0 × 6.0 × 2.1	Broken but good
HSS 14 573	P408839	Šenne; Šilwa-teššup	3.5 × 4.3 × 1.5	Good

Appendix E: Selected Nuzi Corpus (*cont.*)

Documents from Nuzi Generation V included in the Database			
Museum Nr.	**Significant names**	**Size (cm)**	**Condition**
BM 26293	Puḫi-šenni son of Zike	5.8 × 5.6 × 1.4	Good
BM 26268	Puḫi-šenni son of Zike	5.7 × 5.7 × 1.5	Good

Appendix F Published Tigunanum Corpus (as of 2018)

Publication	Collection Nr. or reference	CDLI Nr.	Size (mm)	Remarks
CUSAS 34, 59	MS 1812	P250506	–	Administrative
CUSAS 34, 60	MS 1856/1	P250526	–	Administrative
CUSAS 34, 61	MS 1856/2	P250527	–	Administrative
CUSAS 34, 62	MS 2799	P251845	–	Administrative
CUSAS 34, 63	MS 4995	P254026	–	Administrative
CUSAS 18, 17	MS 2796	P251842	37 × 70 × 28	Liver omen
CUSAS 18, 18	MS 1807	P250501	97 × 103 × 23	Bird's heart omen
CUSAS 18, 19	MS 1805	P250499	110 × 109 × 28	Anomalous birth omen
CUSAS 18, 20	MS 1806	P250500	79 × 89 × 37	Anomalous birth omen
CUSAS 18, 21	MS 2797	P251843	70 × 72 × 34	Anomalous birth omen
CUSAS 12, 3.34	MS 2798	P251844	52 × 85 × ?	Sumero-Hurrian lexical list
Akdoğan & Wilhelm 2010	Erkakan 121, private collection	n/a	70 × 22 × 18	Grain rations, Hurrian names
Zorzi 2017	Private collection	n/a	61.9 × 67.6 × 23.4	Anomalous birth
Salvini 1996	Private collection	n/a	68 × 83 × 25.5	Hurrian fragment
Salvini 1994, 1996	Private collection	n/a	86 × 46 × 19	Letter from Ḫattušili I to Tunip-Teššup
Salvini 1996	Private collection	n/a	c. 220 × 70 each side	Prism listing personnel of King Tunip-Teššup
Salvini 1996	Private collection	n/a	117 × 63 × 28	Anomalous birth omen

Appendix G Mittani Sign-list

MZ Nr.	Value	Amarna Mittani letters	Other Mittani documents	Assyro-Mittanian
1	AŠ			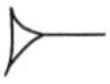
2	ḪAL			
5	BAL			
6	GÍR		–	–
8	BÚR		–	–
9	TAR			
10	AN			
12	MUG	–	–	
14	BA			
15	ZU			
16	SU			
18	ARAD			–
20	ITI	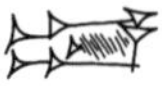	–	–
23	ŠIḪ		–	–
24	KA		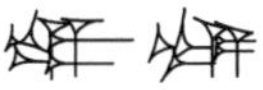	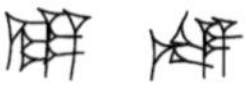 KUB 37·55
26	TU_6	–	–	

Appendix G: Mittani Sign-list (*cont.*)

MZ Nr.	Value	Amarna Mittani letters	Other Mittani documents	Assyro-Mittanian
29	UŠ$_{11}$	–	–	
61	EME		–	
64	NAG	–	–	
65	GU$_7$	–	–	
71	IRI			–
79	ASARI	–	–	
85	LI			 KUB 37.55
86	TU			
89	LA			
91	MAḪ		–	
93	PÚŠ	–	–	
98	MU			
99	QA			
105	GIL		–	
106	KÍD	–	–	
110	NA			
111	RU	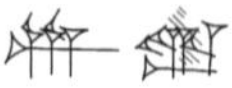 EA 24+25	 TB 11021	

Appendix G: Mittani Sign-list (*cont.*)

MZ Nr.	Value	Amarna Mittani letters	Other Mittani documents	Assyro-Mittanian
112	NU			
113	BE			
115	ŠIR	–	–	
117	NUMUN		–	
118	TI	 EA 24	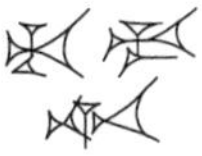	
119	DIN	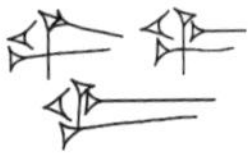		–
120	BAR			
127	AK			
132	ḪU			
134	NAM			
136	IG			
137	MUD		–	
139	RAT			–
140	ZI			
141	GI			

Appendix G: Mittani Sign-list (*cont.*)

MZ Nr.	Value	Amarna Mittani letters	Other Mittani documents	Assyro-Mittanian
142	RI			
143	NUN	–		
148	GAB			
151	SUR	na		
153	INANNA			–
157	GAD		–	
164	EN			
167	TIM	 EA 19	–	–
168	MUN	na	–	
172	SA			
174	GÁN		–	–
176	GÚ		–	
178	DUR	–	–	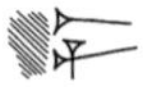
180	GUR		–	–
181	SI			
183	DAR	–	–	
184	SAG			

Appendix G: Mittani Sign-list (*cont.*)

MZ Nr.	Value	Amarna Mittani letters	Other Mittani documents	Assyro-Mittanian
201	MÁ			
207	DIR	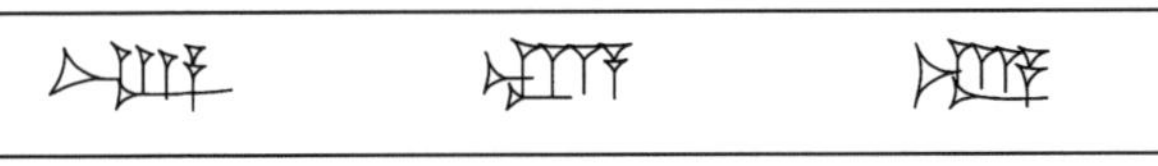		
209	DAB	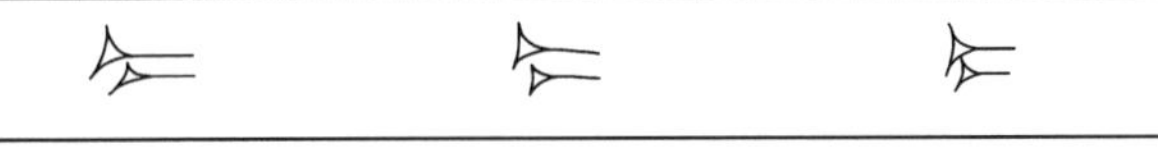		
212	GEŠTIN	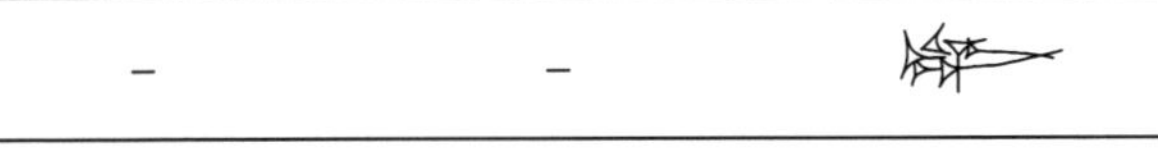		
221	ŠUM	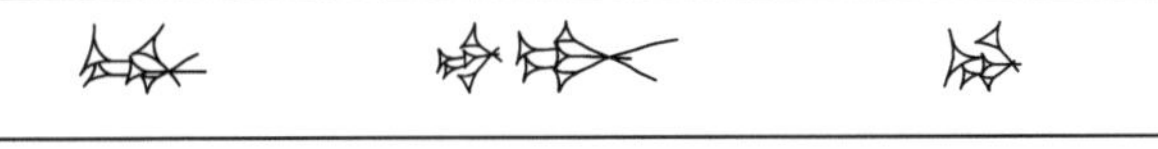		
223	AB	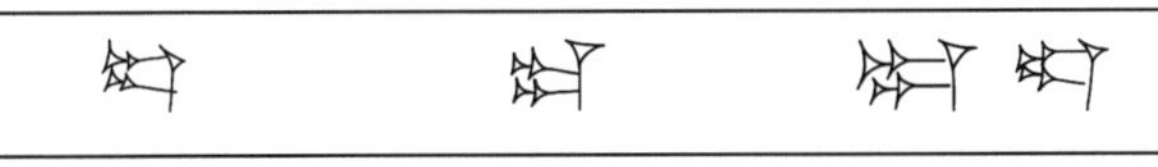		
230	URUDA	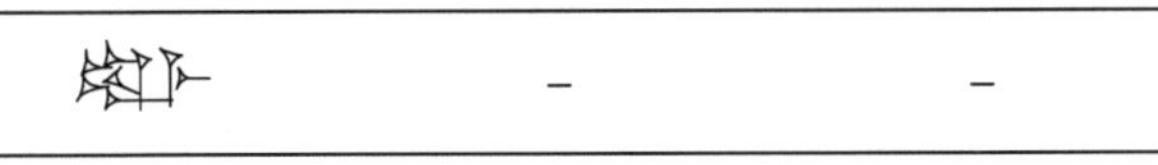		
238	UM	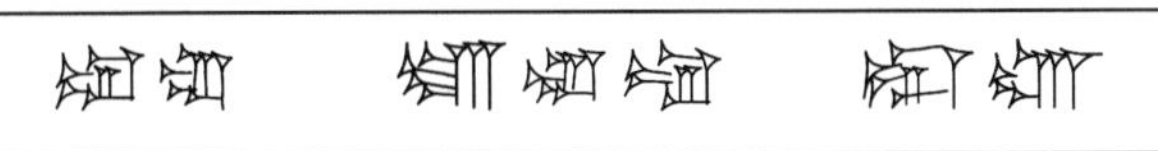		
242	DUB			
246	NAP	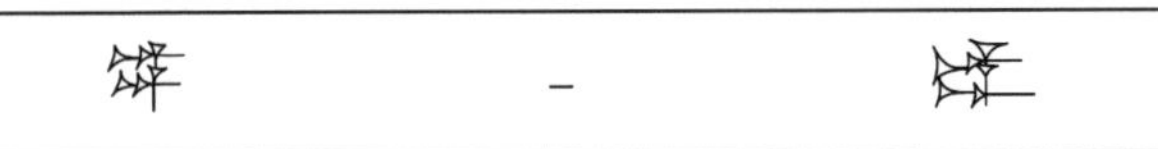		
247	MUL	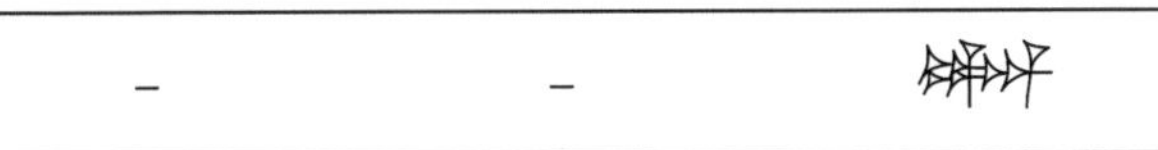		
248	TA	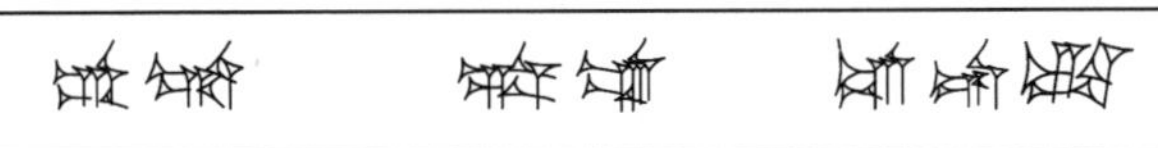		
252	I	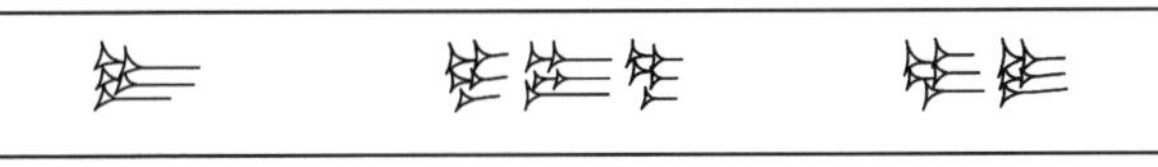		
252b	I+NA	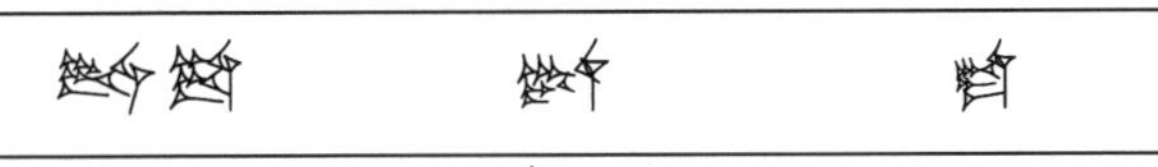		
253	ḪÉ	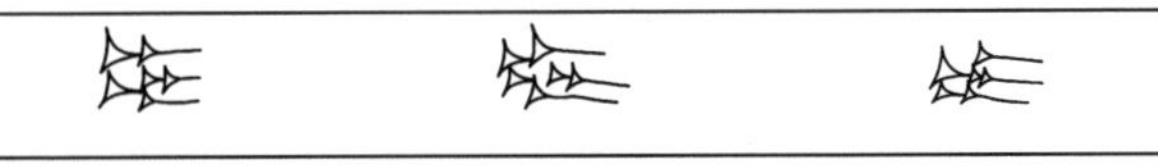		
255	DUMU	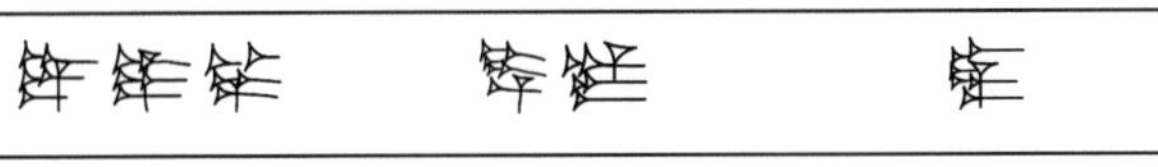		
258	AT	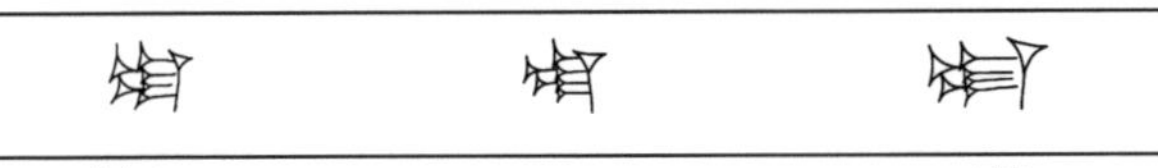		
259	ZÍ	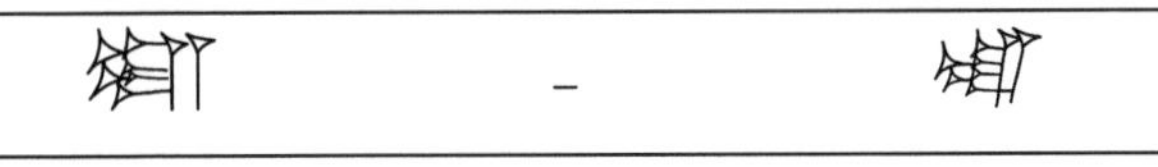		

Appendix G: Mittani Sign-list (*cont.*)

MZ Nr.	Value	Amarna Mittani letters	Other Mittani documents	Assyro-Mittanian
260	IA			
261	IN			
266	LUGAL			–
270	ḪAŠḪUR	–	–	
271	ŠER			
292	SUM	–		–
296	UK	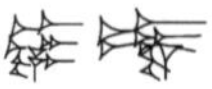	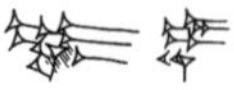	
297	AS	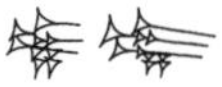		
298	DUḪ		na	
300	EDIN	–		
301	TAḪ		–	
302	KASKAL	–		–
309	AM			
311	UZU	–	–	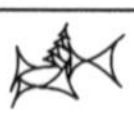
312	BÍL		–	–
313	BÍ		na	
320	ŠÀM	na	–	–
339	KUM	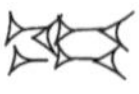		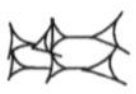

Appendix G: Mittani Sign list (*cont.*)

MZ Nr.	Value	Amarna Mittani letters	Other Mittani documents	Assyro-Mittanian
340	GAZ	–	–	
341	ÚR		–	
348	IL			
350	DU			
352	KAŠ$_4$	–	–	
353	ANŠE			
354	TUM			
356	EGIR			–
357	IŠ			
358	BI			
362	ŠIM		–	–
378	KIB	–	na	–
379	GAG	–	–	
380	NI		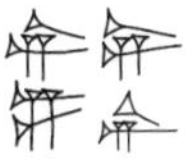	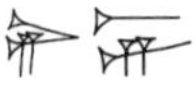
381	UŠ			
385	NA$_4$		–	
387	GÁ	–	–	

Appendix G: Mittani Sign-list (*cont.*)

MZ Nr.	Value	Amarna Mittani letters	Other Mittani documents	Assyro-Mittanian
392	AMA			
408	$SILA_4$			
437	IR			
464	PA			
466	ŠAB			
469	GEŠ			
472	GU_4			
474	AL	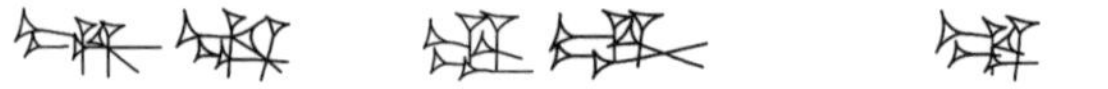		
483	MAR			
484	KID			
486	KIŠIB			
490	Ú			
491	GA			
494	SUKAL			
495	É			
496	DAN			
498	E			
499	DUG			

Appendix G: Mittani Sign-list (*cont.*)

MZ Nr.	Value	Amarna Mittani letters	Other Mittani documents	Assyro-Mittanian
501	UN			
504	UB	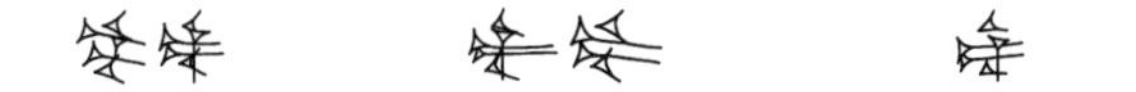		
507	GI_4			
511	RA	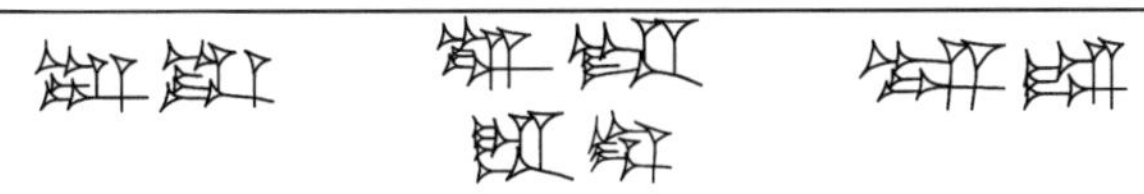		
514	LÚ			
535	ŠEŠ			
540	ZAK			
541	ŠAR			
543	QAR			
545	MÚRU			
548	ÁŠ			
552	MA			
553	GAL			
556	MIR			
558	GIR			
559	BUR			
560	ID	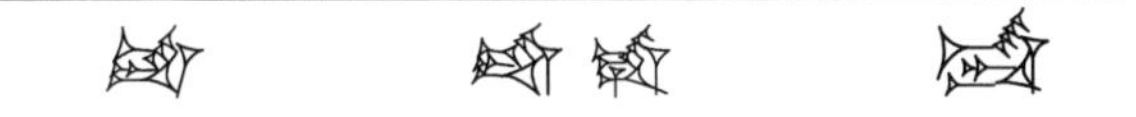	KBo 1.2	

Appendix G: Mittani Sign-list (*cont.*)

MZ Nr.	Value	Amarna Mittani letters	Other Mittani documents	Assyro-Mittanian
561	DA			
566	ŠA			
567	ŠU			
573	ALAM		–	
578	KUR			
579	ŠE			
580	BU			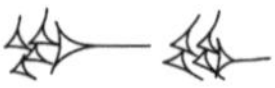
583	US			
585	MUŠ		–	
587	TER		–	na
589	TE			
590	KAR	–		–
591	LIŠ		–	–
596	UT			
596b	ZABAR		–	–
598	PI			
599	ŠÀ		na	

Appendix G: Mittani Sign-list (*cont.*)

MZ Nr.	Value	Amarna Mittani letters	Other Mittani documents	Assyro-Mittanian
608	PEŠ$_4$	–	–	
612	ÉRIN			–
631	ḪI	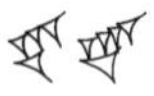	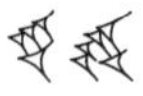	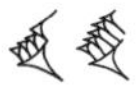
631b	DU$_{10}$.GA		–	–
635	`A		–	–
636	AḪ		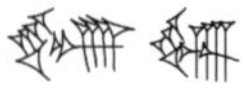	
640	KAM	–	–	
641	IM			
644	ḪUR		–	
645	ḪUŠ		–	–
661	U			
663	UGU			
678	KIŠ	–		
681	MI			
682	GUL		–	–
684	ŠAGAN	–	–	
685	PAN		–	–
686	GIM	–	–	na

Appendix G: Mittani Sign-list (*cont.*)

MZ Nr.	Value	Amarna Mittani letters	Other Mittani documents	Assyro-Mittanian
689	NÁ	na	–	
690	NIM			
693	LAM		–	
698	UL			
701	GÌR		–	
705	GIG	–	–	
708	MAN			
711	EŠ			
712	NIMIN		–	–
724	ŠI	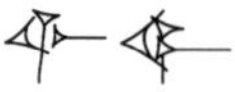	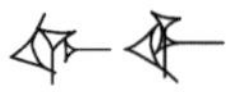	
725	PÀD	–	–	na
726	AR			
731	Ù	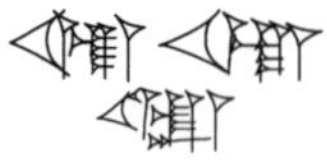		
733	ḪUL	na	–	
736	DI			
737	KI			
742	KIMIN	–	–	

Appendix G: Mittani Sign-list (*cont.*)

MZ Nr.	Value	Amarna Mittani letters	Other Mittani documents	Assyro-Mittanian
744	ŠUL			
745	KÙ		–	–
745b	KÙ.SIG$_{17}$		–	–
745c	KÙ. BABBAR			
746	ŠUK	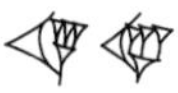		
748	DIŠ			
750	LAL		–	
753	ME			
754	MEŠ	 EA 24+25		
755	LAGAB	–	–	na
760	GIGIR			–
786	TÚL	–	–	
795	SUG		–	–
801	BÚGIN		–	–
804	NIGIN	–	–	
806	NENNI	–	–	
807	IB			

Appendix G: Mittani Sign-list (*cont.*)

MZ Nr.	Value	Amarna Mittani letters	Other Mittani documents	Assyro-Mittanian
808	KU			
812	LU			
815	KIN		–	
816	SÍG	na	–	
821	ŠÉŠ	–	–	
825	MIN		–	
827	TUK		–	–
828	UR			
830	GIDIM	–	–	
833	UDUG	–	–	
834	EŠ$_5$		–	
836	GÍN	–	–	
839	A			
839b	A+NA	na		–
851	ZA			
851b	NÍR		–	–
856	ḪA			
858	GUG		–	

Appendix G: Mittani Sign-list (*cont.*)

MZ Nr.	Value	Amarna Mittani letters	Other Mittani documents	Assyro-Mittanian
859	GAR			
861	ÍA		–	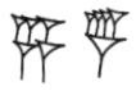
862	ÀŠ			
863	7		–	
864	8		–	–
868	9		–	
869	ŠÚ	–		
870	ÉN	–	–	
883	MUNUS	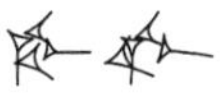		
884	ZUM			
887	NIN			–
889	DAM		na	–
890	GÉME		–	–
891	GU		na	
898	NIG	–	–	
899	EL			
900	LUM	–	–	
905	SIG_4		–	

Appendix H Middle Assyrian Sign-list

MZ Nr.	Value	15th–14th century BCE (Based on Ass. 14446)	13th century BCE (Based on Ass. 14410)
1	AŠ		–
2	ḪAL		
5	BAL		
9	TAR		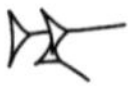
10	AN		
10b	dA.ŠUR		
14	BA		
15	ZU		
16	SU		
18	ARAD		
20	ITI		
24	KA		
71	IRI	–	
85	LI	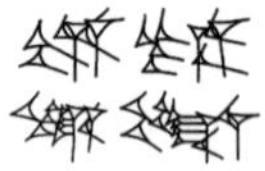	
86	TU		
89	LA		

Appendix H: Middle Assyrian Sign-list (*cont.*)

MZ Nr.	Value	15th–14th century BCE (Based on Ass. 14446)	13th century BCE (Based on Ass. 14410)
92	PAB		
98	MU		
99	QA		
110	NA		
111	RU		
112	NU		
113	BE		
118	TI		
119	DIN		
120	BAR		
127	AK		
130	MÁŠ		–
132	ḪU		
136	IG		–
140	ZI		
141	GI		
142	RI		

Appendix H: Middle Assyrian Sign-list (*cont.*)

MZ Nr.	Value	15th–14th century BCE (Based on Ass. 14446)	13th century BCE (Based on Ass. 14410)
148	GAB		–
151	SUR		
164	EN		
170	LÀL	–	
172	SA	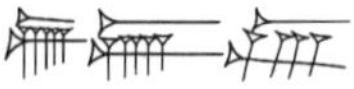	
174	GÁN		–
176b	GÚ.UN		
181	SI		
184	SAG		
209	DAB		
221	ŠUM		
222	KÁ	–	
223	AB		
230	URUDA	–	
238	UM		
242	DUB		
248	TA		
252	I		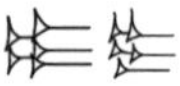

Appendix H: Middle Assyrian Sign-list (*cont.*)

MZ Nr.	Value	15th–14th century BCE (Based on Ass. 14446)	13th century BCE (Based on Ass. 14410)
252b	I+NA		
254	KÁM		
255	DUMU	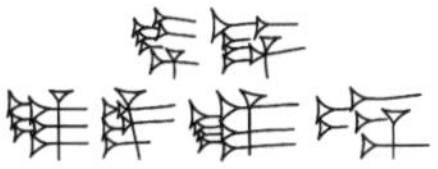	
258	AT		
259	ZÍ		
260	IA		
261	IN	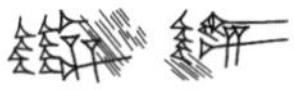	
266	LUGAL		
271	ŠER		
292	SUM		
298	DUḪ		–
300	EDIN		–
302	KASKAL		–
309	AM		
312	BÍL		–
313	BÍ		–
320	ŠÀM	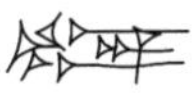	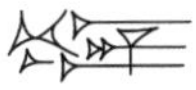

Appendix H: Middle Assyrian Sign-list (*cont.*)

MZ Nr.	Value	15th–14th century BCE (Based on Ass. 14446)	13th century BCE (Based on Ass. 14410)
326	ÁG		–
339	KUM	–	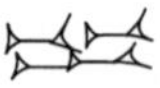
348	IL		
350	DU		
353	ANŠE	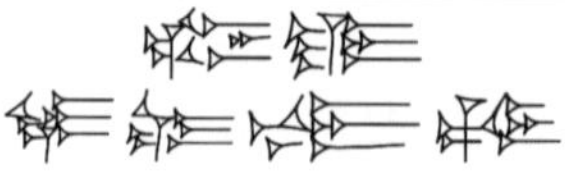	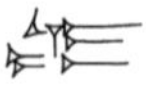
354	TUM	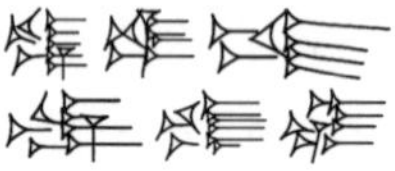	–
357	IŠ		
358	BI		
380	NI	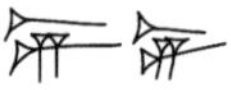	
381	UŠ		–
385	NA_4		
437	IR		
464	PA		
469	GEŠ		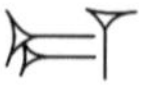
474	AL		
483	MAR	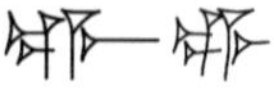	
484	KID		

Appendix H: Middle Assyrian Sign-list (*cont.*)

MZ Nr.	Value	15th–14th century BCE (Based on Ass. 14446)	13th century BCE (Based on Ass. 14410)
486	KIŠIB		
490	Ú	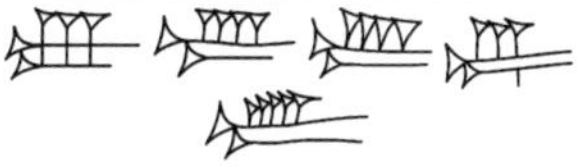	
491	GA		
494	SUKAL		–
495	É		
496	DAN		
498	E		
499	DUG	–	
501	UN		
504	UB		
511	RA		
514	LÚ		
535	ŠEŠ		
540	ZAK		–
541	ŠAR		
543	QAR		
548	ÁŠ		

Appendix H: Middle Assyrian Sign-list (*cont.*)

MZ Nr.	Value	**15th–14th century BCE (Based on Ass. 14446)**	**13th century BCE (Based on Ass. 14410)**
552	MA		
553	GAL	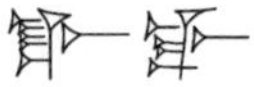	
559	BUR		
560	ID		
561	DA	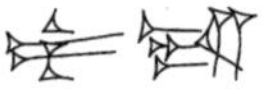	
564	SIG_7		–
566	ŠA		
567	ŠU		
578	KUR		
579	ŠE		
580	BU		
583	US		–
585	MUŠ		
589	TE		
590	KAR		
596	UT		
598	PI		
599	ŠÀ		

Appendix H: Middle Assyrian Sign-list (*cont.*)

MZ Nr.	Value	15th–14th century BCE (Based on Ass. 14446)	13th century BCE (Based on Ass. 14410)
612	LÁḪ		
631	ḪI	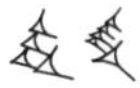	
631b	DU_{10}.GA		
635	ʻA	–	
636	AḪ		
640	KAM	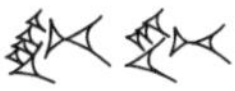	
641	IM		
644	ḪUR		
661	U		
663	UGU		
681	MI		
682	GUL		
693	LAM		–
698	UL		
701	GÌR	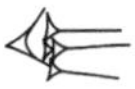	–
704	DUGUD		–
708	MAN		
711	EŠ		

Appendix H: Middle Assyrian Sign-list (*cont.*)

MZ Nr.	Value	15th–14th century BCE (Based on Ass. 14446)	13th century BCE (Based on Ass. 14410)
724	ŠI		
726	AR		
729	SIG_5		
731	Ù		
734	LIM		–
736	DI		
737	KI		
744	ŠUL	–	
745c	KÙ. BABBAR		–
748	DIŠ		
750	LAL		
753	ME		
754	MEŠ		
807	IB		
808	KU		
809	TÚG	–	
810	ZÌ	–	

Appendix H: Middle Assyrian Sign-list (*cont.*)

MZ Nr.	Value	15th–14th century BCE (Based on Ass. 14446)	13th century BCE (Based on Ass. 14410)
812	LU		
815	KIN	–	
825	MIN		
828	UR		
834	EŠ$_5$		
835	UR$_4$		–
836	GÍN		
839	A		
839c	A.GÀR		na
839d	A.ŠÀ		–
851	ZA		
856	ḪA		
859	GAR	–	
861	ÍA		
862	ÀŠ		
863	7		
864	8		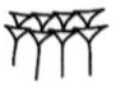
868	9		

Appendix H: Middle Assyrian Sign-list (*cont.*)

MZ Nr.	Value	15th–14th century BCE (Based on Ass. 14446)	13th century BCE (Based on Ass. 14410)
883	MUNUS		
884	ZUM	–	
887	NIN	–	
889	DAM		na
890	GÉME	–	
891	GU		
899	EL		

Appendix I Nuzi Sign-list

MZ Nr.	Value	Contenau 1926	Database 2016
1	AŠ		
2	ḪAL		
3	MUG		–
5	BAL		
9	TAR		
10	AN		
14	BA		

Appendix I: Nuzi Sign-list (*cont.*)

MZ Nr.	Value	Contenau 1926	Database 2016
15	ZU		
16	SU		
18	ARAD		
20	ITI	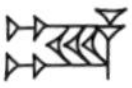	–
24	KA	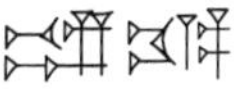	
61	EME	–	
71	IRI	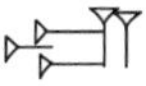	
85	LI		
86	TU	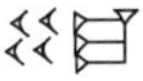	
89	LA	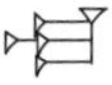	
90	APIN	–	
98	MU		
99	QA		
110	NA	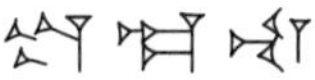	
111	RU		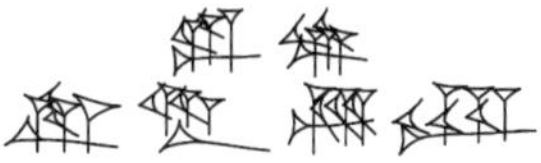
112	NU		
113	BE		

Appendix I: Nuzi Sign-list (*cont.*)

MZ Nr.	Value	Contenau 1926	Database 2016
118	TI		
119	DIN		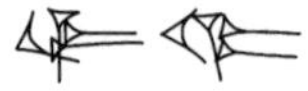
120	BAR		
127	AK	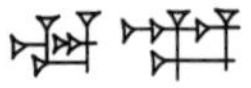	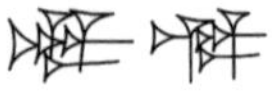
130	MÁŠ	–	
132	ḪU		
134	NAM	–	
136	IG		
140	ZI		
141	GI	–	
142	RI		
148	GAB		
151	SUR		
157	GAD	–	na
164	EN		
165	$BURU_{14}$	–	
172	SA	–	

Appendix I: Nuzi Sign-list (*cont.*)

MZ Nr.	Value	Contenau 1926	Database 2016
173	AŠGAB	–	na
176b	GÚ.UN	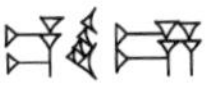	–
180	GUR	–	
181	SI		
184	SAG	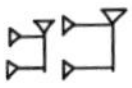	
207	DIR	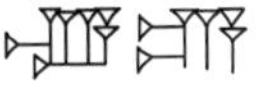	–
209	DAB		
221	ŠUM	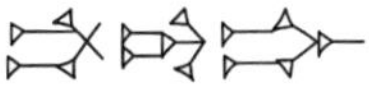	
222	KÁ		
223	AB	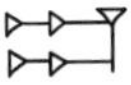	
230	URUDA	–	
238	UM	–	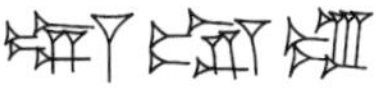
242	DUB		
246	NAP	–	
248	TA		
252	I	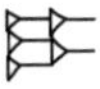	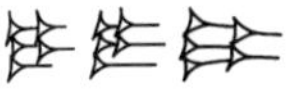
252b	I+NA	–	
253	ḪÉ	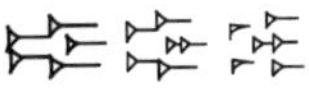	

Appendix I: Nuzi Sign-list (*cont.*)

MZ Nr.	Value	Contenau 1926	Database 2016
255	DUMU		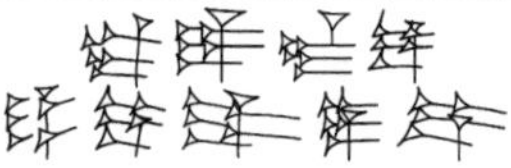
258	AT		
259	ZÍ	–	
260	IA		
261	IN		
266	LUGAL		
292	SUM		
296	UK		
297	AS		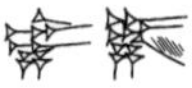
298	DUḪ		–
302	KASKAL	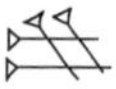	–
309	AM		
311	UZU		–
313	BÍ	–	
336	ZIG	–	na
339	KUM		–
348	IL	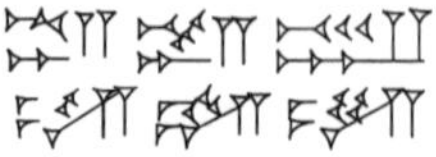	

Appendix I: Nuzi Sign-list (*cont.*)

MZ Nr.	Value	Contenau 1926	Database 2016
350	DU		
353	ANŠE	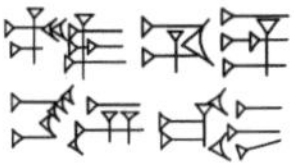	
354	TUM		
356	EGIR		
357	IŠ		
358	BI		
378	KIB		
379	GAG		
380	NI		
381	UŠ	–	
385	NA_4		
437	IR	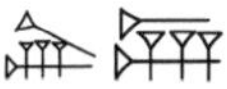	
464	PA		
468	SIPA	–	
469	GEŠ		
472	GU_4	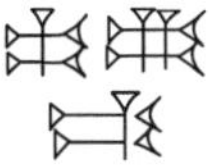	

Appendix I: Nuzi Sign-list (*cont.*)

MZ Nr.	Value	Contenau 1926	Database 2016
474	AL	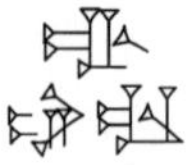	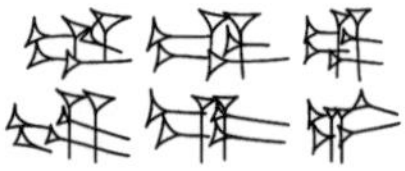
483	MAR	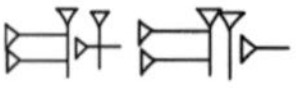	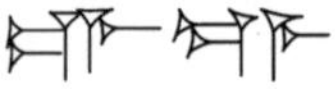
486	KIŠIB	–	–
490	Ú		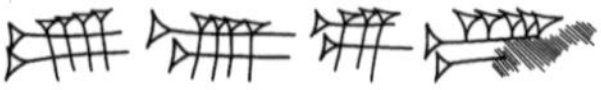
491	GA		
494	SUKAL		
495	É	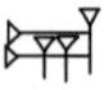	
498	E	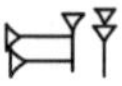	
499	DUG		na
501	UN		
504	UB		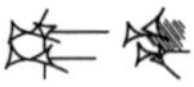
511	RA		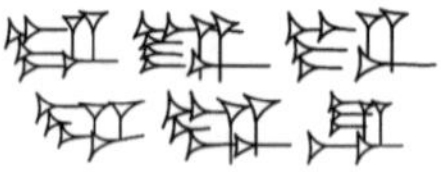
512	DÙL	–	na
514	LÚ		
535	ŠEŠ		
540	ZAK	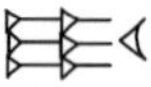	
541	ŠAR		

Appendix I: Nuzi Sign-list (*cont.*)

MZ Nr.	Value	Contenau 1926	Database 2016
543	QAR		
548	ÁŠ	–	na
552	MA	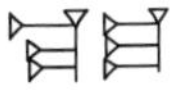	
553	GAL		
559	BUR		
560	ID		
561	DA	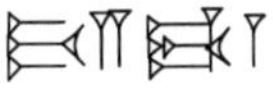	
566	ŠA		
567	ŠU		
570	LUL/NAR	–	
578	KUR	–	
579	ŠE		
580	BU	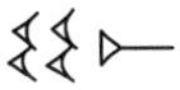	
583	US		
585	MUŠ	–	
589	TE		
590	KAR		–
596	UT		

Appendix I: Nuzi Sign-list (*cont.*)

MZ Nr.	Value	Contenau 1926	Database 2016
598	PI	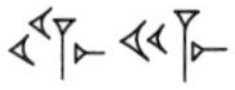	
599	ŠÀ		
612	ÉRIN	–	
631	ḪI		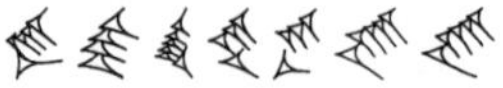
635	ʻA		–
636	AḪ	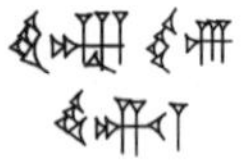	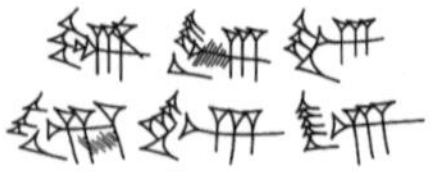
641	IM		
644	ḪUR	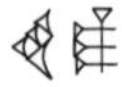	
661	U	–	
663	UGU	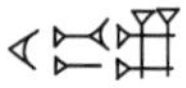	–
672	ÁB	–	
681	MI	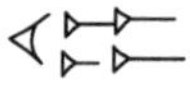	
698	UL	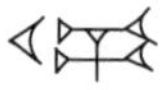	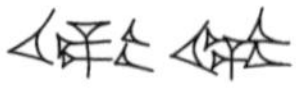
701	GÌR	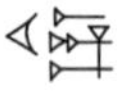	
708	MAN	–	
711	EŠ		
712	NIMIN	–	
714	NINNU	–	

Appendix I: Nuzi Sign-list (*cont.*)

MZ Nr.	Value	Contenau 1926	Database 2016
720	TUL	–	na
724	ŠI	–	
726	AR	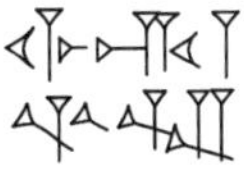	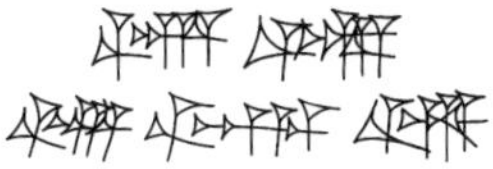
729	SIG$_5$	–	na
731	Ù		
736	DI		
737	KI		
745c	KÙ. BABBAR	–	
748	DIŠ	–	
750	LAL		–
753	ME		
754	MEŠ		
755	LAGAB	–	na
760	GIGIR	–	
786	TÚL	–	
807	IB		

Appendix I: Nuzi Sign-list (*cont.*)

MZ Nr.	Value	Contenau 1926	Database 2016
808	KU		
809	TÚG		–
812	LU		
825	MIN	–	
827	TUK	–	
828	UR		
834	$EŠ_5$	–	
836	GÍN		na
839	A		
839b	A+NA	–	
839d	A.ŠÀ	–	na
851	ZA		
856	ḪA	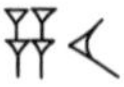	
859	GAR		
861	ÍA	–	
862	ÀŠ	–	
863	7	–	
864	8	–	

Appendix I: Nuzi Sign-list (*cont.*)

MZ Nr.	Value	Contenau 1926	Database 2016
868	9	–	
869	ŠÚ	–	
883	MUNUS		
887	NIN		–
889	DAM		
890	GÉME		
891	GU	–	
899	EL		
905	SIG_4	–	

Appendix J Tigunanum Sign-list

MZ Nr.	Value	Salvini 1994, 1996	Database 2018
1	AŠ		
5	BAL		
9	TAR	–	
10	AN		
14	BA		
15	ZU		

Appendix J: Tigunanum Sign-list (*cont.*)

MZ Nr.	Value	Salvini 1994, 1996	Database 2018
16	SU		
18	ARAD	–	
20	ITI		
24	KA		
85	LI		
86	TU		
89	LA		
90	APIN	–	
91	MAḪ	–	
92	PAB	–	
98	MU		
99	QA		
110	NA		
111	RU		
112	NU		
113	BE		
118	TI		
119	DIN		

Appendix J: Tigunanum Sign-list (*cont.*)

MZ Nr.	Value	Salvini 1994, 1996	Database 2018
120	BAR	–	
127	AK	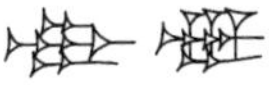	
130	MÁŠ	–	
132	ḪU		
136	IG		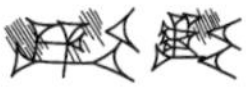
140	ZI		
141	GI		
142	RI		
148	GAB	–	
164	EN		
167	TIM		
172	SA		
174	GÁN	–	
176	GÚ	–	
181	SI		
184	SAG		
203	ÙZ	–	
209	DAB		–

Appendix J: Tigunanum Sign-list (*cont.*)

MZ Nr.	Value	Salvini 1994, 1996	Database 2018
221	ŠUM		
222	KÁ	–	
223	AB		
232	ERI_{11}	–	
238	UM		
242	DUB		–
248	TA		
252	I	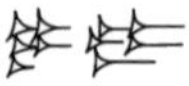	
253	ḪÉ	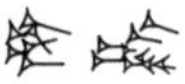	
255	DUMU	–	
258	AT		
259	ZÍ		
260	IA		
261	IN		
266	LUGAL		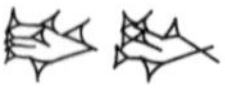
296	UK		
297	AS		

Appendix J: Tigunanum Sign-list (*cont.*)

MZ Nr.	Value	Salvini 1994, 1996	Database 2018
298	DUḪ	–	
302	KASKAL	–	
309	AM		
313	BÍ		–
341	ÚR		
348	IL		
350	DU		
353	ANŠE	–	
354	TUM	–	
357	IŠ		
358	BI		
380	NI		
381	UŠ		
408	SILA$_4$	–	
437	IR		
464	PA		
468	SIPA	–	

Appendix J: Tigunanum Sign-list (*cont.*)

MZ Nr.	Value	Salvini 1994, 1996	Database 2018
469	GEŠ		
472	GU_4	–	
474	AL		
483	MAR	–	
490	Ú	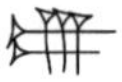	
491	GA		
495	É	–	
496	DAN		
498	E		
501	UN		
504	UB		
511	RA		
514	LÚ	–	
541	ŠAR		
548	ÁŠ		
549	BÁN	–	
552	MA		
553	GAL	–	

Appendix J: Tigunanum Sign-list (*cont.*)

MZ Nr.	Value	Salvini 1994, 1996	Database 2018
559	BUR		
560	ID		
561	DA		
566	ŠA		
567	ŠU		
578	KUR		
579	ŠE		
580	BU		
583	US		
589	TE		
596	UT		
598	PI		
599	ŠÀ		
612	ÉRIN		
631	ḪI		
636	AḪ		
640	KAM		–
641	IM		

Appendix J: Tigunanum Sign-list (*cont.*)

MZ Nr.	Value	Salvini 1994, 1996	Database 2018
644	ḪUR	–	
661	U	–	
681	MI		
685	PAN		–
686	GIM	–	
690	NIM	–	
698	UL		
701	GÌR	–	
708	MAN (20)	–	
711	EŠ		
712	NIMIN (40)	–	
714	NINNU (50)	–	
724	ŠI		
726	AR		
729	SIG$_5$	–	
731	Ù		
736	DI		
737	KI		

Appendix J: Tigunanum Sign-list (*cont.*)

MZ Nr.	Value	Salvini 1994, 1996	Database 2018
748	DIŠ		
753	ME		
754	MEŠ		
755	NIGIN	–	
807	IB		
808	KU		
810	ŠÈ	–	
812	LU		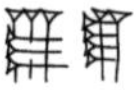
825	MIN (2)	–	
827	TUK	–	
828	UR		
832	ŠANABI (2/3)	–	
834	EŠ$_5$ (3)	–	
839	A		
851	ZA		
856	ḪA		
859	GAR (4)	–	

Appendix J: Tigunanum Sign-list (*cont.*)

MZ Nr.	Value	Salvini 1994, 1996	Database 2018
861	ÍA (5)	–	
862	ÀŠ (6)	–	
863	7	–	
864	8	–	
868	ILIMMU (9)	–	
883	MUNUS		
889	DAM		
891	GU		
899	EL		–
900	LUM		

Appendix K Comparative Sign-list Mittani

MZ Nr.	Value	Tigunanum	Nuzi	Mittanian	Assyro-Mittanian	15th–14th c. Middle Assyrian	13th c. Middle Assyrian
1	AŠ	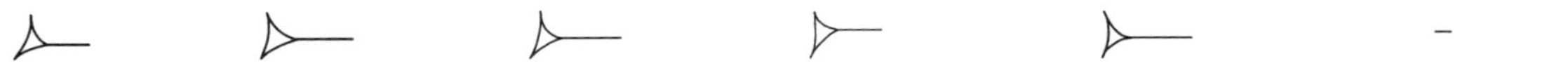					
2	ḪAL						
5	BAL						
9	TAR						
10	AN						
14	BA						
15	ZU						
16	SU						

Appendix K: Comparative Sign-list Mittani (*cont.*)

MZ Nr.	Value	Tigunanum	Nuzi	Mittanian	Assyro-Mittanian	15th–14th c. Middle Assyrian	13th c. Middle Assyrian
18	ARAD				–		
20	ITI		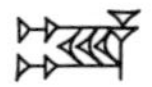	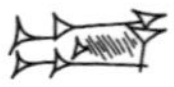	–		
24	KA						
61	EME	–				–	–
71	IRI	–			–	–	
85	LI	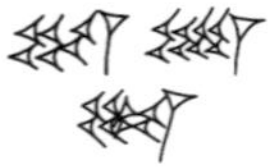					
86	TU	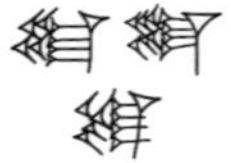					

Appendix K: Comparative Sign-list Mittani (*cont.*)

MZ Nr.	Value	Tigunanum	Nuzi	Mittanian	Assyro-Mittanian	15th–14th c. Middle Assyrian	13th c. Middle Assyrian
89	LA						
91	MAḪ						
92	PAB						
98	MU						
99	QA						
105	GIL						
110	NA						
111	RU						

Appendix K: Comparative Sign-list Mittani (*cont.*)

MZ Nr.	Value	Tigunanum	Nuzi	Mittanian	Assyro-Mittanian	15th–14th c. Middle Assyrian	13th c. Middle Assyrian
112	NU						
113	BE						
117	NUMUN	–	–			–	–
118	TI						
119	DIN				–		
120	BAR						
127	AK						
130	MÁŠ			–	–		–
132	ḪU						

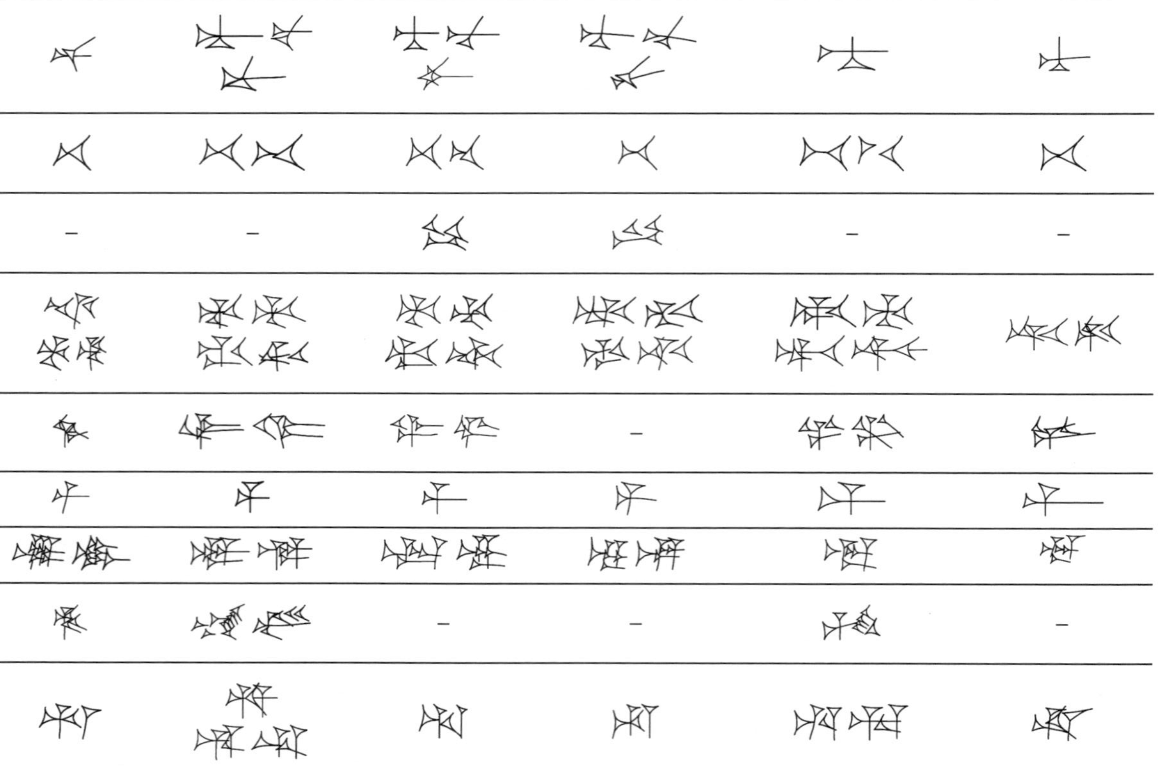

Appendix K: Comparative Sign-list Mittani (*cont.*)

MZ Nr.	Value	Tigunanum	Nuzi	Mittanian	Assyro-Mittanian	15th–14th c. Middle Assyrian	13th c. Middle Assyrian
134	NAM	–				–	–
136	IG						–
137	MUD	–	–			–	–
140	ZI	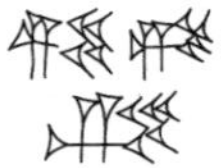					
141	GI		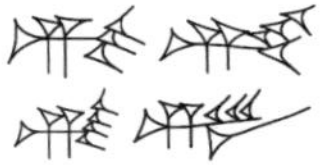				
142	RI		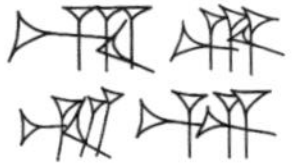				
143	NUN	–	–			–	–
148	GAB						–

Appendix K: Comparative Sign-list Mittani (*cont.*)

MZ Nr.	Value	Tigunanum	Nuzi	Mittanian	Assyro-Mittanian	15th–14th c. Middle Assyrian	13th c. Middle Assyrian
151	SUR	–					
157	GAD	–	–			–	–
164	EN						
172	SA					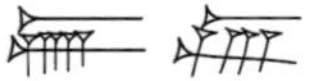	
174	GÁN		–		–		–
176	GÚ		–			–	–
176b	GÚ.UN	–		–	–		
180	GUR	–			–	–	–
181	SI					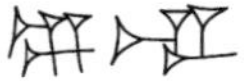	

Appendix K: Comparative Sign-list Mittani (*cont.*)

MZ Nr.	Value	Tigunanum	Nuzi	Mittanian	Assyro-Mittanian	15th–14th c. Middle Assyrian	13th c. Middle Assyrian
184	SAG						
207	DIR	–				–	–
209	DAB						
221	ŠUM						
222	KÁ		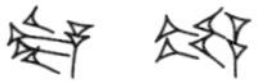	–	–	–	
223	AB						
230	URUDA	–			–	–	
238	UM						

Appendix K: Comparative Sign-list Mittani (*cont.*)

MZ Nr.	Value	Tigunanum	Nuzi	Mittanian	Assyro-Mittanian	15th–14th c. Middle Assyrian	13th c. Middle Assyrian
242	DUB						
246	NAP	–				–	–
248	TA		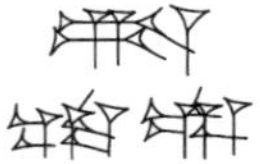	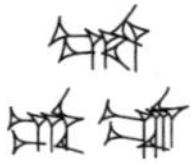			
252	I			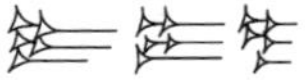			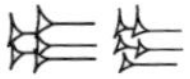
252b	I+NA	na				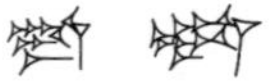	
253	ḪÉ / KÁM						
255	DUMU					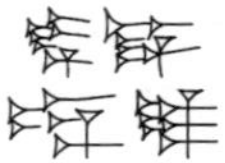	
258	AT						

Appendix K: Comparative Sign-list Mittani (*cont.*)

MZ Nr.	Value	Tigunanum	Nuzi	Mittanian	Assyro-Mittanian	15th–14th c. Middle Assyrian	13th c. Middle Assyrian
259	ZÍ						
260	IA						
261	IN						
266	LUGAL	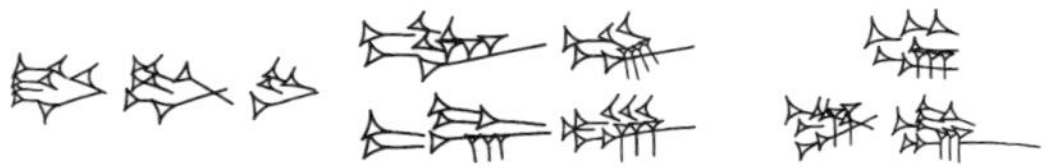			–		
271	ŠER	–	–				
292	SUM	–			–		
296	UK					–	–
297	AS					–	–
298	DUḪ						–

Appendix K: Comparative Sign-list Mittani (*cont.*)

MZ Nr.	Value	Tigunanum	Nuzi	Mittanian	Assyro-Mittanian	15th–14th c. Middle Assyrian	13th c. Middle Assyrian
300	EDIN	–	–				–
301	TAḪ	–	–			–	–
302	KASKAL		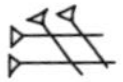		–		–
309	AM						
312	BÍL	–	–		–		–
313	BÍ						–
320	ŠÀM	–	–	–	–		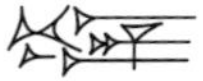
339	KUM	–	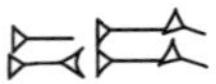			–	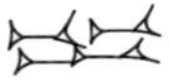
341	ÚR		–			–	–

Appendix K: Comparative Sign-list Mittani (*cont.*)

MZ Nr.	Value	Tigunanum	Nuzi	Mittanian	Assyro-Mittanian	15th–14th c. Middle Assyrian	13th c. Middle Assyrian
348	IL						
350	DU						
353	ANŠE					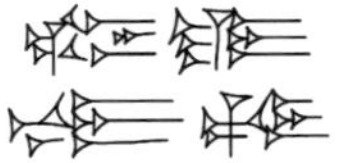	
354	TUM		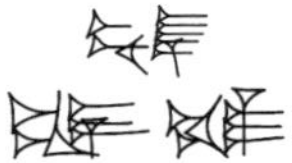	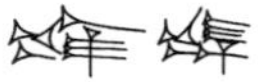		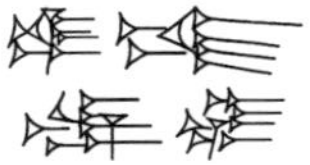	–
356	EGIR	–			–	–	–
357	IŠ		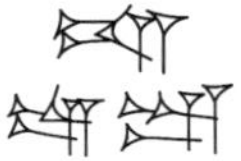				

Appendix K: Comparative Sign-list Mittani (*cont.*)

MZ Nr.	Value	Tigunanum	Nuzi	Mittanian	Assyro-Mittanian	15th–14th c. Middle Assyrian	13th c. Middle Assyrian
358	BI						
379	GAG	–		–		–	–
380	NI						
381	UŠ						–
385	NA_4	–					
437	IR						
464	PA						
466	ŠAB	–	–			–	–
469	GEŠ						

Appendix K: Comparative Sign-list Mittani (*cont.*)

MZ Nr.	Value	Tigunanum	Nuzi	Mittanian	Assyro-Mittanian	15th–14th c. Middle Assyrian	13th c. Middle Assyrian
472	GU_4				–	–	–
474	AL						
483	MAR						
484	KID	–	–		–		
486	KIŠIB	–	–				
490	Ú						
491	GA						
494	SUKAL	–					–
495	É						
496	DAN		–				

Appendix K: Comparative Sign-list Mittani (*cont.*)

MZ Nr.	Value	Tigunanum	Nuzi	Mittanian	Assyro-Mittanian	15th–14th c. Middle Assyrian	13th c. Middle Assyrian
498	E						
499	DUG	–				–	
501	UN						
504	UB						
511	RA	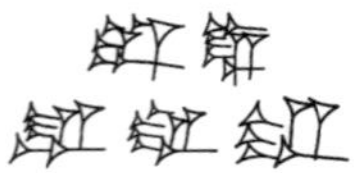				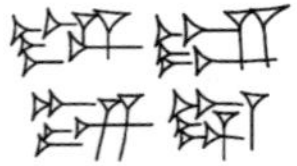	
514	LÚ		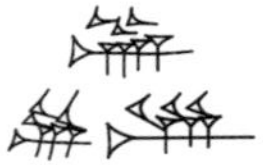				
535	ŠEŠ	–		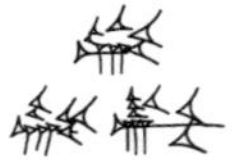	–		

Appendix K: Comparative Sign-list Mittani (*cont.*)

MZ Nr.	Value	Tigunanum	Nuzi	Mittanian	Assyro-Mittanian	15th–14th c. Middle Assyrian	13th c. Middle Assyrian
540	ZAK	–					–
541	ŠAR						
543	QAR	–			–		
545	MÚRU	–	–			–	–
548	ÁŠ		–				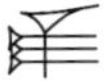
552	MA			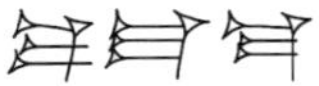		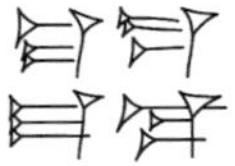	
553	GAL		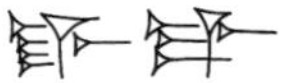			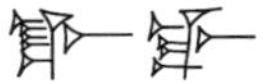	
558	GIR	–	–			–	–
559	BUR			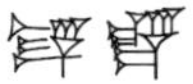			

Appendix K: Comparative Sign-list Mittani (*cont.*)

MZ Nr.	Value	Tigunanum	Nuzi	Mittanian	Assyro-Mittanian	15th–14th c. Middle Assyrian	13th c. Middle Assyrian
560	ID						
561	DA						
566	ŠA	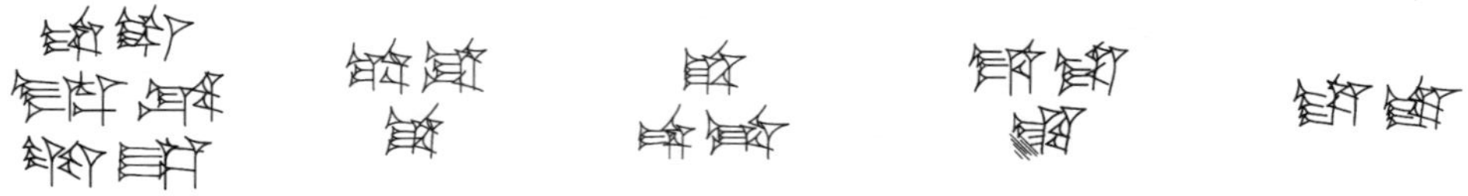					
567	ŠU						
573	ALAM	–	–			–	–
578	KUR						
579	ŠE						
580	BU						

Appendix K: Comparative Sign-list Mittani (*cont.*)

MZ Nr.	Value	Tigunanum	Nuzi	Mittanian	Assyro-Mittanian	15th–14th c. Middle Assyrian	13th c. Middle Assyrian
583	US						–
585	MUŠ	–					
589	TE						
590	KAR	–			–		
596	UT						
598	PI						
599	ŠÀ						
608	$PEŠ_4$	–	–	–		–	–
612	ÉRIN / LÁḪ				–		

Appendix K: Comparative Sign-list Mittani (*cont.*)

MZ Nr.	Value	Tigunanum	Nuzi	Mittanian	Assyro-Mittanian	15th–14th c. Middle Assyrian	13th c. Middle Assyrian
631	ḪI						
631b	DU_{10}.GA	–	–		–	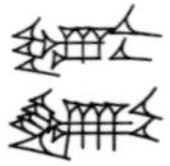	
635	ʻA	–			–	–	
636	AḪ	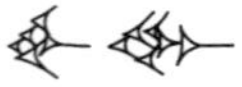				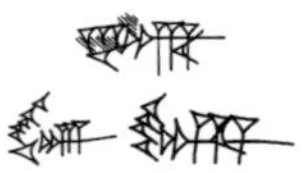	
640	KAM		–	–			
641	IM		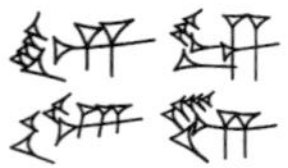				
644	ḪUR						
661	U						

Appendix K: Comparative Sign-list Mittani (*cont.*)

MZ Nr.	Value	Tigunanum	Nuzi	Mittanian	Assyro-Mittanian	15th–14th c. Middle Assyrian	13th c. Middle Assyrian
663	UGU	–					
678	KIŠ	–	–			–	–
681	MI						
682	GUL	–	–		–		
690	NIM		–			–	–
693	LAM	–	–				–
698	UL						
701	GÌR						–
708	MAN						
711	EŠ						

Appendix K: Comparative Sign-list Mittani (*cont.*)

MZ Nr.	Value	Tigunanum	Nuzi	Mittanian	Assyro-Mittanian	15th–14th c. Middle Assyrian	13th c. Middle Assyrian
712	NIMIN				–	–	–
724	ŠI						
726	AR						
729	SIG_5		–	–	–		
731	Ù		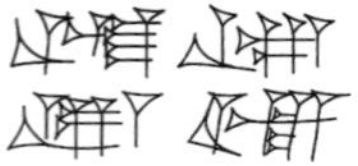				
736	DI						
737	KI	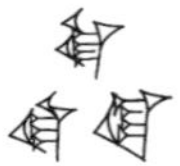	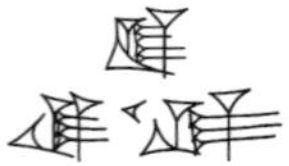				
744	ŠUL	–	–			–	

Appendix K: Comparative Sign-list Mittani (*cont.*)

MZ Nr.	Value	Tigunanum	Nuzi	Mittanian	Assyro-Mittanian	15th–14th c. Middle Assyrian	13th c. Middle Assyrian
745c	KÙ.BABBAR	–					–
746	ŠUK	–	–			–	–
748	DIŠ						
750	LAL	–					
753	ME						
754	MEŠ		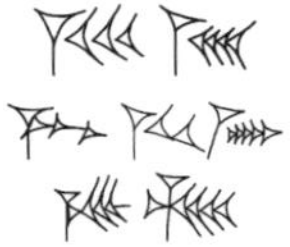				
760	GIGIR	–			–	–	–
786	TÚL	–		–		–	–
807	IB						

Appendix K: Comparative Sign-list Mittani (*cont.*)

MZ Nr.	Value	Tigunanum	Nuzi	Mittanian	Assyro-Mittanian	15th–14th c. Middle Assyrian	13th c. Middle Assyrian
808	KU						
812	LU						
815	KIN	– 	–			–	
825	MIN						
827	TUK				–	–	–
828	UR						
834	EŠ$_5$						
836	GÍN	– 		–			
839	A						
839b	A+NA	– 			–	–	–

Appendix K: Comparative Sign-list Mittani (*cont.*)

MZ Nr.	Value	Tigunanum	Nuzi	Mittanian	Assyro-Mittanian	15th–14th c. Middle Assyrian	13th c. Middle Assyrian
851	ZA						
856	ḪA						
858	GUG						
859	GAR						
861	ÍA						
862	ÀŠ						
863	7						
864	8						
868	9						
869	ŠÚ						

Appendix K: Comparative Sign-list Mittani (*cont.*)

MZ Nr.	Value	Tigunanum	Nuzi	Mittanian	Assyro-Mittanian	15th–14th c. Middle Assyrian	13th c. Middle Assyrian
883	MUNUS		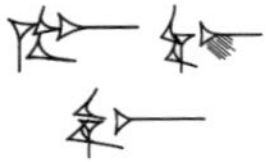	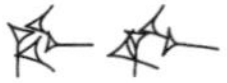			
884	ZUM	–	–			–	
887	NIN	–			–	–	
889	DAM				–		–
890	GÉME	–			–	–	
891	GU						
899	EL						
900	LUM	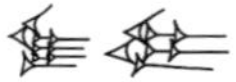	–	–		–	–
905	SIG_4	–				–	–

Bibliography

Abazov, R. (2005). *Historical Dictionary of Turkmenistan*. Lanham: Scarecrow Press.

Abrahami, P., & Lion, B. (2012). L'archive de Tulpun-naya. In *The Nuzi Workshop at the 55th Rencontre Assyriologique Internationale. Studies on the Civilization and Culture of Nuzi and the Hurrians, Vol. 19*. Bethesda: CDL Press.

Adams, R. (2008). Review of 'Inscribed in Clay: Provenance Studies of the Amarna Letters and Other Ancient Near Eastern Texts' by Yuval Goren, Israel Finkelstein, Nadav Na'aman. In *Bulletin of the American Schools of Oriental Research*, 351: pp. 87–90.

Adler, H.-P. (1976). *Das Akkadische des Königs Tušratta von Mitanni*. Kevelaer: Butzon & Bercker.

Albright, W. F. (1934). The Cuneiform Tablet from Beth-Shemesh. In *Bulletin of the American Schools of Oriental Research*, 53: pp. 18–19.

Alexandrov, B. (2014). The Letters from Hanigalbat in the Boğazköy Archives. In P. Taracha & M. Kapełuś (Eds.), *Proceedings of the Eighth International Congress of Hittitology*. Warsaw: Agade.

Amiaud, A., & Méchinau, L. (1887). *Tableau compare des ecritures babylonienne et assyrienne*. Paris: Ernest Leroux.

Anderson, S. E., & Levoy, M. (2002). Unwrapping and Visualizing Cuneiform Tablets. In *IEEE Computer Graphics and Applications*, 22 (6): pp. 82–88.

Archi, A. (2010). When Did the Hittites Begin to Write in Hittite? In Y. Cohen, A. Gilan, & J. L. Miller (Eds.), *Pax Hethitica: Studies on the Hittites and Their Neighbours in Honour of Itamar Singer*. Wiesbaden: Otto Harrassowitz Verlag.

Archi, A. (2015). Remarks on Hittite Augur Rituals and rituals from Arzawa. In *Bibliotheca Orientalis*, 72 (3/4): pp. 282–294.

Aristotle. (c. 350 BCE). Περὶ Ψυχῆς. *On the Soul*. Translated by J. A. Smith. The Internet Classics Archive. Available at: http://classics.mit.edu/Aristotle/soul.3.iii.html (Accessed: August 2016).

Artzi, P. (1997). EA 16. In *Altorientalische Forschungen*, 24 (2): pp. 320–336.

Arvanitis, T., Davis, T., Livingstone, A., Pinilla-Dutoit, D., & Woolley, S. (2002). The Digital Classification of Ancient Near Eastern Cuneiform Data (Virtual Archaeology: Proceedings of the VAST Euroconference). In *British archaeological reports: International series*, 1075: pp. 65–70.

Ascalone, E., & D'Andrea, M. (2013). Assembling the Evidence: Excavated Sites Dating from the Early Bronze Age in and around the Chora of Ebla. In *Ebla and its Landscape: Early State Formation in the Ancient Near East*. Walnut Creek: Left Coast Press.

Ashby, S. (2010). *Artefact Biographies: Implications for the Curation of Archaeological Ivories*. Available at: www.ebur.eu/userfiles/file/Artefact%20biographies%20final%20doc.doc (Accessed: August 2016).

Astour, M. C. (1987). Semites and Hurrians in Northern Transtigris. In *General Studies and Excavations at Nuzi 9/1. Studies on the Civilisation and Culture of Nuzi and the Hurrians* (2). Winona Lake: Eisenbrauns.

Avruch, K. (2000). Reciprocity, equality, and status-anxiety in the Amarna Letters. In R. Cohen & R. Westbrook (Eds.), *Amarna Diplomacy: The Beginnings of International Relations*. Baltimore / London: The Johns Hopkins University Press.

Babak, V., Vaisman, D., & Wasserman, A. (2004). *Political Organization in Central Asia & Azerbaijan: Sources and Documents*. London: Frank Cass Publishers.

Baker, C. (2011). *Foundations of Bilingual Education and Bilingualism* (5th ed.). Bristol: Multilingual Matters.

Barber, A., & Stainton, R. J. (2010). *Concise Encyclopedia of Philosophy of Language and Linguistics*. Amsterdam: Elsevier.

Bard, K. A. (2015). *An Introduction to the Archaeology of Ancient Egypt* (2nd ed.). Chichester: Wiley Blackwell.

Barjamovic, G. (2011). *A Historical Geography of Anatolia in the Old Assyrian Colony Period*. Copenhagen: Museum Tusculanum Press.

Barton, G. A. (1913). *Origin and Development of Babylonian Writing*. Leipzig / Baltimore: J. C. Hinrichs / The Johns Hopkins Press.

Bayer, F. (1927). *Die Entwicklung der Keilschrift*. Rome: Pontificio Instituto Biblico.

Beckman, G. (1999). *Hittite diplomatic texts* (2nd ed.). Atlanta: Society of Biblical Literature.

Bennett, B. P. (2011). *Religion and Language in Post-Soviet Russia*. London / New York: Routledge.

Beran, T. (1957). Assyrische Glyptik des 14. Jahrhunderts. *Zeitschrift für Assyriologie*, 51: pp. 141–215.

Berkooz, M. (1937). The Nuzi Dialect of Akkadian: Orthography and Phonology. *Language*, 13 (1): pp. 5–64.

Bernbeck, R. (2009). Class Conflict in Ancient Mesopotamia: Between Knowledge of History and Historicising Knowledge. In *Anthropology of the Middle East*, 4 (1): pp. 33–64.

Biggs, R. D. (1967). *ŠÀ.ZI.GA Ancient Mesopotamian Potency Incantations* (VOL. II). Locust Valley, New York: J.J. Augustin.

Biggs, R. D. (1973). On regional cuneiform handwritings in third millennium Mesopotamia. In *Orientalia*, 42: pp. 39–46.

Binford, S. R., & Binford, L. R. (1968). *New Perspectives in Archaeology*. Chicago: Aldine Publishing Cooperation.

Bischoff, B. (1990). *Latin Palaeography* Cambridge: Cambridge University Press.

Bloch, Y. (2012). Middle Assyrian Lunar Calendar and Chronology. In J. Ben-Dov, W. Horowitz, & J. M. Steele (Eds.), *Living the Lunar Calendar*. Oxford: Oxbow.

Bonatz, D., & Bartl, P. (2013). Across Assyria's Northern Frontier: Tell Fekheriye at the End of the Late Bronze Age. In K. Aslıhan Yener (Ed.), *Across the Border: Late Bronze-Iron Age Relations between Syria and Anatolia*. Leuven: Peeters.

Borger, R. (2004). *Mesopotamisches Zeichenlexikon*. Münster: Ugarit-Verlag.

Botta, P.-E. (1847). *Mémoire sur l'écriture cunéiforme assyrienne*. Paris: Imprimerie Nationale.

Bourdieu, P. (1972). Esquisse d'une théorie de la pratique, précédé de trois études d'ethnologie kabyle. *Outline of a Theory of Practice*. Translated by R. Nice. Cambridge: Cambridge University Press.

Bramanti, A. (2015). Rethinking the Writing Space: Anatomy of Some Early Dynastic Signs. In *Current Research in Cuneiform Palaeography*. Gladbeck: Pe-We-Verlag.

Brandt, C. (2014). Script as a potential demarcator and stabilizer of languages in South Asia. In H. C. Cardoso (Ed.), *Language Endangerment and Preservation in South Asia*. Honolulu: University of Hawai'i Press.

Breakwell, G. M. (1993). Social Representations and Social Identity. In *Papers on Social Representation / Textes sur les Representations Sociales*, 2 (3): pp. 1–20.

Brenzinger, M. (2007). *Language Diversity Endangered*. Berlin / New York: Mouton de Gruyter.

Brown, B. (2014). Settlement Patterns of the Middle Assyrian State: Notes toward an Investigation of State Apparatuses. In D. Bonatz (Ed.), *The Archaeology of Political Spaces. The Upper Mesopotamian Piedmont in the Second Millennium BC*. Berlin / Boston: De Gruyter.

Brünnow, R.-E. (1889). *A classified list of all simple and compound cuneiform ideographs*. Leiden: Brill.

Brünnow, R.-E. (1890). Die Mîtâni-Sprache. In *Zeitschrift für Assyriologie*, 5: pp. 209–259.

Buccellati, G. (2010). The Semiotics of Ethnicity: The Case of Hurrian Urkesh. In J. F. Fincke (Ed.), *Festschrift für Gernot Wilhelm anläßlich seines 65 Geburtstages*. Dresden: ISLET.

Cammarosano, M. (2015). 3D–Joins und Schriftmetrologie: A Quantitative Approach to Cuneiform Palaeography. In *Current Research in Cuneiform Palaeography*. Gladbeck: Pe-We-Verlag.

Cammarosano, M., Müller, G. G. W., Fisseler, D., & Weichert, F. (2014). Schriftmetrologie des Keils. Dreidimensionale Analyse von Keileindrücken und Handschriften. In *Welt des Orients*, 44: pp. 2–36.

Campo dell'Orto, S. (2004). *Public and private administration in the Middle Assyrian period: The archive of Babu-aḫa-iddina*. MPhil, University of Cambridge. Unpublished (available through Haddon Library, University of Cambridge).

Cancik-Kirschbaum, E. (1996). *Die mittelassyrischen Briefe aus Tall Šēḫ Ḥamad.* Berlin: Reimer.

Cancik-Kirschbaum, E. (1999). Nebenlinien des assyrischen Königshauses in der 2. Hälfte des 2. Jts. V. Chr. In *Altorientalische Forschungen*, 26 (2): pp. 210–222.

Cancik-Kirschbaum, E. (2008). Assur und Hatti – zwischen Allianz und Konflikt. In G. Wilhelm (Ed.), *Ḫattuša-Boğazköy. Das Hethiterreich im Spannungsfeld des Alten Orients.* Wiesbaden: Harrassowitz.

Cancik-Kirschbaum, E. (2012). Middle Assyrian Administrative Documents and Diplomatics: Preliminary Remarks Towards and Analysis of Scribal Norms and Habits. In *Palaeography and Scribal Practices in Syro-Palestine and Anatolia in the Late Bronze Age.* Leiden: Nederlands Instituut voor het Nabije Oosten.

Cancik-Kirschbaum, E., Brisch, N., & Eidem, J. (2014). *Constituent, Confederate, and Conquered Space: The Emergence of the Mittani State.* Berlin / Boston: Walter de Gruyter.

Cancik-Kirschbaum, E., & Mahr, B. (2005). Anordnung und ästhetisches Profil: Die Herausbildung einer universellen Kulturtechnik in der Frühgeschichte der Schrift. In *Bildwelten des Wissens. Kunsthistorisches Jahrbuch für Bildkritik. Band 3.1: Diagramme und bildtextile Ordnungen.* Berlin: Akademie-Verlag.

Charpin, D. (2002). Chroniques du Moyen-Euphrate (Le royaume de Hana: textes et histoire). In *Revue d'assyriologie et d'archéologie orientale*, 96: pp. 61–92.

Charpin, D. (2002). Note sur la localisation de Zalba(r). In *Šapal tibnim mû illakū: Studies Presented to Joaquín Sanmartín on the Occasion of His 65th Birthday.* Barcelona: Editorial AUSA.

Childe, V. G. (1925). *The Dawn of European Civilization.* London: Kegan Paul / Routledge.

Christie, A. (1946). *Come, Tell Me How You Live* (1995 Paperback Edition ed.). Glasgow: Harper Collins.

Clarke, D. L. (1973). Archaeology: the loss of innocence. In *Antiquity*, 47: pp. 6–18.

Clay, A. (1906). *Documents from the Temple Archives of Nippur; Dated in the Reigns of Cassite Rulers* (Vol. 14). Philadelphia: University of Pennsylvania.

Clay, A. T. (1893). *Babylonian Expedition XIV: Documents from the temple archives of Nippur.* Philadelphia: University of Pennsylvania.

Cohen, Y. (2004). Kidin-Gula – The Foreign Teacher at the Emar Scribal School. In *Revue d'assyriologie et d'archéologie orientale*, 98: pp. 81–100.

Cohen, Y. (2009). *The Scribes and Scholars of the City of Emar in the Late Bronze Age.* Winona Lake: Eisenbrauns.

Cohen, Y. (2012). An Overview on the Scripts of Late Bronze Age Emar. In *Palaeography and Scribal Practices in Syro-Palestine and Anatolia in the Late Bronze Age.* Leiden: Nederlands Instituut voor het Nabije Oosten.

Collar, A. (2007). Network Theory and Religious Innovation. In *Mediterranean Historical Review*, 22 (1): pp. 149–162.

Contenau, G. (1926). *Les Tablettes de Kerkouk et les Origines de la Civilisation Assyrienne*. Paris: Geuthner.

Cooper, J., Schwartz, G., & Westbrook, R. (2005). A Mittani-Era Tablet from Umm el-Marra. In *General Studies and Excavations at Nuzi 11/1*. Bethesda: CDL Press.

Cooper, J. S. (1971). Bilinguals from Boghazköi I. *Zeitschrift für Assyriologie*, 61: pp. 1–22.

Cooper, J. S. (1999). Sumerian and Semitic Writing in Most Ancient Syro-Mesopotamia. In *Languages and Cultures in Contact: At the Crossroads of Civilizations in the Syro-Mesopotamian Realm*. Leuven: Peeters.

Cuneiform Digital Forensic Project. (1999). See Woolley *et al.* 2002.

Cuneiform Digital Library Initiative. (2000). A joint project of the University of California, Los Angeles, the University of Oxford, and the Max Planck Institute for the History of Science, Berlin. Available at: http://cdli.ucla.edu/ (Accessed: August 2016).

Cuneiform Digital Palaeography Project (2004). The University of Birmingham and the British Museum. Available at: http://www.cdp.bham.ac.uk/ (Accessed: Offline August 2016).

CuneiformAnalyser. (2014). See Fisseler *et al.* 2014.

Curvers, H., & Schwartz, G. (1997). Umm el-Marra, A Bronze Age Urban Center in the Jabbul Plain, Western Syria. In *American Journal of Archaeology*, 101: pp. 201–227.

d'Alfonso, L., & Cohen, Y. (2008). The duration of the Emar archives and the relative and absolute chronology of the City. In L. d'Alfonso, Y. Cohen, & D. Sürenhagen (Eds.), *The City of Emar among the Late Bronze Age Empires*. Münster: Ugarit Verlag.

Danesi, M. (2010). Edusemiotics. In I. Semetsky (Ed.), *Semiotics Education Experience*. Rotterdam/Boston: Sense Publishers.

Daniels, P. T. (1995). Cuneiform Calligraphy. In *Nineveh, 612 BC: The Glory and Fall of the Assyrian Empire: Catalogue of the 10th Anniversary Exhibition of the Neo-Assyrian Text Corpus Project*. Helsinki: Helsinki University Press.

De Martino, S. (2004). A Tentative Chronology of the Kingdom of Mittani from its Rise to the Reign of Tušratta. In *Mesopotamian dark age revisited*. Vienna: Verlag der Österreichischen Akademie der Wissenschaften.

De Martino, S. (2014). The Mittani State: The Formation of the Kingdom of Mittani. In E. Cancik-Kirschbaum, N. Brisch, & J. Eidem (Eds.), *Constituent, Confederate, and Conquered Space: The Emergence of the Mittani State*. Berlin / Boston: Walter de Gruyter.

De Martino, S. (2015). Mittanian Hegemony in Western and Central Syria. In *Qaṭna and the networks of Bronze Age globalism*. Wiesbaden: Harrassowitz.

De Montfaucon, B. (1708). *Palaeographia Graeca*. Paris: L. Guérin, J. Boudot & C. Robustel.

De Ridder, J. J. (2011). Review: S. Jakob, Die Mittelassyrischen Texte aus Tell Chuera in Nordost-Syrien. In *Bibliotheca Orientalis*, 68: pp. 123–127.

De Ridder, J. J. (2013). 32: A late Old Assyrian sale on a house plot, KAM 10 1. In *NABU*, 2013 (2): pp. 55–57.

Deimel, A. (1922). *Die Inschriften von Fara: Liste der archaischen Keilschriftzeichen.* Leipzig: J. C. Hinrichs.

Delitzsch, F. (1900). *Assyrische Lesestücke* (4th ed.). Leipzig: J. C. Hinrichs.

Delorez, A. (2003). *The Palaeography of Gothic Manuscript Books – From the Twelfth to the Early Sixteenth Century.* Cambridge: Cambridge University Press.

Der Manuelian, P. (1998). Digital Epigraphy: An Approach to Streamlining Egyptological Epigraphic Method. In *Journal of the American Research Center in Egypt,* 35: pp. 97–113.

Descartes, R. (1673). Discours de la Méthode. *Discourse of the Method.* Translated by J. Bennett. Available at: http://www.earlymoderntexts.com/assets/pdfs/descartes1637.pdf (Accessed: August 2016).

Devecchi, E. (2012). *Palaeography and scribal practices in Syro-Palestine and Anatolia in the Late Bronze Age.* Leiden: Nederlands Instituut voor het Nabije Oosten.

Devecchi, E., Müller, G. G. W., & Mynářová, J. (2015). *Current Research in Cuneiform Palaeography.* Gladbeck: PeWe-Verlag.

Diem, M., & Sablatnig, R. (2009). Recognition of Degraded Handwritten Characters Using Local Features. In *10th International Conference on Document Analysis Recognition.* Barcelona: Universitat Autònoma de Barcelona.

Dietrich, M., & Loretz, O. (1981). Die Inschrift der Statue des Königs Idrimi von Alalaḫ. *Ugarit Forschungen,* 13: pp. 201–268.

Dietrich, M., & Mayer, W. (1999). The Hurrian and Hittite Texts. In W. G. E. Watson & N. Wyatt (Eds.), *Handbook of Ugaritic Studies.* Leiden: Brill.

Dietrich, M., & Mayer, W. (2010). *Der hurritische Brief des Dušratta von Mīttānni an Amenḫotep III.* Münster: Ugarit-Verlag.

Digital Hammurabi Project (1999). See Hahn, D. V. *et al.* 2006.

Doble, A., Asaro, F., & Michel, H. V. (1977). Neutron Activation Analysis and the location of Waššukanni. In *Orientalia,* 46: pp. 375–382.

Donbaz, V. (1985). More Old Assyrian Tablets from Assur. In *Akkadica,* 42: pp. 1–23.

Donbaz, V. (2001). 55: The Eponymy of Urad-šerua son of Aššur-bani. In *NABU,* 2001 (3): pp. 54–55.

Duistermaat, K. (2015). The Pots of Assur in the Land of Hanigalbat – The Organization of Pottery Production in the Far West of the Middle Assyrian Empire. In *Understanding Hegemonic Practices of the Early Assyrian Empire. Essays dedicated to Frans Wiggermann.* Leiden: Nederlands Instituut voor het Nabije Oosten.

Duncan, D. D., Hahn, D. V., & Baldwin, K. C. (2007). Non-Laser-Based Scanner for Three-Dimensional Digitization of Historical Artifacts. In *Applied Optics,* 46: pp. 2838–2850.

Durand, J-M (2006). La Lettre de Labarna au roi de Tigunânum, un réexamen. In *Šapal tibnim mû illakū: Studies Presented to Joaquín Sanmartín on the Occasion of His 65th Birthday*. Barcelona: Editorial AUSA.

Düring, B. (2015). The Hegemonic Practices of the Middle Assyrian Empire in Context. In *Understanding Hegemonic Practices of the Early Assyrian Empire. Essays dedicated to Frans Wiggermann*. Leiden: Nederlands Instituut voor het Nabije Oosten.

Ebeling, E. (1927). *Keilschrifttexte aus Assur juristischen Inhalts*. Leipzig: J. C. Hinrichs.

Edzard, D. O. (1960). Die Beziehungen Babyloniens und Ägyptens in der mittelbabylonischen Zeit und das Gold. In *Journal of the Economic and Social History of the Orient*, 3 (1): pp. 38–55.

Edzard, D. O. (1993). Review of Green, M. W. *et al*: Zeichenliste der Archaischen Texte aus Uruk (Ausgrabungen der Deutschen Forschungsgemeinschaft in Uruk-Warka). In *Zeitschrift für Assyriologie*, 83: pp. 136–141.

Edzard, D. O., Calmeyer, P., & Moortgat, A. (1976–1980). *Reallexikon der Assyriologie* (Vol. 5). Berlin: De Gruyter.

Eidem, J. (1997). The Inscriptions. In D. Oates, J. Oates, & H. McDonald (Eds.), *Excavations at Tell Brak: The Mitanni and Old Babylonian Periods*. London: British School of Archaeology in Iraq.

Eidem, J. (2002). *The Clay they Wrote On – Old Babylonian Letters as Artefacts*. London: NABU.

Ernst-Pradal, F. (2008). *Scribes d'Ougarit et paléographie Akkadienne: Les textes juridiques signés*. PhD, Université de Paris IV Sorbonne.

Ernst-Pradal, F. (2015). Paléographie des textes hourrites syllabiques de Ras Shamra / Ougarit (suite): Les vocabulaires à colonne hourrite. In *Current Research in Cuneiform Palaeography*. Gladbeck: Pe-We-Verlag.

Ezaki, M. (2010). Strategic Deviations: The Role of "kanji" in Contemporary Japanese. In *Japanese Language and Literature*, 44: pp. 179–212.

Fincke, J. (2009). KUB 4, 16: utukkū lemnūtu Tafel 6 aus Ḫattuša. In *NABU*, 41: pp. 53–55.

Fincke, J. (2011). The Tradition of Professions within Families at Nuzi. In A. Archi & A. Bramanti (Eds.), *Tradition and Innovation in the Ancient Near East*. Winona Lake: Eisenbrowns.

Fincke, J. (2012). Adoption of Women at Nuzi. In P. Abrahami & B. Lion (Eds.), *The Nuzi Workshop at the 55th Rencontre Assyriologique Internationale. Studies on the Civilization and Culture of Nuzi and the Hurrians, Vol. 19*. Bethesda: CDL Press.

Fine, H. A. (1952). Studies in Middle-Assyrian Chronology and Religion: Part I. In *Hebrew Union College Annual*, 24: pp. 187–273.

Fink, A. (2010). *Late Bronze Age Tell Atchana (Alalakh): Stratigraphy, Chronology, History*. Oxford: Hadrian Books / Archaeopress.

Finkel, I. L. (1985). Inscriptions from Tell Brak 1984. In *Iraq*, 47: pp. 187–201.

Finkel, I. L. (1988). Inscriptions from Tell Brak 1985. In *Iraq*, 50: pp. 83–86.

Fisseler, D., Weichert, F., Müller, G. G. W., & Cammarosano, M. (2014). Extending Philological Research with Methods of 3D Computer Graphics Applied to Analysis of Cultural Heritage. In *Proceedings of the 12th Eurographics Workshop on Graphics and Cultural Heritage*. Aire-la-Ville: The Eurographics Association.

Forrer, E. (1922). *Die Boghazköi-Texte in Umschrift, Erster Band: Die Keilschrift von Boghazköi*. Leipzig: J. C. Hinrichs.

Fossey, C. (1926). *Manuel d'Assyriologie II: Evolution des Cunéiformes*. Paris: Louis Conard.

Foster, B. R. (1982). Administration of State Lands at Sargonic Gasur. In *Oriens Antiquus*, 20: pp. 39–48.

Foucault, M. (1969). L'archéologie du Savoir. *The Archaeology of Knowledge*. Translated by A. M. S. Smit. London / New York: Routledge.

Freu, J. (2007). *Des origines à la fin de l'ancien royaume hittite. Les hittites et leur histoire.* Paris: Harmattan.

Freydank, H. (1988). Zur Paläographie der mittelassyrischen Urkunden. In *Šulmu: Papers on the Ancient Near East Presented at International Conference of Socialist Countries* Prague: Prague University Karlova.

Freydank, H. (1991). *Beiträge zur mittelassyrischen Chronologie und Geschichte*. Berlin: Akademie Verlag.

Freydank, H. (2003). Anmerkungen zu mittelassyrischen texten 4. In *Altorientalische Forschungen*, 30 (2): pp. 244–255.

Friedmann, A. H. (1987). Toward a relative chronology at Nuzi. In *General Studies and Excavations at Nuzi 9/1. Studies on the Civilization and Culture of Nuzi and the Hurrians, Vol. 2*. Winona Lake: Eisenbrauns.

Gamkrelidze, T. V. (1961). The Akkado-Hittite Syllabary and the Problem of the Origin of the Hittite Script. In *Archiv Orientální*, 29: pp. 406–418.

Gardner, A. (2013). Thinking about Roman imperialism: postcolonialism, globalisation and beyond? In *Britannia*, 44: pp. 1–25.

Gasche, H., Cole, S. W., Armstrong, A., & Gurzadyan, V. G. (1998). *Dating the Fall of Babylon: A Reappraisal of Second-Millennium Mesopotamian Chronology*. Ghent / Chicago: University of Ghent / Oriental Institute of the University of Chicago.

Gelb, I. J. (1944). *Hurrians and Subarians*. Chicago: The University of Chicago Press.

Gelb, I. J., Purves, P. M., & MacRae, A. A. (1943). *Nuzi Personal Names*. Chicago: The University of Chicago Press.

Gelb, I. J., & Sollberger, E. (1957). The First Legal Document from the Later Old Assyrian Period. In *Journal of Near Eastern Studies*, 16 (3): pp. 163–175.

George, A. R. (2005). In search of the é.dub.ba.a: The ancient Mesopotamian school in literature and reality. In Y. Sefati (Ed.), *An Experienced Scribe who Neglects Nothing. Ancient Near Eastern Studies in Honor of Jacob Klein*. Bethesda: CDL Press.

George, A. R. (2009). *Babylonian Literary Texts in the Schøyen Collection*. Cornell University Studies in Assyriology and Sumerology, 10. Bethesda: CDL Press.

George, A. R. (2013). *Babylonian Divinatory Texts Chiefly in the Schøyen Collection*. Cornell University Studies in Assyriology and Sumerology, 18. Bethesda: CDL Press.

George, A. R. (2017). *Assyrian Archival Texts in the Schøyen Collection and Other Documents*. Cornell University Studies in Assyriology and Sumerology, 34. Bethesda: CDL Press.

Gibson, J. J. (1979). *The Ecological Approach to Visual Perception*. Boston: Houghton Mifflin.

Giddens, A. (1984). *The constitution of society*. Cambridge: Polity Press.

GigaMesh (2010). See Mara *et al.* 2010.

Giorgieri, M., & Wilhelm, G. (1995). Privative Opposition im Syllabar der hurritischen Texte. In G. W. D. I. Owen (Ed.), *Studies on the Civilization and Culture of Nuzi and the Hurrians (Edith Porada Memorial Volume)* (Vol. 7). Bethesda: CDL Press.

Glock, A. E. (1971). A New Ta'annek Tablet. In *Bulletin of the American Schools of Oriental Research*, 204: pp. 17–30.

Glocker, J. (2011). Ališarruma König von Išuwa. In *Altorientalische Forschungen*, 38: pp. 254–276.

Goetze, A. (1938). Some Observations on Nuzu Akkadian. In *Language*, 14 (2): pp. 134–143.

Goetze, A. (1964). The Kassites and near Eastern Chronology. In *Journal of Cuneiform Studies*, 18 (4): pp. 97–101.

Goodman, N. (1954). *Fact, Fiction and Forecast* (4th edition, 1983 ed.). Cambridge, Massachusetts: Harvard University Press.

Goodman, N. (1956). A world of individuals. In *The Problem of Universals: a symposium*. Notre Dame, Indiana: University of Notre Dame Press.

Goodman, N., & Leonard, H. S. (1940). The Calculus of Individuals and Its Uses. In *The Journal of Symbolic Logic*, 5 (2): pp. 45–55.

Goody, J. (1986). *The Logic of Writing and the Organisation of Society*. Cambridge: Cambridge University Press.

Gordin, S. (2014). The Socio-historical Setting of Hittite Schools of Writing as reflected in Scribal Habits. In *Visualizing Knowledge and Creating Meaning in Ancient Writing Systems*. Gladbeck: Pe-We-Verlag.

Goren, Y., Finkelstein, I., & Na'Aman, N. (2004). *Inscribed in Clay: Provenance Study of the Amarna tablets and Other Ancient Near Eastern Texts*. Tel Aviv: Emery and Claire Yass Publications in Archaeology.

Gosden, C., & Marshall, Y. (1999). The Cultural Biography of Objects. In *World Archaeology*, 31: pp. 169–178.

Gottstein, N. (2013). Ein stringentes Identifikations- und Suchsystem für Keilschriftzeichen. In *Mitteilungen der Deutschen Orient Gesellschaft*, 145: pp. 127–136.

Gottstein, N., & Panayotov, S. V. (2014). *Cuneiform spotlight of the Neo- and Middle-Assyrian signs*. Dresden: Islet-Verlag.

Güterbock, H. G. (1942). *Siegel aus Boğazköy. Zweiter Teil. Die Königssiegel von 1939 und die übrigen Hieroglyphensiege*. Berlin: E.F. Weidner.

Haas, V. (2003). *Materia Magica et Medica Hethitica. Ein Beitrag zur Heilkunde im Alten Orient*. Berlin: De Gruyter.

Hagen, F. (2011). The hieratic dockets on the cuneiform tablets from Amarna. In *Journal of Egyptian Archaeology*, 97: pp. 214–216.

Hagenbuchner, A. (1989). *Die Korrespondenz der Hethiter, 2. Teil: Die Briefe mit Transkription, Übersetzung und Kommentar*. Heidelberg: Winter.

Hahn, D. V., Duncan, D. D., Baldwin, K. C., Cohen, J. D., & Purnomo, B. (2006). Digital Hammurabi: Design and Development of a 3D Scanner for Cuneiform Tablets. In *Proceedings of SPIE 6056*: pp. 130–141.

Hameeuw, H. (2014). *Portable Light Dome System: From registration to Online Publication within the Hour*. KU Leuven. Available at: https://portablelightdome.files.wordpress.com/2014/12/portable-light-dome-system-from-registration-to-online-publication-within-the-hour_1–1.pdf (Accessed: August 2016).

Hameeuw, H., & Willems, G. (2011). New visualization techniques for cuneiform texts and sealings. In *Akkadica*, 132 (2): pp. 163–178.

Harmanşah, Ö. (2012). Beyond Aššur: New Cities and the Assyrian Politics of Landscape. In *Bulletin of the American Schools of Oriental Research*, 365: pp. 53–77.

Haverfield, F. (1912). *The Romanization of Roman Britain*. Oxford: Clarendon Press.

Head, R. (2011). Amarna Messengers and the Politics of Feasting. In *MAARAV, A Journal for the Study of the Northwest Semitic Languages and Literatures*, 18 (1–2): pp. 79–87.

Heidegger, M. (1927). Sein und Zeit. *Being and Time*. Translated by J. Stambaugh. Albany: State University of New York Press.

Herring, S. C. (2004). Computer-Mediated Discourse Analysis: An Approach to Researching Online Behavior. In *Designing for Virtual Communities in the Service of Learning*. New York: Cambridge University Press.

Hethitologie Portal Mainz. (2001). Digital Infrastructure for Hittitology and Related Fields. University of Würzburg. Available at: http://www.hethport.uni-wuerzburg.de/ (Accessed: August 2016).

Hincks, E. (1848). On the Inscriptions at Van. In *The Journal of the Royal Asiatic Society of Great Britain and Ireland*, 9: pp. 387–449.

Hinke, W. J. (1911). *Selected Babylonian kudurru inscriptions*. Leiden: Brill.

Hodder, I. (1985). Postprocessual Archaeology. In *Advances in Archaeological Method and Theory*, 8: pp. 1–26.

Hoffner, H. A. (2009). *Letters from the Hittite Kingdom*. Society of Biblical Literature Writings from the Ancient World 15. Atlanta: Society of Biblical Literature.

Howardy, G. (1904). *Clavis cuneorum: sive, Lexicon signorum assyriorum linguis Latina, Britannica, Germanica*. London: Milford.

Huehnergard, J. (1983). Five Tablets from the Vicinity of Emar. In *Revue d'assyriologie et d'archéologie orientale*, 77 (1): pp. 11–43.

Illingworth, N. J. J. (1988). Inscriptions from Tell Brak 1986. In *Iraq*, 50: pp. 87–108.

InscriptiFact (2003). An Image Database of Inscriptions and Artifacts by the University of Southern California, West Semitic Research. Available at: http://www.inscriptifact.com/ (Accessed: August 2016).

Izre'el, S. (1997). *The Amarna Scholarly Tablets*. Groningen: Styx.

Jakob, S. (2003). *Mittelassyrische Verwaltung und Sozialstruktur*. Leiden / Boston: Brill.

Jakob, S. (2009). *Die mittelassyrischen Texte aus Tell Chuēra in Nordost-Syrien*. Wiesbaden: Harrassowitz.

Jakob, S. (2015). Daily Life in the Wild West of Assyria. In *Understanding Hegemonic Practices of the Early Assyrian Empire. Essays dedicated to Frans Wiggermann*. Leiden: Nederlands Instituut voor het Nabije Oosten.

Jankowska, N. B. (1969). Communal Self-Government and the King of the State of Arrapḫa. In *Journal of the Economic and Social History of the Orient*, 12 (3): pp. 233–282.

Jensen, P. (1890). Vorstudien zur Entzifferung des Mitanni. In *Zeitschrift für Assyriologie*, 5: pp. 260–274.

Jensen, P. (1891). Vorstudien zur Entzifferung des Mitanni II. In *Zeitschrift für Assyriologie*, 6: pp. 34–72.

John, J. A. (1992). Latin Paleography. In *Medieval Studies: An Introduction* (2nd ed.). Syracuse, New York: Syracuse University Press.

Johnson, J. C., & Johnson, A. (2012). Contingency and Innovation in Native Transcriptions of Encrypted Cuneiform (UD.GAL.NUN). In *Agency in Ancient Writing*. Boulder: University Press of Colorado.

Jönsson, C. (2000). Diplomatic Signaling in the Amarna Letters. In R. Cohen & R. Westbrook (Eds.), *Amarna Diplomacy: The Beginnings of International Relations*. Baltimore / London: The Johns Hopkins University Press.

Jursa, M. (1999). *Das Archiv des Bēl-Rēmanni*. Leiden: Uitgaven van het Nederlands Historisch-Archeologisch Instituut te Istanbul.

Jursa, M. (2015). Late Babylonian Epigraphy: a Case Study. In *Current Research in Cuneiform Palaeography*. Gladbeck: Pe-We-Verlag.

Kämmerer, T. R. (1998). *Šimâ milka: Induktion und Reception der mittelbabylonischen Dichtung von Ugarit, Emār und Tell el-ʿAmārna*. Münster: Ugarit Verlag.

Kampel, M., & Sablatnig, R. (2004). 3D Puzzling of Archaeological Fragments. In *Proceedings of the 9th Computer Vision Winter Workshop*. Ljubljana: Slovenian Pattern Recognition Society.

Kant, I. (1787). Kritik der reinen Vernunft. *Edition of the Works of Immanuel Kant in Translation*. Translated by P. Guyer & A. W. Wood. Cambridge: Cambridge University Press.

Kassymova, D., Kundakbayeva, Z., & Markus, U. (2012). *Historical Dictionary of Kazakhstan*. Lanham: Scarecrow Press.

Kim-Renaud, Y.-K. (1997). *The Korean Alphabet: Its History and Structure*. Honolulu: University of Hawai'i Press.

Kitchen, K. A. (1998). The World Abroad. Amenhotep III and Mesopotamia. In D. O'Connor & E. H. Cline (Eds.), *Amenhotep III. Perspectives on his Reign*. Ann Arbor: The University of Michigan Press.

Kleber, F., Sablatnig, R., Gau, M., & Miklas, H. (2008). Ancient Document Analysis Based on Text Line Extraction. In *19th International Conference on Pattern Recognition*. Tampa, Florida: ICPR.

Klengel, H. (1963). Zum Brief eines Königs von Ḫanigalbat (IBoT I 34). In *Orientalia (Nova Series)*, 32 (3): pp. 280–291.

Klengel, H. (2000). Qatna: Ein historischer Überblick. *Mitteilungen der Deutschen Orient Gesellschaft*, 132: pp. 239–252.

Klinger, J. (2001). Die hurritische Tradition in Hattuša und das Corpus hurritischer Texte. In *Kulturgeschichten: Altorientalische Studien für Volkert Haas*. Saarbrücken: Saarbrücker Druckerei und Verlag.

Klinger, J. (2003). Zür Paläographie akkadischsprachiger Texte aus Ḫattuša. In H. A. Hoffner, G. M. Beckman, R. H. Beal, & J. G. McMahon (Eds.), *Hittite Studies in Honor of Harry A. Hoffner Jr: On the Occasion of His 65th Birthday*. Winona Lake, Indiana: Eisenbrauns.

Knudtzon, J. A., & Otto, W. (1915). *Die El-Amarna-Tafeln*. Leipzig: J. C. Hinrichs.

Köcher, F. (1953). Vorwort. In *Literarische Texte in akkadischer Sprache. Keilschrifturkunden aus Boghazköi* (37). Berlin: Akademie-Verlag.

Koliński, R. (2012–2015). *Upper Greater Zab Archaeological Reconnaissance Project*. Available at: http://archeo.amu.edu.pl/ugzar/indexen.htm (Accessed: August 2016).

Koliński, R. (2014). Settled Space. Evidence for Changes in Settlement Patterns of Northern Mesopotamia at the Advent and at the Turn of the Mittani Era. In E. Cancik-Kirschbaum, N. Brisch, & J. Eidem (Eds.), *Constituent, Confederate, and Conquered Space: The Emergence of the Mittani State*. Berlin / Boston: Walter de Gruyter.

Koliński, R. (2015). Making Mittani Assyrian. In *Understanding Hegemonic Practices of the Early Assyrian Empire. Essays dedicated to Frans Wiggermann*. Leiden: Nederlands Instituut voor het Nabije Oosten.

Kopytoff, I. (1986). The cultural biography of things: Commoditization as process. In *Social Life of Things*. Cambridge: Cambridge University Press.

Korzybski, A. (1933). *Science and Sanity: An Introduction to Non-Aristotelian Systems and General Semantics*. Lakeville: International Non-aristotelian Library Publishing Co., Institute of General Semantics.

Koschaker, P. (1928). *Neue Keilschriftliche Rechtsurkunden aus der El-Amarna Zeit*. Leipzig: Hirzel.

Kotsonas, A. (2011). Quantification of ceramics from Early Iron Age tombs. In *Early Iron Age Pottery: A Quantitative Approach. Proceedings of the International Round Table Organized by the Swiss School of Archaeology in Greece (Athens, November 28–30, 2008)*. Oxford: Archaeopress.

Kühne, C. (1999). Imperial Mittani: An Attempt at Historical Reconstruction. In G. Wilhelm (Ed.), *Nuzi at seventy-five. Studies on the civilization and culture of Nuzi and the Hurrians, Vol. 10*. Winona Lake: Eisenbrauns.

Kühne, H. (2015). Core and Periphery in the Assyrian State: The View from Dūr-Katlimmu. In *Understanding Hegemonic Practices of the Early Assyrian Empire. Essays dedicated to Frans Wiggermann*. Leiden: Nederlands Instituut voor het Nabije Oosten.

Labat, R. (1948). *Manuel d'épigraphie akkadienne: signes, syllabaire, idéogrammes*. Paris: Imprimerie Nationale.

Labat, R. (1988). *Manuel d'épigraphie akkadienne: signes, syllabaire, idéogrammes*. Paris: Geuthner.

Lacheman, E. R. (1950). *Excavations at Nuzi: Miscellaneous Texts from Nuzi II* (VOL. XIV). Cambridge, Massachusetts: Harvard University Press.

Lacheman, E. R., & Maidman, M. P. (1989). *Joint expedition with the Iraq Museum at Nuzi VII: Miscellaneous Texts*. Winona Lake: Eisenbrauns.

Leroi-Gourhan, A. (1964). *Le geste et la parole*. Paris: Albin Michel.

Lettner, M., Diem, M., Sablatnig, R., Kammerer, P., & Miklas, H. (2007). Registration of Multi-Spectral Manuscript Images as Prerequisite for Computer Aided Script Description. In *12th Computer Vision Winter Workshop*. St Lambrecht: Institute for Computer Graphics and Vision, Graz University of Technology.

Lettner, M., Diem, M., Sablatnig, R., & Miklas, H. (2008). Registration and Enhancing of Multispectral Manuscript Images. In *16th European Signal Processing Conference*. Lausanne: EURASIP.

Leuven Portable Light Dome (2014). See Hameeuw 2014.

Liebesny, H. (1941). Evidence in Nuzi Legal Procedure. In *Journal of the American Oriental Society*, 61 (3): pp. 130–142.

Liverani, M. (1999). Review: Die mittelassyrischen Briefe aus Tall Šēḫ Ḥamad by Eva Christiane Cancik-Kirschbaum. In *Journal of the American Oriental Society*, 119 (1): pp. 140–141.

Liverani, M. (2000). The Great Powers' Club. In R. Cohen & R. Westbrook (Eds.), *Amarna Diplomacy: The Beginnings of International Relations*. Baltimore / London: The Johns Hopkins University Press.

Liverani, M. (2014). *The Ancient Near East: History, Society and Economy* (S. Tabatabai, Trans.). London / New York: Routledge.

Locke, J. (1690). *An Essay Concerning Human Understanding* (2nd ed.). Project Gutenberg. Available at: http://www.gutenberg.org/ebooks/10615 (Accessed: August 2016).

Lüfkens, M. (2015). *How World Leaders Connect on Twitter*. Twiplomacy. Available at: http://twiplomacy.com/blog/twiplomacy-study-2015/ (Accessed: August 2016).

Luuko, M. (2007). The Administrative Roles of the 'Chief Scribe' and the 'Palace Scribe' in the Neo-Assyrian Period. In *State Archives of Assyria Bulletin*, XVI: pp. 227–256.

Lyon, J. D. (2000). Middle Assyrian Expansion and Settlement Development in the Syrian Jazira: The View from the Balikh Valley. In R. M. Jas (Ed.), *Rainfall and Agriculture in Northern Mesopotamia*. Istanbul: Nederlands Historisch-Archeologisch Instituut te Istanbul.

Maidman, M. P. (2010). *Nuzi Texts and Their Uses as Historical Evidence*. Atlanta: Society of Biblical Literature.

Maidman, M. P. (2011). Tracing the Course of the Arrapha-Assyria War: A Proposal. In *A Common Cultural Heritage: Studies on Mesopotamia and the Biblical World in Honor of Barry L. Eichler*. Bethesda: CDL Press.

Maiocchi, M. (2011). A Hurrian Administrative Tablet from Third Millennium Urkesh. In *Zeitschrift für Assyriologie*, 101 (2): pp. 191–203.

Maiocchi, M. (2015). From Stylus to Sign: a Sketch of Old Akkadian Palaeography. In *Current Research in Cuneiform Palaeography*. Gladbeck: PeWe-Verlag.

Mara, H. (2012). *Multi-Scale Integral Invariants for Robust Character Extraction from Irregular Polygon Mesh Data*. MA, Heidelberg. Available at: http://archiv.ub.uni-heidelberg.de/volltextserver/13890/1/mara_thesis_2012_10_29_FINAL.pdf (Accessed: August 2016).

Mara, H., Krömker, S., Jakob, S., & Breuckmann, B. (2010). GigaMesh and Gilgamesh – 3D Multiscale Integral Invariant Cuneiform Character Extraction. In *Proceedings of the 11th International Symposium on Virtual Reality, Archaeology and Cultural Heritage*. Aire-la-Ville: The Eurographics Association.

Marwell, G., & Oliver, P. (1993). *The Critical Mass in Collective Action: A Micro-Social Theory*. Cambridge: Cambridge University Press.

Marzahn, J. (2015). The Central Syrian States Mirrored in the Amarna Archives. In *Qaṭna and the networks of Bronze Age globalism*. Wiesbaden: Harrassowitz.

Maskevich, A. S. (2014). *Umm el-Marra and the Westward Expansion of the Mittani Empire in Northwestern Syria*. PhD, Johns Hopkins University, Baltimore, Maryland. Available at: http://jhir.library.jhu.edu/handle/1774.2/37037 (Accessed: August 2016).

Mattingly, D. (2002). Vulgar and weak 'Romanization', or time for a paradigm shift? In *Journal of Roman Archaeology*, 15: pp. 536–540.

Mattingly, D. (2011). *Imperialism, Power and Identity Experiencing the Roman Empire*. Princeton: Princeton University Press.

Maul, S. M. (1992). *Die Inschriften von Tall Bdēri*. Berlin: Reimer.

Maul, S. M. (2005). *Die Inschriften von Tall Ṭābān (Grabungskampagnen 1887–1999): die Könige von Ṭābētu und das Land Māri in mittelassyrischer Zeit*. Tokyo: Kokushikan University, Institute for Cultural Studies of Ancient Iraq.

McManus, D. (1991). *A Guide to Ogham*. Maynooth: An Sagart.

Mercer, S. A. (1918). *A Sumero-Babylonian sign list to which is added an Assyrian sign list and a catalogue of the numerals weights and measures used at various periods*. New York: Colombia University Press.

Mertz, E. (2007). Semiotic Anthropology. In *Annual Review of Anthropology*, 36: pp. 337–353.

Messerschmidt, L. (1899). *Mitanni-Studien* (Vol. 4). Berlin: W. Speiser.

Messerschmidt, L. (1906). Zur Technik des Tontafel-Schreibens. In *Orientalistische Literaturzeitung*, 9 (1–6): pp. 185–195; 304–312; 372–380.

Millard, A. R. (1981). Strays from a 'Nuzi' Archive. In *Studies on the Civilization and Culture of Nuzi and the Hurrians (1): In Honor of Ernest R. Lacheman on His Seventy-fifth Birthday*. Winona Lake: Eisenbrauns.

Miller, D. (1985). *Artefacts as categories: a study of ceramic variability in central India*. Cambridge: Cambridge University Press.

Miller, J. (2001). Ḫattušili I's Expansion into Northern Syria in Light of the Tikunani Letter. In G. Wilhelm (Ed.), *Akten des IV. Internationalen Kongresses für Hethitologie: Würzburg, 4.–8. Oktober 1999, Issue 45*. Wiesbaden: Otto Harrassowitz Verlag.

Miller, J. L. (2004). *Studies in the Origins, Development and Interpretation of the Kizzuwatna Rituals*. Wiesbaden: Harrassowitz.

Miller, J. L. (2012). The Palaeography and Ortography of Six Rituals 'Redacted' in the Manner of Arusna. In *Palaeography and scribal practices in Syro-Palestine and Anatolia in the Late Bronze Age*. Leiden: Nederlands Instituut voor het Nabije Oosten.

Mittermayer, C. (2006). *Altbabylonische Zeichenliste*. Fribourg: Academic Press Fribourg.

Mora, C., & Giorgieri, M. (2004). *Le lettere tra i re ittiti e i re assiri ritrovate a Ḫattuša*. Padova: S.A.R.G.O.N Editrice e Libreria.

Morrison, M. A. (1987). The Southwest Archives at Nuzi. In *General Studies and Excavations at Nuzi 9/1. Studies on the Civilisation and Culture of Nuzi and the Hurrians. Vol. 2*. Winona Lake: Eisenbrauns.

Morrison, M. A., Lacheman, E. R., & Owen, D. I. (1993). *Excavations at Nuzi 9/2: Eastern Archives of Nuzi*. Winona Lake: Eisenbrauns.

Mühl, S. (2015). Middle Assyrian Territorial Practices in the Region of Ashur. In *Understanding Hegemonic Practices of the Early Assyrian Empire. Essays dedicated to Frans Wiggermann*. Leiden: Nederlands Instituut voor het Nabije Oosten.

Müller, G. G. W. (1998). *Londoner Nuzi-Texte*. Wiesbaden: Harrassowitz Verlag.

Müller, G. G. W. (1999). The Geography of the Nuzi Area. In *Nuzi at Seventy-Five. Studies on the Civilization and Culture of Nuzi and the Hurrians, Vol. 10*. Bethesda: CDL Press.

Mynářová, J. (2007). *Language of Amarna – Language of Diplomacy*. Prague: Czech Institute of Egyptology.

Mynářová, J. (2014). The Scribes of Amarna: A Family Affair? In L. Marti (Ed.), *La famille dans le Proche-Orient ancien: réalités, symbolismes, et images. Proceedings of the 55th Rencontre Assyriologique Internationale at Paris 6–9 July 2009*. Winona Lake: Eisenbrauns.

Negri Scafa, P. (1995). The Scribes of Nuzi and Their Activities Relative to Arms. In *General Studies and Excavations at Nuzi 9/3. Studies on the Civilization and Culture of Nuzi and the Hurrians, Vol 5*. Winona Lake: Eisenbrauns.

Negri Scafa, P. (1999). The Scribes of Nuzi. In *Nuzi at Seventy-Five. Studies on the Civilization and Culture of Nuzi and the Hurrians, Vol. 10*. Bethesda: CDL Press.

Negri Scafa, P. (2005). Documents from the buildings north of the Nuzi Temple: The 'signed' texts from Square C. In *General studies and excavations at Nuzi 11/1. Studies on the civilization and culture of Nuzi and the Hurrians* (15). Bethesda: CDL Press.

Negri Scafa, P. (2015). *Nuzi_e-DUB.SAR*. Tigris Virtual Lab Project. Available at: http://www.afs.enea.it/project/tigris/project1.php (Accessed: August 2016).

Niedorf, C. (2008). *Die mittelbabylonischen Rechtsurkunden aus Alalaḫ (Schicht IV)*. Münster: Ugarit Verlag.

Nissen, H. J. (1967). Geschäftsleben assyrischer Kaufleute im 14. jhdt. vor Chr. Geb. In A. Falkenstein & D. O. Edzard (Eds.), *Heidelberger Studien zum Alten Orient*. Wiesbaden: Harrassowitz.

Norris, E. (1868). *Assyrian Dictionary: intended to further the study of the cuneiform inscriptions of Assyria and Babylonia*. London: Williams & Norgate.

Novák, M. (2004). The Chronology of the Royal Palace of Qaṭna. In *Egypt and the Levant: International Journal for Egyptian Archaeology and Related Disciplines*, 14: pp. 299–317.

Novák, M. (2007). Mittani Empire and the Question of Absolute Chronology: Some Archaeological Considerations. In *The Synchronisation of Civilisations in the Eastern*

Mediterranean in the Second Millennium B.C. III. Vienna: Verlag der Österreichischen Akademie der Wissenschaften.

Oates, D., Oates, J., & MacDonald, H. (1997). *Excavations at Tell Brak: The Mitanni and Old Babylonian periods*. London: British School of Archaeology in Iraq.

Olsen, B. (2003). Material Culture after Text: Re-Membering Things. In *Norwegian Archaeological Review*, 36: pp. 87–104.

Opitz, D. (1927). Die Lage von Wassuganni. In *Zeitschrift für Assyriologie*, 37: pp. 299–301.

Oppenheim, A. L. (1936). Zur Landessprache von Arrapha-Nuzi. In *Archiv für Orientforschung*, 11: pp. 56–65.

Otten, H. (1959). Ein Brief aus Ḫattuša an Babu-aḫa-iddina. In *Archiv für Orientforschung*, 19: pp. 39–46.

Otto, A. (2014). The Late Bronze Age Pottery of the Weststadt of Tall Bazi (North Syria). In M. Luciani & A. Hausleitner (Eds.), *Recent Trends in the Study of Late Bronze Age Ceramics in Syro-Mesopotamia and Neighbouring Regions*. Rahden: Marie Leidorf.

Owen, D. I. (1995). An Old Assyrian Letter from Nuzi. In *Studies on the Civilization and Culture of Nuzi and the Hurrians, Vol. 7: Edith Porada Memorial Volume*. Bethesda: CDL Press.

Oxford, Reflectance Transformation Imaging for the Study of Ancient Documentary Artefacts. (2010) See Piquette *et al.* 2011.

Panayotov, S. V. (2014). A Bilingual Literary Text from Karkemish Featuring Marduk: Paleographical notes on KH 13 O 1178. In *Orientalia*, 83: Appendix.

Panayotov, S. V. (2015). The Gottstein System Implemented on a Digital Middle and Neo-Assyrian Palaeography. In *Cuneiform Digital Library Notes, 2015 (17)*. Available at: http://cdli.ucla.edu/pubs/cdln/php/single.php?id=70 (Accessed: August 2016).

Paoletti, P. (2015). The Lexical Texts from Ebla: Palaeography, Sign Identification and Scribes in the Early Dynastic Period. In *Current Research in Cuneiform Palaeography*. Gladbeck: PeWe-Verlag.

Papaioannou, G., Karabassi, E.-A., & Theoharis, T. (2002). Reconstruction of Three-Dimensional Objects through Matching of Their Parts. In *IEEE Transactions on Pattern Analysis and Machine Intelligence*, 24 (1): pp. 114–124.

Paradise, J. (1987). Daughters as 'Sons' at Nuzi. In *General Studies and Excavations at Nuzi 9/1. Studies on the Civilisation and Culture of Nuzi and the Hurrians, Vol. 2*. Winona Lake: Eisenbrauns.

Paulissian, R. (1999). Adoption in Ancient Assyria and Babylonia. In *Journal of Assyrian Academic Studies*, 13 (2): pp. 5–34.

Paulus, S. (2011). Foreigners under Foreign Rulers – The Case of Kassite Babylonia (2nd half of the 2nd millennium BC). In R. Achenbach, R. Albertz, & J. Wöhrle (Eds.), *The Foreigner and the Law: Perspectives from the Hebrew Bible and the Ancient Near East*. Wiesbaden: Harrassowitz.

Pedde, F. (2012). The Assyrian Heartland. In D. T. Potts (Ed.), *A Companion to the Archaeology of the Ancient Near East*. Oxford: Wiley-Blackwell.

Pedersén, O. (1998). *Archives and Libraries in the Ancient Near East 1500–1300 B.C.* Bethesda: CDL Press.

Peirce, C. S. (1893–1903). Collected Papers. *The Collected Papers of Charles Sanders Peirce*. Vols. 1–8 (Electronic Edition). Cambridge: Belknap Press of Harvard University Press. Available at: https://colorysemiotica.files.wordpress.com/2014/08/peirce-collectedpapers.pdf (Accessed: August 2016).

Pendlebury, J. D. S. (1951). *The City of Akhenaten III: The Central City and the Official Quarters*. London: Egypt Exploration Society.

Pfälzner, P. (2007). The Late Bronze Age Ceramic Traditions of the Syrian Jazirah. In *Céramique de l'âge du bronze en Syrie, 2, L'Euphrate et la région de Jézireh*. Beyrouth: Inst. Français d'Archéologie du Proche-Orient.

Pfälzner, P. (2013–2015). *The Eastern Habur Survey in Iraq-Kurdistan: Settlement Regions at the Junction between Mesopotamia, Syria and Anatolia*. Paper presented at the 10th ICAANE, Vienna, 25–29 April, 2016.

Pfälzner, P., & Maqdisī, M. (2015). *Qaṭna and the networks of Bronze Age globalism*. Wiesbaden: Harrassowitz.

Pfeiffer, R. G. (1932). *Excavations at Nuzi, Vol. 2: The archives of Shilwateshub son of the king*. Cambridge, Massachusetts: Harvard University Press.

Pfeiffer, R. G., & Speiser, E. A. (1936). The Archives of Tulpunnaya. In *One Hundred New Selected Nuzi texts. Annual of the American Schools of Oriental Research, Vol. 16 (AASOR 16)*. New Haven: American Schools of Oriental Research.

Pfeiffer, R. H., Lacheman, E. R. (1942). *Excavations at Nuzi IV. Miscellaneous Texts from Nuzi I* (Vol. XIII). Cambridge, Massachusetts: Harvard University Press.

Piquette, K. E., Dahl, J., & Green, J. D. M. (2011). Exploring Ancient Writings at the Ashmolean Museum with Advanced Digital Technologies. Available at: http://www.ashmolean.org/departments/antiquities/research/research/rtisad/ (Accessed: August 2016).

Piquette, K. E., & Whitehouse, R. D. (2013). Introduction: Developing an approach to writing as material practice. In *Writing as Material Practice: Substance, surface and medium*. London: Ubiquity Press.

Podany, A. H. (2002). *The land of Hana: kings, chronology, and scribal tradition*. Bethesda: CDL Press.

Postgate, J. N. (1992). The Land of Assur and the Yoke of Assur. In *World Archaeology*, 23 (3): pp. 247–263.

Postgate, J. N. (2013). *Bronze Age Bureaucracy: Writing and the Practice of Government in Assyria*. Cambridge: Cambridge University Press.

Postgate, J. N. (2015). Government recording practices in Assyria and her neighbours and contemporaries. In *Understanding Hegemonic Practices of the Early Assyrian*

Empire. Essays dedicated to Frans Wiggermann. Leiden: Nederlands Instituut voor het Nabije Oosten.

Proust, C. (2010). Mesopotamian Metrological Lists and Tables: Forgotten Sources. In *Looking at it from Asia: The Processes that Shaped the Sources of History of Science* (*Vol. 265*). New York: Springer.

Purves, P. M. (1940). The Early Scribes of Nuzi. In *The American Journal of Semitic Languages and Literatures*, 57 (2): pp. 162–187.

Quirke, S. (2010). Agendas for Digital Palaeography in a Archaeological Context: Egypt 1800 BC. In *Codicology and Palaeography in the Digital Age*, Volume 2. Norderstedt: BoD.

Radner, K. (1995). The Relation Between Format and Content of Neo-Assyrian Texts. In *Nineveh, 612 BC: The Glory and Fall of the Assyrian Empire*. Helsinki: Helsinki University Press.

Radner, K. (2004). *Das mittelassyrische Tontafelarchiv von Giricano, Dunnu-ša-Uzibi*. Turnhout: Brepols.

Rainey, A. F. (2015). *The El-Amarna Correspondence: A New Edition of the Cuneiform Letters from the Site of El-Amarna based on Collations of all Extant Tablets*. Leiden / Boston: Brill.

Reculeau, H., & Feller, B. (2012). *Mittelassyrische Urkunden aus dem Archiv Assur 14446*. Wiesbaden: Harrassowitz.

Reiche, A. (2014). Tell Abu Hafur 'East', Tell Arbid (Northeastern Syria), and Nemrik (Northern Iraq) as Examples of Small-Scale Rural Settlements in Upper Mesopotamia in the Mittani Period. In *The Archaeology of Political Spaces: The Upper Mesopotamian Piedmont in the Second Millennium BCE*. Berlin / Boston: Walter de Gruyter.

Reicher, S., Spears, R., & Haslam, S. A. (2010). The Social Identity Approach in Social Psychology. In *Sage Identities Handbook*. London: Sage.

Richardson, S. (2005). Trouble in the Countryside, ana tarṣi Samsuditana. In W. H. Van Soldt (Ed.), *Ethnicity in Ancient Mesopotamia*. Leiden: Nederlands Instituut voor het Nabije Oosten.

Richardson, S. (2010). *Texts from the Late Old Babylonian Period*. Boston: American Schools of Oriental Research.

Richter, T. (2005). Qatna in the Late Bronze Age. In D. Owen & G. Wilhelm (Eds.), *General Studies and Excavations at Nuzi 11/1. Studies on the Civilization and Culture of Nuzi and the Hurrians, Vol. 15*. Bethesda: CDL Press.

Richter, T., & Lange, S. (2012). *Das Archiv des Idadda: die Keilschrifttexte aus den deutsch-syrischen Ausgrabungen 2001–2003 im Königspalast von Qaṭna*. Wiesbaden: Harrassowitz.

Robson, E. (2001). The tablet house: a scribal school in Old Babylonian Nippur. *Revue d'assyriologie et d'archéologie orientale*, 93: pp. 39–66.

Roshani, D. (2010). *Nation State building or language planning*. Paper presented at the First North American Conference on the Kurdish Language. Available at: http://www.kurdishacademy.org/?q=node/728 (Accessed: August 2016).

Rutz, M. (2006). Archaizing Scripts in Emar and the Diviner Šaggar-abu. In *Ugarit Forschungen*, 38: pp. 593–616.

Rutz, M. (2012). Mesopotamian Scholarship in Ḫattuša and the Sammeltafel KUB 4.53. In *Journal of the American Oriental Society*, 132 (2): pp. 171–188.

Salah, S. (2013). *Die mittelassyrischen Personen- und Rationenlisten aus Tall Šēḫ Ḫamad, Dūr-Katlimmu*. Wiesbaden: Harrassowitz.

Sallaberger, W. (1997). Sign List: Palaeography and Syllabary. In *Administrative Documents from Tell Beydar*. Turnhout: Brepols.

Sallaberger, W., Einwag, B., & Otto, A. (2006). Schenkungen von Mittani-Königen an die Einwohner von Basiru: die zwei Urkunden aus Tall Bazi am Mittleren Euphrat. In *Zeitschrift für Assyriologie*, 96: pp. 69–104.

Salvini, M. (1996). *The Ḫabiru Prism of King Tunip-Teššup of Tikunani*. Rome: Istituti editoriali e poligrafici internazionali.

Salvini, M., & Wegner, I. (1986). *Die Rituale des AZU-Priesters*. Rome: Multigraphica.

Saporetti, C. (1979a). *Assur 14446: la famiglia A: ascesa e declina di persone e famiglie all'inizio del medio-regno assiro*. Malibu: Undena.

Saporetti, C. (1979b). *Gli eponimi medio-assiri*. Malibu: Undena.

Saporetti, C. (1982). *Assur 14446: le altre famiglie: ascesa e declino di persone e famiglie all'inizio del medio-regno assiro, II*. Malibu: Undena.

Sassmannshausen, L. (2008). Babylonische Schriftkultur des. 2. Jahrtausends v. Chr. in den Nachbarländern und im östlichen Mittelmeerraum. In *Aula Orientalis*, 26 (2): pp. 263–293.

Saussure, D. (1916). *Cours de linguistique générale*. (*1972 edition critique préparée par Tullio de Mauro*.) Paris: Payot.

Sayce, A. H. (1890). The Language of Mitanni. In *Zeitschrift für Assyriologie*, 5: pp. 260–275.

Sayce, A. H. (1894). The Cuneiform Tablets. In *Tell el-Amarna*. London: Methuen & Co.

Schiffer, M. B. (1972). Archaeological Context and Systemic Context. In *American Antiquity*, 37 (2): pp. 156–165.

Schoop, U.-D. (2006). Dating the Hittites with Statistics: Ten Pottery Assemblages from Boğazköy-Hattuša. In *Structuring and Dating in Hittite Archaeology: requirements, problems, new approaches*. Istanbul: Ege Yayınları.

Schröder, O. (1915). *Die Tontafeln von El-Amarna*. Leipzig: J.C. Hinrichs.

Schröder, O. (1920). *Keilschrifttexte aus Assur verschiedenen Inhalts: autographiert, mit Inhaltsübersicht und Namenlisten*. Leipzig: J. C. Hinrichs.

Schwartz, G. (2010). Early Non-Cuneiform Writing? Third Millennium BC Clay Cylinders from Umm el-Marra. In S. C. Melville & A. L. Slotsky (Eds.), *Opening the*

Tablet Box (Near Eastern Studies in Honor of Benjamin R. Foster). Leiden / Boston: Brill.

Schwartz, G. M. (2014). Reflections on the Mittani Emergence. In E. Cancik-Kirschbaum, N. Brisch, & J. Eidem (Eds.), *Constituent, Confederate, and Conquered Space: The Emergence of the Mittani State*. Berlin / Boston: Walter de Gruyter.

Schwemer, D. (1998). *Akkadische Rituale aus Ḫattuša. Die Sammeltafel KBo XXXVI 29 und verwandte Fragmente*. Heidelberg: Heidelberger Universitätsverlag.

Schwemer, D. (2005). Lehnbeziehungen zwischen dem Hethitischen und dem Akkadischen. In *Archiv für Orientforschung*, 51: pp. 220–234.

Schwemer, D. (2013). Gauging the influence of Babylonian magic. *Diversity and Standardization: Perspectives on ancient Near Eastern cultural history*: pp. 145–171.

Schwemer, D., & Abusch, T. (2011). *Corpus of Mesopotamian Anti-witchcraft Rituals*. Leiden: Brill.

Singer, I. (2011). The Historical Context of Two Tell Nebi Mend / Qadeš Letters. In *KASKAL*, 8: pp. 161–175.

Singer, M. (1980). Signs of the Self: An Exploration in Semiotic Anthropology. In *American Anthropologist (New Series)*, 83 (3): pp. 485–507.

Smagulova, J. (2008). Language policies of kazakhization and their influence on language attitude and use. In *International Journal of Bilingual Education and Bilingualism*, 11 pp. 440–475.

Smith, G. (1871). *The phonetic values of the cuneiform characters*. London: Williams & Norgate.

Smith, S. P. (2007). *Hurrian orthographic interference in nuzi akkadian: a computational comparative graphemic analysis*. PhD, Harvard University, Cambridge, Massachusetts. Available at: http://www.infinitiv.com/hoina/ (Accessed: August 2016).

Soldi, S. (2008). Recent Considerations About the Origin of Nuzi Ware in the Light of Its Archaeological Contexts. In *Proceedings of the 4th International Congress of the Archaeology of the Ancient Near East*. Wiesbaden: Harrassowitz Verlag.

Sommerfeld, W. (1999). *Die Texte der Akkade-Zeit: Das Dijala-Gebiet – Tutub*. Münster: Rhema.

Speiser, E. A. (1929). A Letter of Shaushatar and the Date of the Kirkuk Tablets. In *Journal of the American Oriental Society*, 49: pp. 269–275.

Speiser, E. A. (1936). Appendix A: On Some Hurrian Numerals. Appendix B: The Linguistic Substratum at Nuzi. *The Annual of the American Schools of Oriental Research*, 16: pp. 131–142.

Speleers, L. (1925). *Recueil des inscriptions de l'Asie Antérieure des Musées Royaux du Cinquantenaire à Bruxelles: textes sumériens babyloniens et assyriens*. Brussels: Vanderpoorten.

Spurkland, T. (2005). *Norwegian Runes and Runic Inscriptions.* Woodbridge: The Boydell Press.

Stanford Cuneiform Tablet Visualisation Project (2002). See Anderson and Levoy 2002.

Starke, F. (1985). *Die keilschrift-luwischen Texte in Umschrift.* Wiesbaden: Harrassowitz.

Starr, R. F. S. (1939). *Nuzi. Report on the excavations at Yorgan Tepa near Kirkuk, Iraq conducted by Harvard University in conjunction with the American Schools of Oriental Research and the University Museum of Philadelphia 1927–1931.* Cambridge, Massachusetts: Harvard University Press.

Stavrakakis, Y. (2004). Jacques Lacan (1901–81). In J. Simons (Ed.), *Contemporary Critical Theorists: From Lacan to Said.* Edinburgh: Edinburgh University Press.

Stein, D. (1989). A Reappraisal of the "Sauštatar Letter" from Nuzi. In *Zeitschrift für Assyriologie,* 79 (1): pp. 36–60.

Stein, G. J. (2002). From Passive Periphery to Active Agents: Emerging Perspectives in the Archaeology of Interregional Interaction. In *American Anthropologist, New Series,* 104 (3): pp. 903–916.

Steve, M. J. (1992). *Syllabaire Elamite: Histoire et Paleographie.* Neuchâtel: Recherches et Publications Neuchâtel.

Stevens, A. (2015). The archaeology of Amarna. *Oxford Handbooks Online.* Available at: http://www.oxfordhandbooks.com/view/10.1093/oxfordhb/9780199935413.001.0001/oxfordhb-9780199935413-e-31 (Accessed: August 2016).

Strassmayer, J. (1886). *Akkadischen Wörter der Cuneiform Inscriptions of Western Asia Vol. II sowie anderer meist unveröffentlichter Inschriften, mit zahlreichen Ergänzungen und Verbesserungen (6 Bände).* Leipzig: J. C. Hinrichs.

Strudwick, N. (2014). Technology and Interpretation. In *A Companion to Ancient Egyptian Art.* Chichester: Wiley Blackwell.

Tajfel, H., & Turner, J. C. (1986). The social identity theory of inter-group behavior. In *Psychology of Intergroup Relations.* Chicago: Nelson-Hall.

Taylor, J. (2011). Tablets as artefacts, scribes as artisans. In *Oxford Handbook of Cuneiform Culture.* Oxford: Oxford University Press.

Taylor, J. (2015). Wedge Order in Cuneiform: a Preliminary Survey. In *Current Research in Cuneiform Palaeography.* Gladbeck: Pe-We-Verlag.

Tenu, A. (2015). Building the Empire: Settlement Patterns in the Middle Assyrian Empire. In *Understanding Hegemonic Practices of the Early Assyrian Empire. Essays dedicated to Frans Wiggermann.* Leiden: Nederlands Instituut voor het Nabije Oosten.

Thureau-Dangin, F. (1898). *Recherches sur l'origine de l'écriture cunéiforme.* Paris: Ernest Leroux.

Thureau-Dangin, F. (1926). *Le Syllabaire Accadien.* Paris: Geuthner.

Tilley, C. (1994). *A Phenomenology of Landscape: Places, Paths and Monuments.* Oxford: Berg.

Tomas, H. (2013). Saving on Clay: The Linear B practice of cutting tablets. In *Writing as Material Practice: Substance, surface and medium.* London: Ubiquity Press.

Toustain, C. F. (1765). *Nouveau Traité de Diplomatique.* Paris: G. Desprez & P-G. Cavelier.

Trigger, B. G. (1989). *A history of archaeological thought.* Cambridge: Cambridge University Press.

Turner, J. C., Hogg, M. A., Oakes, P. J., Reicher, S. D., & Wetherell, M. S. (1987). *Rediscovering the social group: A self-categorization theory.* Cambridge, Massachusetts: Basil Blackwell.

Ungnad, A. (1927). *Babylonisch-assyrisches Keilschriftlesebuch.* München: Beck.

Ur, J., Karsgaard, P., & Oates, J. (2011). The Spatial Dimensions of Early Mesopotamian Urbanism: The Tell Brak Suburban Survey, 2003–2006. In *Iraq*, 73: pp. 1–19.

Van de Mieroop, M. (1999). *Cuneiform Texts and the Writing of History.* London: Routledge.

Van den Hout, T. (1995). *Der Ulmitešub-Vertrag. Eine prosopographische Untersuchung.* Wiesbaden: Harrassowitz.

Van den Hout, T. (2009). A Century of Hittite Text Dating and the Origins of the Hittite Cuneiform Script. In *Incontri Linguistici* 32. Rome: Fabrizio Serra Editore.

Van den Hout, T. (2012). The Ductus of the Alalaḫ VII Texts and the Origin of Hittite Cuneiform. In *Palaeography and Scribal Practices in Syro-Palestine and Anatolia in the Late Bronze Age.* Leiden: Nederlands Instituut voor het Nabije Oosten.

Van der Toorn, K. (2000). Cuneiform Documents from Syria-Palestine Texts, Scribes, and Schools. In *Zeitschrift des Deutschen Palästina-Vereins*, 116 (2): pp. 97–113.

Van Exel, V. J. (2010). Social change at Emar: The influence of the Hittite occupation on local traditions. In *Revue d'assyriologie et d'archéologie orientale*, 104 (1): pp. 65–86.

Van Koppen, F. (2004). The Geography of the Slave Trade and Northern Mesopotamia in the Late Old Babylonian Period. In *Mesopotamian Dark Age Revisited.* Vienna: Österreichische Akademie der Wissenschaften.

Van Koppen, F. (2010). The Old to Middle Babylonian Transition: History and Chronology of the Mesopotamian Dark Age. In *Egypt and the Levant: International Journal for Egyptian Archaeology and Related Disciplines*, 20: pp. 453–463.

Van Lerberghe, K., & Voet, G. (2009). *A Late Old Babylonian Temple Archive from Dūr-Abiešuḫ.* Bethesda: CDL Press.

Van Loon, M. N., & Meijer, D. J. W. (1987). Hammâm et-Turkmân on the Balikh: First Results of the University of Amsterdam's 1986 Excavation. In *Akkadica*, 52: pp. 1–9.

Van Soldt, W. H. (1989). An Orthographic Peculiarity in the Akkadian Letters of Tušratta. In *To the Euphrates and Beyond: Archaeological Studies in Honour of Maurits N. van Loon.* Rotterdam: A. A. Balkema.

Van Soldt, W. H. (1995). Three Tablets from Tell Hammam et-Turkman. In *Studio Historiae Ardens. Ancient Near Eastern Studies Presented to Philo H. K. Houwink ten Cate on the Occasion of his 65th Birthday*. Istanbul: Nederlands Historisch-Archaeologisch Instituut.

Van Soldt, W. H. (1999). The Written Sources. In W. G. E. Watson & N. Wyatt (Eds.), *Handbook of Ugaritic Studies*. Leiden: Brill.

Veldhuis, N. (1999). Continuity and Change in the Mesopotamian Lexical Tradition. In B. Roest & H. L. J. Vanstiphout (Eds.), *Aspects of Genre and Type in Pre-Modern Literary Cultures*. Groningen: Styx.

Veldhuis, N. (2003). On the Curriculum of the Neo-Babylonian School. In *Journal of the American Oriental Society*, 123 (3): pp. 627–633.

Veldhuis, N. (2012a). Cuneiform: Changes and Developments. In *The Shape of Script: How and Why Writing Systems Change*. Santa-Fe: School for Advanced Research Press.

Veldhuis, N. (2012b). Domesticizing Babylonian Scribal Culture in Assyria: Transformation by Preservation. In *Theory and Practice of Knowledge Transfer, Studies in School Education in the Ancient Near East and Beyond*. Leiden: Nederlands Instituut voor het Nabije Oosten.

Vertés, K. (2014). *Digital Epigraphy*. Available at: https://oi.uchicago.edu/research/publications/epigraphic-survey (Accessed: August 2016).

Vignoles, V. L., Luyck, K., & Schwartz, S. J. (2011). *Handbook of Identity Theory and Research*. New York: Springer.

Vita, J.-P. (2009). Hurrian as a living language in Ugaritic society. In *Reconstructing a Distant Past. Ancient Near Eastern Essays in Tribute to Jorge R. Silva Castillo. Aula Orientalis Supplementa* (25). Barcelona: Editorial AUSA.

Vita, J.-P. (2012). Amurru Scribes in the Amarna Archive. In *Palaeography and scribal practices in Syro-Palestine and Anatolia in the Late Bronze Age*. Leiden: Nederlands Instituut voor het Nabije Oosten.

Vita, J.-P. (2013). Alphabet ougaritique et langue hourrite: interactions et adaptations. In *Les écritures mises au jour sur le site antique d'Ougarit (Syrie) et leur déchiffrement*. Paris: Académie des Inscriptions et Belles-Lettres.

Vita, J.-P. (2015). *Canaanite Scribes in the Amarna Letters*. Münster: Ugarit Verlag.

Von Dassow, E. (2004). Canaanite in Cuneiform. In *Journal of the American Oriental Society*, 124 (4): pp. 641–674.

Von Dassow, E. (2005). Archives of Alalaḫ IV in Archaeological Context. In *Bulletin of the American Schools of Oriental Research*, 338: pp. 1–69.

Von Dassow, E. (2008). *State and Society in the Late Bronze Age: Alalah under the Mittani Empire*. Bethesda: CDL Press.

Von Dassow, E. (2014). Levantine Polities under Mittanian Hegemony. In *Constituent, Confederate, and Conquered Space: The Emergence of the Mittani State*. Berlin / Boston: Walter de Gruyter.

Waal, W. (2012). Chronological Developments in Hittite Scribal Habits and Tablet Shapes. In *Palaeography and Scribal Practices in Syro-Palestine and Anatolia in the Late Bronze Age*. Leiden: Nederlands Instituut voor het Nabije Oosten.

Waerzeggers, C. (2014). Social Network Analysis of Cuneiform Archives – a New Approach. In *Documentary Sources in Ancient Near Eastern and Greco-Roman Economic History*. Oxford: Oxbow Books.

Walker, C. B. F. (1987). *Reading the Past: Cuneiform*. London: British Museum Press.

Watson, R. A. (1972). The 'new archeology' of the 1960s. In *Antiquity*, 46: pp. 210–215.

Webster, J., & Cooper, N. J. (1996). *Roman imperialism: post-colonial perspectives*. Leicester: University of Leicester, School of Archaeological Studies.

Weeden, M. (2011). *Hittite Logograms and Hittite Scholarship*. Wiesbaden: Harrassowitz.

Weeden, M. (2012). Assyro-Mittanian or Middle Assyrian? In *Palaeography and Scribal Practices in Syro-Palestine and Anatolia in the Late Bronze Age*. Leiden: Nederlands Instituut voor het Nabije Oosten.

Weeden, M. (2014). State Correspondence in the Hittite World. In K. Radner (Ed.), *State Correspondence in the Ancient World: From New Kingdom Egypt to the Roman Empire*. Oxford: Oxford University Press.

Weeden, M. (2016). Hittite Scribal Culture and Syria: Palaeography and Cuneiform Transmission. In S. Yamada & D. Shibata (Eds.), *Cultures and Societies in the Middle Euphrates and Habur Areas in the Second Millennium BC, I: Scribal Education and Scribal Traditions*. Wiesbaden: Harrassowitz Verlag.

Weidner, E. (1923). *Politische Dokumente aus Kleinasien. Die Staatsverträge in akkadischer Sprache aus dem Archiv von Boghazköi* (Vol. 8). Leipzig: J. C. Hinrichs.

Weidner, E. (1952). Die Bibliothek Tiglatpilesers I. In *Archiv für Orientforschung*, 16: pp. 197–215.

Westenholz, A. (2002). The Sumerian City State. In *A Comparative Study of Six City-state Cultures: An Investigation*. Copenhagen: C.A. Reitzels Forlag.

Westenholz, J. G. (2000). *Cuneiform Inscriptions in the Collection of the Bible Lands Museum Jerusalem: The Emar Tablets*. Groningen: Styx.

Westergaard, N. L. (1845). Zur Entzifferung der achämenidischen Keilschrift zweiter Gattung. In *Zeitschrift für die Kunde des Morgenlandes*, 6: pp. 337–466.

Whitehead, A. N. (1929). *Process and Reality: An Essay in Cosmology* (Corrected). New York: Free Press.

Wiggerman, F. A. M. (2008). A Babylonian scholar in Assur. In *Studies in ancient Near Eastern world view and society presented to Marten Stol* Bethesda: CDL Press.

Wilhelm, G. (1982). *Grundzüge der Geschichte und Kultur der Hurriter*. Darmstadt: Wissenschaftliche Buchgesellschaft.

Wilhelm, G. (1984). Zur Paläographie der Keilschriftbriefe aus Ägypten. In *Studien zur Altägyptischen Kultur*, 11: pp. 643–653.

Wilhelm, G. (1989). *The Hurrians* (J. Barnes, Trans.). Warminster: Aris & Phillips.

Wilhelm, G. (1991a). A Hurrian Letter from Tell Brak. In *Iraq*, 53: pp. 159–168.

Wilhelm, G. (1991b). *Sumerische und akkadische literarische Texte*. Berlin: Mann.

Wilhelm, G. (1992). Zur babylonisch-assyrischen Schultradition in Ḫattuša. In *Uluslararası 1. Hititoloji Kongresi bildirileri (19–21 Temmuz 1990, Çorum)*. Ankara: Uluslararasi Çorum Hitit Festivali Komitesi Başkariliği.

Wilhelm, G. (1994). *Medizinische Omina aus Ḫattuša*. Wiesbaden: Harrassowitz.

Wilhelm, G. (2008). Hurrian. In R. D. Woodard (Ed.), *The Ancient Languages of Asia Minor*. Cambridge: Cambridge University Press.

Wilhelm, G. (2010). Remarks on the Hittite Cuneiform Script. In I. Singer (Ed.), *Ipamati kistamati pari tumatimis. Luwian and Hittite Studies Presented to J. David Hawkins on the Occasion of his 70th Birthday*. Tell Aviv: Emery and Claire Yass Publications in Archaeology.

Wilhelm, G. (2015). Suppiluliuma and the Decline of the Mittanian Kingdom. In *Qaṭna and the networks of Bronze Age globalism*. Wiesbaden: Harrassowitz.

Wiseman, D. J. (1953). *The Alalakh Tablets*. London: British Institute of Archaeology at Ankara.

Wittgenstein, L. (1953). *Philosophische Untersuchungen*. Berlin: Akademie Verlag.

Woodard, R. D. (2008). *The Ancient Languages of Asia Minor*. Cambridge: Cambridge University Press.

Woolf, G. (1997). Beyond Romans and Natives. In *World Archaeology*, 28: pp. 339–350.

Woolley, C. L. (1948). Excavations at Atchana-Alalakh, 1939. In *Antiquaries Journal*, 28: pp. 1–19.

Woolley, C. L. (1955). *Alalakh: An Account of the Excavations at Tell Atchana in the Hatay, 1937–1949*. London: Society of Antiquaries.

Woolley, S. I., Davis, T. R., Flowers, N. J., Pinilla-Dutoit, J., Livingstone, A., & Arvanitis, T. N. (2002). Communicating cuneiform: the evolution of a multimedia cuneiform database. In *Visible language*, 36: pp. 308–324.

Woolley, S. I., Flowers, N. J., Arvantis, T. N., Livingstone, A., Davis, T. R., & Ellison, J. (2001). 3D Capture, representation and manipulation of cuneiform tablets. *Proceedings of SPIE: Three-dimensional Image Capture and Applications*, 4289: pp. 103–110.

Yakubovich, Y. (2010). *Sociolinguistics of the Luvian Language*. Leiden: Brill.

Yoffee, N. (2005). Political Economy in Early Mesopotamian States. In *Annual Review of Anthropology*, 24: pp. 281–311.

Yoffee, N. (2014). The Age of Opportunity: Social and Political Transitions in Mid-Second Millennium BC Mesopotamia. In E. Cancik-Kirschbaum, N. Brisch, & J. Eidem (Eds.), *Constituent, Confederate, and Conquered Space: The Emergence of the Mittani State*. Berlin / Boston: Walter de Gruyter.

Zhu, L., Zhou, Z., & Hu, D. (2008). Globally Consistent Reconstruction of Ripped-Up Documents. In IEEE *Transactions on Pattern Analysis and Machine Intelligence*, 30 (1): pp. 1–13.

Index of Places

Alalaḫ 3, 35–36, 39, 50–52, 55, 94, 96, 118, 151, 183, 185, 190, 193, 195, 234, 253, 270
Anatolia 8–9, 36, 48, 113, 116, 185
Arrapḫa 6, 36, 39, 149, 154, 181–182, 279

Bogazköy 4, 6–7, 26, 39, 48, 56, 58, 79, 113–114, 235, 252, 257, 276–278, 282

Dur-Katlimmu 118, 122, 136–137

Egypt 8, 35, 37, 40–47, 77, 146, 220, 268
Emar 7–9, 184, 224, 261–263, 282
Euphrates 9, 35, 182, 262, 281

Ḫalab 35–36, 53
Ḫana 36
Ḫanigalbat 35, 48–52, 55, 122
Ḫatti 9, 35, 40, 47–49, 280
Ḫattuša 12, 37, 58, 113–114, 186, 252, 257, 269, 278, 280

Iraq 1, 35, 38, 55, 151

Kizzuwatna 36, 51, 257

Mari 12, 118, 183
Mesopotamia 30, 39, 152, 262

Northern Mesopotamia 7–9, 34, 56, 184–186, 218–219, 227, 261, 264, 268, 277, 282

Qaṭna 8, 224, 261–263, 282

Syria 1, 7, 35, 47, 50, 52–55, 185–186, 261

Tall Bazi 36, 39, 53, 96
Tell Brak 4, 36, 39, 52, 54–55, 78, 94, 100, 112, 118, 124
Tell Chuera 36, 118, 125–126, 133, 136
Tell Fekheriye 36, 118
Tigris 181–182, 281
Tunip 36, 50
Turkey 1, 35, 50–52

Ugarit 7–8, 35, 37, 40, 113, 224, 261–263, 282
Umm el-Marra 36, 39, 52–53, 283

Waššukanni 13, 38, 41, 122

Yamḫad 35–36

Index of Names

Adad-nirari 54
Amenhotep III 40–46
Amenhotep IV 40, 46
Artašumara 54
Artatama 38, 53, 116
Aššur-bel-nišešu 120–121
Aššur-nadin-aḫḫe 117
Aššur-nirari 120–121
Aššur-uballiṭ 116, 118, 120–121, 124, 146, 251

Eriba-adad 116, 118, 121, 124

Ḫattušili 9, 35, 48, 183, 186

Labarna 183, 186, 188, 190, 195, 202

Muršili 35

Parattarna 38, 50, 116
Paršatatar 54–55
Pharaoh 37, 41, 43, 46–47, 78, 111, 113, 117, 146, 220, 268–269
Puḫi-šenni 152, 154–155, 181, 269

Salmanassar 122
Šattiwazza 47–48
Šattuara 49
Šaustatar 36, 50–55, 96, 116, 120, 154
Šilwa-teššup 55, 155, 162, 167, 181, 223
Šuppiluliuma 8, 47, 117, 220
Šurki-tilla 155, 162, 181, 269
Šuttarna 38, 51–52, 54

Tiye 45–46, 111
Tukulti-ninurta 49, 122
Tulpunnaya 151, 153–155, 162–163, 170, 176, 223, 269
Tunip-Teššup 9, 182–183
Tušratta 38, 40–47, 54–55, 96, 220, 232–234, 268, 275

Zike 151, 155, 162–163, 181, 269

Index of Subjects

administration 1, 118, 125, 147, 153, 234, 253, 264, 278–279, 281
agency 10, 13–14, 149, 265
Akkadian 4, 8, 16, 36–37, 41, 47–48, 58, 112–113, 115, 146, 150, 181–183, 185, 232–233, 266–267, 269, 277, 279–280
archaeology 10–11, 13–15, 30
Assyrian 48–49, 116–118, 122, 130, 143, 147–148, 150, 152–153, 261
  Old 9, 68, 119, 146 , 182–183, 186, 211, 215, 218, 228, 264, 279, 281
  Middle 4, 5–7, 9, 12, 16, 19, 24–25, 29–31, 34, 38–39, 57–58, 68, 78, 85, 87, 97, 106, 154, 173, 182, 185, 195, 198, 210, 215, 217–218, 220–225, 227–230, 232–239, 241–245, 247–252, 254–257, 262, 264, 267, 269–271, 273, 275–278, 280–282
  Neo 29–31, 123, 136, 220, 223–224, 226, 228–230, 232, 235–237, 247, 264, 267, 269, 282

Babylonian 39–41, 63, 70–71, 78, 85, 104, 113, 140, 146–147, 150, 152–153, 156, 158, 162, 175, 181, 188, 203, 219, 242, 279–282
  Old 9, 12, 35, 68, 131, 149, 183–186, 210–211, 217–218, 220, 223–224, 226, 228–230, 232, 234–236, 239, 243, 245, 247–250, 253, 260, 264, 269, 273
  Middle 6–7, 9, 30, 50, 54, 57–58, 68, 87, 131, 182, 184, 186, 217, 220, 223–224, 226, 230, 236, 244, 248, 252, 262–264, 273
  Neo 6, 242
borrowing 146, 149, 153, 253

catalogue 10, 26, 155
choice 3, 5, 12, 30, 34, 116, 149, 190, 269, 270
clay 11–13, 15, 21–22, 29–31, 40–41, 81, 112, 151, 190, 193, 195, 197, 207, 212, 265–266, 275, 281
correspondence 1, 3–4, 8, 14, 36, 39–44, 46–47, 64, 113, 115, 122–123, 125, 144, 146, 148, 151, 219–220, 232–233, 266–269, 276, 279–280

diplomacy 14–15, 37, 39, 41, 43, 45, 48–49, 57, 113, 115, 123, 125, 146, 148, 153, 181–182, 269, 280

economy 14, 57, 147, 149–151, 181–182, 185, 265, 267, 278
emerging 9, 14, 17, 35, 37, 114, 148, 219

family 9, 17, 41–42, 52, 119, 150–154, 179, 181, 210, 218, 252–253, 265, 269, 279

gifts 41–47, 110, 152, 268

Hittite 8–9, 12, 15, 26, 35, 37, 42, 44, 47–49, 53, 87, 89, 95–96, 113, 116–117, 122, 150–151, 183, 186, 195, 250, 252, 257, 261, 269, 280
Hurrian 3–4, 8–9, 16, 35–37, 41, 44, 47–50, 54, 56, 112–113, 115, 146, 149–150, 152–154, 181, 183–186, 193, 210, 218, 233, 249, 257, 261–262, 266–268, 281

identity 1, 7, 16–18, 21, 34, 37, 48, 112, 114, 146–149, 153, 265–268, 278
inventory 4, 12, 185

knowledge 1–2, 13, 114, 146–147, 282

law 50–52, 123, 146, 150–152, 154–155
loan 119
logogram 42, 44, 160, 184

network 14–15, 33, 116, 144, 153, 266, 279

omen 37, 50, 115, 183–185

palace 8, 34, 40, 51, 54–56, 117, 144, 151–154, 184–185, 253, 267, 283
periphery 7–8, 146, 149–150, 183, 185, 210, 253, 261
politics 1, 6, 9, 11–12, 16–17, 34–37, 44–45, 52, 56, 113–114, 147–148, 183, 264–266, 269, 278–279, 281–282

pottery 12, 15, 35, 53, 118
provenance 11, 40–41, 56, 112, 185, 255

real estate 120, 152
regional 1, 9, 52, 149, 219, 252, 265, 277
religion 17, 37, 151, 185
resistance 35, 149
ritual 4, 9, 37, 39, 57–58, 257, 262
rural 118–119, 181

scribal
-hand 1, 6, 15, 20, 22–23, 34, 37, 67–68, 85, 89–90, 109, 112, 143, 148, 150, 155–156, 158, 172, 174, 179, 188, 195, 218, 230, 232, 266–270
-education 13, 112, 153, 264, 266, 278–280, 283
-school 21–22, 31, 39, 50, 67, 114, 133, 147, 218, 262, 264, 266, 268, 279
-status 267
seal 48, 51–56, 75, 96, 119–120, 124, 154, 160, 234
semiotics 114, 218, 265
standardisation 12, 123, 133, 136, 143, 147, 154, 169, 179, 182, 186, 197, 224, 232, 234, 249, 251–253, 264, 268, 270–273, 275, 279–282
Sumerian 58, 181, 184

tablet
-format 27, 33, 57, 123–125
-shape 11–12, 47, 72, 106, 110, 123–124, 202, 266
-size 11, 44–45, 47, 57, 60, 109–110, 112, 123–125, 233, 235, 266, 275
territory 9, 12, 16, 35, 181–182, 279, 281
transmission 9, 58, 210, 218–219, 264, 282

Urartian 4, 37
urban 36, 50, 52, 54, 118–119

war 35, 37, 49, 54, 154, 182, 279
witchcraft 37, 39, 50, 57–58, 113